ROUTLEDGE LIBRARY OF RAILWAY CLASSICS

No. 1

General Editor: CHARLES E. LEE, M.Inst.T.

OUR IRON ROADS

OUR IRON ROADS

Their History, Construction and Administration

FREDERICK S. WILLIAMS

LONDON AND NEW YORK

Published by Routledge
2 Park Square, Milton Park, Abingdon, Oxfordshire OX14 4RN
711 Third Avenue, New York, NY 10017

First issued in paperback 2014
Routledge is an imprint of the Taylor & Francis Group, an informa business

First edition	1852
Second edition	1883
Third edition	1883
Fourth edition	1883
Fifth edition	1884
Sixth edition	1885
Seventh edition	1888
New impression, with introduction, of Second edition	1968

Transferred to Digital Printing 2006

ISBN 978-0-714-61444-1 (hbk)
ISBN 978-1-138-86602-7 (pbk)

Publisher's Note
The publisher has gone to great lengths to ensure the quality of thisreprint but points out that some imperfections in the original may be apparent

EDITOR'S INTRODUCTION TO THE 1968 EDITION

It was probably the Great Exhibition of 1851 which inspired the son of a Congregational minister to publish the first book on the rise and progress of the railway system designed for the non-specialist reader, "at once stimulating and satisfying a laudable curiosity in reference to this subject". The resources of British railways had never before been so heavily taxed as they were in the summer of 1851. It was a beautiful summer and visitors poured into the great London termini, attracted by the numerous cheap excursion facilities offered. Of the visitors to the Great Exhibition, who totalled 6,201,856, many had come by railway and had seen and used engineering wonders of which they might be expected to seek to know more.

On 18 August 1851 *The Times* had commented that "this morning the railways of the kingdom will disgorge, as usual, their countless swarms of excursionists at every terminus where novelty or amusement is to be found. The power of attraction is not confined to the Great Exhibition alone. Just now all England is on the move".

The first edition of this book appeared with the prefatory date 1 August 1852 from the office of the Illustrated London Library (Ingram, Cooke & Co.) under the title *Our Iron Roads: Their History, Construction, and Social Influences*, by Frederick S. Williams. It included 37 woodcuts showing interesting features of railway construction and working, and its 390 pages were described by *The Economist* as "historic and scientific. It tells us what has been done, and explains the principles of the work. It is anecdotal as well as practically descriptive . . . A great repertory of all kinds of information about rails".

The author, Frederick Smeeton Williams, has been stated already to have been the son of a Congregational minister, but something more of his background is of interest. His father, Charles Williams (1796–1866), was a London man, the son of a foreman in an engine factory, and in early life worked in that factory. He was then employed at a bookselling establishment in Piccadilly, before becoming a Congregational minister at Newark upon Trent, where he remained until 1833. Here Frederick Smeeton was born in 1829. Charles Williams was Editor to the Religious Tract Society from 1835 to 1847, for whom he wrote no fewer than 75 publications, and was the author of a number of books, including *The Seven Ages of England, or its Advancement in Art, Literature, and Science* (1836). Frederick therefore spent his early years in an atmosphere of writing, and with a father who had had some engineering experience. Frederick was educated at University College, London, and entered New College, St. John's Wood, as a student for the ministry in 1850. His production of *Our Iron Roads* at the age of 23 was a remarkable achievement, and the care which he took is exemplified by his acknowledgements "to the Directors, Secretaries, and other Officers of the various railway companies, by whom he has been favoured with special facilities for observation, and with important information in reference to the management of their several lines; and also to those engineers . . . who have materially assisted . . . by the valuable results of their professional experience".

The railways had need of the work of a sympathetic author, for, despite their engineering achievements, they had at this time an unsympathetic Parliament and a bad Press. The period was the aftermath of the Railway Mania. Financial losses (largely through imprudent promotions) had exasperated those in high places, and bitter comments were made in the Press about poor timekeeping, alleged indifference to the safety of passengers, and a general lack of cleanliness. Williams was not insensible to the measure of justification for such criticisms, but he placed them in perspective, and concluded that the railway was " the mightiest physical agency which has been discovered in modern times for the promotion of the comfort and welfare of man ". In the *Dictionary of National Biography*, E. Irving Carlyle described *Our Iron Roads* as " his most important work ".

Our author became Congregational minister at Claughton near Birkenhead, in 1857, and then English tutor and financial secretary at the Congregational Institute, Nottingham, from 1861 until his death at Nottingham on 26 October 1886. He was also an ardent politician, a faithful follower of William Ewart Gladstone, and much of his writing was devoted to religious and political subjects. However, his keen interest in railways persisted, and for many years he occupied his leisure time in the preparation of his other important railway work, *The Midland Railway: Its Rise and Progress*, of which the first edition appeared in 1876. This achieved widespread interest and considerable success.

More than thirty years after the original appearance of *Our Iron Roads*, Williams re-wrote it in extended form, a course necessitated by the enormous development in the intervening years. The total route mileage of public railways in Great Britain was some 6,266 at the beginning of 1852. By 1883, when the second edition of *Our Iron Roads* was published, the total had grown to 15,992. The 321 pages of the main text of the xiv chapters in the first edition had been extended to xvi chapters and 511 pages, but the two appendices of the first edition were not repeated. These were (a) an Abstract of Proceedings of the Committee of the House of Commons on the Liverpool & Manchester Railroad Bill, Session 1825; and (b) Railway Accidents, and Insurance against them. The latter included a table for the half-year ended 31 December 1851 showing the number and nature of railway accidents in Great Britain and Ireland (113 persons killed and 264 injured) related to the totals of passengers on the respective railways (in all 47,509,392) during the same period.

This revised second edition, which is the one here reproduced, appeared under the imprint of Bemrose & Sons, and bore the slightly revised full title *Our Iron Roads: Their History, Construction, and Administration.* The initial 2,000 copies were quickly exhausted, and a further 2,000 (called third edition) followed within a few weeks; 4,000 more (called fourth edition) within a few months; and 3,000 (called fifth edition) in 1884. The sixth edition appeared in 1885, and the seventh in 1888, the last-named after the author's death. All subsequent to the second edition were substantially reprints.

Biographical details of Frederick Smeeton Williams may be found in the *Dictionary of National Biography*, in *Modern English Biography* by Frederic Boase; the *Congregational Year Book* for 1887 (page 250); and the *Nottingham Daily Express* for 28 October and 1 November 1886. Unfortunately, his early works are wrongly credited in the *Gentleman's Magazine* for 1863, and in other places, to Frederick Sims Williams (1811–1863), a barrister who was the author of some legal works.

CHARLES E. LEE

VALE OF LLANGOLLEN VIADUCT.

SHAKESPEARE'S CLIFF, SOUTH EASTERN RAILWAY.

OUR IRON ROADS:

Their History, Construction, and Administration.

BY

FREDERICK S. WILLIAMS,

Author of "The Midland Railway: its Rise and Progress."

A SNOW PLOUGH.

"Now, lads, you will live to see the day when mail-coaches will go by railway, and when it will be cheaper for a working man to travel on a railway than to walk on foot."—GEORGE STEPHENSON.

"Railways have rendered more services, and have received less gratitude, than any other institution in the land."—JOHN BRIGHT.

With Numerous Illustrations.

SECOND EDITION, REVISED.

LONDON:
BEMROSE & SONS, OLD BAILEY,
AND IRONGATE, DERBY.
1883.

PREFACE TO SECOND EDITION

THIRTY years ago the Author had the impression that the rise and progress of our great peaceful and humanising industries should be more interesting and instructive than that which generally fills our books of history—the blood-stained annals of war. Accordingly, though a young writer, he published the first edition of "Our Iron Roads"; and the favour with which his book was honoured showed that, happily, his impression was widely shared. Since then he has been gratified by the reception given by the press and the public to his work—"The Midland Railway: a Narrative of Modern Enterprise"; of which, within a week of its publication, half a large edition was sold, and of which four editions, of 8,000 copies, have nearly been exhausted.

On two occasions "Our Iron Roads" has been recommended to the Author (not knowing who he was) by principal Librarians of the British Museum, one of whom subsequently urged him to bring out a Second Edition; and various requests have reached him from other quarters to the same effect. After careful revision it is now issued, the Author venturing to ask for it the goodwill that its predecessor enjoyed. He hopes that its perusal may help to quicken, especially in the minds of the young, a deeper interest in the social and industrial progress of the people; and that it may also inspire a kindlier appreciation of the endless skill, labour, and cost with which our railway service is carried forward, not only by the chiefs at the head of the administration, but by the hundreds of thousands of workmen, who intelligently and faithfully fulfil their responsibilities for the comfort and safety of the public.

FOREST ROAD, NOTTINGHAM.

CONTENTS.

CHAPTER I.

CHAPTER II.

CHAPTER III.

CHAPTER IV.

CHAPTER V.

CHAPTER VI.

CHAPTER VII.

CHAPTER VIII.

CHAPTER IX.

CHAPTER X.

CHAPTER XI.

CHAPTER XII.

CHAPTER XIII.

LIST OF ILLUSTRATIONS.

OUR IRON ROADS.

CHAPTER I.

Dr. Johnson's Ideal.—"The Coaching Days of Old."—The Troubles of Travel.—Tramroads.—Mr. Outram.—Roger North.—Iron Tramroad in Colebrook Dale.—The Peak Forest Line.—The Edge Railway.—Fish-bellied Rails.—The Surrey Iron Railway Company.—Dr. James Anderson.—Thomas Gray of Nottingham.—Complaints about Canals.—Stockton and Darlington Line Projected.—Wooden Trams and Horses to be Used.—"The Quakers' Line."—Mr. Edward Pease.—The Line Opened.—Joy and Sorrow.—The Engine-wright and the Quaker.—Colliery Engines.—Success of Stockton and Darlington Line.—Rise of Middlesbrough.—Liverpool and Manchester Line Projected.—First English Railway Prospectus.—First Great Parliamentary Railway Battle.—The Northumbrian Engineer before the Parliamentary Committee.—Opposition of Engineers to the Project—The Bill Rejected.—Renewed Efforts.—The Bill Carried.—Anticipated Failure of Railways.—Premium for Locomotives.—The Competition.—The *Rocket*.—The *Sans Pareil*.—The Liverpool and Manchester Line Opened.—Success of Line.—George Stephenson.—Robert Stephenson.

DOCTOR JOHNSON has left it on record that the most pleasing thing in existence is to travel, accompanied by a pretty woman, in a mail coach, at the rate of six miles an hour; and there are some, besides the great lexicographer, who talk of the delights of travelling in "the coaching days of old." They tell, in glowing terms, how the mail was daily examined from pole to boot—wheels, axles, linch-pins, springs, and glasses; how scrupulously each part was cleaned; how every horse was

The initial letter represents a tunnel-mouth in Chee Vale, on the Rowsley and Manchester line of the Midland Railway.

groomed as carefully as if it belonged to the stud of a nobleman; and how, at eight o'clock at night, coach and mettled steeds were ready "on parade," in Lombard Street, to receive the bags.

Perhaps it was a special occasion. The tidings of a military victory had been received—a national foe had been defeated—and the mail would convey the news to ten thousand English homes. Instead of, as now, being silently flashed in a few seconds over the length and breadth of the land, resort was had to more ordinary, and yet more striking means. Horses, men, and carriages were dressed with laurels and flowers, with oak-leaves and ribbons. Coachmen and guards displayed to the best advantage around their rotund forms the royal livery; passengers, in a feeling of national exultation, lost their usual reserve; and, when the noise of the lids locked down on the mail-bags smote on the ear, the trampling of high-bred horses, as they bounded off like leopards, and the thundering of wheels, were soon lost amid the shouts of hosts of spectators. In the remembrance of such scenes, it is scarcely surprising that some regret that they have passed away for ever. We can almost join in the song,—

> "We miss the cantering team, the winding way,
> The road-side halt, the post-horn's well-known air,
> The inns, the gaping towns, and all the landscape fair."

There were also various other sources of innocent enjoyment in the journeyings of our grandfathers of which we have been bereft; and it must, for instance, have been very agreeable "for a lady to be married in her riding habit, and jog off for her honeymoon on her pillion, with her arm round her husband's waist."

Still, the joys even of those days were not without alloy. Stories are told of dreary waitings at road sides in the small hours of wintry mornings for coaches which, when they arrived, were full; of how travellers could not keep awake and dared not go to sleep; of roads "infamously bad," which "the whole range of language could not sufficiently describe;" and of the additional and exciting perils ever and anon of "a race betwixt two stage coaches, in which the lives of thirty or forty distressed or helpless individuals were at the mercy of two intoxicated brutes." To be perched for perhaps twenty hours, exposed to all weathers, on the outside of a coach, trying in vain to find a soft seat, sitting now with the face and now with the back to the wind, rain, or sun; to endure long and wretched winter nights, when the passenger was half starved with cold and the other half with hunger,—was a miserable undertaking, and was often looked forward to with no small anxiety by many whose business required them frequently to travel. Nor were the inside passengers much more agreeably accommodated. To be closely packed in a little straight-backed vehicle, where the cramped limbs could not be in the least extended, nor the wearied frame indulged by any change of posture, was felt by

THE WAY-SIDE INN.

many to be a distressing experience, while the constantly recurring demands of driver and guard, and the exactions of innkeepers, often destroyed the last traces of the fancied romance of stage-coach travelling. In fact, a wet, steaming, dripping coach, swaying along through a village, covered with a compact hood of umbrellas, and looking for all the world like a huge moist green tortoise, was an object sufficiently melancholy for any one to contemplate. Even aristocratic dignity could scarcely be maintained "when, for instance, the Duke of Marlborough's enormous gilt coach broke down in Chancery Lane, when his Grace was entering London in triumph;" and in after days many travellers shared the experience of Charles Dickens, who, when he was a reporter, was "upset in almost every description of vehicle known in this country."

Truth to say, modern wayfarers have little conception of what travelling used to be. It killed hundreds of people; and often in winter a man would get so nearly frozen to death that he could only be got down from the top of a coach in the bent position into which he had stiffened. "The railroad grumblers of to-day know nothing of the sufferings of their Spartan fathers."

"You must be making handsomely out with your canals," was once remarked to the celebrated Duke of Bridgewater. "Oh, yes," rejoined his grace, "they will last my time; but I don't like the look of these tramroads—there's mischief in them." The observation of the duke was, in a sense, prophetic: those wooden roads were the foreshadowing of the Railway system of the present day. Many conjectures have been offered as to the origin of the term "tramroad," but it appears to have been taken from the name of Mr. Outram, who was early connected with their employment; and they would, doubtless, have been called outram-roads, were it not for the well-known custom of Englishmen to reduce their words to the most practical dimensions. The application of the principle on which their value depends, may be traced in the construction of early Italian streets, and especially of those of Milan, where a smooth surface is provided for the passage of wheels, and a rough one on which the horses may tread with security; but the precise date at which they were first used does not appear. It is sufficient to observe that more than two hundred years ago, tramroads existed in the colliery districts; and Roger North, in describing a visit paid by his brother, Lord Guildford, to Newcastle, remarks, that among the curiosities of the region were the way-leaves." "When men," he wrote in 1676, "have pieces of ground between the colliery and the river, they sell *leave* to lead coals over the ground, and so dear, that the owner of a rood of ground will expect £20 per annum for this leave. The manner of the carriage is by laying rails of timber from the colliery down to the river, exactly straight and parallel, and bulky carts are made with four rowlets fitting these rails, whereby the carriage is so easy, that one horse will draw four or five chaldrons of coals, and is of immense benefit to the coal merchants." The hard, smooth, and unchanging surface on which the wheels passed, was then and is now the characteristic of the tramroad.

Towards the close of the last century, wooden tramroads were extensively employed in mining and coal districts, where much heavy material had to be transported; and they rapidly spread in Shropshire, Staffordshire, and the midland counties generally.

An iron tramroad, or railway, as it may be called, was in use at Colebrook Dale—a spot celebrated for having the first iron bridge in the world—about the year 1760; for the price of iron having fallen, it was determined, in order to keep the furnaces at work, to cast plates to be laid on the upper edge of the wooden tramroads; this, it was thought, would diminish friction, and prevent abrasion, while the iron could be sold as "pigs" in case of a sudden rise of price. These "scantlings of iron" were four inches broad, an inch and a quarter in thickness, and five feet long, and were cast with holes so that they might easily be fastened to the wooden rails beneath. So successful, however, was the plan, that the plates remained undisturbed, and rails of solid iron were gradually adopted in those districts. An iron tramway was formed from the collieries near Derby to that town; a second, called the Peak Forest line, was laid down for six miles; and another was constructed near Ashby-de-la-Zouch, which had four miles of double and eight of single rails. In 1811 there were in South Wales no fewer than 180 miles completed, of which thirty belonged to the Merthyr Tydvil Company.

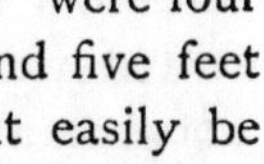

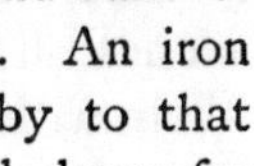

Shortly after the experiment at Colebrook Dale cast-iron rails with an upright flange were invented, and they seem to have been first used at the colliery of the Duke of Norfolk, near Sheffield. They were originally fixed on cross sleepers of wood, but stone blocks were afterwards substituted. The "edge railway" was introduced at the slate quarries of Lord Penrhyn in Carmarthenshire. The "metals," as they are called, were between four and five feet long, their section representing an oval, as seen in the diagram. The wheels were formed with a grooved tire, so as to run easily on the rail; but it was subsequently found that the groove became so deepened by wear as to fit the rail tightly, and thus to occasion unnecessary friction. To obviate this difficulty, the bearing surface of the rail and the corresponding part of the wheel were made flat; and two horses were then able, with comparative ease, to draw a train weighing twenty-four tons, and they could conduct a traffic which, on a common road, would have required four hundred.

Experience suggested various improvements in the construction of the tram-rail. "Fish-bellied" rails, as they were denominated, were made three or four feet in length, with their greatest strength in the middle; they were secured one to another in the "chair," or iron box, and this was so fixed to the sleeper that the whole was safe.

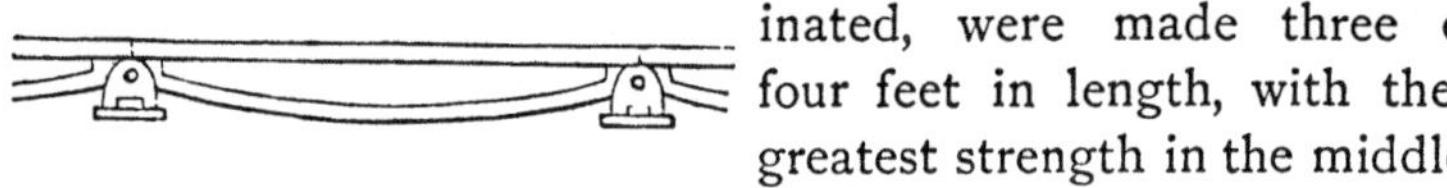

In 1801 the "Surrey Iron Railway Company" obtained an Act for the construction of a tramway for general merchandise from Wandsworth to Croydon, and the advantages it presented were subjected to a practical test. The draught of a horse on a good road is about fifteen hundredweight, and strong horses can, under ordinary circumstances, draw two thousand pounds. Twelve wagons were on this occasion loaded with stones till each weighed about three tons, and a horse then drew them with apparent ease a distance of six miles in an hour and three quarters. At each stoppage, other wagons were added to the train, with which the horse resumed his journey, with apparently undiminished power; and the attending workmen, to the number of about fifty, also mounted the wagons, without any apparent effect on the horse. The load at the end of the journey was found to weigh more than fifty-five tons.

"I found delight," said Sir Richard Phillips, "in witnessing, at Wandsworth, the economy of horse-labour on the iron railway. Yet a heavy sigh escaped me, as I thought of the inconceivable millions of money which had been spent about Malta; four or five of which might have been the means of extending double lines of iron railway from London to Edinburgh, Glasglow, Holyhead, Milford, Falmouth, Yarmouth, Dover, and Portsmouth."

In connection with the history of tramroads, the name of Dr. James Anderson is well deserving of notice. In 1800 he published a book, entitled "Recreations in Agriculture," in which he proposed the adoption of lines of railway along the sides of turnpike roads, both for heavy loads at slow rates, and for accelerated motion. Dr. Anderson proposed that they should be tried between the metropolis and the docks then projected at the Isle of Dogs, and also along the western road to Hounslow; after which, if successful, he recommended that they should be more fully applied on the turnpike from London to Bath. He estimated that heavily-laden wagons could be drawn with one-tenth of the force and cost of the common modes of traffic; and he recommended that the whole should be "kept open and patent to all alike who shall choose to employ them, as the king's highway, under such regulations as it shall be found necessary." He subsequently described the method in which these railways might be constructed; their width, height, gradients, curves, bridges, and even "short tunnels." "Dr. Anderson's description might pass for that of a modern rail-road."

A thoughtful man in the north of England visited one of these tramways which connected the mouth of a colliery with a wharf at which the coals were shipped; and, after watching the passing trains for some time, he turned to the engineer of the line, and said, "Why are not these tramroads laid down all over England, so as to supersede our common roads, and steam-engines employed to convey goods and passengers along them, so as to supersede horse-power?" The engineer looked at the questioner and replied,—"Just propose you that to the nation, sir, and see what you will get by it! Why, sir, you will be worried to death for your pains." The conversation on this topic terminated; but Thomas Gray, of Nottingham, did not allow the matter to escape him. Tramroads, locomotive steam-engines, and the superseding of horse-power, filled his mind. "It was his thought by day; it was his dream by night. He talked of it till his friends voted him an intolerable bore. He wrote of it till the reviewers deemed him mad."

Meanwhile, the growing demands of commerce had led to general discontent with the means of intercommunication through the country. The tramroads were detached and isolated undertakings; and the proprietors of canals, thinking themselves secure in their possession of a monopoly, were extravagant in their charges as well as inefficient in their administration. The dissatisfaction that resulted was specially strong in the coal districts of the north, where the burdens to be carried were large and heavy. One of the richest coalfields in the country lay to the west and north-west of Darlington, a long way from the sea; and it is not surprising that here the great practical problem of transport eventually found its solution. The story of that time has been admirably told by Dr. Smiles, in his "Lives of the Stephensons." How it was proposed to overcome the local difficulties by the construction of a canal, but nothing was done; how Stockton waited twenty years for Darlington, and Darlington for Stockton; how, at length, the Stocktonians, who adopted as the motto of their company, "Meliora speramus," held a public meeting to discuss the "better things" to come, and appointed a committee to inquire into the advantages of forming a *railway* or canal; how the Darlington committee went to sleep, woke up, made a report, but could not decide; and how imperial wars arose and general apathy ensued: all this and much more is narrated by Dr. Smiles with the fidelity of the historian and the vividness of the painter.

In estimating the possible results of their work, if a railway were made, the friends of the enterprise were modest indeed. The line itself was to be a wooden tramway, over which coal trucks and other vehicles were to be drawn either by horses or by ropes attached to stationary engines, and it was estimated that "one horse of moderate power could easily draw downwards on the railway, between Darlington and Stockton, about ten tons, and upwards about four tons of loading, exclusive of the empty wagons." By the advice of George Stephenson, who was appointed engineer and surveyor to the line, iron rails were substituted for wood; and, as he gradually gained the confidence of the directors, he urged upon them, at length successfully, to employ a locomotive engine, such as that which he had already constructed and was working successfully at Killingworth colliery. The export trade in coal it was calculated, "might be taken, perhaps at 10,000 tons a year," about a cargo a week. No allusion in any of the reports was made to the carriage of passengers. At length, towards the end of 1816, a company was formed for constructing the railway, and the requisite capital was raised, though not so much by faith in the undertaking as by faith in the character of its friend and advocate,

Edward Pease. The leading men of the district ridiculed or opposed the idea; and even the merchants of Stockton, who had most to gain in the enterprise, were so lukewarm in its support that Mr. Pease was not able, with all his energy, to dispose in the whole town of twenty shares! That he succeeded in the end was through the help of his immediate personal friends. "The two principal Quaker families next to his own, the Backhouses and the Richardsons, gave their liberal support to Edward Pease, having unbounded faith in his wisdom; and it was with their help, and that of other members of the Society of Friends, that he was finally enabled to establish the company and obtain an Act of Parliament for the construction of the Stockton-Darlington railway." No wonder that the people of the district gave the undertaking a name it still retains, "the Quakers' line."

In looking back, many years afterwards, on the origin of this railway, Mr. Henry Pease observed that it was remarkable that the world should have had to be many thousands of years old "before it was thoroughly known to what extent two simple parallel bars, laid at a given distance, would facilitate the intercourse of mankind." It was not that the principle was new, but it was to a certain extent developed by the early pioneers of railways. At that time, also, the power of the locomotive was little known. Its opponents said, "It is folly: you will not get your wagons to travel on the railroad," and the answer they received was, "On our two parallel bars our horse shall carry eight tons at twice the speed that your horse can carry one." "I am sorry to find," said Lord Eldon, "the intelligent people of the north country gone mad on the subject of railways." Another authority declared: "It is all very well to spend money; it will do some good, but I will eat all the coals that your railroad will carry." "He did not live," said Mr. Henry Pease, "until the year 1874, when 127,000,000 of tons of coal were carried by railway, and I hope that he had many good dinners on much more digestible material. You will not wonder that the farmers were in array against the railway system, for their landlords said to them, 'You will be ruined, as there will be no demand for horses.' But they were not men of sufficient perception (and there are probably very few now who can look forward fifty years) to look forward to 1874, when a Committee of the House of Commons had to sit to consider what should be done to overcome the dearth of English horses. Whether those gentlemen have yet found out a law by which they can contravene the law of supply and demand, I do not know, as they have not yet been good enough to inform us. There was also the absence of the cash. Persons said, 'This is a very foolish scheme; I will not put my money into it.' One year the bill was thrown out of Parliament, and the second year it could not have gone to Parliament if one of the promoters had not said at the last moment, 'I would rather risk £10,000 more than this bill should not be lodged in the House of Commons.'"

Such were the remarks of Mr. Henry Pease at the Jubilee Celebration of the Stockton and Darlington line. On that occasion Mr. Moon said: I was present twenty-five years ago in this town, when Mr. Joseph Pease pointed out to me the tree from which George Stephenson took his first survey for the Stockton and Darlington line—a tree which I hope the inhabitants will take care to preserve. He told me, in addition, that the engineer only charged for his survey the modest sum of £115, a sum which, I need not say, is very different from what we railway directors know it takes to complete a survey of a railway at the present day."

The Stockton and Darlington scheme had three times to present itself before it received the sanction of Parliament. The application of 1818 was defeated by the Duke of Cleveland, because the line threatened to interfere with one of his fox-covers. Certain road trustees, also, spread the report abroad that the mortgagees of the tolls would suffer; and to meet this objection, Edward Pease had to disarm opposition by a public notice that the company's solicitors were ready to purchase these securities at the price originally paid for them.

In 1821, however, the Bill passed; and on Tuesday, the 27th of September, 1825, the line was opened. "The scene on the morning of that day," said Mr. Pease, fifty years afterwards, "sets description at defiance." Many who were to take part in the event did not the night before sleep a wink, and soon after midnight were astir. The universal cheers, the happy faces of many, the vacant stare of astonishment of others, and the alarm depicted on the countenances of some, gave variety to the picture." At the appointed hour the procession went forward. The train moved off at the rate of from ten to twelve miles an hour, with a weight of eighty tons, with one engine—"No. 1"—driven by George Stephenson himself; after it six wagons, loaded with coals and flour; then a covered coach, containing directors and proprietors; next twenty-one coal wagons, fitted up for passengers, with which they were crammed; and lastly, six more wagons loaded with coals.

"Off started the procession, with the horseman at its head. A great concourse of people stood along the line. Many of them tried to accompany it by running, and some gentlemen on horseback galloped across the fields to keep up with the engine. The railway descending with a gentle incline towards

OPENING OF THE STOCKTON AND DARLINGTON LINE.

Darlington, the rate of speed was consequently variable. At a favourable part of the road, Stephenson determined to try the speed of the engine, and he called upon the horseman with the flag to get out of the way," and Stephenson put on the speed to twelve miles, and then to fifteen miles an hour, and the runners on foot, the gentlemen on horseback, and the horseman with the flag, were soon left far behind. "When the train reached Darlington, it was found that four hundred and fifty passengers occupied the wagons, and that the load of men, coals, and merchandise amounted to about ninety tons."

On that memorable day "a dark shadow fell on the home

of Edward Pease. At the very moment when the old Quaker was counting upon enjoying to the full a triumph which would recompense him for countless days of labour and nights of anxiety, the Angel of Death entered his dwelling, and the day which had promised to be one of triumphant joy, was, in the mysterious dispensations of Providence, converted into a day of desolation and anguish. He was bereaved of his best-loved son. If the ringing cheers of the immense crowd which hailed the arrival of 'No. 1' and her lengthy train from Brusselton reached as far as the well-known house in Northgate, they fell upon the ears of one to whom they seemed but empty sounds compared with the terrible reality of death. For there, in an inner chamber, his son Isaac, who had lived by his father's side for two-and-twenty years, lay dead. He had always been a delicate boy, and the fond heart of the old man had gone out towards the weakly member of his numerous household. . . . The day which brought to Edward Pease the crowning triumph of his active life, also bore with it the greatest grief that ever humbled him in anguish before the throne of his Maker. Thus it was that while crowds were shouting and bands were playing and the new era was being born, he who had done more than any one to bring about the triumph of that day, was in his house, alone, crushed by the stroke of bereavement."

The part taken in that opening ceremony by the locomotive "No. 1" was interesting; but it was the beginning of more important events. The engine cost only £500; it was the pioneer of multitudes far more costly and powerful. But we must here retrace our steps a few years, and recount some incidents that had already occurred. One day, in the spring of 1821, George Stephenson, the Northumberland engine-wright, had called upon the wealthy Quaker and manufacturer of Darlington. "Burly men they were both; strong in mind, too, as in body; and one may fancy how they stood, face to face, and eye to eye, to read each other's character." As was the alliance of Bolton with Watt, so was that of Stephenson with Pease. Pease found the railway, and Stephenson the locomotive. Some of the main facts with regard to locomotives had already been determined. In certain districts were small engines, which, "with much clanging and rattling, puffing and smoking, with both a chimney and a steam vent, drew along, at the sufficient pace of two or three miles an hour, a dozen or more small iron wagons loaded with coal. A man would walk by the side to open gates, remove impediments, or assist at a difficulty. The colliers themselves would sometimes get into the empty wagons, as a tired carter will get into his empty dung cart, or sit on the shaft." Stationary engines had come to a high degree of perfection, but the "tramway" of those days consisted of light bars of iron, stretching from block to block, of wood or stone, which had worn for themselves sockets in the soft ground. But when the Stockton and Darlington was projected, there was no intention of employing the locomotive for the work of transport. In the preamble of the first Act, it was stated that the proposed line would "be of great public utility, by facilitating the conveyance of coal, iron, lime, corn, and other commodities"; and power was taken to provide "for the making and maintaining of the tramroads, and for the passage upon them of wagons and other carriages, with men and horses, *or otherwise*"; but, though the margin—"otherwise"—was wide, it was not expected that the locomotive would fill it. Mr. Pease afterwards said: "I was so satisfied that a horse upon an iron road would draw ten tons for one ton on a common road, that I felt sure that before long the railway would become the king's highway." George Stephenson, moreover, in his memorable interview, induced Edward Pease to visit Killingworth; he there saw for himself what a locomotive could do, and he consented to try to obtain power to work the railway by means of locomotives, and also to employ them for the haulage of passengers as well as of goods.

The results of the opening of the Stockton and Darlington line were in many respects surprising. Though the conveyance of passengers had formed no part of the original scheme, yet on the first day many hundreds of persons rode from Darlington to Stockton and back, and passengers soon insisted upon being taken regularly. Hence it became necessary to provide carriages adapted to their requirements. It was not, however, till October, 1825, that the company began to run a coach of their own. They announced that "the company's coach, called the Experiment," would run from Darlington to Stockton and back, except Sunday, making one journey each way each day, and occupying two hours in its completion. Each passenger was allowed to take "a package of not exceeding 14 lbs." The fare was 1*s*.

The great work of the new railway was in the conveyance of minerals and goods. A single engine could draw after it, at the rate of five miles an hour, a train weighing ninety-two tons. The rate, too, per ton for the carriage of merchandise was reduced from 5*d.* to the one-fifth of a penny per mile; the price of the carriage of minerals declined from 7*d.* to 1½*d.* per ton per mile; coals at Darlington fell from 18*s.* to 8*s.* 6*d.* per ton; and, as one consequence, a much larger tonnage passed along the railway than had been anticipated. "An export trade," said a writer of the time, "is now certain, for an order has been already contracted for for 100,000 tons of coals annually for five years by one house alone in London, the produce of which alone to

THE FIRST RAILWAY PASSENGER CARRIAGE.

the company will more than pay 4 per cent. on their whole expenditure. The shares are at £40 premium each; plenty of would-be purchasers, but no sellers."

Meanwhile the administration of the line and the line itself had to be improved. Additional passing places had to be provided, and the road had to be doubled. Stronger engines were made; and when the engine-men put on the power of the steam too rapidly, they had to be taught better manners. "There were no buffers on the trains then, the wagons got knocked together most cruelly, and the coals were thrown out of them to the great annoyance of the coalowners, who could not deliver them as put into the wagons."

The Corporation of the borough of Stockton welcomed the railway to their port, but they acted in a shortsighted manner as regarded the accommodation of the traffic which it brought.

The Stockton and Darlington Company were accordingly compelled to provide for themselves elsewhere. They purchased 500 acres of land a few miles below Stockton, on the mud-banks of the river, where one solitary farmhouse had stood among the green fields, and here they erected staiths and other conveniences for the loading of coal. And here, as if by magic, Middlesbrough arose, and that farmhouse became the centre of a town of more than 50,000 inhabitants.

The success at Darlington of the initial movement in railway enterprise could not be without effect elsewhere; and in various directions hopes arose that relief might be obtained from the inefficiency and the exactions of canal proprietors. For when an application was made for a reduction of charge, and an increase of accommodation, a decided negative was returned, and a *hauteur* was manifested by the canal proprietors, which naturally gave great offence. But pride went before a fall. A declaration was signed by a hundred and fifty leading men of Liverpool, that new means of communication were indispensable; and measures were adopted which eventually led to the establishment of means of communication between that town and Manchester incomparably superior in every respect to those that had previously existed.

The first English railway prospectus ever issued was that of the Liverpool and Manchester company. It was drawn up by Mr. Henry Booth, was signed by the chairman, Charles Lawrence, and was dated Oct. 29th, 1824. It set forth that "railways hold out to the public not only a cheaper but far more expeditious mode of conveyance than any yet established"; and it stated that "in the present state of trade and of commercial enterprise despatch is no less essential than economy. Merchandise is frequently brought across the Atlantic from New York to Liverpool in twenty-one days; while, owing to the various causes of delay above enumerated, goods have in some instances been longer on their passage from Liverpool to Manchester. But this reproach must not be perpetual. The advancement in mechanical science renders it unnecessary; the good sense of the community makes it impossible. Let it not, however, be imagined that were England to be tardy other countries would pause in the march of improvement." Among the advantages that would be secured by the new system, the prospectus said : "Increased facilities for the general operations of commerce, arising out of that punctuality and despatch which will attend the transit of merchandise between Liverpool and Manchester, as well as an immense pecuniary saving to the trading community. But the inhabitants at large of these populous towns will reap their full share of direct and immediate benefit. Coal will be brought to market in greater plenty at reduced price ; and farming produce of various kinds will find its way from greater distances and at more reasonable rates. To the landholders also, in the vicinity of the line, the railroad offers important advantages in extensive markets for their mineral and agricultural produce, as well as in a facility of obtaining lime and manure at a cheap rate in return. Moreover, as a cheap and expeditious means of conveyance for travellers, the railway holds out the fair prospect of a public accommodation the magnitude and importance of which cannot be immediately ascertained." This prospectus may be pondered as a great historical document.

The first great parliamentary battle for a railway was fought over the proposal to construct the line between Liverpool and Manchester. The Committee of the House of Commons, to whom the Bill was referred, met for the first time on Monday, March 21st, 1825. The chair was occupied by General Gascoigne, then member for Liverpool. At the present day no member for a locality affected by a Railway Bill is allowed to be a member of the Committee by whom it is to be considered, though he may give such advice and assistance as his local knowledge and position may render useful. Manchester was not then represented on the Committee, nor even in the House. The Company appeared by counsel, the chief of whom were Serjeant Spankie and Mr. Adam ; while arrayed against the Bill was a phalanx of canal-owners, road-trustees, and landed proprietors through whose property the intended line was to pass. The legal talent engaged on their side appeared overwhelming.

Before that august array George Stephenson, a self-taught mechanic, appeared to prove by arguments and facts,—stated with a Northumbrian dialect and "burr" so decided as to make him scarcely intelligible to southerners,—that a certain work was possible and desirable which public opinion and the most distinguished engineers of the day had declared to be impracticable and absurd. "Clear though the subject was to himself, and familiar as he was with the powers of the locomotive," sixteen of which he had built, "it was no easy task for him to bring home his convictions, or even to convey his meaning, to the less informed minds of his hearers, in the face of the sneers, interruptions, and ridicule of the opponents of the measure, and even of the Committee, some of whom shook their heads and whispered doubts as to his sanity."

"Have you any doubt," he was asked, "that a locomotive engine could be made to take the weight of forty tons, at the rate of six miles an hour, with perfect safety?"—"An engine," he replied, "may go six miles an hour with forty tons; that is, including the weight of the carriages." "Have you any doubt that the power of the engine might be so increased as to take that weight at any speed between six and twelve miles an hour?"—"I think the power of the engine may be increased to take that weight." "To what extent do you conceive the power of the engine could be increased to take that weight of goods?"—"I can scarcely state that to you: the power of the engine may be increased very greatly." "As much as double?"—"I think it might." "If you had such an engine, in your opinion could it be made to go with perfect safety twelve miles an hour, with relation to the bursting of the boiler?"—"Yes, I think it might." "At the rate you go at Killingworth, are the engines easily managed,—easily stopped?"—"Very easily." "Is their pace easily slackened?"—"Yes." "Easily started again?"—"Yes." "In short, they are easily manageable?"—"They are." "Do you think they could be made perfectly manageable to go at the rate of eight miles an hour?"—"Yes, I conceive they might at eight miles an hour."

But in the speech with which he summed up the evidence given, Mr. Alderson declared: "I say there is no evidence upon which the Committee can safely rely, that upon an average, more than three and a half or four and a half miles an hour can be done. Consider the nature of the engine: it consists in part of a large iron boiler, and the elastic force of steam is the moving force, and that depends upon the quantity of heat; the water is enclosed in a boiler of iron, a most rapid conductor of heat, and which must move in storms of snow, in storms of rain, and during the times of frost. At all those times it will be extremely difficult to keep up the elastic force of the steam: I do not say it is impossible, but extremely difficult."

With regard to Chat Moss, which the proposed line had to cross, Mr. Harrison declared that "it rises in height from the rain swelling it like a sponge, and sinks again in dry weather; and if a boring instrument is put into it, it sinks immediately by its own weight. The making of an embankment out of this pulpy wet moss is no very easy task. Who but Mr. Stephenson would have thought of entering into Chat Moss, carrying it out almost like wet dung? It is ignorance almost inconceivable. It is perfect madness." "No engineer in his senses," said Mr. Francis Giles, C.E., "would go through Chat Moss if he wanted to make a railroad from Liverpool to Manchester. In my judgment," he added, with amusing self-contradictoriness of style, "a railroad certainly cannot be safely made over Chat Moss without going to the bottom of the Moss."

The Committee sat for thirty-eight days. On the 31st of May, after thirty-seven witnesses, and an indefinite number of speeches, had been heard against the Bill, the preamble was declared to have been proved by a vote of thirty-seven to thirty-six. The contest was continued on the clauses. On the 1st of June, the thirty-eighth day of the Committee's sitting, the room was cleared, and counsel, agents, and parties were then summoned to be informed that the proposal that the Company should have power to make a railway had been "put and negatived."

A first failure was not, however, conclusive. Steps were at once taken with a view to a renewed application to Parliament, and Messrs. John and George Rennie were engaged as engineers, with instructions to make a new survey, it being thought that their recognised reputation as engineers would strengthen the case. The promoters also determined to adopt a more southern route, although it involved a tunnel, the Olive Mount rock cutting, and other works, which made it necessary that the capital should be increased from £400,000 to £510,000.

The third reading of the Bill was carried in the Commons by a majority of 88 to 41. The cost of obtaining the Act was £27,000. Mr. George Stephenson was now appointed principal engineer, with a salary of £1,000 a year.

When the works of the new line were at length approaching

completion, it was necessary that a decision should be made as to the motive agency to be employed. Horse-power was now regarded as inadequate, and the choice lay between locomotive and stationary engines. If the latter had been selected, a rope would have been carried along the line, between the rails, and would, at certain intervals, have been coiled round large drums or cylinders, worked by fixed steam engines. To this rope the wagons containing passengers or goods would have been attached, and been drawn from station to station.

In the spring of 1829, the directors of the Company instructed Messrs. Stephenson, Locke, Walker, and Rastrick to collect information from the managers of the various railways of the country as to the comparative merits of locomotive and fixed engines; and those gentlemen visited the railways in the north of England, made most careful inquiries as to the methods adopted upon them, and gave the results in separate reports. These, on the whole, were in favour of stationary engines; but it was admitted that improvements were being effected in the construction of locomotives which made it probable that their efficiency would be materially increased. It was thought that, in the stationary system, accidents would be less frequent; but that when they occurred, they would be more injurious, as they would extend to the whole line; whereas in the locomotive system they would be confined to the engine that was disabled, and to its train. In the stationary system perfect uniformity from end to end must be preserved; in the locomotive system, one engine, with its train, by passing to the sidings, might be detained without inconvenience to others. Eventually it was decided that locomotive engines should be employed upon the line generally, but that two fixed engines should be placed at Rainhill and Sutton, to draw the locomotive engines, as well as the goods and carriages, up the inclines at these places. Hitherto the transport of passengers had not formed any special feature in these arrangements: it was now suggested that locomotives might possibly be so constructed as to convey passengers at a speed equal to that attained by coaches. Accordingly, in order to attract the attention of men of science to the subject, a premium of £500 was publicly offered for the best locomotive that could, under certain stipulations, be constructed; and though that amount was comparatively insignificant, it was obvious that on the successful engineer would devolve the construction of the entire "stud" of locomotives for the new line. The company required of the competing engines, that they should consume their own smoke; that, if they weighed six tons each, they should be capable of drawing a train of twenty tons weight, including the tender, at a speed of ten miles an hour, on a level railway; that each should have two safety-valves,—one beyond the control of the engine-driver; and that their height, of the engine including the chimney, should not exceed fifteen feet. It was also announced that preference would be given to an engine of less weight, if it performed an equal amount of work; that the company was to be at liberty to test the machinery; and that the price of the engine of the successful competitor was not to exceed £550.

Now that the results of railway enterprise are before the world, it is curious to observe how completely many of them were unforeseen. One distinguished writer, who resided in a coal country, and under whose windows locomotives had been working for years, has left his disclaimer on record in a published work. "It is far from my wish," said he, "to promulgate to the world that the ridiculous expectations, or rather professions, of the enthusiastic speculatist will be realized, and that we shall see engines travelling at the rate of twelve, sixteen, eighteen, and twenty miles an hour. Nothing can do more harm towards their general adoption and improvement than the promulgation of such nonsense"!

"As to those persons," said the *Quarterly Review*, "who speculate on making railways generally throughout the kingdom, and superseding all the canals, all the wagons, mails, and stage-coaches, post-chaises, and, in short, every other mode of conveyance, by land and by water, we deem them and their visionary schemes unworthy of notice. The gross exaggerations of the powers of the locomotive steam-engine (or, to speak in plain English, the *steam-carriage*), may delude for a time, but must end in the mortification of those concerned. We should as soon expect the people to suffer themselves to be fired off upon one of Congreve's *ricochet* rockets, as trust themselves to the mercy of such a machine, going at such a rate."

The merits of the competing engines for the Liverpool and Manchester Railway were determined by the directors, assisted by Messrs. Rastrick, Kennedy, and Nicholas Wood. On the day appointed, the *Rocket*, constructed by Mr. George Stephenson; the *Novelty*, by Messrs. Braithwaite & Ericson; and the *Sans Pareil*, by Mr. T. Hackworth, entered the lists, on a piece of railroad which had been selected between Liverpool and Manchester. In consequence of this space being little more than a mile and a half long, each engine had to travel the whole distance backwards and forwards ten times, making a journey of thirty miles. In order that the performances of each might be accurately tested, a judge was stationed at each end of the real running course, who noticed the exact time at which the engines passed; the additional ground at each end being allowed to them for getting up their speed. When the *Sans Pareil* was examined, it was found not to have been constructed in precise accordance with the stipulations of the company, and therefore was, in strictness, disqualified; but it was resolved that a trial should be made, and that, if it displayed marked superiority, it should be recommended to the favourable consideration of the directors. On its eighth trip, however, the pump that supplied the water failed, and the accident terminated the experiment. The *Novelty* succeeded only in passing twice between the stations, the joints of the boiler then gave way. The *Rocket* having been supplied with water, was weighed, and the load of seventeen tons was then attached. This engine twice performed the distance of thirty miles; the first time in about two hours and a quarter, and the second in about two hours and seven minutes. Its greatest speed was at the rate of thirty miles an hour, and the average about fourteen. The marked superiority exhibited by the *Rocket* was owing to the admirable contrivance of the steam blast, and the use of a tubular boiler, pierced with twenty-five copper tubes, through which the heated air passed on its way to the chimney, the tubes being surrounded by the water of the boiler, an arrangement by which a very large

THE NOVELTY.

surface was brought in contact with the fire, and a proportionate amount of steam generated. This engine, also, consumed less coal than the others, in the proportion of eleven to twenty-eight. The boiler consisted of a cylinder, six feet in length, having flat ends; the chimney issued from one extremity, and to the other the fire-place was attached, which, externally, had the appearance of a square box.

The opinion has been confidently expressed to the writer, that after all the *Sans Pareil* was as good an engine as the *Rocket.* The accident that led to its withdrawment from the competition was trifling, and could now-a-days have been repaired in two minutes. "But it frightened the driver, and he gave in. It was a wonderful little engine," remarked our informant, "and for

THE ROCKET.

years did a deal of work. After the competition it was bought by the Bolton and Kenyon Junction Railway people; and it ran from Bolton by Kenyon Junction to Liverpool and back twice a day. When the traffic increased the runnings had to be rearranged, and it did not come farther than the junction, but ran the ten miles to and from Bolton from seven o'clock in the morning till about nine at night—120 miles a day—for years. The *Sans Pareil* was only about five tons weight; it carried a tub of rainwater for the boiler, and three or four barrow-loads of coke for the furnace. The boiler had one tube, a return tube. The fireman rode on the foot-plate, but the driver stood at the front end of his engine on the buffer-plank, and he had a seat on one side boarded in. But he was out in the open during rain, hail, or sunshine; and this arrangement lasted as long as the engine lasted."

Mr. Stephenson, having thus been the successful competitor, was appointed to build the engines of the railway, and from that period to his death he conducted the engineering department of the company.

The construction of the works of the Liverpool and Manchester Railway required immense and unremitting labour. Besides the embankment over Chat Moss, to which we shall have again to refer, there was the building of viaducts, the formation of cuttings and embankments, the erection of sixty-three bridges, and the construction of a tunnel near Liverpool;

THE SANS PAREIL.

besides the laying down of the permanent way, the erection of stations and warehouses, and the preparation of the engines, carriages, and wagons. The cost was as follows:—

Cuttings and Embankments	£199,763
Chat Moss	27,719
Tunnel	47,788
Land	95,305
Fencing	10,202
Bridges	99,065
Formation of Road	20,568
Laying of Blocks and Sleepers	20,520
" Rails (£12 10s. per ton)	60,912
Surveying, Law, Parliamentary, and Incidental	157,341
	£739,183

The opening of the line took place on the 15th of September, 1830, when the Duke of Wellington, Prime Minister, Mr. Peel, Home Secretary, Mr. Huskisson, and a number of other distinguished persons, were to pass in the first train with the directors. A gay *cortege* of thirty-three carriages, accompanied by bands of music, started from Liverpool, amidst the acclamations of a countless multitude of observers, and with all the splendour of an ancient pageant. But soon the enjoyment of the scene was marred. While the engines were stopping to take in water at Parkside, Mr. Huskisson, with some other gentlemen, strolled along the line. As they were returning to their seats, another train of carriages came up. All ran for shelter; but, unhappily, Mr. Huskisson hurried to the side of the train, and, opening the door, attempted to enter; the door swung back at the moment—he fell to the ground, and was in an instant overthrown and crushed beneath the wheels of the advancing carriage. His thigh was fractured and mangled, and his own first expression, "I have met my death," proved too true, for he died that evening in the neighbouring parsonage of Eccles. The train passed on to Manchester without further accident; but the contemplated festivities were forgotten amidst the gloom occasioned by this tragedy.

Referring to the events of that memorable day, Lord Brougham said: "When I saw the difficulties of space, as it were, overcome; when I beheld a kind of miracle exhibited before my astonished eyes; when I surveyed masses pierced through, on which it was before hardly possible for man or beast to plant the sole of the foot, now covered with a road, and bearing heavy wagons, laden not only with innumerable passengers, but with merchandise of the largest bulk and heaviest weight; when I saw valleys made practicable by the bridges of ample height and length which spanned them; saw the steam railway traversing the surface of the water, at a distance of sixty or seventy feet perpendicular height; saw the rocks excavated, and the gigantic power of man penetrating through miles of the solid mass, and gaining a great, a lasting, an almost perennial conquest over the power of nature, by his skill and industry; when I contemplated all this, was it possible for me to avoid the reflections which crowded into my mind—not in praise of man's great success, not in admiration of the genius and perseverance he had displayed, or even of the courage he had shown in setting himself against the obstacles that matter offered to his course—no! but the melancholy reflections that all these prodigious efforts of the human race, so fruitful of praise, but so much more fruitful of lasting blessings to mankind, have forced a tear from my eye, by that unhappy casualty which deprived me of a friend and you of a representative."

"I know nothing," said Mr. George Leeman, M.P., many years afterwards, "comparable in the history of science to that triumphant march—for such it was—when the Liverpool and Manchester Railway was opened, with George Stephenson himself driving the *Northumbrian* engine; Robert Stephenson, his son, the *Phœnix;* Joseph Locke, the *Rocket;* Alcard, the *Comet;* Thomas Gooch, the *Dart;* and Frederick Swanwick, the *Arrow*—all young engineers of that day who had imbibed the spirit and practical genius of George Stephenson—men whose names, as well as those of others who have followed, have become part of our railway history—men who are to be found, not only in our own country, but who have gone forth over the whole earth, and have spread their names wherever civilization is to be found, and have themselves been the great pioneers of civilization itself."

Next day the business of the railway began. The *Northumbrian* drew a train of 130 passengers from Liverpool to Manchester in an hour and fifty minutes; and before the close of the week six trains were running daily. Instead of thirty stage-coaches that had plied between the two towns, there was only one left; but, instead of 500 passengers, there were 1,600. On one occasion one of the engines travelled thirty-one miles in less than an hour; and in February, 1831, the *Samson* accomplished the greater feat of conveying 164 tons from Liverpool to Manchester in two hours and a half, a load that would have required seventy horses to draw.

The advantages that accrued to the public from the opening of the Liverpool and Manchester line were great, but it did not realize the precise results expected. The goods traffic had been estimated at £50,000 a year, but did not produce £3,000; and coals, which had been put at £20,000, yielded less than £1,000. The tariff of the canal was lowered to that of the railway, and speed and attention to the accommodation of customers were increased. The canal also possessed this important advantage over the railway, that, as it wound through Manchester it touched the warehouses of the merchants and manufacturers, and it terminated at the Liverpool docks, thereby avoiding expense in cartage. On the other hand, the passenger traffic, which had been calculated at £10,000, brought in tenfold that amount; and instead of the passengers by the twenty or thirty coaches that had run between the two towns, there were more than 1,000 a day. The saving to manufacturers in the neighbourhood of Manchester, in the carriage of cotton alone, soon amounted to £20,000 a year; while some houses saved £500 per annum. New factories were established and new coal-pits were sunk near the line, giving increased employment; and while reducing the claimants for parochial relief, the line paid one-fifth of the poor-rates in the parishes. The shareholders of the company, also, by the latter part of the year 1835, were receiving a dividend at the rate of 10 per cent. per annum.

The success of the Liverpool and Manchester line destroyed all doubt as to the possibilities of the railway system, and it was not long before its advantages were sought in other parts of the country. Branches were made from the main line to Warrington on the south, and to Bolton on the north, besides others of minor importance. At a later period, Birmingham was united to Warrington, and consequently with Liverpool and Manchester, by the Grand Junction Railway.

It was subsequently resolved to form a line from London to Birmingham, and in 1830 two companies started on this enterprise. By one it was proposed to proceed through Oxford; by the other to pass near Coventry. Eventually the promoters of the two schemes decided to unite; the Coventry route was preferred; surveys were made of the country through which the line was to pass, estimates of the expense of the works were completed, and an application was made to Parliament for the necessary Acts. In 1832 the Bill was read a third time and passed in the Commons, but a few days afterwards it was thrown out in the Lords, on the ground that it was undesirable to force "the proposed railway through the land and property of so great a proportion of dissentient landowners and proprietors." In the following year the Bill was again brought before Parliament, and received the sanction of both Houses.

Some further reference should now be made to two men whose names are identified with the rise and progress of the railway system. George Stephenson was born in a small cottage, in the village of Wylam, on the banks of the Tyne, near Newcastle. He was the son of a collier, and had early to labour for his share of the household bread. Heavy were the demands upon him. When "too young to stride across the furrow" he went to plough. Then we find him picking bats and dross from the coal-heaps, at twopence a day, and he was still so small that he often hid himself when the overseer passed, lest he should be thought too little to earn his wages. Shortly after he entered his teens he worked as brakesman on a tramway, and subsequently became stoker to an engine on an estate of Lord Ravensworth, often having to rise at one and two o'clock in the morning, and to work till a late hour at night. Thankful in the receipt of a wage of a shilling a day, he declared, when this amount was doubled, that he was "a man for life." He was still a stoker—but a thoughtful and observant one—showing the native ingenuity that dwelt beneath his rough exterior in the execution of some repairs that were required in the machine he tended. Yet his circumstances were far from cheering. In the year 1800 the scourge of war, with famine in its wake, was raging over Europe. Wages were low and food was dear, while the militia and the pressgang imperilled the occupation of the artisan ; and we find George Stephenson seriously thinking of the New World as a more fitting field for his labours. With a keen and painful recollection of the embarrassments of that period, he afterwards remarked to one who was well acquainted with him : "You know the road from my house at Killingworth, to such a spot. When I left home and came down that road, I wept, for I knew not where my lot would be cast."

As his prospects somewhat improved, he gave up the thought of emigration, and when he reached the age of twenty-two, he married. In 1803, his only child, Robert, was born. With increasing responsibilities the father became, if possible, still more industrious. He tried his hand at all kinds of work, and while he availed himself of every opportunity of personal improvement, he cut out clothes for the pitmen, taught the pitmen's wives, and made shoes for his poorer relatives.

Meanwhile, his powers of contrivance and invention had been

developed in various ways, and had created for him what may be designated a local reputation. So decided was his ability, and so great was the confidence Lord Ravensworth and the Killingworth owners had in him, that they supplied him with money to make a locomotive, and in the month of July, 1814, it was tried on a tramway. "Yes," said Stephenson himself, in a speech which he delivered at the opening of the Newcastle and Darlington Railway, in June, 1844, "Yes, Lord Ravensworth & Co., were the first parties that would intrust me with money to make a locomotive engine. That engine was made thirty-two years ago. I said to my friends, that there was no limit to the speed of such an engine, provided the works could be made to stand. In this respect, great perfection has been reached, and, in consequence, a very high velocity has been obtained. In what has been done under my management, the merit is only in part my own. I have been most ably assisted and seconded by my son. In the earlier period of my career, and when he was a little boy, I saw how deficient I was in education, and made up my mind that he should not labour under the same defect, but that I would put him to a good school, and give him a liberal training. I was, however, a poor man ; and how do you think I managed. I betook myself to mending my neighbours' clocks and watches at night, after my daily labour was done ; and thus I procured the means of educating my son. He became my assistant and my companion. He got an appointment as under reviewer, and at night we worked together at our engineering. I got leave to go to Killingworth to lay down a railway at Hetton, and next to Darlington ; and after that I went to Liverpool, to plan a line to Manchester. I there pledged myself to attain a speed of ten miles an hour. I said I had no doubt the locomotive might be made to go much faster, but we had better be moderate at the beginning. The directors said I was quite right ; for if, when they went to Parliament, I talked of going at a greater rate than ten miles an hour, I would put a cross on the concern. It was not an easy task for me to keep the engine down to ten miles an hour ; but it must be done, and I did my best. I had to place myself in that most unpleasant of all positions—the witness-box of a Parliamentary Committee. I could not find words to satisfy either the committee or myself. Some one inquired if I were a foreigner, and another hinted that I was mad." "I put up," he continued, "with every rebuff, and went on with my plans, determined not to be put down. Assistance gradually increased—improvements were made—and to-day, a train, which started from London in the morning, has brought me in the afternoon to my native soil, and enabled me to take my place in this room, and see around me many faces which I have great pleasure in looking upon."

George Stephenson's connection with the Liverpool and Manchester railway brought him into the front rank of the engineers of his day. He became an extensive locomotive manufacturer at Newcastle, a railway contractor, and a great colliery and iron-work owner, particularly at Clay Cross. It is recorded of him, that in reply to the inquiry of a lady, he said, in review of his past career:—" Why, madam, they used to call me George Stephenson; I am now called George Stephenson, *Esquire*, of Tapton House, near Chesterfield. And, further, let me say, that I have dined with princes, peers, and commoners, with persons of all classes, from the humblest to the highest. I have dined off a red-herring when seated in a hedge-bottom, and I have gone through the meanest drudgery. I have seen mankind in all its phases, and the conclusion I have arrived at is this,—that if we were all stripped, there is not much difference."

Robert Stephenson, when a lad, served for three years as a coal-viewer to Mr. Nicholas Wood; and, as better prospects opened up to his father, he attended the University of Edinburgh for a session. During that period there was not a more diligent student there. He knew the value of knowledge, applied himself earnestly to its pursuit, and learned how to teach himself. In 1822 he returned from Edinburgh, and commenced his apprenticeship to engineering, under his father, who had just established a steam-engine factory at Newcastle. But two years of laborious application to the study and practice of his profession, gave evidence, in his failing health, of the fact that he was doing too much even for his robust frame. It happened at that time that an expedition had been arranged for exploring the silver and gold mines of Venezuela, New Grenada, and Colombia, the charge of which was offered to him, and it was accepted. The change of work and of climate were the means of restoring his health, and on his way home, in

1828, he met with Mr. Trevithick, the engineer, from whom he gathered much information in reference to the mines of Cornwall, and this tended, by its application to the construction of locomotives, to his ultimate success in that department.

During the absence of Robert Stephenson from England, a new era had arisen in our railway history. The *Rocket* was nearly completed. The success of that engine encouraged Robert Stephenson to devote his attention to the construction of locomotives ; and, by simplifying the working parts of the engine, enlarging the steam-generating capacities of the boiler, and varying the proportions of several parts of the engine, he obtained a great increase both of power and speed. The engines that issued, month by month, from the factory, were a continuous improvement on their predecessors, until the Newcastle factory became the largest and most famous in the world. As railways increased, it sent engines to all the countries of Europe, and to the United States, and it manufactured about a thousand locomotives. A writer in October, 1850, said, while speaking of the achievements of railway enterprise, especially under the auspices of Mr. Stephenson, that we then had about 5,000 miles of railway, in the construction of which 250,000,000 cubic yards, or not less than 350,000,000 tons of earth and rock had, in tunnel, embankment, and cutting, been moved.

On the completion of the London and Birmingham, the Stephensons undertook the formation of the Birmingham and Derby, North Midland, York and North Midland, Manchester and Leeds, Northern and Eastern Railways, and for ten years were incessantly engaged upon the surveys, plans, parliamentary battles, and construction of the vast network of lines stretching in all directions throughout the kingdom. During this period, Robert Stephenson, as engineer-in-chief, executed the great iron cross of roads which, on the one hand, unite London with Berwick, and on the other, Yarmouth with Holyhead, making, with the lines in connection with them, not fewer than 1,800 miles of the iron highways of the country. They also planned the construction of an extensive system of railways in Belgium, extending on the one hand from Ostend to Liege, and on the other, from Antwerp through Brussels, to be connected through Mons with Valenciennes, altogether 347 miles of railway.

In the year 1846 Robert Stephenson visited Norway to

examine the country for the purpose of a railway between Christiania and the Myosen Lake; and he had honours conferred upon him, in acknowledgment of his able services, by the King of Norway and Sweden, as previously he had received distinctions from the King of Belgium.

"It was but as yesterday," said Robert Stephenson in 1850, "that he was engaged as an assistant in tracing the line of the Stockton and Darlington Railway. Since that period, the Liverpool and Manchester, the London and Birmingham, and a hundred other great works, had sprung into vigorous existence. So suddenly had they been accomplished, that it appeared to him like the realization of fabled powers, or the magician's wand. Hills had been cut down, and valleys had been filled up; and where this simple expedient was inapplicable, high and magnificent viaducts had been erected; and where mountains intervened, tunnels of unexampled magnitude had been unhesitatingly undertaken. Works had been scattered over the face of our country, bearing testimony to the indomitable enterprise of the nation, and the unrivalled skill of its artists. In referring thus to the railway works, he must refer also to the improvement of the locomotive engine. This was as remarkable as the other works were gigantic. They were, in fact, necessary, to each other. The locomotive engine, independent of the railway, would be useless. They had gone on together, and they now realized all the expectations that were entertained of them."

"Healthy-bodied and healthy-minded," said a writer in the *Westminster and Foreign Quarterly Review*, "apt in emergencies, and yet of slow, and generally of sound judgment, Robert Stephenson may be regarded as the type and pattern of the onward-moving English race, practical, scientific, energetic, and, in the hour of trial, heroic. Born almost in the coal-mine, of the racy old blood of the north, with a father strong in mother-wit, stern of purpose, untiring in patience, careful of his small resources, keenly conscious of the bounded sphere his want of early education had kept him in till a later period of life, and determined to pare off from himself all luxuries, all but the merest necessaries, in order that his after-coming should start fair in life with that knowledge he himself held above all price —born thus, Robert Stephenson was emphatically *well-born.*

With natural talents, good education, a healthy frame, the rising *prestige* of his father's name, little money, and a large demand for original work in a working and energetic old world, he went forth to the New World, and in the mines of South America and their environs added new manners and customs to his varied stock of knowledge. More than all this, the genial spirit that ever looked kindly on his fellow-creature, with the intellect that could generally winnow the false from the true, marked him out for a leader of men. Not to his mere mechanical skill does he owe his success in life. That might have been thwarted in five hundred ways by interested rivals; but men wish not to thwart those whom they love; and probably no chief of an army was ever more beloved by his soldiers than Robert Stephenson has been by the noble army of physical workers, who under his guidance have wrought at labours of profit,—made labours of love by his earnest purpose and strength of brotherhood."

TRENT BRIDGE, NOTTINGHAM.

CHAPTER II.

Change of Public Feeling towards Railways.—Wordsworth's Indignation.—Alarm of Vested Interests.—Colonel Sibthorpe.—Opposition of Northampton, Oxford, and Eton.—Hatred "even unto Death."—Prophecies of Disaster Falsified.—Progress of Railway Enterprise.—Select Committee of House of Commons.—Excellent Dividends.—Unwelcome Truths.—Railway Mania.—Extraordinary Excitement.—Gambling and Suicide.—"Stags."—George Hudson.—Remarkable Career.—The Railway King.—Decline and Fall.—Deposit of Plans at Board of Trade.—November 30th, 1845.—Sharp Practice.—Statistics of Railways.—Cost of Railway Mania.—Disastrous Issues.—Confidence Returning.

DURING the events that witnessed the successful establishment of the railway and the locomotive, the indifference or contempt with which both had been regarded came gradually to be exchanged for other sentiments. Surprise, gratification, admiration, and hostility were warmly felt and expressed, according to the point of view from which the great innovation was regarded. Perhaps no feeling was so strong as that of those who feared that their vested interests or privileges were likely to be imperilled; and those who had these alarms did not fail assiduously to impart them to others. A rumour that it was proposed to bring such a thing as a railroad within a dozen miles of a particular neighbourhood, was sufficient to elicit adverse petitions to Parliament, and public subscriptions were opened to give effect to the opposition. Newspaper editors and pamphleteers ridiculed the delusiveness of the particular project. Householders were told that their homes would be hourly in danger of being burned to the ground, and farmers were assured that their hens would not

The initial letter represents the mouth of a tunnel on the Lledyr Vale line, North Wales.

lay nor their cows graze, and that game would fall dead to the ground if they attempted to fly over the poisoned breath exhaled by the engines. A poet laureate, when he heard of a proposal to bring a line from Kendal to Windermere, indignantly demanded—

> "Is there no nook of English ground secure
> From rash assault? Schemes of retirement sown
> In youth, and 'mid the busy world kept pure
> As when their earliest flowers of hope were blown,
> Must perish; how can they this blight endure?
> And must he, too, his old delights disown,
> Who scorns a false, utilitarian lure
> 'Mid his paternal fields at random thrown?
> Baffle the threat, bright scene, from Orrest-head,
> Given to the pausing traveller's rapturous glance!
> Plead for thy peace, thou beautiful romance
> Of nature; and if human hearts be dead,
> Speak, passing winds; ye torrents, with your strong
> And constant voice, protest against the wrong!"

Hundreds of innkeepers and thousands of horses would, it was said, have nothing to do. Labour for the poor would be lessened, and rates for the poor would be increased. Canals would be destroyed; those who lived by them would become beggars; and houses would be crushed by falling embankments. The 27,000 miles of turnpike-roads in Great Britain, to say nothing of the other public and cross roads of the country, would, it was averred, be made useless. Politicians declared that the railway system was "a monopoly the most secure, the most lasting, the most injurious that can be conceived to the public good;" and that directors were "induced by no motive to action but their own selfishness, swayed by every gust of prejudice and passion, and too often as profoundly ignorant of even their own real interest, as they are exclusively devoted to its advancement." Medical men asserted that the gloom and damp of tunnels, and the deafening peal, the clanking chains, and the dismal glare of the locomotives would be disastrous alike to body and mind. Hundreds of thousands of persons would be ruined for the benefit of a few. An eminent parliamentary lawyer affirmed that it would be an impossibility to start a locomotive in a gale of wind, "either by poking the fire, or keeping up the pressure of steam till the boiler is ready to burst." A well-known engineer deprecated "the ridiculous expectations, or rather professions, of the enthusiastic speculator that we shall see engines travelling at the rate of twelve, sixteen, eighteen, or twenty miles an hour. Nothing could do more harm towards their general adoption and improvement than the promulgation of such nonsense." "I hate these infernal railways," said the energetic Colonel Sibthorpe, "as I hate the devil."

Nor did this opposition exhaust itself in words; it expressed itself in active hostility to the various schemes projected. The London and Birmingham line was compelled to change its intended route through Northampton, and to keep at a respectful distance; lest, said some of the worthies of that shoe-making town, the wool of the sheep should be injured by the smoke of the locomotives (though they burned coke); and therefore—philanthropic souls!—they required that the purity of their fleeces should be preserved unsullied from the plutonic cloud, at the cost of the farmers of Blisworth and its neighbourhood. One consequence of this opposition was that the line had to be carried through the famous Kilsby Tunnel at an additional expense of £300,000. It was declared of the London and Birmingham Railway, that it would be "a drug on the country;" that "its bridges and culverts would be antiquarian ruins;" that "it would not take tolls sufficient to keep it in repair;" that "the directors were making ducks and drakes of their money;" that agriculture would be stopped; that springs would be dried up, and meadows become sterile. "Like an earthquake, it would create chasms and upheave mountains;" and it was added that "the railway promoter was like an evil Providence, unrighteously attempting that which Nature was too kind to effect."

Nor was such hostility confined to Northampton. Those seats of learning, Oxford and Eton, would not permit the Great Western bill to pass without the insertion of special clauses to prohibit the formation of any branch to Oxford, or of a station at Slough; while it was declared by the authorities of the school, that anybody acquainted with the nature of Eton boys would know that they could not be kept from the railway if it were allowed to be constructed. When the directors subsequently attempted to infringe the conditions with which they had been bound, by only stopping to take up and set down passengers, proceedings were commenced against them in Chancery, and they were interdicted from even making a pause.

The hatred of railways, even to a late period, was cherished by some "even unto death." A curious illustration of this was shown by a will proved in 1868 at Carlisle. The testator, a yeoman of Abbey Cowper, entertained a great objection to the construction of the Carlisle and Silloth Bay Railway, which passed through his property, and in order to show to the last his disapprobation of the undertaking and its promoters, he bequeathed one farthing to each of nine persons who took an active part in promoting it, and £750 to a land surveyor who valued his land for him when the Company took it. The bulk of the property was left to a distant relative, hampered, however, with the conditions that he "shall not at any time travel in or upon the Carlisle and Silloth Bay Railway;" and, further, that in case three local promoters of the line—whom he named—or any of them, or any of the sons of one of them, should call at Abbey Cowper on business, or for any other purpose, the legatee "shall not receive them into his house at Abbey Cowper aforesaid, nor entertain them with meat, drink, or otherwise."

But prejudice, vested interests, abuse and poetry, could not avert the advance of railways. The prophecies of disaster to landlords and farmers were alike unfulfilled: farmers could buy their coals, lime, and manure with less money, and could find readier access to the best markets for their produce. Cows still gave milk, sheep fed and fattened, and at length even skittish horses ceased to shy at the passing trains. "The smoke of the engines did not obscure the sky, nor were farm-yards burnt up by the fire thrown from the locomotives." The farming classes found that their interests were promoted by the extension of railways; and landlords discovered that they could get higher rents for estates situated near a line. Even the proprietors of the canals were astounded to see that in the face of railway competition, their own traffic receipts continued to increase; and that they fully shared in the expansion of trade and commerce which had been promoted by the extension of railways. Horse-flesh, too, increased in value as railways spread; and the coaches running to and from the new stations gave employment to a greater number of horses than under the old stage-coach system. "Those who had prophesied the decay of the metropolis, and the ruin of the suburban cabbage growers, in consequence of the approach of railways to London, were disappointed; for, while the new roads let citizens out of London, they also let country-people in. Their action, in this respect, was centripetal as well as centrifugal. Tens of thousands who had never seen the metropolis could now visit it expeditiously and cheaply; and Londoners who had never visited the country, or but rarely, were enabled, at little cost of time or money, to see green fields and clear blue skies, far from the smoke and bustle of town. The food of the metropolis became rapidly improved, especially in the supply of wholesome meat and vegetables. And then the price of coals—an article which, in this country, is as indispensable as daily food to all classes—was greatly reduced. What a blessing to the metropolitan poor is described in this single fact!"

The press, too, aided the cause of progress, and hastened to make known facts illustrative of the triumphs of the means of locomotion. Thus, so early as 1838, the proprietors of a Scottish periodical announced that, before their next number was published, in consequence of the sending of the mails to Warrington by the railway, the people of Edinburgh would receive their letters and papers an entire day sooner than during the time of the late war, namely, in thirty-one instead of fifty-five hours; and a return by post between London and Edinburgh, which twenty years before occupied a week, would then be accomplished in three days and a half; and the *Railway Magazine* mentioned, as a prodigy of expedition, that a gentleman had lately gone from Manchester to Liverpool in the morning, and purchased a hundred and fifty tons of cotton, which he immediately took back with him to Manchester. He there sold the lot, returned to Liverpool, purchased a second lot, and delivered it the same evening.

The report of the Board of Trade stated that, in the year 1843 no fewer than 24,000,000 of passengers had travelled, the average journey of each being fifteen miles.

The lines sanctioned by Parliament during the year 1844 were brought forward partly on account of their intrinsic merits, and partly as measures of self-defence, adopted by established Companies to exclude rivals. So energetically were these steps taken, and so enterprising was the spirit of those connected with these lines, that at a meeting of the Midland Railway Company upon this subject, the proprietors voted two millions and a half of money to be applied, at the discretion of the directors, to the formation of lines of which no definite plans were then decided on.

Another class of projects consisted of branches or junctions, formed as connecting links between existing lines, but the precise course of which seriously affected the question as to which main line would attract the largest amount of traffic from the intermediate districts. The new undertakings of various kinds brought before the public during the year 1844, numbered no fewer than a hundred and fifty.

Early in the Session of 1844, a Select Committe of the House of Commons was appointed to consider the Standing Orders relating to railways, and also to examine the whole subject of railway legislation. That Committee recommended several modifications of the existing orders, which were adopted. By these a reduction was made in the deposit required by Parliament before introducing a railway bill, to one-twentieth of the amount of capital, instead of one-tenth, which had been demanded under the regulations of 1837. The Committee also recommended a new method of investigating the merits of railway bills, by referring them to a Select Committee consisting of members whose constituents had no local interest in the measure, and who were themselves in no way personally involved in the bill referred to them.

The results of the labours of the Railway Committee were brought before the House in several subsequent reports, upon which a bill was founded, which required that one train should pass from one end to the other of every trunk, branch, or junction line, once at least each way on every week-day; that the time at which these trains should start should be fixed by the Lords of the Committee of Privy Council; that each train should travel at an average rate of speed of not less than twelve miles an hour, including stoppages; that it should take up and set down passengers at every passenger station on the line; that the carriages should be protected from the weather, and provided with seats; that the fare should not exceed a penny a mile; that half a hundred weight of luggage shall be allowed to each passenger, any excess being charged at a regulated rate. It was further enjoined, that children of three years old shall be conveyed without charge, and that from that age up to twelve, the rate should be one-half the amount of an adult passenger.

A remarkable feature of the railway history of the year 1845 was the number of amalgamations made between individual lines, and the arrangements of the principal companies to lease the minor lines connected with their own undertakings. But there were a large number of cases which, after an agreement for such an union of interests had been made by the directors, and sanctioned by a public meeting of proprietors, were "repudiated" at subsequent meetings in consequence of a rise in the market value of the stock, or of the prospect of obtaining more favourable terms with another company.

But we have drawn near to a great epoch, not only in the history of the railway, but of the monetary world. Up to the year 1843, and during part of 1844, railways may be regarded as honestly working their way through good and evil report into the public appreciation of their value, not only socially and generally, but as a means for the investment of capital. The security and profit they offered were so great that there was a rapid flow of capital in the new direction. The dividends paid by the London and Birmingham, by the Liverpool and Manchester, and by the York and North Midland Companies were at the rate of 10 per cent. per annum, while the Grand Junction was paying 11, and the Stockton and Darlington 15 per cent. The temptation of such dividends could not be resisted. Enterprise outran prudence, and railways became for the time popular beyond every other kind of investment. There had been a brief mania for new lines in 1836, but it had not reached fever-heat; and the reaction, with the consequent losses, had not induced caution. Money was abundant. The Bank rate of discount was 2½ per cent. Consols were above par, and everything seemed to promise the continuance of a golden age. This surplusage of capital and the growing manufacturing wealth of the country proved the occasion for the outbreak of one of those periodical manias which appear, and (like the South Sea Bubble) leave their black mark behind. Unemployed engineers and attorneys, with the tribe of promoters, jobbers, and speculators were not slow to perceive the advantages they might derive. Exaggerated accounts were spread of the vast wealth to be easily gained.

Popular cupidity was inflamed, and railway investment became a fashion and a frenzy. To doubt the profits was branded as ignorance, and to deny the success was madness. From week to week during the winter of 1844 the delusion spread.

Meanwhile the Report of the Select Committee on Joint Stock Companies, in 1844, announced many unwelcome truths. It stated that when a company was to be formed, the prospectus was usually first issued, sometimes without the names of directors, in the expectation that parties would form themselves into a direction for its support; and advertisements were issued of the new project. As soon as the scheme attracted attention, applications were made, in the hope that the shares would come out at a premium, however small; and if that was secured, every species of influence was employed to obtain an allotment which could be sold. Mr. Duncan, M.P., stated that frequently the shares were not attended to at all, for the applications of persons were not made with a view to investment, but for the immediate premium. "The reason," he said, "why these letters can be dealt in, is because the company's bankers, not knowing one from another, take money from everybody who brings a letter of appropriation, and they give a receipt. This receipt is taken to the company's office and exchanged for a scrip certificate to bearer, and then the title of the buyer of the letter is complete. If there be much risk about the company, or no great soundness, or if it be ill supported by the directory, a second call can never be obtained. The consequence is, that after from six to twelve months' duration, the company is dissolved, and dies a natural death, and the deposit is found to be eaten up by expenses."

Such were the facilities at the command of those who embarked in what came to be known as the Railway Mania, and every event was made to contribute to the excitement. In January, 1845, sixteen new companies were registered; in February and March this number was more than doubled, and in April fifty-two additional companies were formed. Popular enthusiasm was hastening forwards in an unjustifiable and insane career.

Amidst a great number of *bonâ fide* undertakings appeared a multitude of bubble projects, concocted by those who cared only to prey on the honesty or credulity of others. Out of a true spirit of legitimate enterprise arose a mania, in the midst of which many a needy rogue was transmuted into what society calls "a gentleman." One chief object was to get possession of the deposit money, and to spend it in preliminary expenses (*i.e.* their own), and in lawyers' bills. The capital required was small. A few knaves engaged an office, bought a map, struck out a railway in what appeared to be a suitable direction, gave it a plausible title, and with a sheet of foolscap and a "Court Guide" made a prospectus, on which they placed the names of a few noble lords, right honourables, ex-M.P.s, and merchants, to which an engineer, banker, and lawyer were added, and the whole was "served up," with imaginary advantages, and with the assurance of at least ten per cent. dividend. The excitement of the times prevented much chance of the detection of the fraud, and the inexperienced who wished to speculate were taken in. Shares were advertised at £2 or £2 10*s.* for the first instalment, only a certain number being allotted, that they might bring a full price, while "stags" were actively engaged in inquiring for shares which they never intended to purchase, and only asked for to give them a fraudulent value in the market; or perhaps they bought a few with the deposit-money which subscribers had paid, in order to produce the same result. As soon as the premium was reached the price was forced upwards, and then the shares were placed as fast as possible upon the market. The profits thus realized were, in many instances, enormous; cabs were set up, "tigers" were hired, and good coats and clean shirts began to be worn by men who had been strangers to these luxuries for many a day!

The successes of both honest men and of knaves in share-speculating encouraged large numbers of both classes to embark in the enterprise, and the mania proportionately increased. The *Manchester Guardian* reported that during one week eighty-nine new schemes had been announced in three newspapers, the capital required for which was estimated at more than eighty-four millions; while in the space of a month three hundred and fifty-seven railway projects were advertised in the same journals, having an aggregate capital of three hundred and thirty-two millions sterling.

> "Old men and young, the famish'd and the full,
> The rich and poor, widow, and wife, and maid,
> Master and servant—all, with one intent,

> Rushed on the paper scrip ; their eager eyes
> Flashing a fierce unconquerable greed—
> Their hot palms itching—all their being fill'd
> With one desire."

Lord Clanricarde mentioned in the House of Lords that a clerk named Guernsey, in a broker's office, with twelve shillings a week wage, and the son of a charwoman, had his name down as a subscriber for shares in the London and York line for £52,000. Bland country vicars became "bears," curates were "stags," and old maiden ladies became "bulls," on the Stock Exchange. Servants wrote for shares in their master's names; and there is a story told of a butler at the West-end giving notice to his mistress to quit, as he had realized several thousand pounds by shares. On the lady asking him how this was, "Why, ma'am," he said, "I applies for the shares, and gives a reference here; and, as I opens the door myself, and answers the reference, I always gives myself the wery highest character for property and all that, and so I gets the shares and sells them." And thus we have the living prototype of *Jeames* of *Buckley Square*, renowned in song and story.

A voluminous return, subsequently made in conformity with an order of the House of Commons, shows the general excitement in these speculations. It includes the names of all who subscribed for *less* sums than £2,000; and among them may be recognised many of the leading nobility, the largest manufacturing firms, and individuals well known from their connection with various departments of science, literature, and art. The juxtaposition of the professions or engagements of some is very amusing. Side by side are "peers and printers, vicars and vice-admirals, spinsters and half-pays, M.P.s and special pleaders, professors and cotton-spinners, gentlemen's cooks and Q.C.s, attorneys' clerks and college scouts, writers at Lloyd's, relieving officers and excisemen, barristers and butchers, Catholic priests and coachmen, editors and engineers, dairymen and dyers, braziers, bankers, beer-sellers, and butlers, domestic servants, footmen, and mail-guards; with a multitude of other callings unrecorded in the Book of Trades."

"Every man of the present day," said Cruikshank in his Table Book, "is a holder of shares in a railway; that is, he has got some pieces of paper called scrip, entitling him to a certain proportionate part of a blue, red, or yellow line drawn across a map, and designated a railway. If the coloured scratch runs south to north, it is generally called a Trunk Line; if it 'turns about and wheels about' in all directions, leading to nowhere on its own account, but interfering with every railway that does, ten to one but it is a Grand Junction; and if it lies at full length along the shore, it is a Coast Line. Trunk lines are generally the best, because the word trunk naturally connects itself in the mind of the public with the idea of luggage, and a good deal of traffic is consequently relied upon. Grand Junctions are good speculations, as troublesome customers, likely to be bought off by larger concerns, which would consider them a nuisance; and as street nuisances generally expect a consideration for moving on, a Grand Junction may ask a good price for taking itself off from an old-established company."

The localities of railway enterprise were curious. From Moorgate Street issued nearly ninety prospectuses of railways, the capital required for which amounted to as many millions sterling. In Gresham Street twenty were planned, requiring for their construction the sum of more than seventeen millions, and eight of them having originated in one house. Well might *Punch* say, "As many as seventeen thousand newspapers have been found in the General Post Office with their covers burst. The reason of the newspapers bursting is accounted for by the fact that they contain so many railway bubbles."

The "manufacture" of the managers and officers of companies was in many cases on an equally wholesale system. Taking the list of the members forming the provisional direction of twenty-three companies, one man was discovered who belonged to them all; two, each of whom figured on nineteen companies; three who had given their names to seventeen companies; fourteen who belonged to fourteen companies; twenty-two to ten; twenty-three to eight; and twenty-nine to seven. These twenty-three provisional committees divided among themselves 352,800 shares, at the rate of 2,800 a-piece.

The Irish railways furnished even a more ample list of pluralist directors; and it is asserted that there was no difficulty in pointing out several who held office in no fewer than thirty railway directions. The same parties even appeared as the promoters of rival lines; and individuals were the avowed patrons of three competing companies at the same time. Specific instances could easily be cited.

The names of gentlemen wholly unconnected with railways, and who would have utterly repudiated association with the men who advocated them, were unhesitatingly employed for the purpose of lending a supposititious countenance to bubble companies. One line was declared to enjoy the patronage of four gentlemen who had been dead for several months; and ten others had no knowledge of the existence of the scheme till they saw it paraded before the public, avowedly under their own sanction. In another case, the three leading projectors of a very costly railway were notoriously "living by their wits," and could not have raised a hundred pounds among them except by fraud. The course usually adopted when gentlemen protested against the unwarranted use of their names, was to assure them that it was quite a misunderstanding; but after many apologies, its use was continued till public exposure was threatened, or the object was secured.

Affairs went on in this manner for some time, all men knowing that a crash must come. "The prospect becomes more serious," said a writer, "when it is discovered in what feeble hands great masses of this speculation rest; in what manifold ways the mischief has descended through all classes of society; to how many persons a reverse will be utter ruin, not to themselves only, but to helpless numbers whom they have deceived, with whose funds they have been gaming, or to whom they owe debts that can neither be paid nor spared. We tremble to think how much more of the like vice and folly, now concealed under this surface of bustle and feverish excitement, may be at this moment struggling in the grasp of the same evils, and preparing other lamentable scenes of failure, shame, and madness. It is a vice which we fear is becoming an utter plague in the land—a pestilence destructive of things infinitely more precious than even the fortunes or maintenances which it rashly hazards. Every day brings us some new instance of its hateful effects upon private happiness and public character. Now we are told of shameful disclosures affecting the honour of men in office,—persons whom it was our English boast, for the last half century at least, to proclaim to the world as above the suspicion of any foul handling of lucre. Now we are called to deplore the utter ruin of a household, dashed down from decent competency into beggary and disgrace, in the frantic pursuit of sudden wealth. The next moment we hear of a pious defaulter for hundreds of thousands ; and, turning from him in disgust, we stumble on the body of a suicide ! "

The sinews of war, once obtained, were quickly put into requisition to further the objects of the projectors of the line. It was on the deposits which thus came into their hands that directors, without money themselves, counted to carry on the management. The company, once started, could prosecute its operations on a large scale. " Confidence, generosity, cash, were sure to command success. Crack engineers were engaged at large salaries, and received *carte blanche* for their surveys and surveying parties. Advertising agents were directed to be active and liberal ; they boasted to editors and proprietors of newspapers of their instructions. The newspapers puffed, and charged like heroes ; the directors and secretaries bragged to the newspaper writers ; surveyors composed epics on the capabilities of the lines ; and shareholders listened to the lay, with the vague, swelling, dreamy delight of opium-eaters under the influence of their drug. All concerned assumed that the nominal capitals of all the projected companies would be actually forthcoming ; all counted upon the share in the plunder which they had in imagination allotted to themselves, being as sure as if they had already held it in gold."

The " stags," who performed so important a part in the Railway Mania, should not go unnoticed. They were an unique race, though there were several grades of this remarkable calling, each with its appropriate designation. A regular thoroughbred stag was perhaps some forty years old, or upwards, with a face wearing a peculiarly sinister expression, tainted with colours suggestive of strong drinks. His apparel was worthy of his vocation, but varied according to the circumstances of the case, or the occasion. Sometimes he disported a faded suit of black —then he appeared in drab unmentionables and gaiters ; but there was almost invariably a tint about his garments, which is only to be expressed by the word—*seedy*. Some individuals of the species had an appearance akin to that of those " sporting gents " who are to be found near the betting places on the course, and they all had a taste for sporting. They indulged in small transactions of this kind, and did not eschew skittles; and if a stag had his hand in his pocket, he was generally fumbling a greasy halfpenny, which he called into frequent requisition in order to decide, by tossing up, any disputed point in reference to which his veracity might be called in question. This, however, was in his easier moods. A writer who sketched this interesting class, thus described the stag when professionally engaged:—"When sneaking into an office as a slate quarry proprietor, or great railway capitalist, he has a subdued air, and the clerk in his teens, and first experience of railway business, listens to his inquiries with becoming deference, and ushers him into the presence of the secretary, or sees him carefully lay up the letter of application in his enormous pocket-book, to which his multifarious memoranda are consigned, and which contains a list of all the applications he has under hand, entered systematically, with the several names and addresses made use of. The clerk little thinks that the bulk in his coat pocket consists of several enormous bundles of prospectuses, greasy outside, and bound up with red tape. It is needless to say, that the stag has long since been in the position of having no character to boast of, having gone through all the several stages of whitewashing, remand, and imprisonment in Whitecross Street, with perhaps some experience of the criminal jurisprudence of his country. He has a knowledge of business, for he has failed in it; and he is disinclined to begin again, as he is an uncertificated bankrupt. He hates work, and prefers misery. Where he lives no one knows. His letters are generally addressed to the Old Kent Road; but it is doubtful whether he have any residence at all. His mornings begin by carefully examining all the daily papers at a pot-house or cheap coffee-house, where he makes copious memoranda of all the places to be called at for prospectuses and forms of application. He then gets his letters, and if he has the good luck to get any shares allotted, he proceeds to sell the latter among his brethren; and glad is he if he can take a few shillings home. Besides looking after prospectuses, he occasionally varies his pursuits by signing deeds, to make up the parliamentary subscription list. This he does for the consideration of, perhaps, five shillings per name,—going in, it may be, with a pair of spectacles on, and signing the deed, and then returning without the spectacles, and signing in some other capacity. A well-known hotel and tavern-keeper in Covent Garden is reputed to contract occasionally for supplying these vagabonds with such things, and with the carrying out schemes for plundering the small tradesmen, and other unfortunate individuals having money, who get dealings with them." The stag passed the evening, if lucky, in the pot-house.

Our history at this period would be incomplete were not some allusion made to the remarkable but changeful fortunes of one whose name is indissolubly associated with this era of our railway system. George Hudson was born in 1800, served his apprenticeship in the ancient city of York, and subsequently carried on business there as a linendraper, and became a man of considerable property. "The happiest part of my life," he said, many years afterwards, "was when I stood behind the counter and used the yard measure in my own shop. My ruin was having a fortune left me. I had one of the snuggest businesses in York, and turned over my thirty thousand a year, when a relation died and left me a goodish fortune. It was the very worst thing which ever happened to me. It led me into railways and to all my misfortunes since." The results that had attended the opening of the Liverpool and Manchester line had attracted the attention of the country at large; and while various schemes of railways were proposed for different parts of the country, the people of York also determined to have their own railway. A line between York, Leeds, and London was proposed; Mr. Hudson was appointed one of the provisional committee; and, on the passing of the bill into law, he was made the chairman of the board. His efforts in this capacity were so satisfactory, that the cost of the land he procured for the railway averaged only £1,750 a mile, while that of the North Midland had amounted to upwards of £5,000. "Hudson's line," as the people called it, was opened on the 29th of May, 1839, and on the 1st of July of the following year the linendraper of York had the great satisfaction of seeing the first locomotive speed on its way from the old archiepiscopal city, his native place, to the metropolis.

These successes were only an incentive to fresh efforts. To avoid rivalry between his own and a neighbouring line, he proposed that the latter should be leased to himself and friends for thirty-one years; the plan was approved; the result, in a pecuniary sense, was gratifying; and other great schemes were undertaken by him, his most determined opponents shrinking before his enterprise and influence. The shareholders of the North Midland, for instance, were involved in difficulty. Mr. Hudson appeared before them, and in a remarkable speech contended that their expenses might be reduced nearly one-half, enforced his arguments with facts and figures, and offered to guarantee double the then dividend if his scheme of amendment was adopted. He was made chairman of a committee of shareholders, the directors resigned, and Mr. Hudson was appointed instead. His reforms were vigorously carried out, the efficiency of the line was increased, the cost halved, and the shares doubled in value. Other great plans were successfully undertaken — embarrassed lines were relieved — weak ones were strengthened—rivals were subdued. Ever active, vigorous, and energetic, his capacity for business was singular; and it may without dispute be asserted, that up to a particular period of his history his efforts were highly advantageous to the railways with which he was connected. He found himself chairman of 600 miles of railway, extending from Rugby to Newcastle. "His name became an authority on railway speculation, and the confidence reposed in him was unbounded. For a time the entire railway system of the north of England seemed under his control. What herculean energy was in the man may be gathered from a couple of days' work. Under Mr. Hudson's direction, on the 2nd May, 1846, the shareholders of the Midland Company gave their approval to twenty-six bills, which were immediately introduced into Parliament. On Monday following, at ten o'clock, the York and North Midland sanctioned six bills, and affirmed various deeds and agreements affecting the Manchester and Leeds and Hull and Selby companies. Fifteen minutes later he induced the Newcastle and Darlington Company to approve of seven bills and accompanying agreements; and at half-past ten took his seat as a controlling power at the board of the Newcastle and Berwick. During these two days he obtained approval of forty bills, involving the expenditure of about £10,000,000." He was looked upon with feelings of admiration and wonder, as one at whose magic touch everything turned into gold.

Many pictures might be drawn of the strangely varied

career of the "Railway King." One has been sketched by an eye-witness: "The place was the drawing-room of a well-known noble patron of the fine arts, the occasion was a semi-public *conversazione* connected with national objects, at which representative men—'men who had done something'—were present by the hundred. England's greatest authors, sculptors, painters, inventors, philanthropists, statesmen, physicians, engineers, captains, jostled each other in the crowded rooms. Amid the constellation of celebrities there were two men round whom the crowds circled, both receiving the deference of the great and noble. One was the late Prince Consort, the other was George Hudson. They looked rival monarchs, each with his obsequious courtiers round him, and divided pretty equally the honours of the evening. Those who were not able to come within speaking distance of these great men waited patiently, and as near to the charmed circles as they could. Suddenly there was a movement, and a gentleman was seen to pass from the Prince Consort's followers and to make his way to the little court which hemmed in the Railway King. It was like a plenipotentiary carrying a message between neighbouring potentates. 'The Prince has asked to be introduced to Mr. Hudson.'"

After a while the enthusiasm cooled, and the tables were turned. Mr. Hudson's connection with the Eastern Counties Railway, and the truth that ultimately came to light, that dividends had been paid out of capital; the method in which he had conducted the business of some other companies; and the fact that many sustained fearful losses by the fall in the value of their property, produced a revulsion in the public mind in reference to their hero. Probably much of the invective poured upon him came from those of whose purity there was little to boast. The fox that loses his tail is persecuted by all the foxes; the rook that is maimed is cawed out of the rookery. Mr. Hudson may be regarded as the type of the period in which he acted so prominently,—as an illustration of the spirit of that epoch in the history of manias. He had been held up to adulation because he had accumulated great wealth—his highest achievement, in the view of thousands, was the fact that he had made £100,000 in one day—and he was deified because he enabled others to be successful too.

"The truth is," said a writer of that time, "Mr. Hudson is

neither better nor worse than the morality of 1845. He rose to wealth and importance at an immoral period; he was the creature of an immoral system; he was wafted into fortune upon the wave of a popular mania; he was elevated into the dictatorship of railway speculation in an unwholesome ferment of popular cupidity, pervading all ranks and conditions of men; and whatever may be the hue of the error he committed, it is rather too much to expect of him that he should be purer than his time or his associates. The commercial code of 1845 was, as far as railways were concerned, framed upon anything but moral principles. The lust of gain blinded the eyes of men who, before that period, could see clearly enough the difference between right and wrong, between trading and gambling, and between legitimate and illegitimate speculation. Men who would have scorned to do a dishonest act towards any other real tangible living man, did not scruple to do acts towards that great abstraction, the public, which no morality could justify."

In his old age, it was rumoured among some of the former friends of George Hudson, that he was in poverty; it was said that he frequently went hungry to bed; whereupon a fund was raised sufficient to purchase him an annuity of £600 a year—a kindness and help for which he was deeply grateful. In his later days he would freely chat over the events, great and small, of former times. "The speeches he made when at the height of his prosperity; the quiet grave in the little Yorkshire churchyard which he bought for himself long ago, and which he went down to visit from time to time; the social fun he had in former days with 'old George Stephenson, the best of fellows and the best of friends;' his civic triumphs as Lord Mayor of York, and the quaint piece of plate which he insisted that holders of that high office are required to use while at the Mansion House; his dealings with his lady customers when he kept a shop; his visits to the nobility; his victories at railway boards; the way he was run after by the great world of London, and the zest with which he enjoyed the *éclat* and the fun of it all; the respect with which he was listened to when speaking in the House of Commons; the opinions he had enforced in various great commercial enterprises, and how others were profiting by them, were wont to be quoted and expatiated on by him with a hearty interest. He was fond, too, of telling the origin of his title of Railway King. 'Sydney Smith, sir, the Rev. Sydney Smith, the great wit, first called me the Railway King; and I remember very well that he made a very pretty speech about it, saying, that while some monarchs had won their title to fame by bloodshed and by the misery they inflicted on their fellow creatures, I had come to my throne by my own peaceful exertions, and by a course of probity and enterprise.'"

But we are approaching another epoch in the history of railways. Parliament had required that plans of proposed railways should be deposited at the offices of the Board of Trade, on or before Sunday night, the 30th of November, 1845, and extraordinary efforts were necessary on the part of numerous railways to have their documents completed for that occasion; while the supply of labour in every department being greatly exceeded by the demand, its value proportionately increased in all directions. Innumerable surveyors and levellers were required, and in many instances they made from six to fifteen guineas a-day; while numbers of persons were employed who were acquainted with only the rudiments of the art, and who, by their blunders, subsequently occasioned even fatal inconvenience to the enterprises in which they were concerned. The extravagant payment that was offered, also induced great numbers to leave situations they occupied in order to learn the new business; while professors, lecturers, and teachers announced classes, lectures, and private instruction, which with almost magical celerity would convert all persons of ordinary powers into practical men earning enormous payments. Still the supply was not equal to the wants of the case, surveyors and levellers became "worth their weight in gold," and countless amateurs presented themselves. A peddling stationer, who long itinerated in Northumberland and Durham, earned "five guineas a day and his expenses" on a southern railroad; and the *Lancaster Guardian* stated that a fat neighbour, long unemployed, obtained an engagement of three guineas. "I could have had five," said he, "but it would have been in a country where the gradients were severe, and too trying for my wind;" and he preferred three guineas and a level line. No fewer than eighty surveyors arrived in Lancaster in one day for the York and Lancaster line only, and they were followed by another "batch" a few days afterwards. During the month of November scarcely a copperplate could be obtained, all the large houses having received as many orders as they could complete; and not unfrequently the money was paid in advance, to secure their execution. During the last week, some of the most eminent engravers did not consider it beneath their professional dignity to aid in the work. Lithographic and zincographic draughtsmen were collected from all the large towns in England, and many from France and Germany, who made their own terms with their employers. Prices rose with the demand, and at last almost any sum was paid to those who would undertake to execute the work.

During the last few days of November, engravers and printers laboured night and day; but in many instances, only the outlines of the plans were engraved; and mere tracings were deposited with the plans, the figures being filled in by hand. Most of the engineers had from twenty to a hundred assistants thus engaged; and as the work approached completion, many had not been in bed for a week.

On the 29th and 30th of November, the work of depositing the plans remained to be accomplished. By a strange oversight the Sabbath had been made the last day on which the documents could be deposited at the offices of the Board; and the excitement and bustle were in entire disaccord with the proprieties of the occasion. The majority of the papers had to be transmitted from the provinces. The opponents of the lines were also on the alert, and a variety of tricks were resorted to to frustrate the designs of the projectors. Some of the companies on whose lines express trains had been ordered for the conveyance of the plans, and who felt that their own interests were in danger from the proposed lines, interposed almost every conceivable obstacle, and one of them ultimately refused to convey the required documents to London. The friends of the new rival, however, were not to be out-generalled, and they resorted, for the accomplishment of their object, to an original *ruse*. On receiving a peremptory denial to their demand for the means of transport, the promoters of the competing line hired an *undertaker's hearse*, and having placed the plans, sections, and clerks inside, they conveyed it to the station, and it was unhesitatingly forwarded with its contents to the metropolis. Six special trains had been ordered on the

Great Western line for nearly the same hour, for each of which, it is said, £80 were paid.

Various other illustrations of "sharp practice" were furnished on this occasion. Horses had been engaged at one of the principal hotels by the promoters of the Dudley, Neadely, and Trowbridge line, to convey their papers to Stafford. The cattle had been kept in the stable during four days, in order that they might be thoroughly ready for their journey; but on being "turned out" at the required time, they did not go at a greater rate than four miles an hour. The attorney in charge failed by request, demand, and intimidation, to produce any effect on the postboys, and he came to the conclusion that they had received a handsome consideration from the opponents of the line; so, finding that exceptional means must be resorted to if he expected to arrive at his destination within the required period, he leaped from the carriage, detached the traces, and thrashed the postboys till they roared for mercy. He then resumed his seat, and the remainder of the stage was performed at the speed of fifteen miles an hour. Nor were these solitary instances of the determination required, and of the fertility of resource exhibited, on the part of the friends of the proposed lines, in the fulfilment of their important commissions.

In the year 1844, the number of projects, in respect of which plans were lodged with the Board of Trade, had been 248; the number in 1845 was 815. The projectors of most of the Scottish lines, with characteristic prudence, lodged their plans on the Saturday. The Irish projectors, and the old established companies seeking powers to construct branches, were among the earliest, but upwards of six hundred plans remained to be deposited on the Sabbath. The excitement was extraordinary; and as the time rolled away, it increased to a painful intensity till the last hour of the Sabbath arrived. A large establishment of clerks had been in attendance to go through the necessary formalities, and the arrangement proceeded very well till eleven o'clock, when the delivery increased so rapidly that the officials were unable to keep pace with the arrivals. Vehicles, however, of all sorts and sizes continued to dash up, and in breathless haste to discharge their contents of documents and projectors. The entrance hall was crowded, and as the allotted period was gliding away, the expression of anxiety on the countenances of those assembled indicated their apprehension that, after all their efforts, they should be unable to complete the required arrangements within the time that remained. Eager inquiries were made, and speculations offered on the probabilities of those who arrived with their plans before the hour had elapsed being allowed to complete the business afterwards; and their countenances brightened when they were assured that this privilege would be granted. As the clock struck twelve, the doors of the office were about to be closed when a gentleman with the plans of one of the Surrey railways arrived, and with the greatest difficulty succeeded in obtaining admission.

Despite every effort, however, some were unsuccessful. "The witching hour of night, when churchyards yawn and graves stand tenantless," never seemed half so terrible to the rustic as it did to the unfortunate wights who, hastening to the offices of the Board of Trade, failed to reach it when "the iron tongue of midnight" smote upon their ear, and told them that the 30th of November, 1845, had passed away for ever. A lull of a few minutes now occurred in the hall of the Board; but just before the expiration of the first quarter of an hour, a post-chaise with reeking horses drove up in hot haste to the entrance. Three gentlemen immediately alighted, and rushed down the passage leading to the office door, each bearing a plan of huge dimensions. On reaching it, and finding it closed, their countenances fell; but one of them, more valorous than the rest, and prompted by the by-standers, gave a loud pull at the bell. It was answered by Inspector Otway, who informed the ringer that it was too late, and that his plans could not be received. The agents did not wait for the conclusion of the unpleasant communication, but, taking advantage of the open door, threw in the papers, which broke the passage lamp in their fall. They were, however, soon tossed back into the street, and again into the office; and this "was kept up for nearly half an hour, to the great amusement of the crowd." The projectors, however, were unsuccessful, and discomfited, were obliged to retire.

The statistics of railways at this time show the wholesale way in which great schemes had been undertaken without any idea of their cost, or of the resources from which they were to be carried out. We find that in November, 1845, the enormous number of 1,428 lines were either made, or authorised to be made, or announced to the public, and registered. The vastness of these enterprises will be seen by comparison with the lines which had been at that time completed, or were then in progress. Including the session of 1845, rather more than four hundred Railway Acts had been passed, relating to about two hundred and fifty lines, some of which had not been completed. Of these nearly a hundred new lines were authorised during the preceding session, three times as many as in any previous session. Only forty-seven lines were, between 1823 and the end of 1844, actually completed. Passing next to the cost of these railways, the aggregate sum which Parliament had empowered Companies to raise, whether as capital or by loan, was £154,716,937, including the earlier and ruder descriptions of railways constructed for the carriage of coals and ore, from 1801 to 1825. It also includes the relinquished lines. The forty-seven lines completed from 1823 to the end of 1844, cost £70,680,877. The number of railways then in progress was 118, their aggregate mileage 3,543, and their estimated cost was £67,359,325. By adding, therefore, to the actual cost of all the completed lines the estimated cost of all lines then in progress, we arrive at the aggregate capital of the railway undertakings of the country as it then stood, amounting to £138,040,202. Of the projected lines there were 1,428, with an estimated capital of £701,243,208, and a deposit of £49,592,816. On one scheme £40,000,000 was to be expended.

The cost of the Railway Mania was enormous. Worthless and fraudulent as were many schemes, they involved as much preliminary expense as if they had been good. Offices, agents, lawyers, engineers of every class, advertising and meetings to puff, were not to be obtained at any reasonable outlay. It is computed, on high authority, that on the proposed capital at least one per cent. was expended for the above-mentioned purposes. "We will answer for it," says a competent writer, "that during the two or three months immediately preceding the late salutary check, as much as a hundred thousand pounds a week were spent in railroad advertisements alone." This statement was made on November 8, 1845, and the advertising still continued.

But a change now "came o'er the spirit of the dream" of railway enterprise. Thousands had bought stock in the hope of realizing profit by the speculation, but, having no intention of permanent investment therein, were anxious to back out of the concerns with which they were identified. Projectors of bubble Companies, too, were obliged to meet their shareholders, and, in the most gentlemanly terms, to intimate their deliberate and conscientious conviction, that though some eighty or a hundred thousand pounds had been expended, yet that, on the whole, it would scarcely be expedient to proceed with the line. Holders of shares, having discovered the manner and extent to which they had been duped, uttered threats of exposure and of the terrors of the law, and were then rewarded for their trouble by the discovery that the projectors were not worth punishing ; or before legal proceedings had commenced saw their acquaintances comfortably reading the morning newspaper on board a Boulogne or Ostend steam-packet, whither they were going with their ill-gotten plunder. Railway speculations were found to be alike in this, that—"a hook's the end of many a line."

To sell scrip connected with new lines, even at any sacrifice, was now almost impossible; and the only relief which great numbers of holders looked for was, that the bills would be thrown out by Parliament, and that some unappropriated funds would remain. This hope was cherished with respect even to some lines which, a few months before, were regarded as most promising ; and it was said by competent authorities that probably there was not at that time a single new railway undertaking on which the majority of the shareholders would not have voted for its abandonment. The most doubtful schemes were even regarded as the best for holders, inasmuch as the Parliamentary Committee would strangle them in the birth.

Pay-day came at last, and, as every thinking man had seen was inevitable, there was disappointment and misery for thousands. Well was it said, in imitation of the well-known words of the poets :—

"Oh ! many a stag, late blithe and brave,
Forlorn 'mounts the ocean wave ;' *

---

* "Say, mounts he the ocean wave, banish'd forlorn,
Like a limb from his country cast bleeding and torn ?"
Campbell's Lochiel.

And many a 'letter' has been torn, †
And countless scrip to trunks be borne;
And many an antler'd head lies low,
Which whilom made a glorious show!
And many a fast coach now 'crawls slow'!"

The process of "breaking up" manifested itself in various forms, according to the circumstances of the case, or the temperament of the individuals concerned. "Internal dissensions," said a writer in *Tait's Magazine*, "are breaking out among directors and their coadjutors, hurrying them before mayors and bailies, preparatory to more regular campaigns in the courts of law." Newspapers sent in their bills for advertising, and pressed for payment, and boards audited the bills, called for vouchers, and quarrelled with the charges. Surveyors were clamorous for wages, and secretaries for overdue salaries. Parties to whom scrip was allotted refused to pay deposits for what they now regarded as an unsuccessful concern; boards, to accelerate the payment of deposits, reduced the amount of their calls; and impatient holders, who were precipitate in paying up, asked to have the excess refunded,—out of an empty treasury. Tart remarks and bitter rejoinders grew into decided acts. "One angry man goes with quiet concentrated malice, at white heat, to consult his lawyer; another rushes, roaring like a boy that has been soundly thrashed, into a mayor's court to tell his 'pitiful story.' The newspapers, as usual, blow the coals, for every 'excitement' promotes sale. The public mutters, 'Try the responsibilities of directors in a law court;' and deeply-staked directors respond to the hint by advertising a Defensive Association. The genius of Westminster Hall laughs, crows, and claps its wings; nay, it did so months ago. In July, the *Law Magazine* coolly discussed the various points likely to arise when this crisis came: the hoodie crows croaked their consultations anent picking bones, in the ears of their unheeding victims."

† "And many a banner shall be torn,
And many a knight to earth be borne;
And many a sheaf of arrows spent,
Ere Scotland's king shall pass the Trent."
Scott's Marmion.

A parody which appeared about this time, described the position of affairs with great accuracy: *

"There was a sound that ceased not day or night,
Of speculation. London gathered then
Unwonted crowds, and, moved by promise bright,
To Capel Court rushed women, boys, and men,
All seeking railway shares and scrip; and when
The market rose, how many a lad could tell,
With joyous glance, and eyes that spake again,
'T was e'en more lucrative than marrying well;—
When, hark! that warning voice strikes like a rising knell.

"Nay, it is nothing, empty as the wind,
But a 'bear' whisper down Throgmorton Street;
Wild enterprise shall still be unconfined;
No rest for us, when rising premiums greet
The morn, to pour their treasures at our feet;
When, hark! that solemn sound is heard once more,
The gathering 'bears' its echoes yet repeat—
'T is but too true, is now the general roar,
The Bank has raised her rate, as she has done before.

"And then and there were hurryings to and fro,
And anxious thoughts, and signs of sad distress,
Faces all pale, that but an hour ago
Smiled at the thoughts of their own craftiness.
And there were sudden partings, such as press
The coin from hungry pockets—mutual sighs
Of brokers and their clients. Who can guess
How many a stag already panting flies,
When upon times so bright such awful panics rise?"

Time rolled on, and exercised its healing powers. The first railway panic subsided. The apprehensions of many were found to be unreasonable; and though fraud had characterized railway speculation, there was still much substantial good. Railway authorities gave the best account of the Companies with which they were severally connected, confidence was gradually restored, and railway works began to be prosecuted with vigour. Trunk lines guaranteed interest to the shareholders of branches

* "There was a sound of revelry by night."
Childe Harold.

and extensions which were feared as rivals; they were accepted as *feeders*, for a time they proved to be *suckers*. People wondered, but they did not distrust; shares continued at a premium; satisfactory dividends were declared; and the railway world went on in fancied security.

But before long it was found that, though large sums in the form of dividends were divided among shareholders, calls were frequently threefold as great. These at last created a suspicion that all was not right, vague impressions arose, which were in some cases proved to be correct, that the glittering dividends were paid out of what ought to have been regarded as capital, and that the expenses of railway management were too great to allow of even moderate dividends, without a change of system.

The result was inevitable—shares sank in an extraordinary degree, and everything seemed to be going from bad to worse. Where was the remedy for the evil? "Confine the total amount of calls," said a writer in one of the railway journals, "during the whole of the next year, 1849, to £6,000,000; that sum will be ample to finish lines nearly completed, and to open them for traffic. Reduce the rate of interest on loans to four per cent." Besides this, a publication of the accounts of the Companies was indispensable. The "balance-sheet of a railway Company," said the *Times*, "has now no more effect than a sheet of waste paper; and as it would be perfectly easy to give accounts that would make everything clear, and these accounts are not given, it is naturally inferred that the market would not be benefited by the prospect they would indicate; and hence, that, although the end cannot be known, there is a certainty, at all events, that it has not yet been reached. If there is a single Company that is considered by its Directors to have fallen too low in the market, they can set the matter right. There are plenty of shrewd people at this moment, notwithstanding the hardness of the times, waiting with money in their pockets to find investments. Give them a statement such as they would require, and such as any city accountant, with the materials at his command, would prepare in a form that the simplest tradesman might understand it, and forthwith they will bid within a fraction of the true value of the shares."

The Companies were at length impressed with the importance of these considerations, several of them were led to publish their accounts, which showed their real condition to be in some respects better than had been believed; and by the promises to limit their calls for the future, and their announcements on other matters, they succeeded in allaying the popular fears, stock rose in the market, and confidence began to be restored.

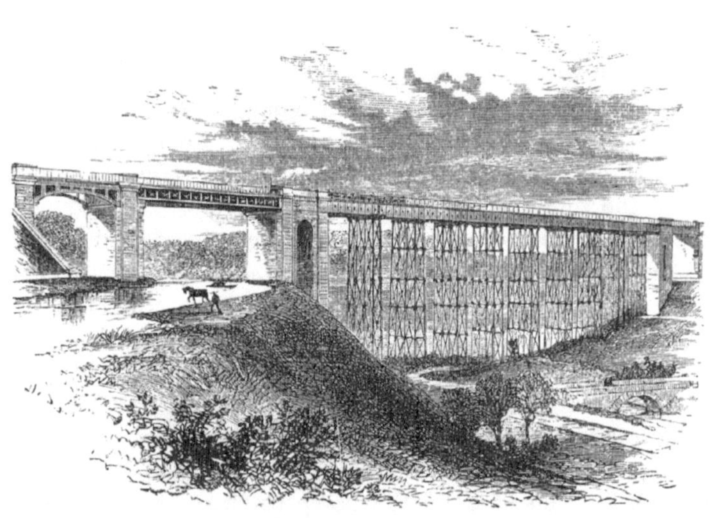

BARNSLEY VIADUCT.

CHAPTER III.

A New Railway Project.—The Prospectus.—Advertisement.—Deposit Money.—Flying Levels.—The Course of a Line.—Opposition to Survey. —Mr. Gooch.—A Clergyman Outwitted.—The Breadalbane People — "The Battle of Saxby Bridge."—Experience of Surveyors.—Mr. Sharland Snowed Up.—Deposit of Notices.—Fighting for the Act.—Theory and Practice of Parliamentary Committees.—"The Railway Session."— "The Minting Age."—The Hon. John Talbot and Mr. Charles Austin. —Scenes in Railway Committee Rooms.—Amusing Displays of Forensic Genius.—The Defence and the Attack.—Witnesses.—Professional Reputations.—Sir Edmund Beckett.—Cheap Amusement.—Buying oft Opposition.—Enormous Prices for Land.—A Curious Bill.—Compensation.—A Pleasing Exception.—Buying an Editor.—Mr. Venables, Q.C., on Compensation.—Decisions of Parliamentary Committees.—The Preamble Proved.—Cost of Parliamentary Contests.—Cost of Railways.

THE circumstances under which railway enterprises are now undertaken are essentially different from those in which, in former days, some of them came into being. For many a year their origin was, as we have seen, more or less speculative. "Project money," was perhaps paid for the idea. Directors of supposed business habits, with possibly "a lord" or two for ornamental purposes, were selected by the projectors of the scheme, and a secretary, an engineer, a banker, and a solicitor, were chosen chiefly under the influence of private considerations. A prospectus was then privately circulated, and was inserted in the principal daily and local newspapers, in which an enlightened and a discriminating public was informed of the important project which had been devised. In due time a newspaper reaches the

The initial letter represents George Stephenson's birthplace.

breakfast-table of the happy owner of a little uninvested capital, who unfolds the packet, still as damp as the sheets of a German bed. His eye glances over subjects dramatical, political, poetical, and paragraphical,—now he alights on this piece, and then he flutters off to that; and after running up one column and down another, like an aide-de-camp on a battle-field, disregarding the accomplishments of nursemaids, or the number of housemaids who want situations "where a footman is kept;" wondering, for an instant, how a gentleman, no more than fifty, who possesses, according to his own candid confession, "all the virtues out of heaven," and £500 a-year to boot, should be reduced to the unpleasant necessity of advertising for a wife; and meditating for an instant on a variety of other equally momentous problems, the prospectus of "the Grand Diddlesex Junction," of which he has already heard, attracts his attention. Therein he reads that a "direct, cheap, and convenient railroad" is to be constructed through a populous and wealthy district, situated in a county or in counties whose manufacturing, mining, agricultural, trading, or commercial resources are minutely and vividly delineated. The document expatiates on the inconveniences which are at present caused by the inadequacy of the means of communication; and the assurance is given to all in whose neighbourhood the line will pass, that it will be a boon to trade, and will revive or augment all its commercial interests. The cost of the required land is either "moderate," or a comparatively "trifling" item; the whole line, with necessary appendages, can be completed at an expense of so many hundreds of thousands sterling; and the annual return on the traffic arising from passengers and goods will yield, at moderate rates of tonnage, satisfactory dividends. The date is added at which the Act of Parliament will be applied for in order to incorporate the subscribers as a Company, with all usual and necessary powers for carrying out the proposed scheme, and for the proper conduct and regulation of its affairs. The time and place at which the annual general meeting will be held; the number and value of the shares to be raised; the bank into which the money is to be paid; and an invitation to all persons who wish to take shares, to apply to the chairman of the Provisional Committee, usually follow this part of the statement; the assurance being added, that the present defective nature and the expense of the means of communication between districts so important, which "have been so often and loudly complained of," render unnecessary any apology for the present undertaking.

The logic and eloquence of the prospectus overcome the reader, and before his last cup of now luke-warm coffee is swallowed, he resolves to write, without delay, to the Provisional Committee of the "Grand Diddlesex Junction," and to request, in accordance with the prescribed "form of application" which is subjoined to the prospectus, that there may be "apportioned" to him "shares in the above proposed railway;" and he engages to pay "the deposit of £2 10*s*. per share upon such allotment," and to sign its subscription contract required by Parliament, and also the subscribers' agreement.

With the deposit money thus obtained from subscribers, preparations are commenced for gaining the sanction of the Legislature to the proposed Company. The route of the line has to be definitely determined, and the plans and sections for the Parliamentary Committee to be prepared. In doing all this the considerations that have to be regarded are numerous, complicated, and weighty. The relative importance of various towns and villages which lie in the direction of the railway, and the traffic which may be expected; the character and resources of the district, whether agricultural, commercial, or manufacturing; the number and nature of the population, and other statistical intelligence, must be collected from the best sources, and prepared in legal form. Take the map. There are the termini, and there are the intermediate towns. And what about these "intermediates?" Nothing, some reply. Select your termini, they say, and run your line between them as straight as you can. It is not even necessary that there should be a single house upon the route. Open the line, and as people flock to the banks of that first great highway, a river, so they will flock (we are assured) to your railway; and in due time, the direct line, in which there is no original error to correct, will pass through a large and rich population which it has itself attracted or created; will have feeders by branches to all the towns that stood out of its route when projected; and there will be no more notion of a competing line to it, than there would have been in former days to the Appian Way. Such were the opinions boldly avowed as to the principle on which a decision should be made of the route of the line. But that was at a time when railways were few and far between.

It is said that when the Emperor Nicholas of Russia was asked to give his decision respecting the construction of a railway between St. Petersburg and Moscow, he indignantly threw aside the plans submitted to him, exhibiting lines more or less curved, and asking for a fresh map, laid his sword from the new to the old capital of Holy Russia, and drawing a straight line between the two points, he tossed the map over to the astonished engineer, "Voilà votre chemin de fer." But this is not at any rate the conventional method; with the Ordnance map in his hand, and the mountain barometer in his pocket, with which to take "flying levels," the engineer—"monarch of all the surveys"—has to visit the districts through which the line may pass, and perhaps make a selection from three or four eligible routes, each of which may be liable to a variety of modifications as discretion may dictate; while the magnitude of the question at stake gives an importance to his decisions which few can appreciate if they have not felt the weight of similar responsibility. The acquaintance with the features of the country which is requisite may be illustrated by the fact, that when Mr. R. Stephenson was determining the route of the London and Birmingham Railway, he is said to have walked over the intervening districts no fewer than twenty times. Meanwhile, trial-shafts and borings are made by the assistants of the engineer, which reveal the geological formation of the various strata, and which may present important facts which will have to be regarded.

The difficulties which arise in planning the course of a railway are sometimes great. A few years ago an engineer of eminence was sent by the Grand Junction Railway Company to ascertain the best route for a line from Lancaster among the valleys of the North of England. On returning, he declared that, though he had been able to see his way as far as a certain place in Westmoreland, no man living could construct a railway farther in that direction, and that the project must be abandoned. In less, however, than two years, a country surveyor produced plans of a line which, without a tunnel, or any other work of special difficulty, except a long climb up and over the hill of Shap, runs to Carlisle and on to Scotland by the western side of the island.

Having completed his observations, and collected the information of his assistants, the engineer sums up the evidence, and marks out the route which the line shall take; and few are the instances in which the decisions thus arrived at have been open to subsequent impeachment. Rivers and streams are crossed as near their sources as possible; hills and valleys are skirted; towns and places where land is expensive are cautiously approached; pleasure grounds and gentlemen's seats are avoided; and a general estimate is made for setting off the amount of cuttings or embankments as nearly as possible against one another.

A LEVELLING PARTY.

The route of the line must now be surveyed and levelled with the utmost precision. Surveying may be described as the art of determining the form and dimensions of tracts of ground, with any objects that may exist thereupon. A representation on paper is made of all these objects, and also a delineation of the slopes of the hills, as the whole would appear if projected on a horizontal plane. The ground has also to be levelled in order that it may be ascertained how much higher or lower is any given point on the surface of the earth from any other. The engineer is thus able to adopt measures for reducing the whole of the new line to a level, or to such gradients as may be deemed most expedient to adopt.

The work of surveying and levelling for railways has often been attended with no small difficulty, apart from the natural obstacles to be encountered. The annoyance felt by the owners of pleasure grounds at the invasion, or even the immediate proximity, of railways, has occasioned many serious quarrels between the surveyors and the agents of the proprietors. The opposition thus raised, however, seldom caused any ultimate inconvenience to the projectors, who contrived, by some means or other, to accomplish their design.

This hostility was shown at the commencement of railway enterprise, as the following evidence, given before the Committee of the House of Commons, on the 27th of April, 1825, will indicate. The questioner was Serjeant Spankie, and the respondent George Stephenson :—

"You were asked about the quality of the soil through which you were to bore in order to ascertain the strata, and you were rather taunted because you had not ascertained the precise strata ; had you any opportunity of boring ?" "I had none ; I was threatened to be driven off the ground, and severely used if I were found upon the ground." "You were quite right, then, not to attempt to bore ?" "Of course, I durst not attempt to bore after those threats." "Were you exposed to any inconvenience in taking your surveys in consequence of those interruptions ?" "We were." "On whose property ?" "On my Lord Sefton's, Lord Derby's, and particularly Mr. Bradshaw's part." "I believe you came near the coping of some of the canals ?" "I believe I was threatened to be ducked in the pond if I proceeded ; and, of course, we had a great deal of the survey to make by stealth, at the time when the persons were at dinner ; we could not get it by night, for we were watched day and night, and guns were discharged over the grounds belonging to Captain Bradshaw, to prevent us ; I can state further, I was twice turned off the ground myself by his men ; and they said, if I did not go instantly they would take me up, and carry me off to Worsley." Here the Committee inquired : "Had you ever asked leave ?" "I did, of all the gentlemen to whom I have alluded ; at least, if I did not ask leave of all myself, I did of my Lord Derby ; but I did not of Lord Sefton, but the Committee had—at least I was so informed ; and I last year asked leave of Mr. Bradshaw's tenants to pass there, and they denied me; they stated that damage had been done, and I said if they would tell what it was, I would pay them, and they said it was two pounds, and I paid it, though I do not believe it amounted to one shilling." "Do you suppose it a likely thing to obtain leave from any gentleman to survey his land, when he knew that your men had gone upon his land to take levels without his leave, and he himself found them going through the corn, and through the gardens of his tenants, and trampling down the strawberry beds, which they were cultivating for the Liverpool market?" "I have found it sometimes very difficult to get through places of that kind."

In some cases large bodies of navvies were collected for the defence of the surveyors; and being liberally provided with liquor, and paid well for the task, they intimidated the rightful owners, who were obliged to be satisfied with warrants of committal and charges of assault. The navvies were the more willing to engage in such undertakings, because the project, if carried out, afforded them the prospect of increased labour. Great difficulties were encountered in making the surveys for the London and Birmingham Railway; and though it is probable that in every case as little injury as possible was done, because it was the interest of those concerned to conciliate the landed proprietors, yet in several instances the opposition was very decided, and even violent. In one case no skill nor ingenuity could, for a considerable time, evade the watchfulness and resolution of the lords of the soil, and the survey had to be made at night, by the aid of dark lanterns. On another occasion, when Mr. Gooch was taking levels through some of the large tracts of grazing land a few miles to the west of London, two brothers, by whom the land was occupied, came to him in great anger, and insisted on his immediately leaving the property. He contrived to learn from them that the adjoining field was not theirs, and therefore remonstrating only briefly with them, he walked quietly through a gap in the hedge into the next field, and planted his level on the highest ground he could find—his assistant remaining at the last level station, about one hundred and sixty yards distant, apparently quite unconscious of what was taking place, although one of the brothers was hastening towards him, for the purpose of sending him away. Had the assistant moved his staff before Mr. Gooch had taken the sight at it through the telescope of his level, all his previous work would have been lost, and the survey would have had to be completed by some other means, or not at all. The moment Mr. Gooch began looking through the telescope at the staff held by his assistant, the farmer nearest him, spreading out the skirts of his coat, tried to place himself between the staff and the telescope, to intercept the view, and at the same time shouted violently to his comrade, desiring him to make haste and knock down the staff. But before this could be done, the observation was completed.

In another instance a clergyman offered such decided opposition to the intruders, that the expedient was resorted to of surveying his property during the time he was engaged in his public duties on the Sabbath. A strong force of surveyors were in readiness to commence operations by entering the grounds on one side, at the time that they saw him fairly off on the other; and, by an organised arrangement, each completed his task just as the reverend gentleman ended his sermon.

In the surveying of the land for a railway at Glenfallach, a serious affray took place between the Breadalbane people and the agents of the projectors. The first survey of the line had been completed; but it was found necessary that an engineer should be sent to re-examine a small portion near Crainlarich. Some days elapsed after the original parties had retired, and as the new comer had only one attendant with him, he at first attracted little attention. But at length the hated theodolite was recognised, and the miners of Clifton were summoned to the defence of the land from the assaults of the railway intruders. It was said that the surveyor drew a sheath knife; but whether in his own defence, or for the purpose of removing the screen of plaids interposed between him and the measuring-rod, was doubtful; but the survey being almost completed, the conflict ended.

Another disturbance took place near the village of Appleton, eight miles from York, between some "watchers" and a railway surveyor and his assistant, who had been employed by the Cambridge and Lincoln Company. It appears that the party attempted to enter a field of Sir W. Milner, Bart., but their progress was opposed, and a serious struggle ensued, the surveyors making a determined attack on the men who obstructed them. The servants of the baronet, however, obtained a reinforcement, and the aggressors were taken in custody to York. On the following day the defendants were brought to the Castle, and charged with committed assaults, one man being dangerously wounded in the head, and two others being severely injured. After much mutual recrimination, the magistrates bound the surveyor and his assistants over to keep the peace for six months; and as their work was nearly completed, they cheerfully complied with the requirement.

One of the most determined struggles of this kind took place on the estate of Lord Harborough. That nobleman gave notice to the friends of the Peterborough and Nottingham Junction Railway that he should not permit their surveyors to enter his land. In the maintenance of this resolution a struggle ensued at Saxby, near Stapleford Park. The contest began by one of his lordship's men standing before the surveyor, and preventing his carrying the chain forwards, on which the latter drew a pistol and threatened to shoot him. Undaunted, the keeper replied, "Shoot away!" and a slight scuffle ensued, in which the pistol was, fortunately, not discharged. This event was called "the Battle of Saxby Bridge," as one of the surveyors subsequently remarked to us, "and we were lodged in Leicester jail as 'first-class misdemeanants.'" An effort, also, was made to survey the park from the towing-path of the Oakham Canal, which was considered to be a public road, whereupon a number of Lord Harborough's people obstructed the surveyors, seized their instruments, and put the parties themselves in a cart, to take them before a magistrate. His worship, however, being from home, it is said that his lordship's steward ordered them to be turned out of the cart, and while this was being done, some of the surveying instruments were broken. The solicitor of the Company subsequently saw the steward, and declared his proceedings were unjustifiable, but intimated that, if no further obstruction were offered, legal measures would not be resorted to.

The experiences of surveyors, even when not opposed by violence, have sometimes been unpleasant. Such was the case in 1869, on the part of one who attended to the survey for a new line to reach the Cleveland iron district in Yorkshire. "For some weeks," said a local writer, "strangers have been about the Cleveland Hills, their object being to get a road through the hills to the plain of Cleveland. Of course this work has been done 'on the quiet' as much as possible, but, nevertheless, the errand has oozed out. Dispersed into parties this week, one gentleman (name unknown, but hat bearing the initials 'W.L.L.') had a dreadful night of it on Tuesday, showing that railway prospecting, without a guide, in the wild moorlands of North Yorkshire, is no joke. Starting for a 'push on' from the Grosmont Junction towards Scarborough, this gentleman, in a dense fog, found night come on, in which he became bewildered, and eventually rode or slid down a clayey slopement into the Black Beck. Here he lost horse and hat, and had himself great difficulty in regaining *terra firma.* Once there, nothing remained but a night on the moor, and there he stopped till daylight ensued, and a kindly shepherd housed and warmed him in a moor-hut. Having recovered, the 'prospector' was taken to a railway station, and left for London."

When Mr. Sharland was engaged in staking out the centre line of the then intended Settle and Carlisle line of the Midland Company, and had taken up his quarters at a little inn on Blea Moor, a bare and bleak hill 1,250 feet above the level of the sea, and miles away from any village, he was literally snowed up. For three weeks it snowed continuously. The tops of the walls round the house were hidden. The snow lay eighteen inches above the lintel of the front door,—a door six feet high. Of course all communication with the surrounding country was suspended; and the engineer and his half-dozen men, and the landlord and his family, had to live on the eggs and bacon in the house. In another week their stock would have been exhausted; and it was only by making a tunnel, engineer-like, through the snow to the road they could even get water from the horse trough to drink.*

The surveys for the projected line being at length completed, it is required that copies of the document be deposited with the clerks of the peace of the counties through which the line is intended to pass, and also with the parochial and other authorities; and every landholder receives a section showing the depth of cutting or embankment across his estate.

---

* "The Midland Railway: Its Rise and Progress." By Frederick S. Williams.

These and other preliminaries being settled, the duty of "fighting for the Act," as it is termed, commences. If this is obtained, the petition is transmuted into an Act of Parliament, and by it the subscribers are authorized to incorporate a Company for executing the proposed design and are provided with the powers requisite for their work.

The theory and the practice of Parliamentary Committees on Railway Bills have during late years undergone considerable modifications. At one period the Committee was open to the visit and the vote of the members of the boroughs and the counties through which and adjoining which the projected line was to pass; and sometimes a "whip" was applied to secure the passing or the rejection of a Bill or of a clause. Since the year 1844, however, members who have been in any way connected with the particular line have been excluded from taking any direct share in the decision on the matter. But the most memorable period in the history of Parliamentary Committees on Railways was after the great Railway Mania. The excitement of what was emphatically called the "Railway Session" was unexampled. Cabs rushed in and out of Palace Yard in fearful haste; clerks and witnesses in their hurry tumbled over one another; while the avenues were thronged with anxious groups of engineers, surveyors, and shareholders, waiting for the meeting of the committees. Lobbies and ante-rooms were besieged by crowds of railway projectors, parliamentary agents, and others connected with the great work of the day; and the approaches to the committee-rooms were every now and then blocked up by sturdy porters and messengers, struggling under the weight of maps, plans, and sections. The old cloisters of the Westminster Palace rung with cabalistic sounds of "datum level," "gradient," "goods traffic," "loop-line," and other foreign technicalities.

Counsel learned in the law hurried from their chambers to the committee-room, in obedience to the golden voice that invited them; and those who divided the spoil of the railway Companies had good reason to remember that "minting age." The desire of the promoters of railways to retain particular counsel in their several cases was—in accordance with the spirit of the times—a mania; and though, doubtless, the gentlemen so courted had created the demand for their services by the ability they had previously displayed in that particular line of practice, and though the handsome fees with which their labours were rewarded, would, under ordinary circumstances, have secured their best exertions on behalf of the undertaking, yet, as they had not the power of ubiquity, their efforts were necessarily limited. Often they had to rush from one committee-room to another before they had said half they wished in advocacy of the views of their clients: and thus they spent the hours from eleven to four almost in a state of bewilderment—the only idea that presented itself clearly before them being that, for all this bustle and work, they were perhaps receiving fees to the amount of £200 or £300 a-day. It is affirmed that practice before Committees of the House of Commons has, in many cases, produced three times larger incomes than ever have been acquired in the regular pursuit of the profession. Among others, Mr. Cockburn was very successful. Mr. Charles Austin, also, got into practice at the Parliamentary bar when that profession "was in its palmiest condition, and his marvellous gifts as an advocate gave him a position there, the like of which was never attained by any other man in any branch of its profession. His income in the year 1847—the great railway year—was something fabulous. His reputation was so great that he received many briefs merely in order to prevent his appearance on the other side; and this, no doubt, is the origin of the story (mythical or not) of his being out riding in Hyde Park on one of the busiest days of the session. 'What in the world are you doing here, Austin?' was the inquiry. 'I am doing equal justice to all my clients.'" He is said to have made, for four years, an average of £40,000 a-year. The Hon. John Talbot is known to have received more than £12,000 a-year; and juniors, who never obtained £200 a-year at Westminster Hall, made £3,000 or £4,000 per annum before committees during those three years.

While counsel thus performed such valuable services in the cause of railways, there was another class scarcely less important—the witnesses. Hundreds and thousands of these were in request. There were plenty of people to be had, who, having nothing else in the world to do, for an adequate consideration could express a very decided, and of course competent, opinion in reference to a new line, or on the resources of a town in their neighbourhood. Many, doubtless, were honest and sincere enough; but numbers did the whole thing as a matter of business.

Amusing displays of the forensic genius of the counsel and of the engineers, pitted against each other, were made on these occasions. The counsel who appears on behalf of the line extols its virtues to the skies; while at the same time he declares that in an engineering point of view he cannot conceive that any difficulty can possibly arise. If a mountain, or a range of mountains stands in the way, he penetrates its depths with the utmost facility; and gives so eloquent a description of the ease with which the work can be accomplished, that the Committee almost begin to think that tunnel-making is an elegant recreation, or that it is as easy to hammer and blast a route through whinstone coeval with the creation, as to thrust a red-hot poker through a keg of Irish butter. If a broad river opposes the course of the new line, it can quickly be spanned by a bridge; if a valley intervenes, a viaduct can be thrown across which shall be as inexpensive as it is durable; if a series of gradients are indispensable, such as have never before been attempted, he has already provided against any evil arising therefrom, and has, indeed, rendered them a positive benefit; for they are so planned, that the impetus gained in the descent of the one incline shall be more than sufficient—whichever way the train may be going—to enable it to ascend the other. In short, there never was a line having a greater accumulation of positive advantages, and a greater absence of everything to discourage those connected with it.

The opposing counsel rises. He has the utmost confidence in the ability of his learned friend, but he has on this occasion the misfortune to differ from him. The engineers have examined the proposed line with the greatest care, and they have shown that the route which his friend has selected is, on the whole, the most judicious that could have been chosen, this only proves how wrong it is to attempt the formation of a line at all, since the best is, in effect, impossible. The engineering difficulties are extreme; and though the abilities of his learned friend in the advocacy of the scheme are distinguished, yet the cost that would be incurred, if it were attempted to be carried out, would be ruinous to the shareholders, and the works, if completed, most hazardous to the public. How is it possible, he asks with confidence, to tunnel through miles of quicksands and basaltic rock, which have been obviously arranged by Nature in such strata as to prevent any such undertaking? What engineering skill shall be competent to carry an embankment over marshes, in comparison with which

> —"The great Serbonian bog,
> 'Twixt Damiata and Mount Casius old,
> Where armies whole have sunk,"

sinks into insignificance? How can the piers of a viaduct be properly supported on a quagmire, or a cutting be made through a mass of floating mud? And all this is proposed to be undertaken in order to unite two towns which have not two interests or commodities in common, except one everlasting feud, which may be traced from son to sire back to the time of the Wars of the Roses! On the whole, therefore, he has been driven to the deliberate and conscientious conviction,—though upon personal grounds he should have greatly preferred that it had been otherwise,—that a more dangerous, impracticable, and worthless line has never been submitted to the consideration of Parliament.

In the same temper the evidence and the witnesses are dealt with. An atrabilarious lawyer, whose keen eyes twinkle as he thinks he has found a point which will be fatal to his opponent, endeavours, "with the voice of an exasperated cockatoo," to make the opposing engineer contradict himself; but that gentleman is not to be confused. He is the hero of a hundred committees; he replies with an amiable tranquillity not surpassed by that which characterized the illustrious Sam Weller; and he sometimes returns his answers with equally damaging effect. If, perchance, he should be close pressed, he occasionally avails himself of one safe retreat, and escapes into a thicket of algebra, from which he shoots forth a furious volley of arguments and terms about the reduction of the horizon, the curvature of the surface of the triangle in relation to the ellipticity of the earth; about azimuths and longitudes, sines and cosines, logarithms and chord angles, optical squares, box-sextants, zenith distances, equatorial axes, and terrestrial arcs, into which neither counsel nor members care or dare to follow him; and fortified with the mysteries of his craft, he can defy the universe.

During that memorable "Railway Session," many an odd scene occurred within the walls of committee rooms. The scrip of a particular company is running up or down, according to the eloquence of the learned counsel or the want of it on either side. Business is proceeding listlessly ; one or two members are asleep ; others are chatting or comparing the horticultural specimens in their respective button-holes, while a junior counsel is examining some witness who demonstrates that the line may cross a particular turnpike without disturbing the equanimity of mind of one thistle-browsing donkey, or of one nervous gosling. Immediately on his conclusion, a "leader" on the other side has elbowed his way through the crowd, and, to the horror of the junior, starts up and formally announces that he has a proposition to make which must settle the whole question, and which is at the same time so advantageous to all parties that no objection can possibly be urged by the other side. The committee discard the flowers and other minor considerations, and listen with attention to the proposal ; before it is concluded, the affrighted junior has dispatched half a dozen attorney's clerks for his leader ; and in reply to the query of the chairman as to what he is prepared to say in answer to the unanswerable suggestion, he begs permission to wait a few moments.

One of the messengers has at length found the principal in the middle of a speech in reference to another line on the merits of which he is descanting. He has, perhaps, just stated that he shall now proceed to demonstate the necessity of the line of which he is the advocate when a mysterious whisper reaches his ear ; and, without the alteration of his countenance, he adds, 'But the case is so clear that it would be altogether a work of supererogation to proceed with it ; and I shall therefore leave the witnesses in the hands of my learned friend, Mr. So-and-so, and beg permission of the committee to withdraw for a few minutes. Away he goes ; arrives just in time to save his junior from going into a fit of apoplexy ; and having received from him certain instructions, he pours forth a torrent of declamation against the aforesaid unanswerable proposition, till his presence is required elsewhere.

Of one class of speeches, a description, not excessively overcoloured, was given by a writer in *Blackwood's Magazine*, in 1845 : "I swear to you, Bogle," he says, "that no later than a week ago, I listened to such a picture of Glasgow and the Clyde from the lips of a gentleman eminent alike in law and letters, as would have thrown a diorama of Damascus into the shade. He had it all, sir,—from the orchards of Clydesdale to the banks of Bothwell; the pastoral slopes of Ruglen, and the emerald solitudes of the Green. The river flowed down towards the sea in translucent waves of crystal. From the parapets of the bridge you watched the salmon cleaving their way upwards in vivid lines of light. Never did Phœbus beam upon a lovelier object than the fair suburb of the Gorbals, as seen from the Broomielaw, reposing upon its shadow in perfect stillness. Then came the forest of masts, the activity of the dockyards, and

> 'The impress of shipwrights, whose hard toil
> Doth scarce divide the Sunday from the week.'

Farther down, the villas of the merchant-princes burst upon your view, each of them a perfect Sirmio; then Port Glasgow, half spanned by the arch of a dissolving rainbow; Dumbarton grand and solemn, as became the death-place of the Bruce; Ben Lomond, with its hoary head swathed in impenetrable clouds; and lo! the ocean and the isles. Not a Glasgow man in the committee-room but yearned with love and admiration towards the gifted speaker, who certainly did make out a case for the Queen of the West, such as no matter-of-fact person could possibly have believed. And all this was done by merely substituting a Claude Lorraine glass for our ordinary dingy atmosphere. The outline was most correct and graphic; but the secret lay in the handling and distribution of the colours. I shall not wonder if the whole committee, clerk included, come down this autumn to catch a glimpse of that terrestrial paradise."

The reputation acquired by some Parliamentary counsel is of decided though not entirely flattering character. One of the most eminent of these is Sir B. Denison, Q.C. "His learned friend," said Mr. Mereweather on one occasion of Mr. Denison, "in private life was as amiable as anybody could desire, but before these tribunals he seemed to forget all that gentle manner, and there could be no two more distinct persons than Mr. Denison, his private friend, and Mr. Denison, his public opponent." He was therefore satisfied that in private his learned friend would regret having, by a careless expression, trampled upon the dead genius of a great man like Mr. Brunel."

Sir Edward Watkin, speaking before a meeting about a Bill

in which he was interested, said: "Well, then, we had one of those mild and gentlemanly attacks with which Mr. Denison, Q.C., honours us at different periods, whenever we do anything that he does not approve of. He particularly fell foul of me, which he was quite welcome to do, for it might amuse him, and did not hurt me. He spoke of my 'long-cherished design of fixing my claws in the Great Northern.' Well, now, while I have always been ready, as you know, that this railway should enter into a closer alliance with the Great Northern, I have never on any single occasion been the originator of the numerous 'nibbles' which the Great Northern has made at this property. The Great Northern look at us with that mild and anxious benevolence which distinguishes those who wish to enjoy a treat, but have not the moral courage to pay the proper price for it. But we were told by Mr. Denison that we not merely came for the Coal Bill, but to stick our claws into the Great Northern And Mr. Denison being particularly severe upon me, seemed to consider that I was the prime conspirator in all these matters. Now, I must say that my personal relations with the Great Northern, I think, ought to have protected me from any attack, from either Mr. Denison or anybody else connected with the Great Northern. They surely have not forgotten that it was from a nice sense of what was due to you and due to the Great Northern that, holding a very profitable appointment at that time under your service, I resigned it because I believed, first of all, that the agreement made with the Midland was contrary to your interests; and, secondly, because I believed it was contrary to good faith with the Great Northern. And such was the opinion of the chairman of the Great Northern upon that matter, for I remember going to King's Cross to deliver up my ivory pass, and being requested by the chairman to receive that pass back from his hands, disconnected as I was then from every English railway, with a request that I would keep it for life, in testimony of the chairman's high opinion of the conduct I had always pursued towards the company over which he presided. Therefore, anybody attacking me on the part of the Great Northern reminds me very much of the old story of the turtle and the scorpion. Fleeing from a burning wood, the scorpion managed to persuade a good-natured turtle to take him upon his back and swim with him across a lake and land him on the other side in a haven of safety. But the poor unfortunate turtle, as he was going across, had a very uncomfortable time of it, for the scorpion poked his sting between the scales of the friend who was doing him this service. On questioning the reptile, when they got to the other side, as to what he meant by such conduct, the scorpion replied, 'I did not mean to injure you at all; I assure you I have no malice against you; I am extremely grateful for what you have done for me, but *it is my nature.*' Well, gentlemen, I suppose it is Mr. Denison's nature, and there we will leave him."

It is said that Mr. Denison was once asked why a man of his high position and great wealth troubled himself to continue the toils of his profession. "Well," he replied, "the doctor says I ought, for the good of my health, to take a great deal of amusement; and this is the cheapest way in which I can get it." And certainly its cheapness can be guaranteed, since, instead of costing him anything, it is said to have brought him in busy sessions £20,000 to £30,000 a year.

While the arguments and evidence have thus been advanced within the committee-rooms, great efforts have been made "out of doors" by the friends of the Bill. If possible, the landowners have been induced to concur in the scheme, and to signify their assent thereto. Merchants, manufacturers, and tradesmen have been brought from the towns through which the intended line will pass, to express their opinion in its favour. Objectors to the railroad are conciliated, and opposition even "bought off." When landowners have been asked by the company if they approved the general design of the proposed railway, they have given their answer in the negative, although they have privately avowed their anxiety that the railway should be made; and they have admitted that their sole object in opposing the line was to obtain from the company a larger sum of money for their land.

The grounds of the opposition made were various. "The Trent Valley Railway, when proposed in 1836, was thrown out," said Mr. Robert Stephenson, "in consequence of a barn, of the value of about £10, which was shown upon the general plan, not having been exhibited upon an enlarged sheet. In 1840, the line again went before Parliament. It was opposed by the Grand Junction Railway Company, and no less than four hundred and fifty allegations were made against it. A sub-committee was engaged twenty-two days in considering these objections. They ultimately reported that four or five of the allegations were proved, but the Standing Orders' Committee, nevertheless, allowed the bill to be proceeded with. Upon the second reading, it was supported by Sir Robert Peel, and had a large majority in its favour. It then went into committee. The committee took sixty-three days to consider it, and ultimately Parliament was prorogued before the report could be made. Such were the delays and consequent expenses which the forms of the House occasioned, that it may be doubted whether the ultimate cost of constructing the whole line was very much more than the amount expended in obtaining permission from Parliament to make it."[1]

One noble lord had an estate near a proposed line of railway, and on this estate a beautiful mansion. Naturally averse to the desecration of his home and its neighbourhood, he gave his most uncompromising opposition to the Bill, and found, in the committees of both Houses, sympathizing listeners. Little did it aid the projectors that they urged that the line did not pass within six miles of that princely domain; that the high road was much closer to his dwelling; and that, as the spot nearest the house would be passed by means of a tunnel, no unsightliness would arise. But no arguments affected the decision of the proprietor, and it was found necessary to appeal to other considerations. His opposition was ultimately bought off by a promise of £200,000, to be paid when the railway reached his neighbourhood. Time wore on, funds became scarce, and the company decided that it would be best to stop short at a particular portion of their line, long before they reached the estate of the noble lord. Accordingly, in a second bill they sought to be released by Parliament from the obligation of constructing that portion of the line which had been so obnoxious. What was their surprise at finding this very man their chief opponent, and that fresh means had now to be adopted of silencing his objections!

Other instances may be given. A line had to be brought near the property of a certain member of Parliament. It threatened no injury to the estate, either by affecting its appearance or its

[1] Address to the Institute of Civil Engineers.

worth; on the contrary, it afforded him a cheap and expeditious means of communication with the metropolis. But the proprietor, being a legislator, had power at head-quarters, and by his influence he nearly turned the line of railway aside; and this deviation would have cost the projectors the sum of £60,000. Now it so happened that the house of this honourable member, who had insisted on such costly deference to his views, was afflicted with the dry rot, and threatened every hour to fall upon his head. To pull down and rebuild it would require the sum of £30,000. The idea of a compromise, beneficial to both parties, suggested itself. If the railway company rebuilt the house, or paid £30,000 to the owner of the estate, and were allowed to pursue their original line, it was clear that they would be £30,000 the richer, as the enforced deviation would cost £60,000; and, on the other hand, the owner of the estate would obtain a secure house, or receive £30,000 in money. The proposed bargain was struck, and £30,000 was paid by the company. "How can you live in that house," said some friend to him afterwards, "with the railroad coming so near?" "Had it not done so," was the reply, "I could not have lived in it at all." *

Sums of money ranging from £5,000 to £120,000 were given ostensibly for strips of land, but really to purchase consent. In one neighbourhood it was found expedient to buy off opposition at a price which, under the ordinary calculation of railway profits, would oblige the company to raise £15,000 per annum of additional tolls. In another case a nobleman demanded £30,000 as the price of coming across an angle of his estate, to which the Company agreed; but finding afterwards that the line could be more conveniently made by slightly changing the route, they proposed to do so; whereupon the nobleman, reluctant to lose the £30,000, threatened them with such powerful opposition that it was judged prudent to pay the money, although not a foot of the land was touched. In another case, a man who had demanded four bridges to connect his property, found, after the signing of the agreement, that half the money they would cost would be more serviceable to him; and he proposed this as a compromise, which the directors accepted,

* *Fraser's Magazine.*

paying him the money in addition to what he had received for the land. An account once sent in to the Eastern Counties Company may serve as a humble specimen of the demands of some tenants. We quote it verbatim :—

	£	s.
1838 To Hy Finch		
May A Bridge laid across River for Parth over four Meddows of grass—the crops of grass very much beated abought with Men and Dogs—I have found five large dogs with as many Men in the crops at a time—almost afrade of being put into the river by them	20	0
When the hay on the cock sadley puled about and spoiled—have found 3 Men at a time laying in the hay cocks—the hay sadley dameged	10	0
A horse drove into the river—cast—and so much drowned as never Stood any more	15	0
4—5 and 6 Cows at a time milked, drove from their lodging and sadley disturbed	52	0
Removing post and rail fence across the third Meddow—carring away and laying up	3	0
Loss of growing 5 cwt. Cattle Cabbage Seed at 3*s.* lb. . . .	84	0
Loss of 2 Acers for parths 4 years	40	0
Profit of the 2 acers 4 years	16	0
Trafick of timber Carriages, Horses, Carts &c., over the 4 meddows	5	0
Repearing Gates, locks and fences the 4 years	4	4
Sloping up hedges to ceap cattle from straying the 4 years . .	8	4
Garden fence broken, robed and plundered the 4 years	2	0
Manewer as mendment on the 2 Acers, Land in Spring of 1838—40 load 10*s.*	20	0
	£279	8

The case went into court, occupied ten hours, and the jury eventually gave a verdict for £49.

On one occasion, a trial occurred in which an eminent land-valuer was put into the witness-box to swell the amount of damages, and he proceeded to expatiate on the injury committed by railroads in general, and especially by the one in question, in *cutting up* the properties they invaded. When he had finished the delivery of his evidence, the counsel for the Company put a newspaper into his hand, and asked him whether he had not inserted a certain advertisement therein. The fact could not be denied, and the advertisement proved to be a declaration by the land-valuer himself, that the approach of the railway would prove exceedingly beneficial to some property in its immediate vicinity, then on sale.

An illustration of the difference between the exorbitant demands made by parties for compensation, and the real value of the property, may be mentioned. The first claim made by the directors of the Glasgow Lunatic Asylum on the Edinburgh and Glasgow Railway is stated to have been no less than £44,000. Before the trial came on, this sum was reduced to £10,000; the amount awarded by the jury was £873. In another case only one-fiftieth of the amount demanded by the owner of land was, by arbitration, finally awarded.

The opposition thus made, whether feigned or real, it was always advisable to remove; and sums of £35,000, £40,000, £50,000, £100,000, and £120,000 have thus been paid. An honourable member is said to have received £30,000 to withdraw his opposition to a Bill before the House; and "not far off the celebrated year 1845, a lady of title, so gossips talk, asked a certain nobleman to support a certain Bill, stating that, if he did, she had the authority of the secretary of a great company to inform him that fifty shares in a certain railway, then at a considerable premium, would be at his disposal. This, of course, is no bribery; but we wonder whether it explains the reason of some people having so many friends in Parliament." * Exceptions there have been to this spirit. It was of such that Sir Robert Peel spoke, when, on turning the first sod of the Trent Valley line, he said to its directors: "I assure them that there are many persons in this neighbourhood who have not scrupled to sacrifice private feeling and comfort, by consenting to their land being appropriated to the Trent Valley Railway. They have given that consent from a conviction that this undertaking was one conducive to the public benefit, and that considerations of private interest should not obstruct the great one of the public good."

One pleasing circumstance, highly honourable to the gentleman concerned, must not be omitted. The late Mr. Labouchere had made an agreement with the Eastern Counties Company for a passage through his estate, near Chelmsford, for the price of £35,000: his son and successor, the Right Honourable Henry Labouchere, finding that the property was not deteriorated to the anticipated extent, voluntarily returned £15,000. The Duke

---

* *Herapath's Journal.*

of Bedford, also, after the lapse of many years, returned £150,000 paid for land taken by a railway, on the ground that his estate was benefited, and that no compensation was due.

The cost of purchasing land, and for compensation, has been stated by Mr. Laing, in a paper appended to the evidence given by him before a select Parliamentary committee on railways, as follows :—

Newcastle and Carlisle Railway . . .	£2,200	per mile.
Grand Junction	3,000	"
South Western	4,000	"
Manchester and Leeds	6,150	"
London and Birmingham, and Great Western .	6,300	"

while, on three other lines, the expenditure has averaged £14,000 per mile. "There can be no doubt," says Mr. Noble, "that, in every instance, the price claimed and paid, either by agreement or under award, has been largely in excess of the actual value of the property sold, notably so in the case of railways; although it is impossible for a railway to be constructed through an estate without largely increasing its value, enormous claims have been made, and allowed, as compensation for imaginary injuries." Mr. Laing estimated that the *waste* of capital incurred in this country, under the head of land and compensation, amounted to more than two millions and a half sterling,—a sum immensely augmented since.

The practice of buying off opposition has not been confined to the proprietors of land. We learn from one of the Parliamentary reports, that in a certain district, a pen and ink warfare between two rival companies ran so high, and was, at least on one side, rewarded with such success, that the friends of the older of the projected lines thought it expedient to enter into treaty with their literary opponent, and its editor soon retired on a fortune. It is also asserted that in a midland county, the facts and arguments of an editor were wielded with such vigour, that the opposing company found it necessary to adopt extraordinary means on the occasion. Bribes were offered, but refused; an opposition paper was started, but its conductors quailed before the energy of their opponent; every scheme that ingenuity could devise, and money carry out, was attempted, but they successively and utterly failed. At length a director hit on a Machiavelian plan—he was introduced to the proprietor of the journal, whom he cautiously informed that he wished to risk a few thousands in newspaper property, and actually induced his unconscious victim to sell the property, unknown to the editor. When the bargain was concluded, the plot was discovered; but it was then too late, and the wily director took possession of the copyright of the paper and the printing-office, on behalf of the Company. The services of the editor, however, were not to be bought: he refused to barter away his independence, and he retired, taking with him the respect of friends and foes.

In speaking of the subject of compensation generally, Mr. Venables, Q.C., in 1873, remarked: "I remember hearing an agent of the Duke of Newcastle give evidence that the duke could ride on his land twenty-four miles straight on end. How could a railway be made in such a country if it does not go through his estate? The park of Clumber alone consists of upwards of 4,000 acres, which is something of a protection to the house. I remember perfectly well when there was a ball at Clumber in the dead of winter, a great many of the visitors left somewhere about four or six o'clock in the morning, and they drove about in the park till daylight at eight o'clock, not being able to find their way out of it. That park alone is a tolerable protection to the privacy of the house. When people are on a very great scale, it is just like a very stout man not being able to get through a hole as well as a slimmer man—a very big duke cannot get about the country without being interfered with by those who must necessarily claim the right to cross his territory.

"Then our opponents give in detail the cases of severance of the duke and his tenants. There is no doubt they will all be fully compensated. There are farmers some of whose farms we traverse, and how can an estate of enormous magnitude—34,000 acres—expect that there shall be no railway across it. And if railways come across they will cut up the fields; and when railways do so, it always happens that the fields are cut off from the farm-house at exactly the very part of the farm that it is particularly important they should not be cut off. But, in fact, they will not be cut off, for there will be all sorts of crossings and bridges and accommodation works of some kind; and every one knows that though railways look so shocking before they are made, when they are made people get exceedingly well used to them. The people will have their money, and with their money they will be very happy, and will no longer think about any grievance connected with the railway."

At length the arguments and witnesses before the Parliamentary Committees, in reference to the proposed line, are concluded ; and, after due deliberation, a decision has to be made. It would be unreasonable to expect that this should always be in accordance with wisdom ; it is indisputable that in some instances grievous and irreparable errors have been committed. In the case of the Brighton line, of the three brought before the Committee, it is declared that the worst, and the shortest by only a trifling distance, was selected. One route was proposed, which, passing through a natural gap in the hills, avoided the necessity of tunnelling, and the outlay and inconvenience consequent thereon.

The decision of a Committee is at last about to be announced, and on more than one occasion we have been present at the critical moment. One day we were only just in time. We had been busy all the morning, and were now seated in one of the voluptuous chairs in the magnificent "Reading-Room" of the "Midland Grand" at St. Pancras, rewarding our industry by a leisurely scanning of the papers, when, as the clock in the tower solemnly boomed forth the half-hour past three, we remembered that that was about the time at which a certain Commons Committee were expected to pronounce its decision on a railway measure which the Midland Company had projected. We dropped our paper with so much more precipitancy than decorum that an old gentleman looked up with astonishment, and gazed at us over his spectacles as if he had a vague impression that we had suddenly gone out of our mind ; and, hieing our way over the rich and noiseless carpets of the corridor and staircase, were soon in eager colloquy with a hansom cabman.

"Palace Yard in fifteen minutes!" we exclaimed.

"Can't do it," he replied. "'Taint worth while ; break the knees of a thirty-pound horse, and get summoned for furious! 'Taint worth it, for half a crown," he added in a deprecatory and persuasive tone.

"Well, then, as quick as you can."

The three-quarters was struck by Big Ben as we rounded the

curve from Trafalgar Square into Parliament Street, and in about four minutes more we walked briskly up beneath the majestic roof of Westminster Hall, and then on through the corridors and lobbies to the Commons Committee-rooms. Here we found a throng of eager railway agents, eminent railway officials, and be-wigged and be-robed counsel, learned in railway law, passing in and out of the Committee-rooms like bees clustering around a row of hives. Earnest deliberations were going on in subdued voices, for unexpected contingencies had at the last moment to be provided for ; new complications of railway diplomacy had to be adjusted ; a new departure had to be arranged, or a concession agreed upon ; and there was an anxious look upon many a face which the light chat or occasional raillery of friend or foe could scarcely conceal. And no wonder : for on the skill or resource, or want of it, of the next few days, or even hours, the destiny of a trade or a town, and the fate of perhaps a million of money would be determined.

We were just in time, and only just. The case had ended ; the Committee-room had been cleared, and as we entered the decision was about to be pronounced. For a moment there was a pause, and we had time to glance around. The noble apartment was crowded by an eager throng. The windows, with their stone mullions, looked out on the quiet river, and across to the opposite shore to the stately piles of St. Thomas's Hospital. The walls of the room, from ceiling to floor, were occupied by gigantic maps, whereon sundry railway lines were marked upon them in various colours. Across the middle of the room was a "bar," immediately within which another "bar" had just taken their seats ; to their right and left were directors and officials connected with the case ; in front were the chair and table of the shorthand writer, who sat pencil in hand ; and also the chair and table recently occupied by the witnesses ; while beyond, and of course facing the counsel, were the five members of Parliament upon whose decision, so far as one estate of the realm was concerned, rested the fate of the Bill. They are seated, as is their wont, covered. A question is asked by the chairman concerning the bearing of a certain clause ; a learned counsel, in a sharp, rapid, conversational way, replies ; and a sentence by way of rejoinder is uttered by a portly counsel on the other side. "Who are they ?" we whispered to a lawyer's clerk who stood beside us in the throng. "That's Ursa Major," he answered, pointing covertly to the former speaker; "splendid man, dreadfully clever, but a bear." "And who is the other counsel?" "Oh, that's the Busy Bee," he continued; and so we came to learn that, even within the arena of law and in the High Court of Parliament itself, pleasantries abound.

The critical moment has come. Every sound is hushed; and all eyes are turned towards the chairman, as pausing for a moment, as if to add to the suspense, he slowly says: "I am directed

PARLIAMENTARY COMMITTEE-ROOM.

to state that the Committee are of opinion that the preamble of the Bill is proved, and to report to the House accordingly."

The Committee rise, and immediately the throng breaks up. It is a Midland Bill, and Midland people are strongly represented. The chairman, Mr. Ellis, comes from his seat within the bar, looking as courteous and as resolute as ever. Mr. Allport, whose tall figure might a moment before have been seen bending eagerly forward as he awaited the fate of his policy, walks out into the corridor with a sunny smile on his face; while his then chief secretary, who follows him, playfully parries the thrust which some humorous competitor has levelled at him. Counsel, agents, and officials hustle one another in their flight down the staircase, and as we cross the lobby and hear the great clock bell sound four, we learn that "Mr. Speaker is at prayers."

On the occasion of the decision being given on the London and York—eventually the Great Northern Railway, which was fought through the Committees of both Houses with special perseverance and acrimony, the moment that it was pronounced there were shouts from stentorian lungs of "Bravo! hurra!" accompanied by the stamping of feet and umbrellas, and then a general fight for the door, at which a fearful struggle took place. The confusion was complete, and after repeated demands for "Order," which were utterly ineffectual, the chairman could only give expression to his indignation by declaring that the conduct of those present was "exceedingly indecent."

The announcement thus made has sometimes been rendered useful to parties interested. One darts away, perhaps by special means he has provided for the purpose, and succeeds in selling or buying on 'Change a lot of shares, during the five minutes that intervene before the arrival of the intelligence; and is thus enabled, at the expense of others, to save himself from the loss he would otherwise have incurred, or to make a handsome profit on the strength of his early information.

Of the labour, intellectual and physical, to which honourable members were exposed in the interminable discussions of the "Railway Session," the reader will already have some idea. Flesh and blood might well revolt at the task. How would it be possible for them to enter with vigour on the great public questions of the day! It has been remarked, that if, after three days' patient hearing of the witnesses and lawyers on some of these conflicting interests, a Committee-man had one tangible idea floating in his head, he must have been either an Alcibiades or a Bavius—a heaven-born genius, or the incarnation of a fool!

The sanction of the Legislature thus obtained empowers the Company to take possession of a width of land for the line, inclusive of that needed for giving the necessary inclinations to the sides of cuttings or embankments. The requirements of the Government on railways are enforced under the supervision of a department of the Board of Trade. No new line can be opened without the previous inspection, and certificate of approval, of the Inspector, who is, however, not responsible for the capability of the works to fulfil the duty to be required of them. All accidents must be reported to this department of the Board of Trade within forty-eight hours of their occurrence.

The dimensions to which Railway Acts sometimes extended were enormous. Subsequently, however, a Railway Clauses Consolidation Act was passed, with a view to the diminution of these difficulties, and of the expense consequent thereon.

The expenditure incurred in procuring legislative authority to construct railways has been, in many cases, scarcely credible. While the parliamentary, surveying, and engineering costs of the Kendal and Windermere Company amounted to little more than two per cent. on the total outlay of the railway, we are assured that the parliamentary costs of the—

Brighton Railway averaged . . .	£4,806 per mile.
Manchester and Birmingham . .	5,190 "
Blackwall	14,414 "

The Brighton line had to contend with three or four other Companies during two successive sessions, and when its Bill was before the Committee, the expense of counsel and witnesses was stated at £1,000 daily, extending over fifty days. The London and Birmingham line escaped much of this cost by coming earlier into the field; but the parliamentary and surveyors' expenses even then amounted to £72,000,—a reproach on a system of legislation that permits impediments to be thrown in the way of works of great public use. It is also affirmed that "the solicitor's bill of the South-Eastern Railway contained ten thousand folios, occupied twelve months in taxation before the Master, and amounted to £240,000." One Company had to fight so hard for their Bill, that they found, when at length they reached the last stage—that of receiving the Royal assent—that their preliminary undertakings had cost nearly half a million of money,—a sum which had been expended in merely acquiring the privilege of making a railway, and the interest of which has now to be paid by the passengers and goods that travel thereon.

Of the cost of projects which were ultimately unsuccessful, a single illustration may be given. In the celebrated battle of the

Stone and Rugby Railway, the inquiry continued during sixty-six sitting-days, from February to August, 1839, and, having been renewed in the following year, the Bill was finally defeated at an expense to its promoters of £146,000. The capriciousness of Parliamentary tribunals may be shown by the following facts :—Six Bills rejected by the Commons in 1844 were passed in the following year on precisely the same evidence. Of eighteen Bills rejected in 1845, seven were passed unaltered in 1846. Of six Bills thrown out by Committees of the House of Lords in 1845, four were adopted by other Committees in 1846.

Much as it is to be regretted that costs so enormous have been incurred in the construction of railways, it must be admitted that, in many instances, the Companies are less to be blamed than pitied, as the victims of systematic and determined extortion. In favourable situations, English lines have been made at the rate of £10,000 per mile. One of these, the Northampton and Peterborough branch, about forty-seven miles in length, was constructed at a cost of £429,409; and the York and Scarborough, forty-two miles, was made at an average of £6,000 per mile. Some single lines have cost, for land and everything, not more than £5,000 a mile, the undertakings being promoted by land proprietors whose interest was in economy. Of cheap Scotch lines, the Peebles branch of the North British is an illustration.

VIADUCT NEAR MANSFIELD.

CHAPTER IV.

Commencement of a Railway.—Turning First Sod.—The Ceremony.—Bedford and Bletchley Line.—Difficulties in the Construction of Railways.—Gradients.—Theoretical and Practical Considerations.—Undulating and Level Lines.—The Desborough Bank.—Special Precautions.—The High Peak Railway.—The Lickey Incline.—Spragging and Skidding.—The Righi Incline.—The Fell Line over Mont Cenis.—Working of this Line.—Curves.—The Great Horse-shoe Curve.—Commencement of Works.—Making Cuttings.—Making the Running.—Angle of Repose.—Illustrations.—Retaining Walls.—Ditches and Drains.—The Great Enemy of Cuttings.—The Road-bed.—Crest Ditches and Spade Drains. Embankments.—The Haslingden Cutting.—Three Remarkable Cuttings.—Vicissitudes.—A Terrible Storm.—Slips.—Chemical Combination of Soils.—Precautions.—Covering the Slopes of Cuttings.

IN the actual commencement of a great undertaking special interest is usually taken, and time-honoured customs are observed. So with a new railway. The noble and the peasant, the philosopher and the schoolboy, the poet and the ploughman, consider "the turning of the first sod" of a new line an occasion of moment. And though some may have capacity or inclination to look only to the benefits which may, perhaps, accrue to themselves from the undertaking, others will think of social, commercial, and national interests that are involved, and rejoice in an era in which science and art have lent such aids to the prosperity and happiness of man.

On such an occasion, there is usually an assemblage of the people of the neighbourhood, and of navvies "in their best." A marquee, for the accommodation of the Directors and the

The initial letter depicts Olive Mount Cutting.

visitors specially invited, is provided ; and at the appointed time appear the leading gentry of the county and neighbourhood, in their carriages, on horseback, or on foot. A procession has sometimes been formed accompanied by a band of music ; and the company then form into a circle round the spot where the first sod is to be dug. The chairman, of course, delivers an eloquent address, consisting of popularized selections of the prospectus which had been issued ; and he informs his enlightened auditory of the benefits that the line will confer on the neighbourhood; and perhaps intimates,—as did Mr. D. Salomons, at the commencement of the Reading, Guildford, and Reigate line,—that it may attract around it a population large enough to claim the privilege of representation in the Commons' House of Parliament.

The assistant-engineer then presents to the chairman a handsome spade of polished mahogany, with a silver blade ; and a wheelbarrow, of similar materials and elegant design, is brought upon the scene. The spade is struck into the ground and the barrow filled, amidst the cheers of the assembly. The contents are trundled along a plank, and then emptied. Other gentlemen go through a similar process ; the company then proceed to do honour to the occasion in the true John Bull style, of "having something to eat," and move off to the marquee erected on the grounds, where a *déjeûner* has been duly prepared. The navigators who are present, and who are to aid in carrying out the work thus auspiciously commenced, retire to a similar scene of operations, where roast beef and plum pudding are plentifully provided.

The commencement of the Bedford and Bletchley line was an exception to the ordinary proceedings on such occasions, the ceremony being performed by Her Grace the Duchess of Bedford. The duke had engaged to preside, but was suddenly summoned to the metropolis on public business ; and, to avoid disappointment, the duchess, assisted by Lord Alford, consented to officiate. Her grace was accompanied to the ground by the railway directors, and other officials, and by many members of the principal families in the county. A salute of cannon and a band of music greeted her arrival ; and the Chairman of the Company having made a few preliminary observations, handed her grace the spade, and requested her to do honour to the proceedings by commencing the works. Acknowledging the compliment, she pressed the spade into the earth; and Lord Alford, having addressed the company, threw off his great coat and hat, and, amidst the cheers of the bystanders, filled the barrow. The barrow was of beautifully-grained oak from the Woburn estate, and was richly ornamented with silver. His lordship then wheeled the barrow along the platform, and led the way to the marquee which had been erected. After several toasts had been drunk, the duchess entered her carriage amid the cheers of the people and the report of cannon, taking with her, at the request of the contractors, the barrow and spade with which the work had been performed.

It is now necessary for the engineer to complete his plans, if he has not already done so, for the intended railway. The various works are perhaps indicated by the accompanying diagram. The gradients must accordingly be determined with

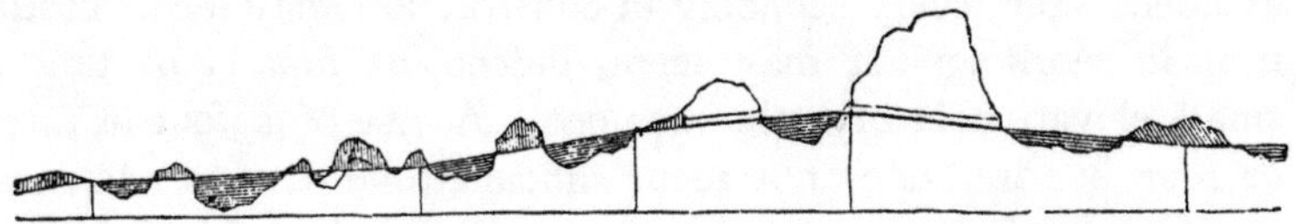

reference to the amount of the earth-works; for, if the line were constructed at too low an average level, there would be a superabundance of material, from the cuttings being disproportionately deep and extensive; while, if it were so carried too high, a large amount of soil would have to be conveyed, at great cost, from various places off the line to construct the embankments. The chief object, therefore, is to have just enough earth-work to remove from the cuttings to form the embankments; and just enough embankment to use up the material from the cuttings.

The execution of the works is seldom in the hands of the actual executive of the company. Railway directors are usually connected with city life, perhaps unacquainted with the details of the matters over which they have the supreme authority; and are really capable of conducting only the general administration of the company. Contracting for railway making has thus become a great business; and experienced and wealthy men will undertake the completion of the entire works of a long line. Meanwhile the chief engineer has appointed his own staff of agents to superintend the work as performed by the contractors. Over each portion of from thirty to fifty miles a "Resident" is aided by inspectors of the earth-works, masonry, mining, and of permanent way, each with a special district under his observation, the chief contractors perhaps sub-let the different works to sub-contractors, giving the earth-works to one, the masonry to another, and the ballasting to a third; and sometimes the sub-contractors again let out lesser portions to those who may be called sub-sub-contractors. The last make their arrangements with various individuals for what are designated "little jobs," in which are included the cartage of bricks, rails, or sleepers, for given distances, and for the hire or feed of horses.

A chief characteristic of a railway is the uniformity of surface secured by its construction. The increased power of locomotives has, indeed, of late, permitted a much nearer approach to the natural form of the earth in the formation of lines than was before admissible; and vast cost in construction has been thus avoided. But every economy in construction may mean costliness in working. It may seem, indeed, at first sight that a small elevation is of little moment. A rise of a foot in three or four hundred does not seem difficult to be reached; but one in a hundred does not only mean one inch in a hundred, but one mile in a hundred; that is to say, the traveller, in running on such a gradient a distance less than that between London and Birmingham, would reach a perpendicular elevation of a mile.

It used to be said that to mount a gradient of 1 in 300 required a tractive force nearly twice as great as was sufficient to move the same load at an equal speed along a level line; and it was affirmed that to ascend an elevation of thirty feet demanded as great a power as would suffice to propel an equal weight along a mile of level railway. These computations have, however, undergone important modification through the enormous improvements made in the power of locomotives; and engineers have been able to conduct lines through districts, which a few years since were declared to be impassable. So important were these advances that, even as early as 1845, the Report of the Board of Trade said, that "such gradients as were before thought objectionable are now adopted every day as a matter of course; and as the capabilities of the locomotive have been enlarged, gradients of a class which would have been, a few years ago, altogether impracticable, have come into general use."

The ascents made by means of a gradual inclination are sometimes considerable, and when it is remembered that what is lost in the upward journey is, in a great measure, gained in the descent by trains coming from the opposite quarter, it must not be regarded as altogether a loss of power. Many of our readers who have travelled from London on the Birmingham line, would be surprised to be informed, when they reached Tring, which is thirty-two miles from London, that they have ascended a perpendicular height of about three hundred and thirty feet since they left Euston Square, and that they are four hundred and twenty feet above the level of the sea. Yet many minor inclines have been ascended and descended on that journey.

Gradients constantly vary, and vary considerably as we may see by the finger-boards placed on the lines for the guidance of the engine-driver, that tell us now that we are ascending at the rate of one in 296, and then again we are descending at one in a 100. Thus some parts of the inclined plane between Euston and Camden stations rise at the rate of one in sixty-six and one in seventy-five; that by which the Manchester and Leeds Railway is connected with the Victoria Station, at Manchester, descends at the ratio of one in fifty-nine for about 1000 yards, and one in forty-nine for 640 yards; and that by which the line from Edinburgh is conducted into Glasgow, has a slope of one in forty-two, for a distance of a mile and a quarter. Though, with heavy trains and "greasy" weather, an additional engine may be required, locomotives are exclusively employed. The Lickey incline, on the Birmingham and Gloucester line, has a gradient of one in thirty-seven and a-half, for a length of more than two miles.

It was long contended that the only proper principle upon which to lay out a railway was, to secure as near an approximation as possible to a level surface; for though it involved a larger original outlay, it afforded the best means of satisfactorily working them when completed. On the other hand, it is maintained that lines formed on a series of undulations are equally advantageous with those that are perfectly level, because the impetus acquired in descending would be equivalent to that lost in mounting the inclines. The "undulating theory," as it may be styled, would, according to some, work well if applied in the form of a series of severe gradients, varying from thirty to forty feet a mile; and the North Union Railway, from Parkside to Preston, has been cited in illustration, five miles of which out of twenty-two have gradients of one in a hundred, yet it is worked at less expense than some more uniform lines.

The London and Birmingham Railway may be regarded as an illustration of the uniform system. It was constructed on the principle of obtaining the most perfect level for the purpose of economic working, the amount of original outlay being a secondary consideration. The ordinary gradient never exceeds one in three hundred and thirty, with the exception of the Euston and Camden incline, which was intended to be worked, and for some years was worked, by stationary engines.

When a railway has to be carried over a considerable elevation, the question has arisen whether the rise and fall should be distributed, or whether the gradients should be concentrated in a few steep planes. The latter course was adopted on the Liverpool and Manchester Railway. The main line has no slope exceeding one in eight hundred and forty-nine, with the exception of two inclined planes, each of about a mile and a half in length, near Rainhill, where the ascent is one in eighty-nine and one in ninety-six, and where passing trains used to have the aid of an auxiliary engine. Similar means are adopted to overcome the Euston incline, on reaching the summit of which, at Camden the pilot engine is detached.

When the South Western Line was undertaken, this subject had a thorough investigation. The project for this line was opposed in Parliament by the Great Western Railway Company, and one of the grounds of opposition involved the question of gradients. The Great Western line was laid out so as to be almost a dead level over nearly one hundred and twenty miles, the only important inclination being arranged within a very short space, by means of two gradients, one of which is a very steep ascent. The London and South Western Railway, on the other hand, has long steep gradients, and enormous earthworks, though it has none of the gigantic viaducts, bridges, or tunnels to be found on some lines. Lichfield is the summit level, being nearly four hundred feet above the termini at London and Southampton. One of the gradients extends from

Lichfield tunnel, fifty-four miles from London, for a distance of seventeen miles, and is one in two hundred and fifty. It was indeed stated by the first engineer, who laid out the line, in his Report to the Parliamentary Committee, that the aggregate of the earthworks between London and Southampton would be sixteen million cubic yards—a mass sufficient to form a pyramid having a base of 150,000 square yards, and a thousand feet in height. The length and steepness of the gradient was principally occasioned by the extraordinary height of the ridge of country which runs east and west through Hampshire near the middle of the line, and which it was necessary to cross.

The line was laid out so as to undulate with a series of gradients, the prevailing one being at the rate of one in two hundred and fifty, or about twenty feet a mile. It was on the propriety of this arrangement that a contest took place before a Committee of the House of Lords; and Dr. Lardner was employed by the London and South Western Company to ascertain—so far as could be done by theory and experiment—what would be the probable effects of such an undulating line on the moving power.

It was argued by the friends of the flat gradients of the Great Western, that such a line as the projected South Western would be worked under disadvantages so enormous, owing to the resistance of the gradients, that it would be wiser to select another, if circuitous course, but thereby securing a nearly level line. A portion of the Great Western itself could form part of such a circuitous route; and thus the theory expounded and the interests of the opposing Company were made to coincide. Dr. Lardner, in reply, contended that upon the undulating line there would be a compensating power in descending the slopes, which would to a great extent balance the disadvantages in ascending them; that in a journey backwards and forwards on such a line, the expenditure of power would not be materially greater than upon a dead level; that the average speed would not be much less, although in the course of the complete journey it would be much more variable; that on the ascending gradients the engine would have to overcome a greater resistance, to expend more power, and to move more slowly, but that this loss would be to a great extent made up in the descending gradients, where the resistance would be less considerable and the speed higher.

This theory—for experience had not then established it—was fiercely attacked and ridiculed; but it prevailed: the Bill for the South Western Company was obtained, the line was constructed, and it has been worked with great success.

Some years ago we were travelling by the 8.40 Midland train from Nottingham to London. After passing Market Harborough and approaching Desborough, the speed of the train slackened. "We are going very slowly," remarked one of the company. "What can be the reason?" said another. "The signals must be against us," said a third. "No, that isn't the cause," we interposed. "We're going slowly because of the Crimean war!" Our friends laughed at the seeming paradox; but it was true. When the Leicester and Bedford line was projected the country was at the height of the Russian war. Money was dear, men were difficult to get, and the Midland shareholders could not be persuaded to provide more than a million of money with which to construct a line sixty miles long. "Now, Charles Liddell and John Crossley," said old John Ellis (and John Crossley told us this story), "there are £900,000 to make your line with. If it can't be done for that, it can't be done at all. So you must put all your fine notions into your pockets and go and do it for £15,000 a mile. And then there is the rolling stock to find." "It took," Mr. Crossley said, "a great deal of scraping to get it done; and the Desborough bank had to be left as it is to-day, rising fifty feet a mile for four miles, and falling fifty feet a mile for four miles more, and all because of the hardness of the war-times and the shortness of money and of men when the line was made." Nearly two hundred and fifty trains every day toil slowly up one slope or the other of that incline; and all the loss and cost incurred are part of the penalties still paid, and for long years will have to be paid, for one of the many needless and heedless wars in which England has been engaged. To avoid the daily delay and expense of this bank was one of the reasons why the Midland Company have opened their new route to London *viâ* Kettering, and to avoid another similar bank—made at the same time as that at Desborough, between Irchester and Sharnbrook—have recently constructed a deviation line on a better level and through a tunnel somewhat farther east. It re-unites with the old line near Sharnbrook station.

The heavy inclines on one railway in England have for many years been worked by a curious combination of locomotive and stationary engines. The High Peak Railway in Derbyshire was at one time one of the great thoroughfares of England. Travellers and merchandise came on to it from the Manchester district down to the Cromford Canal, and thence by the various navigations of the Erewash valley and the Soar to Leicester and the South. But these arrangements have been superseded, and a friend of the writer recently told his experiences in one of the last journeys taken by passengers on the High Peak Railway.

"It was in August, 1877," he said, "and thinking I should like to see the country through which it passed, I went to Stonehouse, generally called 'Stonnis,' just by the Black Rocks, where the railway crosses the Wirksworth Road, and inquired of a man in the office for the train. 'Do you mean the "fly"?' was the reply. 'Yes.' But the official not knowing whether the 'fly' had passed or not, went out to inquire, and brought back word that it had gone, but that if I followed it up the line, I might catch it at the siding; and if not, I should be sure to overtake it at 'Middleton Run.' I accordingly gave chase, and at length caught sight of it being drawn up the incline by a rope and a stationary engine. A man at the bottom inquired if I wished to catch the 'fly,' and added, 'I will stop it for you at the top,' which he did by a signal. A quarter of a mile ahead I joined it. My fellow-travellers were then a young woman and a child, and the vehicle in which we sat was like an old omnibus. The guard stood in the middle and worked the brake through a hole in the floor. A locomotive now drew us three or four miles to the foot of another incline, up which we were drawn by a rope. When reaching the summit the guard remarked: 'We may have to wait at the top.' 'How long?' I inquired. 'Oh, it may be five minutes,' he replied, 'or a few hours. It all depends upon when the engine comes to take us on. Yesterday,' he added, 'it did not come at all.' To while away the time I walked along the line, and my fellow-passengers went mushrooming. In about three hours an engine came from Whaley Bridge to fetch us, and after the driver, fireman, and guard had refreshed themselves at a little public-house not far away, and had freely commented on their 'horse,' they went back along the line, brought up the 'fly,' and having refreshed themselves again, we started. At one part of the journey a flock of sheep were quietly feeding or resting on the line. 'Just see them,' said the guard as we approached, 'jump the walls;' and they did it like dogs. We reached Park Gates, about a mile from Buxton, at seven o'clock, after a journey of about twenty miles, in six hours. Not long after my journey, a traveller on this line was killed, and the Company decided to close it against passenger traffic. The High Peak may be seen as it joins the Midland Railway on the western side of the line in a wood a little north of Whatstandwell station. Its summit level is 1,254 feet above the sea."

The existence of steep inclines involves the adoption of special precautions. Before the descent begins, care must be taken by the driver to have his engine well under command; and additional brake vans may have to be attached to the trains. The Lickey Incline, on the Birmingham and Bristol section of the Midland Railway is one of the steepest on a through main line, and its successful administration for so many years reflects the greatest credit on the gentleman under whose charge it has long been. It is not simply that the gradient is steep, but that the condition of the rails and the power of the brakes to act upon them may, in a few minutes be changed. A fall of snow or a shower of rain has so altered the "bite" of the wheels that, whereas the control was complete, the wheels now glide over the glass-like surface almost or entirely uncontrolled; and, in years gone by, a heavy mineral train has been known, with all its brakes on, and its wheels "spragged," to sweep unhindered down the incline through the Bromsgrove station, and to run a mile and more away along the flat line at the foot before its course could be arrested. At night, too, the sight has sometimes been strange. The wheels being "spragged," and not turning, of course the particular part that pressed on the rail became hotter and hotter, so hot as to throw off fibres and flakes of molten metal twisted into all conceivable forms, and every wheel sent out a blaze of heat and light so as almost to make the train appear to be on fire. "I have seen," said a gentleman to the writer, "tons of bits of metal, that have thus been burned off the old iron tires, lying on the ballast of the Lickey Incline." Still, despite these difficulties, Mr. Stalvies, the Midland engineer at Bromsgrove, has carried on the traffic, not only without accident, but in so orderly a manner that the main local and mineral trains pass up and down with perfect regularity and success. We may add that the wheels are now never, as formerly, allowed to "skid." It is found that to allow them to move slowly round is to secure a firmer bite upon the rail than if they were at rest. The spirit in which Mr. Stalvies has discharged the duties of his office may be illustrated by a remark he once made to a friend: "I believe," he said, "if an accident did happen at the Lickey, it would kill me." Pilot engines have, of course, to be used to assist the trains in ascending the Lickey, but the heaviest trains are the mineral that descend it in going to the west.

The steepest and highest incline on any railway in Europe is that which ascends the Righi Mountains near Lucerne, in Switzerland. It is designed to convey passengers to the top of the mountain, from which there is a view so celebrated as to attract large numbers of visitors. Hitherto the only means of ascent had been by walking, or by horses, or by *chaises a porteurs*. A few years ago M. Riggenbach, the superintendent of the railway workshops at Olten, proposed to make a railway to the summit. On account of the height, 4,500 feet, an unusually steep gradient, about one in four, was necessary. The necessary concessions were obtained from the Cantonal Governments, and the railway was commenced in 1869. It was delayed during the war of 1870, by the non-delivery of some rails ordered in France, but it was opened in 1871. The line commenced at Vitznau, on the Lake of Lucerne, and is about four miles long. The rolling-stock at present consists of three locomotives,—they have upright boilers, and their driving axles are furnished with cog-wheels, which secure them a firm hold or grip on a cogged rail; three large passenger carriages, with accommodation for 54 persons each; and two smaller ones having thirty seats each.

Another line with extraordinary inclines was the mountain railway of Mr. Fell. He actually succeeded in carrying it, and working it, over Mont Cenis itself, by methods he had previously tested on the High Peak Railway in Derbyshire. Its chief characteristic was the centre rail. The two outer rails were of the ordinary flat bottom section, without chairs, spiked down upon transverse wood sleepers, and they carried the weight of the engine. The "centre-rail" was double-headed, laid on its side instead of its edge, supported by and bolted to wrought-iron "saddle chairs," fastened to a longitudinal sleeper resting upon the transverse sleepers. The upper edge of the "centre-rail" was nine inches above the surface of the side rails, and its two "heads" stood out clear of the chairs, ready to receive the lateral pressure of the four friction wheels of the engine. The "centre rail" was laid only on the steep inclines, its ends being tapered off to blunt points, so that the friction wheels might enter upon and leave it gradually. The locomotive was a complicated machine, and contained about as many working parts as two ordinary engines.

The practical working of the line, however, at first was hindered by many discouraging facts. "I regret to inform you," wrote a correspondent of the *Times*, in the autumn of 1868, "that the Mont Cenis Railway Company has come to considerable grief, and that the communications between France and Italy are in a very disturbed and uncertain state. We hear of one train having been stuck for eight or nine hours in the snow, frozen to its place. In short, the concern seems to have completely broken down, the disaster being apparently mainly due to want of sufficient locomotive power, but accelerated by the unusually early and very heavy fall of snow. The locomotives furnished to the Mont Cenis Company were not of the best description, and they have failed to do the work allotted to them. It is a fact that an engine which has performed a return journey across the mountain almost invariably needs more or less repairs on getting back to St. Michel, where there is a lack of means to repair it. Fresh pieces have to be got from a distance, and much delay ensues. The wear and tear is great in locomotives constructed on the Fell system. It was naturally sought to show the utmost possible advantage in speed over the old mode of crossing the mountain, and five and a quarter hours were fixed as the time for performing a journey which due consideration for the engines ought to have extended to seven hours. It was something like making a steady roadster do a racer's work. The animal, overstrained, knocked up." Subsequently, however, a telegram announced that Lord Mayo, *en route* to India, had made the passage across Mont Cenis in four hours by the Fell Railway, and the line continued for several years in successful operation.

The degree of *curvature* that may be given to a railway, in order that, if necessary, it may thread its course among hills, valleys, parks, and lakes that lie in its route, is a matter of importance. When railways were first projected, great apprehensions were entertained, not only of the resistance which might be produced by curves, but of the danger of passing over them at any considerable speed; and standing orders were adopted in Parliament, which required that all curves having a less radius than a mile should be the subject of special inquiry. In the course of investigations made by Dr. Lardner, in 1838, he ascertained that the effect of curves in producing resistance was infinitely less than had been supposed. Curves, having a radius of three-quarters, or even half a mile, did not produce the slightest increase of resistance at any speed which the trains attained.

In the construction of curves upon railways, the outer rail is placed at a somewhat higher elevation than the inner; the effect of which is to make the carriage lean slightly inwards, so that its weight has a tendency to resist the centrifugal force attending the curvilinear motion. An animal when moving in a circle spontaneously assumes such a position; and the leaning inwards will depend on the velocity of the motion and the smallness of the circle; and similarly, the elevation of the outer rail must depend upon the radius of the curve and the velocity of trains that will pass over it. Experience has, in some instances, led to the adoption of curves of smaller dimensions than those formerly allowed. On the Newcastle and Carlisle line there is a succession of curves, the radii of which are very small; and though some of these are found on steep inclines, the line is worked with economy and safety. On the Manchester and Leeds Railway are two curves, each of 220 yards radius, distant from any station, and there is one in a gradient of one in eighty-two, over which the trains have run with security and speed for several years. On the other hand, some curves have been found so inconvenient that their radii have been altered. Thus, on the Lancashire and Yorkshire line, at Charleston, the radii of several have been increased from 660 to 2,000 feet; and on the Midland line at Shipley, near Bradford, the radius of the curve by the removal of a hill of rock will be greatly improved.

Some of the most remarkable curves are on the American

lines. This is not surprising considering the bold outline of many districts of the country through which some of these railways are carried. One of them is known as the "Chiques

CHIQUES ROCK CURVE.

Rock Curve." Hence the road is cramped for space between the hills and the river. From the summit of the Rock a lovely landscape may be surveyed.

HORSE-SHOE CURVE, KITTANNING POINT, U.S.A.

One of the most remarkable curves in the world is that at Kittanning Point, on the Pennsylvania Railroad, two hundred and forty-two miles from Philadelphia. The curve is reached shortly after leaving Altoona station, from which there is a rise for many miles of over ninety feet to the mile. The gorge continually deepens as the train ascends, until the tops of the tallest trees are far below, and the few houses visible seem lost in an impenetrable chasm. Soon the valley, which the road has followed for six miles, separates into two chasms neither of which could be made available for further progress. But engineering science and skill proved equal to the task. By the grand Horse-shoe Curve represented in our engraving, the road crosses both ravines on a high embankment, cuts away the point of the mountain dividing them, sweeps around the stupendous western wall, and leads away to a more tractable pass. The sides of the curve are parallel with each other, thus giving trains travelling the same way the appearance of moving in entirely different directions. Reaching the new pass, the road continues its steady ascent through the very heart of the great dividing range of a continent.

The route of the railway being now determined, the deviations, if any, permitted by Parliament being arranged, the work let to the contractors-in-chief, and underlet to subordinates, the undertaking commences at the part where there is most to be done. The reason of this is that the line has to be completed throughout as nearly as possible simultaneously. Those portions that lie between heavy cuttings and embankments are levelled, and rails laid down, so that the material from the one may be used to form the other. A few scores of navvies may now be seen on the face of the hill through which the cutting is to pass; the hill is laid open, and a "gullet" excavated. This term is applied to a cutting made just large enough to receive a row of the wagons that are to bear away the earth; and into the gullet the tramway is run. The wagons can now be brought close alongside the material to be moved, and several men being set to work at each, the soil is flung into them with ease and celerity. Meanwhile, as the stuff is removed the gullet is opened farther and farther into the hill, while earth is showered into the wagons from all sides. When these are filled, they are secured together in a train, and, if the inclination of the ground permits it, they run down by their own velocity, being regulated by a breakman, who stands on the last wagon, and who applies his feet to a lever when he wishes the trucks to be stopped. His duty, however, is anything but pleasant, for, what with the roughness of the roads, and the action of the springless vehicle on which he rides, the shaking he receives in his journey seems sufficient to reduce every joint in his body to a most unsatisfactory condition of laxity. On reaching his journey's end he consigns the laden trucks to the embankment men, and assists in driving the horses which are to draw the empty trucks back.

MAKING A CUTTING.

In the interim a fresh supply of empty wagons has been brought into the cutting, and the men are now filling these as they did the others. When a large number of navvies are employed, the trains of wagons are very numerous, but care is usually taken that the limited room they are obliged to occupy shall not occasion one to hinder another.

Other considerations have also to be regarded. In the formation of cuttings, springs are frequently tapped which discharge large quantities of water, and which must be conveyed away by means of drains. Sometimes, too, if rainy weather comes on, large quantities of water unexpectedly pour from the sides of cuttings, and this has to be turned into temporary channels till permanent drains are constructed. The excavators are usually paid according to the number of loads filled, though prices are necessarily conditioned on the nature of the soil.

When the stuff has been removed, and the gullet can lay a reasonable claim to the appellation of a cutting, the rails are moved so as to bring the wagons immediately alongside the wall of earth on either hand, and thus two trains may be filled at the same time. Meanwhile barrows laden with earth are trundled from all directions and the contents overturned into the trucks. *Runs*, as they are called, are also made, by laying planks up the sides of the cutting, on which barrows may be wheeled. The *running* is performed by strong men, round the waist of each of whom is a belt, and fastened to it is a rope running up the side of the cutting, turning on a wheel at the top, and at its end is a horse. The barrow being laden, a signal is given, the driver leads the horse quickly out a given distance into the field, and the barrow and man are drawn up the acclivity ; the contents of the barrow are emptied, the horse being led back the rope is slackened, and the man runs down the plank again, drawing the empty barrow after him.

This practice of running, though common, is dangerous, for the man rather hangs to than supports the barrow, and it at once becomes unmanageable if there is any irregularity in the motion of the horse. If the barrow man finds himself unable to control it, he tries, by a sudden jerk, to raise himself erect ; then throwing the barrow over one side of the board or "run," he swings himself round and runs down to the bottom. Should both fall on the same side, there is risk of the barrow with its contents falling on him before he can escape. Although there were from thirty to forty horse-runs in the Tring cutting, which was made in this way, and they were constantly working during many months, and nearly all the labourers were thrown down the slopes several times ; yet from continual practice, and sure-footedness, only one fatal accident occurred. A moving platform was invented by the engineer to supersede the necessity of thus perilling life and limb, but the men, considering it designed to diminish their labour and wages, broke it. The accompanying cut gives a vivid delineation of the process; and when we see the angle at which the ascending stages are laid, it will be imagined that it is not an easy thing for the workmen to maintain their "centre of gravity within the base."

If in the formation of a cutting more earth is excavated from it than is required for the neighbouring embankments, it be-

MAKING THE RUNNING.

comes necessary to lay the surplus materials on a piece of land adjoining the line; this is called "putting it to spoil." Where, on the other hand, there is an excess of embanking or deficiency of excavation, it is sometimes necessary to make a cutting out of other land; this is designated "side cutting." In both cases the expense of forming the road is increased. Cases sometimes occur where the distance between the cutting and the embankment is such, that the expense of conveying the earth from one part of the line to the other is greater than the cost of making a side cutting from which to form the embankment; and it may be better to deposit the earth from the cutting which ought to have formed the embankment upon waste ground alongside, or of "putting it to spoil." These are considerations which are left to the judgment of the engineer. The cutting being at length reduced to something like its intended proportions, the brick and timber work required for drainage and other purposes is made.

The importance of avoiding the trouble, danger, and cost of accidents from slips in cuttings is obvious; and much patient attention has been given to the subject. The degree of the inclination required by the sides of cuttings or embankments depends on the nature of the strata of which they are composed. The soils intersected, include peat, clay, and mud, are sometimes stratified with seams of clay, shale, sand, and shells, often of considerable dip, and with an extreme tendency to slip. When saturated with water, the soil swells, and can move laterally only towards the unresisting opening of the cutting. "Drying again, this ground cracks; the fissures rapidly fill with dust or sand washed or blown in, another saturation thus produces another swell, with a further movement, until a fall or slip occurs. When the ground is usually full of water, certain clays or marl will become so soapy or greasy as almost to destroy the friction between the strata, which, in inclined seams, is all that holds the upper soils in place. In some, the soil may so far dissolve as to run over in a semi-fluid state, thus undermining solid earth above."

All materials, however, have a certain position at which they will rest, which is denominated the *angle of repose,* but this is affected not only by the character of the material themselves, but by the influence that weather has on those materials. If the strata vary the slope would have to be flatter than in homogeneous earth. Alternate strata of clay and sand are especially treacherous; separate strata will not absorb water and swell equally; and a comparatively impervious stratum like clay will hold all the water that comes to it. This will swell and move forward towards the face of the slope, the movement being on the surface of the next stratum which is like a smooth lubricated floor. The action is of course more decisive if the strata are inclined. In the strata through which railway cuttings are made, and from which embankments are often formed, the slopes of the sides are usually about a foot and a half horizontal to one foot vertical, and from this they vary from three or four feet horizontal to one vertical. Chalk has usually great stability. This is illustrated in the town of Dover, a con siderable portion of which lies beneath a high range of chalk cliffs, and yet has long been perfectly secure. On the other hand, it is sometimes very insecure. In the well-known Merstham cutting, on the Brighton line, which passes through stratified chalk the sides of which are nearly perpendicular, there is a falling of pieces which sometimes renders the attendance of watchers by night and day indispensable. This is especially the case in frosty weather, when the jutting pieces begin to give way, and after a while many of them come tumbling down. Their rattling and crumbling, however, give notice to the workmen, and thus they are enabled to provide against accident to passing trains.

When cuttings are formed through rocky strata, no considerable inclination is required, as in the case of the stone cutting on the London and Birmingham line between the Wolverton and Blisworth stations. The Olive Mount cutting, on the Liverpool and Manchester Railway, is in some parts more than a hundred feet deep. It is indeed a narrow ravine cut for nearly two miles through the solid rock, and 480,000 cubic yards of stone were removed in its excavation.* In such instances tunnelling would generally be less expensive, but in this case the material was required for the formation of an embankment in the vicinity. So small is the sacrifice of land, and the amount of superfluous material necessary to be removed when there is no angle of repose, that cuttings through clay, gravel, or other loose substances are nearly as expensive as those made in rock.

Other materials require different degrees of inclination to give them the desired stability. Thus the London clay has been made to stand at one to one, and has slipped at one to three, its firmness depending greatly on its dryness when cut through, or, in the case of embankments, when it is tipped. If it contains much water, it is peculiarly difficult to manage;

---

* See page 91.

and in the cutting which extends for some distance between the Euston and Camden stations, the clay is only retained in its position by walls seven bricks in thickness at the foundation, and three at the top; they are twenty feet in height. They are also curved inwards to give them additional security. The walls by themselves, however, were insufficient to sustain the pressure; and it was found necessary to support them by no fewer than forty-four massive iron beams, which stretch across over head, and provide a counterpoising lateral pressure. A similar arrangement had to be made when the Midland line

RETAINING WALLS, HAVERSTOCK HILL STATION.

was carried by Haverstock Hill station. With steep slopes the bottom is often supported by a low retaining wall or revetment of stone or earth.

Another illustration of the difficulties which have occurred in working the London clay may also be mentioned. In the formation of a cutting on the London and Birmingham Railway at Highgate, near what is called the Archway Road, a gullet had been formed and a temporary tramway laid down. Excessive wetness set in, but the works were continued with persevering energy, when one morning the treacherous material gave way, the gullet was filled up, the labour of weeks, estimated at £800, was destroyed by an accident which could not have been anticipated.

Sometimes the work is made secure with comparative ease. Thus, in all the excavations on the Newcastle and Carlisle line, through a district sixty-two miles in length, the slopes are made at one and a half to one, and they have stood well. The sand cuttings through the Corvan Hills, on that line, are 110 feet deep, and it is interspersed with thin layers of clay, yet it has remained firm with a slope of one and a half to one. Cuttings on the Birmingham and Gloucester line fifty feet deep in pure gravel, have stood well at one to one, and on the same line is a cutting eighty-six feet deep, with a spoil bank on the top of twenty-four feet, making a total depth of 110 feet in gravel and sand, which has stood at one and a half to one.

In the construction of cuttings, retaining walls are sometimes built to save excavation. They are calculated to resist the pressure of the earth behind them, estimating that pressure as "equal to the weight of a prism of earth slipping upon the face of the natural slope due to the character of the soil." But if water collects behind the wall and saturates the earth, then the pressure equals the weight of the column of semi-fluid resting against the wall. The plan has sometimes been adopted of building buttresses opposite each other along the faces of a perpendicular cutting. These buttresses may easily be kept apart, by a reversed arch below the track and by a brick beam overhead, the beam being arched both on its upper and under sides. The intermediate faces of the cutting are supported by concave retaining walls.

In cuttings the track has, more or less, a slope towards each end, both to reduce the quantity of excavation and to keep the side-ditches clear. Where the incline is steep, the side-ditches are sometimes lined with stone, in order to save excavation and to prevent the ditch from wasting. Such a ditch would be perhaps thirty-three inches deep, eighteen inches open at the top, paved with three-inch flagging stone at the bottom, and lined with walls of twelve to fifteen inches in thickness. "On the London and North Western line cross underground drains of circular and perforated tiles are used to a considerable extent, placed well below the ballast. In some of the deep chalk cuttings some of the side drains are of large bricks, running the whole length underground, with cesspools, or eyes, at convenient distances to take off the surface water. Semicircular half-brick open drains are used for the sides of some of the cuttings." In very wet cuttings, covered drains are made under the centre of the road-bed; some are oval, three feet in vertical diameter, and two feet wide, the bottom being from four to five feet below the surface of the ballast. But with all the care taken to remove underlying water, accidents from this cause will occur, although perhaps rarely. In dealing with drainage upon such a vast scale as is involved in railway works, a knowledge of geology is very useful. Every geologist knows the *strata* that probably underlie each other, and where there is water. In cuttings where the land is in transverse section, ditches are made on both sides at the top, called "crest ditches," which discharge themselves at the end of the cutting, if it is not too long, or they fall down its sides, and the water has to be carried off by drains that have some fall also.

The great enemy of cuttings, whether in making or maintaining them, is water. If it runs over the surface of earthworks, it dissolves and washes it away, soaks the road-bed of the line, and chokes the ditches. One curious and serious effect of this is, that no matter how high the mass of matter that is in contact with the water, and whether it be loam, sand, or clay, the water will rise by absorption to the top. The road-bed also becomes saturated, the ballast sinks, the sleepers, when a train passes, deflect deeply, and in doing so, oppose a heavy grade to the wheels, and enormously increase the wear and tear of the road. In wet weather mud oozes from beneath the sleepers, and in dry seasons this is dissipated in clouds of dust. Clay soils, soaked with water, will, on the return of dry weather, shrink and crack in every direction; and whatever may thus disturb the road-bed disturbs the sleepers, the fastenings are strained, the chairs are broken, the metals are rusted, and the road is rotted. "In an economical view," says one authority, "the damage occasioned by water is far greater than the utmost cost of its removal." "Wherever water is known, or suspected to exist," remarked Robert Stephenson, "its immediate source should be traced, and every possible means adopted for diverting it from the slopes and adjacent surfaces." All running water must be cut off from any point that comes within three feet below the rails. "No excellence of ballast can keep a road-bed dry except the surface is fully three feet above the reach of water."

To this end the ditches on the side of cuttings must be straight and clean, with an inclination that prevents their containing stagnant water, and with free outlets to neighbouring watercourses.

The surface of the slope may be intersected by numerous shallow "spade drains" as they are called, running either straight down from the top to the bottom, or diagonally each way, so as to form a continual outline like the letter W on the face of the work.

Numerous illustrations of the difficulties attending the making of cuttings might be given. In the formation of a cutting on one of the railways in the north of England, it was estimated that about 50,000 cubic yards of earth would have to be removed. The computation was unexpectedly found to be fallacious. The soft earth was supported by a seam of shale, and no sooner was it severed than a mass of earth slipped down into the railway, which required the removal of no less than 500,000 cubic yards of material.

The Haslingden cutting, on the East Lancashire line, was probably one of the most difficult works of the kind ever undertaken. Nearly half a million yards of peat, gravel, and sand were removed from it, and it had to be cut through a bog-hole, the material of which, being saturated with water, sometimes came in faster than it could be taken out. The peat was twenty feet or more in thickness; and for three months, during the summer of 1848, all the earth that two locomotives and their trains could bring was carried away to form an embankment without obtaining a foundation. The difficulty was at length overcome by the company's engineer, Mr. Perring, who sunk large masses of stone at the required points, and these, forcing away the peat, provided a solid bed over which the line could be carried.

The three great cuttings on the London and Birmingham line are at Denbigh Hall, Roade, and Blisworth. The last passes through limestone and clay, and upwards of 1,000,000 cubic yards of earth had to be removed in its formation, about a third of which was limestone, nearly as hard as flint. Beneath the rock was the clay, and under that were beds of loose shale so soaked with water that for a year and a half they resisted all efforts to pump them dry. To hold the sides of the cutting in their place, strong retaining walls had to be erected, behind which drains were built through which the water might escape. More than 800 stonemasons, miners, labourers, and boys were at work at this spot, directed by experienced engineers, and aided by horse and steam-power, with "all appliances and means to boot;" twenty-five barrels of gunpowder were consumed weekly, or 3,000 in all, in blasting. The cost of the

BIRKETT CUTTING.

work was about a quarter of a million of pounds sterling. This cutting has lately been doubled in width.

The largest cutting on the London and Birmingham line is at Tring. It passes through the flintless chalk ridge of Ivinghoe for nearly two miles and a half, and is crossed by three bridges of three arches, besides a smaller bridge. Its average depth is forty feet; for a quarter of a mile it is fifty-seven feet deep; 1,500,000 cubic yards of chalk were removed in its excavation by horse runs, and they form an embankment to the north six miles long and thirty feet high, besides vast "spoil banks" of superfluous material.

Roade cutting is a mile and a half long, and in some places sixty-five feet deep, cut through clay and hard rock. Constant pumping was necessary. The contractors gave the work up, and the company had to take it in hand. Steam-engines were set to pump, locomotives to draw, and 800 men and boys to dig, wheel, and blast, and 3,000 barrels of gunpowder were used.

Two other cuttings are deserving of special notice. The one is the Birkett cutting, a little south of Birkett tunnel, about two miles and a half south of Kirkby Stephen on the Settle and Carlisle line. It is of rock, and has been made through

BARON WOOD CUTTING.

what is known as the Great Pennine Fault. It passes through shale, mountain limestone, magnesian limestone, grit, slate, iron, coal, and lead ore in thin bands, all within a hundred yards. "The most curious combination," remarked Mr. Crossley, "I have ever seen." In the same side of the hill the strata rise up from a horizontal position till they are not far from perpendicular.

The other is on the same railway somewhat south of Armathwaite. The line runs through a long ancient forest, called Baron or Barren Wood, in some places thickly timbered with oak and ash, fir and beech; and in others covered with brushwood and bracken. A heavy cutting then runs through the wood for a distance of nearly a mile; the hill slopes 150 feet to the water's edge. Here, among beautiful views, are the remarkable rocks that raise, for perhaps 100 feet, their "shattered and fretted summits," and form the entrance to what is known as Samson's Cave. The water washes their base. The view is depicted in our engraving as seen from the other side of the beautiful river Eden. The rocks of Samson's Cave are in front.

The vicissitudes that arise in the prosecution of railway work are sometimes very serious. Before us lies a letter of a young

DOVE HOLES CUTTING.

engineer, named Sharland, to whose memory we have elsewhere paid a tribute, in which he describes an accident that occurred when making the cutting at the north end of the Blea Moor tunnel on the Settle and Carlisle line. "We have had," he says, "a terrible storm. A waterspout burst over our tunnel. The men were all at work as usual, when without two minutes' warning a sheet of water came tearing down the tunnel hill like an immense wave, five feet in height. Down it came, right into a cutting where fortunately there were only seven men at work; but before the poor fellows could run ten yards it was on them, and two of them were drowned immediately; also a horse, which was in the act of drawing a wagon towards the tip, was overtaken, and in less than twenty minutes, both horse and wagon were buried under some hundred tons of *débris* from the mountain side. You never saw a more perfect wreck than now appears in the beautiful valley of Dent: seven road bridges are washed away bodily, and what was formerly the public road is now the bed of the river. One solid block of marble 10 ft. × 4′ 6″ × 1′ 8″ was washed fifty-four yards down stream; this gives some idea of the force of the torrent; stone walls, trees, etc., are washed away, and as I have said before, the wreck is most complete on all sides. The greatest wonder to me is that

DOVE HOLES CUTTING CLEARED.

there was not a greater loss of life. A rain-gauge in Dent Valley showed that there had been 2½ inches of rain in three-quarters of an hour."

Of course the deeper a cutting is carried the costlier it becomes, until a point is reached at which it is cheaper to run underground. At the mouth of the Dove Holes tunnel, near Buxton, on the Midland, the cutting was 72 or 73 feet, a depth at which the cost of cutting or of tunnelling would about balance one another. Here, in the summer flood rain of 1872, the cutting slipped in, and presented the appearance depicted on the previous page; when, eventually, it was cleared out, the engineers decided to arch over part of the cutting, as indicated on the second engraving, which we transfer to these pages from our history of "the Rise and Progress" of the Midland Railway.

Other considerations may also affect the choice between cuttings and tunnels. Thus, as Mr. Barlow, the engineer-in-chief of the Midland Company informed us, in the formation of the Rowsley and Buxton Extension northwards towards Manchester, he in some instances substituted tunnels for cuttings,

WOODHOUSE TOWER AND CUTTING, ON THE CALEDONIAN RAILWAY.

the line being also moved a little nearer to the rocks in order to prevent the embankments running into the channel of the river and displacing the current. Difficulty would also have been found in securing space whereon to deposit the material from a cutting. These alterations received the sanction of the Board of Trade.

The difficulties connected with cuttings do not end when the works are completed. In many instances their sides have stood securely for weeks, or months, or even years after they were finished, and have then loosened and fallen. Sometimes these misfortunes arise from the unexpected accumulation of water behind the earthwork, sometimes from the disturbed drainage of adjoining lands, and sometimes from chemical action. The chemical combinations that are thus created are very curious and embarrassing to the railway engineer. The walls of tunnels, for instance, on the Midland Railway, both at Miller's Dale and on the Settle and Carlisle, stood perfectly for years, and it was thought they would continue to stand of themselves: they had then, at great inconvenience and expense—for the traffic must be carried on—to be lined with brick. So with the sides of cuttings. An unintelligent observer sees that a slip has taken place upon a railway, and thinks that the engineer is at fault—that he ought to have made the slope greater. But with some materials no sloping of the side of a cutting will arrest the active chemical process that, under some conditions of weather and time, will be developed. Thus, for instance, with the Ampthill cutting on the Bedford and London line of the Midland. "You may lay that stuff on its back," remarked Mr. Crossley the engineer to us, "but it will kick up its heels. I will show you some nearer London," he added, "which lies nearly on the flat, but it is always boiling up and turning over."

In the winter of 1841 and 1842, landslips took place in the New Cross cutting of the Croydon line. The cutting is in some parts eighty feet deep, and in the autumn about 50,000 cubic yards of earth suddenly gave way, immediately after the passing of a train, from the western slope, and covered both lines of rails to a depth of nearly twelve feet and for a length of 360 feet. Other slips subsequently occurred near the same spot, and upwards of 250,000 cubic yards of earth had to be removed. The works were carried on day and night without intermission, but it required three months before the trains could run as before.

Similarly, in the autumn of 1876, a landslip took place on the North British Railway line, near Dunfermline. About 8,000 tons of sand and rock gave way at a cutting about forty feet deep, and covered the line for some forty yards to a depth of fifteen feet. A special cattle train ran into the heap, fourteen wagons were smashed, and the engine was thrown across the opposite line of rails. The line was not cleared for five days.

Wherever possible the slopes of cuttings and embankments are covered with a layer of soil, procured from the base of the embankments or from the top of the cuttings when they are commenced ; this is spread about six inches in thickness, or as thick as the amount of soil will allow. The soil should be laid on as soon as possible after the excavation is made, or the embankment is consolidated, and it should be either sown with grass or clover, or both, in order to have a turf upon it before the slopes are affected by the weather. By attending to these matters, slopes will stand when otherwise they would crumble.

A WELSH RAILWAY STATION.

CHAPTER V.

Levelling of the Round Down Cliff.—Blasting on the Londonderry and Coleraine Railway Embankments.—Making an Embankment.—The Tip.—Disappearance of an Embankment.—Embankments on Marshes.—Chat Moss.—Embankments Chained with Iron Cables.—Hanwell Embankment.—Intake Embankment.—Embankments on Loch Foyle.—A Baked Embankment.—Earthworks of Railways.—Comparison of Labour of Ancients and Moderns.—Market Gardens on Railway Banks.—Navigators and their Characteristics.—Cunning of Navvies.—Comparison of English and Foreign Navvies.—Nicknames of Navvies.—Courage and Recklessness of Navvies.—Management of Navvies.

IN the ever-varying exigencies that arise in the formation of a railway, abundant opportunities are afforded for testing the skill and experience of the engineer. An illustration in the construction of the South Eastern line, is worthy of special consideration. Towards the west, in the direction of Folkestone, the line of sea-face is terminated by Abbot's Cliff, and to the east, adjoining Dover, by the well-known Shakespeare's Cliff.* These hills are separated from the "Heights" by a narrow valley, from which they slope upwards by gentle courses to their escarpment, which has a majestic perpendicular front, about five miles in extent, looking to the ocean, and of an average height of 350 feet. This front is varied by occasional bold projections, which divide the beach at their base into corresponding spaces. One of these protruding rocks was the Round Down Cliff: it rose 375 feet above the sea, and was the highest point of the chalk cliffs between Folkestone to Dover. How then, was the railway to be carried in a direct line to

* *Vide* Frontispiece. The initial letter represents the viaduct and tunnel near Penmaenmawr.

Shakespeare's Cliff. To tunnel was impossible, if such a word is found in the vocabulary of the engineer of the present day; to dig it down would have occasioned a delay of twelve months, and an expense of £10,000. Although the obstacle to be removed was nothing less than a mass of chalk rock, 300 feet in length, of still greater height, and averaging 70 feet in thickness, the engineer of the line, Mr. William Cubitt, devised a new

ABBOT'S CLIFF.

method of accomplishing the desired work. It was by the explosion, by galvanism, of 19,000 pounds of gunpowder.

At the time appointed, a number of distinguished visitors reached the Downs, and joined the directors and the scientific corps at a commodious pavilion erected near the edge of the cliff, at a distance of about a quarter of a mile from the point of explosion. "When the arrangements were completed, and the spectators assembled, curiosity was at its height, and the most strange and fearful speculations were entertained by the people assembled as to the possible contingencies which might arise. 'What,' said Professor Sedgwick, 'what if there should be a concealed fissure—a blinded chasm—in the cliff behind us? A smart vibration *might* throw it open.' 'What then?' inquired a ghastly querist. 'We shall be swallowed up!' muttered one in response; while another sighed, 'We shall be swallowed *down!*' Still the fascination was irresistible, and though many were uneasy, and wished to be gone, no one withdrew. After a long suspense of half an hour the discharge of half a dozen blasts on the face of Abbot's Cliff occasioned a great sensation. When two o'clock arrived, the time appointed for the explosion, the interest which pervaded the multitude became most intense. The 'choughs and crows that winged the midway air' were distinctly heard amidst the profound calm that prevailed. The signal which announced it to be fifteen minutes before firing having been given, all the other flags were hoisted. The air was still, the sea was calm, and the murmuring surges gently laved the cliff's huge base. A quarter of an hour now passed, and a shell with a lighted fusee was thrown over the cliff, from which it bounded to the beach, where it burst with an astounding report, followed by echoes from the hills, which had the effect of sharp fusillades of musketry. The flags were then hauled down, and at length the 'one minute before firing' arrived.

"The excitement of the people was now painfully intense, while their courage was put to its severest test. 'Now! now!' shouted the eager multitude, and a dull, muffled, booming sound was heard, accompanied for a moment by a heavy jolting movement of the earth, which caused the knees to smite. The wires had been fired. In an instant the bottom of the cliff appeared to dissolve, and to form by its melting elements a hurried sea-borne stream. The superincumbent mass, to the extent of about five hundred feet, was then observed to separate from the main land, and as the dissolution of its base was accomplished it gradually sank to the beach. In two minutes its dispersion was complete. The huge volleys of ejected chalk, as they swelled the lava-like stream, appeared to roll inwards upon themselves, crushing their integral blocks, and then to return to the surface in smaller and coalescing forms. The mass seemed to ferment under the influence of an unseen, but uncontrollable power. There was no roaring explosion, no bursting out of fire, and, what is very remarkable, not a single wreath of smoke; for the mighty agent had done its work under an amount of pressure which almost matched its energies: the pent-up fires were restrained in their intensity till all smoke was consumed. A million tons of weight and a million tons of cohesion held them in check. When the turf at the top of the cliff was launched to the level of the beach, the stream of *débris* extended a distance of 1,200 feet, and covered a space of more than fifteen acres!"

The moment the headlong course of the chalk had ceased, and the hopes of the spectators were realized, a simultaneous cry arose of "Three cheers for the engineer!" and William Cubitt was honoured with a hearty huzza from the lips of a grateful people. An era in the history of engineering had passed, and a precedent had been established, the results of which none could anticipate. It had been demonstrated that the most powerful and mysterious agency in nature was under computable regulations, and in no small degree under the control of science. The congratulations thus re-echoed were borne to the gloom of the battery house, and at once dissipated the apprehensions of the operators; for so slight was the noise and the shock that the impression made on their minds was that the experiment had failed, for their situation prevented their witnessing the result. The ruins of the Round Down Cliff may now be observed stretching towards the sea at the mouth of the Shakespeare tunnel. "Nothing," says Sir John Herschel, "can place in a more signal light the exactness of calculation which could enable the eminent engineer by whom the whole arrangements are understood to have been made, so completely to task to its utmost every pound of power employed as to exhaust its whole effort in useful work—leaving no superfluous power to be wasted in the production of useless uproar or mischievous dispersion, and thus saving at a blow not less than £7,000 to the railway company."

A similar blasting, on a small scale, was made on the Londonderry and Coleraine line. It having been found necessary to hurry on the works, it was determined to throw a hill into the sea, through which a tunnel had been commenced.

This took place in June, 1846. A heading or gallery was formed in the rock from the side of the cliff, fifty feet in length, at the end of which a shaft was sunk, for twenty-two feet, to the level of the railway, and again another gallery was made at the bottom, running at right angles to the first, and farther into the rock. At the end of this was placed 2,400 pounds of powder, the earth was well filled in, and the wires for

MAKING THE WOLVERTON EMBANKMENT.

the passage of the electric fluid carefully arranged. The smaller charge of 600 pounds was then placed higher up in the rock. On the explosion being made, the bottom of the mass heaved outwards for a moment, trembling with the force exerted on it, and then, cracking into a thousand fissures, rolled into the sea. The amount of material removed was upwards of 30,000 tons.

When the level of a railway has to be raised, it is usually

done by an embankment. The material, as we have seen, is generally obtained from a neighbouring cutting;—the engineer in laying out the railway, having arranged that the embankments and its cuttings shall in amount about equal one another. The distance along which the stuff is conveyed to the embankment is called "the lead." The first thing in the formation of an embankment is the shaving off to the thickness of six inches of the turfs, if any, at the base of the intended line, and they are put aside for sodding down the slopes of the work when finished. By these means also a good bottom, free from vegetable matter, is obtained. All stumps, brush, or other obstructions, which, by their disturbance of the integrity of the bank, or by their decay, might cause sinking or slips, are then removed. The culverts being laid in cement are allowed ample time to set before the filling commences. The material of which the embankment is made is conveyed along the lead by different means. If possible, the loaded wagons run down the tramroad, by their own gravity, to the embankment. In some instances, each load has to be drawn along the lead by horses, in other cases by engines, which are themselves conveyed to the scene of operations on what are called "drugs." To take so weighty an affair as a locomotive along a common road, is not a trifling matter, especially if the distance it has to travel be considerable, and hills intervene. Then may the old turnpike-road be seen invaded by a team of sixteen or eighteen contractor's horses, each pair under the guidance of an appointed driver; while the gleaming brass-work, the black funnel, and the metal ribs of the engine, form a striking contrast to the rural simplicity and tranquillity that stretch around.

In the formation of an embankment, it is of much importance that it should be constructed with great firmness, and with due consideration of the nature of the material of which it is composed, and of the probable weight which it is designed to support. To this end the embankment will be made at first to the full intended width, for material subsequently added does not readily unite with the original mass. If additions become necessary the side of the bank is, perhaps, "stepped." An embankment is sometimes commenced from two directions, which at last unite in the middle. A train of wagons being brought on to the part of the embankment already finished, preparations are made to empty them. A tramroad has already been formed to the end of the bank, and at its extreme verge a stout piece of timber is secured to prevent the wagons when their contents are discharged, from being precipitated over it. One of the trucks is then detached from the train, and being brought within a few hundred yards of the end of the embankment, the horse that draws it is made to trot and then to gallop, so as to give the required impetus to his load The uninitiated observer fancies that both horse and driver must be killed, or hurled over the embankment; but when they have approached very near to the edge, the driver loosens

THE "TIP."

the horse from the wagon, gives him a signal which he has been taught to obey, both leap aside with the greatest celerity, and the wagon alone rushes on till it is suddenly stopped at the end of the embankment by the piece of timber, and the shock makes the hinder part tip up and discharge the load. The horse is immediately brought up again and hooked on, the truck rights itself, and is drawn away to form part of the empty train which will soon return to the cutting. If the works of the railway are proceeding with moderate rapidity, two lines of rails, and two or three sets of wagons, horses, and men, are simultaneously at work. Care is of course necessary that the elevation of the embankment be rightly adjusted: this is ensured by the erection of posts at intervals along the line, fitted with cross pieces that indicate the height to be observed.

When the general outline of the embankment has thus been given, it is trimmed so as to have the required uniformity of appearance, and the necessary material is conveyed to the spot, in little three-wheeled carts, the contents of which are tipped over the side, and then spread with the spade.

The face of a slope, according to the analogy of nature, is strongest when curved so as to be flattest at the base, where the pressure is greatest, and to counteract the effect of time and of weather in gradually washing down the slopes. In districts where stone is abundant, embankments and excavations are extensively faced with it. Embankments must also be made strong enough to withstand the vibration caused by the passage of fast trains. This has been detected in some cases at one and a half mile distance. At the astronomical observatories, the disturbance has at the distance of a mile from the passing train sensibly affected the instruments. "The blows of a pile engine, in driving piles in some kinds of ground, are sufficient to unsettle the foundations of contiguous buildings. This was the case at Lincoln, on the Great Northern line, where the station was supported by iron screw-piles in order to avoid this danger." Vibration may be an important cause of the failure of earthworks many years after the opening of a railway.

How unexpected difficulties arise in the prosecution of great engineering works, may be illustrated in the case of embankments. On one occasion an embankment was observed, without any apparent cause, gradually to sink, and the adjoining fields to rise; the mass having penetrated some less solid stratum below, and by expanding at its base had elevated, without otherwise disturbing, the adjoining surface. The Hanwell embankment on the Great Western line, fifty-four feet high, once broke through the covering of a clay stratum beneath. The swollen ground "forced up on one side of the embankment extended for 400 feet, with a width of eighty feet, a height of nearly ten feet, and had been removed horizontally for about fifteen feet. Had this embankment been made originally with flatter slopes, the extension of base, by distributing the weight over a greater area, would have saved the failure. As it was, this extensive work actually absorbed more material in its repair than in its original construction." It is also asserted that an embankment on a railway in North America suddenly disappeared from view, and sank in sixty feet of water. The cause was ascribed to the fact that an extensive lake had, in the course of ages, been covered with various deposits, which at length formed a soil of sufficient stability to withstand the operations of agriculture; but being oppressed by the weight of so extraordinary a contrivance as a railway embankment, it declined to be thus burdened, and deposited its load beneath its waters.

The embankment of the Great Eastern line which crosses Stratford Marshes has a peculiarity worthy of notice. In order to facilitate its construction, by enabling the workmen to tip more wagons than usual in a given time, Mr. Braithwaite constructed a kind of scaffolding or stage in advance of the end of the embankment; and by leaving some of the timber framework of the scaffolding in the earth of the embankment, it is so bound together as to enable it to more effectually withstand the action of the heavy floods to which the valley of the Lea is subject, than if it had been constructed in the ordinary way.

Other curious difficulties have arisen in the formation of embankments across marshy districts. Thus it was found with one at Ashton, that the materials disappeared as fast as they were deposited, owing to the unsound state of the valley at the base; the surface outside the railway actually burst, in consequence of the enormous pressure; and a culvert near the spot was destroyed. The power of a culvert to sustain an embankment fifty feet high may be supposed to be great; but its construction upon a soft foundation is a task on which no engineer, however cautious and skilful, can calculate upon with certainty.

A similar difficulty occurred in the case of a portion of the Newcastle and Darlington line, which crosses a spot called Morden Carr, about eight miles north of Darlington. The soil consists of peat, and is of great depth, being probably the remains of a primæval forest; while, from its low position, compared with the surrounding hilly country, it has in winter the appearance of an immense lake. At such times the line has been overflowed, and sometimes to such a depth as almost to extinguish the engine fires. On one occasion, a portion, to the extent of between fifty and sixty yards, gave way, and it was necessary to transfer the passengers and luggage across the gap, to other trains. Meanwhile, a great number of workmen were collected to repair the injury, but incessant rain reduced the ground to such a state, that as ballast was laid upon the depressed part, the additional weight only caused a further sinking, and rendered the attempt abortive. Under these circumstances a temporary way had to be constructed, which avoided the marshes, and united the sound portions of the line, and with great difficulty the line was restored to a condition for safe working.

One of the most important of the lines carried across a morass was the Liverpool and Manchester line. Chat Moss was nothing less than a huge bog, of soft or flowing moss, covered with spagni, or bog-mosses, stretching over an area of twelve square miles, from twenty to forty feet in depth, and estimated to contain at least sixty million tons of vegetable matter, held up by a saucer-shaped stratum of clay and sand, and of so pulpy a nature that cattle could not walk on it, and in many parts a piece of iron sank into it by its own weight. It will readily be imagined that to traverse this place with an embankment and a secure road, was no small undertaking; and when the railway was under discussion, an eminent opposing engineer declared "that no man in his senses would attempt a railway over Chat Moss;" and he affirmed that it would cost not less than £227,000.

In order to deprive the moss of some of its water, its drainage was commenced; but, in many instances, the drains filled up almost as quickly as they were dug. A pathway between the drains was laid of ling or heather on which a man could safely walk; light iron rails were placed on sleepers, along which a little wagon could be pushed by boys; and then followed a thin layer of gravel, and sleepers, chairs, and rails.

Greater difficulty still was found at one part where, as the materials were deposited, the whole mass gradually sank; and when the embankment was finished, although the actual level of the railway was only four or five feet above the original surface, the quantity of earth deposited would have made, on ordinary ground, an embankment twenty-four or twenty-five feet high. With such materials, therefore, as clay and gravel, it would have been impracticable to form an embankment over Chat Moss, for the quantity required and the expense involved would have been enormous. But George Stephenson here made a layer of dry moss, of considerable tenacity; and upon this he placed, transversely, hurdles nine feet long and four broad, wickered with heather, and where the moss was soft, two were used. The bank, however, had "scarcely been raised three or four feet in height when the stuff broke the heathery surface of the bog and sank overhead. More moss was brought up and emptied in with no better result; and for many weeks the filling was continued without any embankment having been made. Sometimes the visible work done was less than it had appeared a fortnight or a month before." The resident engineer himself was greatly disheartened, and his directors had seriously to discuss the question whether the work should not be abandoned.

But George Stephenson's one word was—persevere. "There is no help for it," he said. "The stuff emptied in is doing its work out of sight, and if you will but have patience it will soon begin to show." "And so," remarks Dr. Smiles, "the filling went on; several hundreds of men and boys were employed to skim the moss all round for many thousand yards by means of sharp spades, called by the turf cutters 'tommy-spades'; and the dried cakes of turf were afterwards used to form the embankment, until at length as the stuff sank and rested upon the bottom, the bank gradually rose above the surface, and slowly advanced onwards, declining in height and consequently in weight, until it became joined to the floating road already laid upon the moss. In the course of forming the embankment, the pressure of the bog turf tipped out the wagons caused a copious stream of bog-water to flow from the end of it, in colour resembling Barclay's double stout; and when completed, the bank looked like a long ridge of tightly-pressed tobacco-leaf." Nearly 700,000 cubic yards of raw moss eventually formed only about half that amount of solid embankment. Strange to say, the road across Chat Moss proved to be not only one of the best portions of the railway, but also one of the cheapest. Its cost had been estimated by Mr. Giles at £270,000, but it amounted to only about one-tenth of that sum. The example thus set has been successfully followed elsewhere, and the South Devon line, for instance, crosses the once unfathomable swamp of Cockwood.

Some of the embankment work of the Great Western railway was curiously constructed. It is near the Swindon junction, at the northern edge of the great range of Wiltshire Downs. The directors "could not stay to cart the earth from the cuttings to the places where it was required for embanking; so where they excavated thousands of tons of clay they purchased land to cast it upon out of their way, and where they required an embankment they purchased a hill, and bodily removed it to fill up the hollow. They could not stay for the seasons, for proper weather to work in, and in consequence of this their clay embankment thrown up wet and saturated, swelled out, bulged at the sides, and could not be made stable, till at last they drove rows of piles on each side, and chained them together with chain-cables, and so confined the slippery soil. They drove these piles, tall beech trees, twenty feet into the earth, and at this day every train passes over tons of chain-cables hidden beneath the ballast." *

The biggest bank on the Great Western Railway is at Hanwell. It is about seventy feet high, and three-quarters of a mile long, through clay chalk, and, as we were expressively informed by the authorities, "all sorts of other things."

Another embankment, on the Settle and Carlisle line of the Midland Company, was most difficult to make. It is the Intake embankment, and is a little south of Kirkby Stephen. It is about one hundred feet high, and the tipping actually proceeded *for twelve months without the embankment advancing a yard.* The tip rails during the whole of that period were unmoved, while the masses of slurry, as indicated in the engraving, rolled over one another in mighty convolutions, persisting in going anywhere and everywhere except where they were wanted.

A remarkable embankment has been raised on the Londonderry and Coleraine Railway. It not only serves the ordinary purpose of such a work, but reclaims 22,000 acres from the sea, at Lough Foyle. This is a large lough on the northern coast of Ireland, covering an area of about 60,000 acres, in which the tide did not usually rise more than six feet, while at low water

---

* *Fraser's Magazine.*

a great part of it was perfectly dry,—a rich alluvial deposit. Of the reclaimed land, 12,000 acres were set apart to cover the expenditure of the railway, and were inclosed and sold.

Difficulties have sometimes arisen in the construction of railway works against which no precautions could have been made. The Wolverhampton embankment had been nearly completed, when it was observed to display certain unaccountable volcanic indications. It first began to smoke, then became exceedingly hot, and a slow smouldering flame might at night be seen to rise from it. The people in the neighbourhood were filled with alarm: by some it was confidently affirmed that the embankment would certainly blow up; and a lady reminded her friends of the opinion she had uniformly expressed during the progress of the railway, that "the devil was at the bottom of it!" The embankment for some time carried on this freak of spontaneous combustion, and having burned the sleepers, at last exhausted itself. It was found that the phenomenon had been occasioned by a large quantity of sulphuret of iron, or pyrites, contained in the earth.

INTAKE EMBANKMENT.

The earthworks of a railway, as the cuttings, levellings, and embankments are denominated, are frequently enormous. In lines that traverse comparatively level districts they are unimportant; but in others they are great and costly. According to the estimate laid before the Parliamentary Committee by the engineer of the South Western Railway, it was computed that the aggregate amount of earthwork on the earlier lines of that company would be about 16,000,000 cubic yards, an average of 200,000 cubic yards a mile. Almost every portion of the London and Birmingham line consisted of embankments or cuttings; so that by the original section the latter were estimated at about 12,000,000, and the embankments at more than 10,000,000 cubic yards. On the Settle and Carlisle railway of the Midland Company, a farmer declared to us that "there wasn't a level piece of ground on the whole line big enough to build a house upon."

Mr. Lecount made some interesting calculations, illustrative of the labour involved in the formation of the earthworks of the London and Birmingham Railway. He declared that it was the greatest public work ever executed. "If we estimate its importance," he said, "by the labour alone which has been expended on it, perhaps the great Chinese wall might compete with it; but when we consider the great outlay of capital which it has required, the great and varied talents which have been in a constant state of requisition during the whole of its progress, together with the unprecedented engineering difficulties, which we are happy to say are now overcome, the gigantic work of the Chinese sinks wholly into the shade."

He then proceeded to institute a comparison between the railway and the Great Pyramid of Egypt. "After making the necessary allowances for the foundations, galleries, etc., and reducing the whole to one uniform denomination, it will be found that the labour expended on the Great Pyramid was equivalent to lifting 15,733,000,000 cubic feet of stone one foot high. This labour was performed, according to Diodorus Siculus, by 300,000 men; according to Herodotus, by 100,000 men; and it required for its execution twenty years. If we reduce in the same manner to one common denomination the labour expended in constructing the London and Birmingham Railway, the result is 25,000,000,000 cubic feet of material (reduced to the same weight as that used in constructing the Pyramid) lifted one foot high, or more than 9,000,000,000 cubic feet more than were lifted one foot high in the construction of the Pyramid; yet this immense undertaking has been performed by about 20,000 men in less than five years."

It has been proposed that the sloping sides of a railway embankment, well sunned and sheltered, might be used for purposes of cultivation. "There are miles of embankment," we are assured, especially in the south and west of England, where vines would flourish and grapes ripen, while ordinary wall fruit, supported on trellises, would be in a capital situation. Green figs, too, the cultivation of which is neglected, could not have a better place for growing than on the side of a sunny embankment.

"I had the pleasure," writes a correspondent of the *Gardener's Magazine*, "of seeing perhaps half an acre of strawberries the other day on a railway embankment. They were planted thickly and broadcast, the whole ground being covered with them, and they were loaded with bloom. Perhaps this is the best way of growing strawberries on railway embankments, as the whole ground is thus covered with them; and the fierce sunshine, though intensified by the slope of the ground, cannot burn the roots."

Another advantage of planting the slopes of embankments with trees is found in the fact that their roots, at least of those which do not penetrate with a straight tap root, bind together the surface soil, which they permeate and interlace. In Scotland, where there is a steep slope, more especially if it consist of what is called "travelled" earth, it is closely planted to guard it against landslips. It has, we presume, been somewhat playfully added, that if embankments were covered with trees, a train might indeed leave the rails, but we should read no more of their being "precipitated to the bottom of a lofty embankment." It might be possible for a railway carriage to get "up a tree," but it would be difficult for it to get "down a hole."

In Belgium a plan has been adopted of thus turning railway fences to advantage. They consist of wooden posts 4½ feet high, connected by four lines of wires, across which four long thin sticks are tied obliquely. In front of and between each post are planted cordon apples and pears, which are trained along the oblique sticks. "The trees," says a writer, "appeared healthy, and likely to be very productive."

Having thus considered some of the earthworks of a railway,

we may refer to the special race of men of whose labours they are the outcome.

The word "navvie" is an abridgment of "navigator," a class of men first employed in the construction of the canals that immediately preceded the railway era. Many were "bankers" from the lowlands of Lincolnshire and Cambridgeshire, where they had made the banks and cut the canals by which waste lands were recovered from marsh and sea. The wages offered by railway contractors drew great numbers of other men from all parts of the country, especially from the hills of Lancashire and Yorkshire, and they had the boldest characteristics of the Anglo-Saxon stock. Their great strength, their knowledge of embanking, boring and well sinking, and their familiarity with the nature of clays and rocks, gave them special qualifications for making railway earthworks.

The navvie of the period wandered from one place to another. He usually "wore a white felt hat with the brim turned up, a velveteen or jean square-tailed coat, a scarlet plush waistcoat with little black spots, and a bright-coloured kerchief round his herculean neck, when, as often happened, it was not left entirely bare. His corduroy breeches were retained in position by a leathern strap round the waist, and were tied and buttoned at the knee, displaying beneath a solid calf and foot encased in strong high-laced boots. Joining together in a 'butty gang,' some ten or twelve of these men would take a contract to cut out and remove so much 'dirt'—as they denominated earth-cutting—fixing their price according to the character of the 'stuff,' and the distance to which it had to be wheeled and tipped. The contract taken, every man put himself to his mettle: if any were found skulking, or not putting forth his full working power, he was ejected from the gang." Their powers of endurance and their consumption of flesh food were alike enormous. They seemed to disregard danger, and they were as reckless of their earnings as of their lives. Pay day was usually once a fortnight, when a large amount of their earnings was squandered in dissipation. A sum equal to £1,000 a mile on all the railways of England, has, it is said, thus been wasted. Ignorant and violent as some of them were, they were open-handed to their comrades, and would share their last penny with their friends who were in distress. They also often had a shrewdness, and even a cunning, which got many a one into a scrape and many another out.

An illustration of their keenness is given by Sir Francis Head. During the construction of the London and Birmingham line a landlady at Hillmorton, near Rugby, of a "very sharp practice, which she had imbibed in dealings for many years with canal boatmen, was constantly remarking aloud that no navvie should ever 'do' her; and although the railway was in her immediate neighbourhood, and although the navvies were her principal customers, she took pleasure on every opportunity in repeating the invidious remark.

"It had, however, one fine morning scarcely left her large, full-blown, rosy lips, when a fine-looking young fellow, walking up to her, carrying in both hands a huge stone bottle, commonly called 'a grey neck,' briefly asked her for 'half a gallon of gin'; which was no sooner measured and poured in than the money was rudely demanded before it could be taken away.

"On the navvie declining to pay the exorbitant price asked, the landlady, with a face like a peony, angrily told him he must either pay for the gin or instantly return it.

"He silently chose the latter; and accordingly, while the eyes of his antagonist were wrathfully fixed upon his, he returned into her measure the half-gallon, and then quietly walked off; but having previously put into his grey-neck half a gallon of water, each party eventually found themselves in possession of half a gallon of gin and water; and, however either may have enjoyed the mixture, it is historically recorded in all Hillmorton that the landlady was never again heard unnecessarily to boast that no navvie could 'do' her."

The methods in which railway excavation work was executed on the Continent as compared with England, would have excited the scorn of the navvie. "Hereabouts," in the neighbourhood of Pisa, wrote William Chambers in 1862, "signs of railway construction are apparent. The digging is effected by a sort of adze, and the loosened material is deliberately lifted by a long-shanked scoop and carried away in small baskets on the heads of women and girls. A sorrowful spectacle, these bands of bare-footed female navvies, each in turn casting her modicum of earth to swell the slowly accumulating heaps,"—a service for which she was paid a few pence a day. Ordinarily, in constructing railways the hollows are filled from the heights, "but here every spot is made to depend on itself; the material for the excavations is piled mountains high, along the sides of the line, by that dreary basket-carrying process; and, to form the embankments, acres of the adjoining fields are mercilessly stripped of several feet of their soil—the waste of land, the toil, and the stupidity of the whole thing being absolutely pitiable."

The contrast between the characteristics of the early makers of the French railways, and the English navigator, may also be illustrated: In excavating a portion of the first tunnel east of Rouen towards Paris, a French miner dressed in his blouse, and an English navvie in his white smock jacket, were suddenly buried alive together by the falling in of the earth behind them. Notwithstanding the violent commotion which the intelligence of the accident excited above ground, Mr. Meek, the English engineer who was constructing the work, after having quietly measured the distance from the shaft to the sunken ground, satisfied himself that if the men, at the moment of the accident, were at the head of "the drift" at which they were working, they would be safe.

Accordingly, getting together as many French and English labourers as he could collect, he instantly commenced sinking a shaft, which was accomplished to the depth of fifty feet in the extraordinary short space of eleven hours, and the men were thus brought up to the surface alive.

The Frenchman, on reaching the top, suddenly rushing forwards, hugged and embraced on both cheeks his friends and acquaintances, many of whom had assembled, and then, almost instantly overpowered by conflicting feelings,—by the recollection of the endless time he had been imprisoned, and by the joy of his release,—he sat down on a log of timber, and putting both his hands before his face, he began to cry aloud most bitterly.

The English navvie sat himself down on the very same piece of timber—took his pit-cap off his head—slowly wiped with it the perspiration from his hair and face—and then, looking for some seconds into the hole or shaft close beside him, through which he had been lifted, as if he were calculating the number of cubic yards that had been excavated, quite coolly, in broad Lancashire dialect, said to the crowd of French and

English who were staring at him as children and nursery-maids in our London Zoological Gardens stand gazing half terrified at the white bear: "Yaw've bean an infernal short toime abaaowt it!"

One of the most curious characteristics of navvies is their use of nicknames. It is said that a gentleman was once inquiring for the house of one Richard Millwood, or some such name, in a village, and just as the young woman who piloted him was about to give up the search in despair, she exclaimed, "Hang it! thou means my feyther! why doosn't thee ax for Old Blackbird?" The names of navvies are very suddenly given, and are almost immovable. "I have known a simple fellow all at once styled 'Rush,' after the notorious murderer, for no conceivable reason whatever, and by that name was he almost exclusively known afterwards. A gentleman—an engineer—once walked through his engine-shed, and saw three men by the furnace, apparently asleep. He hurried towards them to see who they were, but that mysterious telegraph which is always at work when the master is about, warned the men, and they ran off too quickly for him to get a sight of their faces. 'Who were those?' he demanded of a man who was near the spot. Of course the man interrogated declared at first he did not know, but finding his superior very much in earnest, he admitted that he knew them; that they were the Duke of Wellington, Cat's Meat, and Mary Anne; and, preposterous as it may sound, he knew them by no other names. The nose of the first, the previous profession of the second, and the effeminate voice of the third, gained these attractive titles. So, one known as Gorger was so called because he had been seen to eat a whole shoulder of mutton; Hedgehog had a whimsical resemblance to his namesake; while, through singing a favourite negro melody, Uncle Ned had lived and was killed, known to very few by any other name."

Of their extreme recklessness, as regards life or limb, numerous illustrations have been mentioned to the writer by engineers and contractors under whom they have served. In the formation of the Kilsby tunnel, two or three were killed in trying to jump one after another across the mouth of the shafts, in a *game* of "Follow my Leader." When the Blisworth cutting was in course of excavation, and the material from thence was taken to the Wolverton embankment, the men were accustomed to ride down on the tip-wagons to their dinners, and in doing this the wagons not unfrequently ran off the rails, and their contents, of workmen and stone, were precipitated in a heterogeneous mass upon the ground. On one of these occasions, a few days after a fatal accident under similar circumstances had taken place, some wagons were thrown off the rails, and several men buried beneath the limestone. One stalwart fellow scrambled out from the heap, and feeling his arm, said to a more fortunate comrade, "It's broke, I maun go home;" and, after waiting to ascertain the fate of his fellow-sufferers, he strode off to his dwelling, six miles distant, supporting the broken limb with the sound one. A fine, handsome boy, who by the same accident had his foot crushed into a shapeless mass of flesh and bone, gave vent to his feelings by crying. A rough-looking ganger who stood by, took the pipe from his lips, and in a blunt, advisory way, said: "Crying 'ill do thee no good, lad;" and then, as if acquainted with the mysteries of the scalpel, added, "thou'dst better have it cut off above the knee."

Their coolness and daring was also extreme. A workman employed on the Scottish Central Railway had lighted the fusees connected with some charges of gunpowder by which a blast was to be effected, and having given the signal to be drawn up, the rope slipped, and the poor fellow was suspended but a few feet above the spot where the explosion was about to take place. His presence of mind, however, did not forsake him. He called out that he might be lowered again, and then approaching the burning fusees, he extinguished them one after another, and his life was saved. They had burned within half an inch of the powder!

It may be easily conceived that the management of large bodies of such men was no easy task to those on whom it devolved. Yet it has been found that a little tact and wit would ordinarily suffice, if judiciously employed, in guiding and subduing them, when any attempt at force would have been fatal either to the one party or the other. A bold demeanour, a few words of advice well applied, associated with a kind interest in them, almost invariably commanded their respect and obedience. A few illustrations may be mentioned.

On one occasion the resident engineer, Mr. Shedlock, afterwards the Rev. Jno. Shedlock, M.A., of Paris, on one portion of the Great Western Railway was engaged in some professional duties on the Saturday afternoon, when a messenger arrived at his house in breathless haste, and said that the men had been greatly enraged about some matter relating to their pay, and that they had left their work, and were coming down *en masse.* "Bring a horse," said the engineer; and in a few minutes he galloped up to the scene of action, and met the whole gang, to the number of about three hundred, crossing the field with their tools on their shoulders. They were evidently extremely angry, and manifested their rage by the most terrible oaths and threats. Decisive measures were requisite. The engineer rode into the midst of them, and throwing the reins on the neck of his horse, exclaimed, in a voice which all could hear: "What are you doing here? What is the use of your coming to complain to me? You know I have nothing to do with your pay; * I have only to see you do your work well. You know I am always your friend if you are in the right; but you are not now, so go back and mind your work. And mark," he added, "if there is any row, or one drop of blood spilt, I shall know that you, and you [singling out two or three of them] are the ringleaders!" The men knew their master, and turned back to the line; yet it was only such a decisive course that kept that mass of men from enacting one of those scenes of drunkenness, violence, and debauchery which made them, in many cases, a terror to the neighbourhood. When once excited by liquor it was useless to attempt to restrain them; the engineer never stopped then to parley with them, but as he passed along the roads on horseback, where the men might be standing in the way, an authoritative "Whar off!" was the only remark made as the horseman rode past.

Among those of the navvies who worked together for any length of time, there was much of what may be called a coarse kind of fine feeling. Accidents occurring to their companions sometimes produced strong manifestations of sympathy. On one occasion, Mr. Shedlock was standing near the edge of a deep gravel cutting, on the side of which some men were working. Suddenly a great mass of soil gave way at the top of the cut-

---

* This was the contractor's business.

ting, beginning within a few inches of the feet of the engineer, who escaped ; but one of them was crushed beneath the weight, another was flung into one of the trucks, and a third was hurled completely over them with great violence. So heavy was the mass of earth by which the first was killed, that a case-knife he had in his pocket was snapped in two. The accident occurred in a beautiful summer evening, and the men might, and would, under ordinary circumstances, have worked several hours longer, but so strong was their sympathy with their late companion that they refused to do so ; the night fires which had been kindled were extinguished, and they all went away with sad and heavy hearts to their habitations.

That the men not only knew how to value a competent and kind master, but also to cherish a grateful feeling towards him, may be illustrated by the fact that when, during the formation of the Great Western Railway, a number of navvies broke open a Roman urn they had found, one of them seized with his huge grip a handful of some sixty silver coins, for which the men were scrambling, and said, "These are for Mr. Shedlock," to whom they were handed over.

Mr. Chadwick has stated that the contracts for the execution of railway works were often undertaken at prices which the engineer, if he was a competent man, knew could not pay the contractors. "I have been informed," said he, of one piece of work undertaken by a few contractors, who will lose by the work itself, but who will make upwards of £7,000 by the truck* of beer and inferior provisions to the workmen. Here the interests of the contractors in the sale of beer were greater than in the good execution of the work, and men under their arrangements were often at work in a state of intoxication."

The life and habits of the navvies in lonely places, during the period of railway construction, have been very low. Mr. Robertson has stated that he was a witness of the condition of the men engaged in the formation of a large tunnel on the Sheffield, Ashton-under-Lyne, and Manchester Railway. There was no town or village in which the labourers could reside, and rude hovels were erected for their "accommodation" near the mouth

* Sold under what is called the "truck" system, at a "tally" or beer and provision shop owned by the contractor or his "sub."

of the shafts that penetrated the surface of the bleak moor, and at the two ends of the works. The huts were mostly composed of stones without mortar, and the roof was of thatch or flags, built by a workman who lodged a number of other labourers. As many as fourteen or fifteen men were in one hut that contained only two apartments. Some of the rooms were white-washed and cleanly; others were filthy hovels; and here from ten to fifteen hundred men were crowded together, for a period of six years.

In some cases the conduct of the men led to open rioting. On one occasion a conflict took place at Gorebridge, near Dalkeith, in which a policeman was killed by some Irish labourers. By way of retaliation, a thousand Scotchmen and Englishmen assembled, and after driving the "islanders" from the line, proceeded to burn down their turf and wooden huts, and the tumult was only quelled by the interference of a large body of police, aided by dragoons. When the pay-days of the English and Irish labourers engaged on the Lancaster and Carlisle line took place, it was several times found necessary to keep a regiment of infantry and a troop of yeomanry cavalry in readiness to prevent dangerous and perhaps fatal riots.

It is only fair to add that there were, on the other hand, some excellent exceptions. In a report made to the magistrates of Bangor by the police authorities, it was stated that eight or ten collegians, who for some weeks had been residing in the town, had been more riotous and disorderly than all the six or seven hundred labourers employed within Bangor parish in making the Chester and Holyhead railroad.

A touching incident was told us by Mr. Bayliss, the railway contractor. Just to the north, he said, of Bugsworth station, on the Ambergate and Manchester line, is a tunnel, and the men were making it. One day some of the directors and chief officers of the Midland Company went into the northern end to inspect the progress of the work. Having done so they left; and they had scarcely done so when the end of the tunnel fell in with a crash. Having expressed their pleasure at their narrow escape, they were alarmed at the condition of those who were buried alive within. What was to be done? To dig the whole of the tunnel entrance out again was in the time, and with the nature of the soil impossible, and the engineers resolved at once to sink a short shaft from above through which the prisoners might be brought; and, after some three and twenty hours of most strenuous work by relays, the men were reached. They were found to be lying, exhausted from want of air, upon the floor, and their candles were flickering in their sockets; but they were saved. It was then learned that, when the tunnel end fell in, one of the men had exclaimed to the others: "Well, chaps, we shall never get out alive, so we may as well go on with 'our bit' while we can." And they went on till they could go on no longer.

We will conclude this chapter with a vivid picture of the life of a colony of navvies, admirably sketched, we believe, by a writer of renown.*

"After the late rains the sun rises in unclouded splendour, kindling into smiles the sullen dark green of the fells, and making rainbows of the mists that still linger around the summits of Ingleborough and Whernside, and wreathe themselves among the crags of Penyghent. The becks and gills which plunge impetuously down the steep mountain sides are so many rills of silver; and as the sun falls upon the smoke that is lazily drifting upward from the chimneys of Batty Wife-hole, even that dismal abiding-place of navvies looks almost picturesque in the distance. I am just in time to miss Mr. Ashwell, the contractor, who, I am told, has gone 'up the line'; and I set out to follow him. 'The line' is a temporary way which winds deviously across the hollow, already partly spanned by the huge skeleton viaduct.

"I scramble along somehow, through knee-deep bogs, on to piers whose foundations are just level with the surface, past batches of stone-hewers hammering away industriously at great blocks of blue stone for the piers of the viaduct; then I find myself among these, and in the labyrinthine scaffolding that encircles them—looking up at trucks and engines traversing tramroads at a dizzy height, at derricks and blocks and pulleys, at noisy little fixed engines, and at silent, busy masons. From the hollow below the viaduct I make my way somehow on to the embankment leading to it, and pick my road through the deep mire on its surface, now balancing myself on the rails that

* *Daily News*, Oct. 29th, 1872.

run along it, now making a stepping-stone of a sleeper, now plunging mid-leg into half-liquid mud. I find that the great tunnel is a mile and more from the end of the viaduct, and that the interval is composed partly of cutting through the wild high-lying moorland morass, with the deep gully of a stream on the left. I step aside to let engines pass with trains of trucks attached, full of earth or stones, the latter going on toward the viaduct, the former, waste as it is, being shot away down into the gully.

"As I arrive at the beginning of a deep cutting, and pause in hesitation whether to go on or to turn back, there overtakes me the clergyman of the navvies, a wiry elderly gentleman with a long white beard. It would do a fashionable curate a world of good to undertake this worthy man's work for a few months in the winter season, traversing these miry cuttings, and plunging through the bogs and the marshes on visitation duties to the outlying navvie settlements. His headquarters are in Batty Wife-hole, his church being the school-room, and last Sunday evening, as he tells with something like pride, he had a congregation of ninety. He is one of the missionaries of the Manchester City Mission, and was detailed to this work on the application of the Midland Railway Company. Rough as the place is now, it must have been much rougher when he first came, some fifteen months ago. Drinking and fighting were all but universal; now they are of considerably less common occurrence. Still, in such work there is little encouragement to a clergyman, and his influence must be of a passive rather than of an active kind. Every one we passed greeted him civilly, some of the lads even with affectionate respect, and the old gentleman's face glowed again with pleasure when a gigantic navvie, whom he did not know, having sheepishly saluted him, said, in answer to a question, that he remembered him some years ago on some works in another part of the country. The 'parson,' as most called him, was plodding his muddy way up through Jericho, past the barracks 'up tunnel,' and so to Denthead at the opening into the further valley, to uplift the 'school money,' and bring it back to the treasury. Mr. Ashwell has organized a school system along his contract. At Batty Wife-hole there is a schoolmaster, and at Jericho and Sebastopol schoolmistresses. A nominal school fee is charged, and he sustains the rest of the expense.

"We again miss Mr. Ashwell by a hair's-breadth, but meet Frank Moodie, his henchman, a stalwart Northumbrian, with a fine homely breadth of North-country accent, and a profound pride in his navvies. Frank has the portion of line between Sebastopol and Denthead, the heaviest work in the whole section. Hither come all the best men, where the work is all piecework, and best paid because it is the most severe. There has been a slip in a cutting, and twenty-five men are clearing out the slipped ground, working by the yard. As they toil they are the embodiment of physical force in its fullest development of concentrated energy. No man stops to lean for breath on the head of that pickaxe he wields so strenuously; the heave of the shovels is like clock-work. The navvies, bare-throated, their massive torsos covered but by the shirt, their strong, lissom loins lightly girt, and the muscles showing out on their shapely legs through the tight, short breeches, and the ribbed stockings that surmount the ankle-jacks, are the perfection of animal vigour. Finer men I never saw, and never hope to see. Man for man, they would fling our Guardsmen over their shoulders; they have all the height and breadth of the best picked men in a Prussian Grenadier regiment of the Guards Corps, without their clumsiness. For there is no heaviness in the muscular strength of these navvies; they sway to their work with as much suppleness as a coal-porter sways under his load in unison with the vibration of the plank. Their countenances are manly and ingenuous, and as I look on them I can realize what an influence for good it is possible for such an one as the authoress of 'English Hearts and English Hands,' to exercise over the stalwart, gentle-hearted, giant navvie. The stiff, greasy, blue-black clay melts away bit by bit from before their indomitable, energetic onslaught, each man working as if he wrought for his life. A 'waster' among such men would stand ignominiously confessed before the morning's work were half done.

"Five and twenty more equally fine men are labouring on the face of a harder and deeper cutting a little farther on. Seven of them abreast are plying their picks with a persistent zeal that speaks of piecework in every stroke—others are wheeling mighty barrow-loads over a narrow bridge, and tipping them down into a hollow. Moodie explains with pride that these two gangs are composed of the best men on the working.

No ganger is needed over them; indeed, they would not brook supervision.

"'The way the country has come to think now,' explains Moodie, 'good men wonna stand to be ordered about'—only he uses a stronger expression. 'They wonna have a foreman cursing and bullying about among them.' And piecework saves the contractor the expense of supervision. All that is needed is to see that the levels are right, and to have an engineer to measure the work done every fortnight, against the pay-day settlement. They allot their duties among themselves, and 'the best man' among them is the man who can do the most work, and a skulker could not live among them for an hour. They are all Englishmen. I ask whether there are no Irish among them? 'Irish!' is the reply. 'They'd take up an Irishman by the back of the neck and throw him over the bank into the river.' These men heap fuel lustily into the furnace of their vital energy. Many of them eat eighteen pounds of beef in the week. Beef is their fare. Mutton they reckon of little account, and bacon is only used to fill up the interstices. As we look at them, the 'tommy-truck' makes its appearance behind an engine. It is a peak-roofed structure, like the cabins shepherds sleep in on the Downs, and it is full to the eaves of great sides of beef that have been sent up from Settle. A firm in Batty Wife-hole supply nearly the whole of the edibles to the navvie communities along this section, sending carts daily or bi-weekly across the moors to the different villages. There is no truck direct and hardly any inferential truck. I make no doubt any other tradesman, if he found it worth his while, might oppose the Batty Wife-hole 'tommy-shop.'

"Bidding adieu to Jericho, after an outside inspection of a chaotic heap of stones, which I am profoundly surprised to find is hollow, and contains indeed what, for want of a better name, must be called a public-house, we return to the cutting, which is now nearing the mouth of the tunnel, and which as yet has not been excavated at this point within some thirty or forty feet of the intended level. Within a couple of chains of the mouth of the tunnel we come upon a shaft, down in the depths of which twenty-five Cornish and Devonshire miners are excavating to right and to left of them along the level intended for the permanent way. They are working in blue-stone rock, hard as the nether millstone,—not a spoonful, to use the phrase of my companion, comes out without powder. We hear the clink of their drills, and every now and then the dulled report of a blast. Tub after tub comes to the surface laden with jagged fragments of the stone. There is still the tunnel to be visited, where over some 500 men are steadily burrowing through the heart of the rocky Blea Moor, and where alone Irishmen labour alongside of Englishmen. But time does not serve for the present, and I should prefer to be accompanied in a visit to a work of so great magnitude by Mr. Ashwell himself.

"I came up on foot, but Moodie undertakes that I shall be sent back on wheels. When a man in authority here desires to ride, he calls, not for his carriage, but for his engine. If he had guests, and chose, in imitation of the lavish gentleman with the curricles, to order more engines, I have no doubt that his behests would be fulfilled. 'Your engine waits,' says Moodie, and we ascend. We stand with our feet on a narrow ledge, and clutching with our hands a bar on either side of the boiler of the puffing, screeching, impetuous, and yet docile little 'Curlew,' and having had fastened on behind a few trucks containing stones, we move on. I need not say that the temporary rails laid down for service during the construction of a railroad, differ totally from an orthodox permanent way. You must lay your account with bumps, jerks, miscellaneous and incomprehensible wobbling, and a seemingly tipsified character of things in general. You go, as a matter of course, down declines that would make the hair on the head of a Government Inspector stand on end, and labour up inclines that would wind a foot passenger. Presently there is a shout, and the engine halts—the last truck has lumbered off the rails. There is a rush of all surrounding hands, and it is prised and purchased back in an incredibly short time. We make progress, but at the top of an incline over against Sebastopol the engine itself quits the rails, and I quit it, preferring to perform the rest of my journey on foot. Paying another passing visit to Sebastopol, I find in the rear of it an outlying suburb of excellent detached huts standing upon a dry gravelly soil. This suburb bears, I find, the high-sounding title of 'Belgravia,' and is probably the fashionable quarter of the settlement.

"Returning through Batty Wife-hole, I encounter a gigantic navvie in a huge moleskin monkey-jacket, with a round bundle on his back, and a great deal more inside him than was good for him. He was about to quit this happy valley. He had begun drinking on Saturday, and had sedulously pursued that walk of life ever since, having drunk all his wages, a Whitney pea-jacket with mother-o'-pearl buttons, six flannel shirts, two white linen ditto, sundry pairs of stockings, a pair of boots, and a silver watch, with a gilt chain. Now he was going to try his luck elsewhere, with the meagre remnant of his kit contained in the little bundle on his shoulder. He insisted on treating me, and we tumbled over each other into one of the dogholes which do duty in Batty Wife-hole for tap-rooms. About half through the second pot, the tone of his conversation suddenly altered, and he developed the keenest anxiety to engage me in a pugilistic encounter, ultimately substituting for that aspiration a burning zeal to 'kick my head off.' The landlady came and addressed him in accents of gentle chiding, which he took so much to heart that he began to weep, accused me of being his brother, and having departed from his first impulse to kiss me in recognition of the relationship, ultimately went to sleep with his head on his bundle."

WILLERSLEY CUTTING.—A WINTER SKETCH.

CHAPTER VI.

Tunnels.—Shape of Tunnels.—Shafts.—The Horse-Gin.—Timbering.—Driftways.—Air Shafts in Kilsby Tunnel.—"Cut and Cover" Tunnels.—Cost of Tunnels.—Vicissitudes of Tunnel Making.—Drainage of Tunnels.—Lining of Tunnels.—Making of Tunnels.—Box Tunnel.—Woodhead Tunnel.—Kilsby Tunnel.—The Deepest Tunnel in England.—The Longest Tunnel in England.—The Metropolitan Railway.—A Tunnel Carried Under a Tunnel.—Construction of the Underground Railway.—Moorfields Chapel Underpinned.—Potholes.—Tunnel Under the Thames.—Tunnel Under the Severn.—Lost in a Tunnel.—Length of Tunnels.—The Channel Tunnel.—Mont Cenis Tunnel.—St. Gothard Tunnel.—Spruce Creek Tunnel.—Shugborough Tunnel.

N the construction of a railway of considerable length it is often found that tunnels are necessary. When the depth of the excavation, for some distance, is more than 60 feet, it is usually economical to tunnel, unless the material happens to be required for some neighbouring embankment. Cost is the chief test in this matter; for, in the advanced state of engineering, a tunnel may be made of almost any length, and through almost any substance, from granite to quicksand.

One of the most important considerations in the formation of a tunnel is its size and shape. Its width on the narrow gauge should be about 30 feet; and in depth it must extend 5 or 6 feet below the intended line of the rails, so that space may be allowed for the inverted arch, the ballasting, and the drainage. Where, however, the excavation is carried through rock sufficiently hard to form the bottom and side walls, 25 to 26 feet in width, and about 26 feet in height are sufficient. The brickwork, from the invert upwards, is oval, whereby greater resistance to side pressure is obtained than if the side walls were perpendicular. The shape of the tunnel will also be determined by the nature of the ground through which it has to pass. In a wet quicksand approaching the nature of a fluid, the form will approximate to that of a circle.

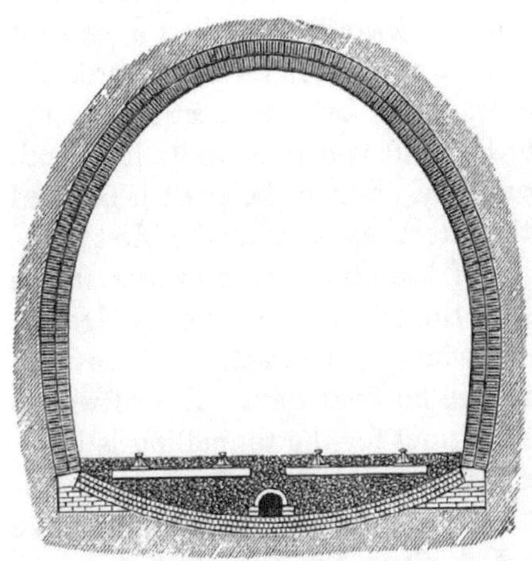

INTERIOR OF A TUNNEL.

When a tunnel is about to be commenced, the cuttings that approach the opposite ends are carried on towards the points where the boring is to begin; and the men are set to work at the tunnel itself. Short tunnels are excavated from the ends only; but when they are of considerable length, vertical shafts are sunk from the hill top down to the required

THE HORSE-GIN.

level. This was formerly done with the aid of the horse-gin, now replaced by the steam-engine; and, by the material raised, the engineer and the contractor learn the nature of the strata through which they have to pass. The shafts are usually some 9 feet in diameter, including the brickwork lining laid in cement 9 inches in thickness. The ends of the bricks are towards the shaft. The brickwork of the sides is built in sections as the workmen descend ; and when the shaft is carried to its full depth the lining, as it is called, is complete. When the shaft is finished the men proceed to execute the lateral excavations by first forming a drift way along the level of the upper part of the future tunnel, and this is sometimes continued through its entire length. It also has the advantage of showing the character and position of the strata, and the obstacles to be overcome. A driftway is occasionally made before the contract for the tunnelling is let.

The manner in which the brickwork is laid is of great importance. In a quicksand it has been found necessary to make the lining twenty-seven inches thick in the sides and top, and eighteen inches in the invert, Roman cement being used. This, however, is not the greatest strength frequently required. Each brick should be well bedded with a wooden mallet ; and, when the curvature of the tunnel requires it, the bricks may be moulded of a taper form. In the arch they are laid in concentric rings, half a brick thick, taking care that the additional number of bricks requisite for each additional ring is inserted.

Where the material tunnelled will stand without timbering—as in the case of rock and chalk—the operation of tunnelling is of the simplest character. The only thing against which it is especially necessary to guard, is the first displacement of the strata ; and this can generally be prevented with only slight timbering, judiciously placed. But if this be not watched and provided against in time, a slip of rock will perhaps take place and bring with it enough to leave a great cavern, which has to be filled up solidly in order to prevent future accident. The diagram shows the manner in which such timbering is arranged : and it is similar to that used in the Abbot's Cliff tunnel made through the lower chalk between Folkestone and Dover. The sides are first excavated, a pillar being left in the middle, which serves as a prop, from which to support the roof, and also to carry the centres used in turning the arch.

TEMPORARY PROPS IN A TUNNEL.

The arrangements made by which the several portions of a tunnel shall at last meet together, are such that the result is usually attained with surprising accuracy. This was tested on the Leicester and Swannington Railway in the following manner: Before the visit of the directors on the completion of the work, twenty-five candles were fixed at intervals along one side of the tunnel, at a distance of two inches and a half from the wall; and when they were lighted it was found that their relative position did not vary a quarter of an inch from the required line. In the Bletchingly tunnel also, with eight shafts, it was only a single inch from a perfectly straight line. In a length of more than fifteen hundred feet between two shafts of the Box tunnel, which has an incline of one in a hundred, the junction of the two workings was perfectly effected as regards the level, and did not deviate more than an inch and a quarter at the sides. The drift-ways of the principal tunnel of the Sheffield and Manchester Railway—which goes for three miles through rock formation, and is at one part more than six hundred feet below the surface of the hill—were also effected with great exactness. Five shafts were opened, from which the work was carried on; and while these were in progress, driftways were made from each face of the mountain, extending to nearly a thousand yards at the eastern side, and a hundred and eighty yards from the next shaft. When these were completed, the levels were tested, and found to have varied less than an inch, and the range was within two inches of being geometrically true. Though the difficulty is greatly augmented in the formation of curved tunnels, yet extraordinary accuracy is attained; and thus in those on the Glasgow and Greenock Railway at Bishopton, the deviation nowhere exceeded two inches.

To prevent the accumulation of foul air in the workings ot tunnels, and to assist in dispelling the otherwise impenetrable gloom, small air or light shafts of three or four feet in diameter are sometimes sunk by the contractors. They are formed in a similar manner to the working shafts, the masonry at the lower ends resting on a cast-iron ring secured in the roof of the tunnel. They are built, at the upper ends, about ten feet above the surface, and are coped with stone.

In the Kilsby tunnel, more than a mile and a third in length, there are two large air-shafts, besides smaller ones. Their appearance is curious. The visitor has perhaps walked from one end of the tunnel to the shaft, and when he reaches it, he hears a deep thunder muttering in the distance, and some advancing body is seen to darken the little horizon of the tunnel mouth, while the bright gleam of fire and the noise tell that it is a train. On it comes,—the hollow walls flinging forward the sound, and condensing it into harsh murmur. He stands back in the recess of the shaft, where he can see the thundering mass as it approaches, emerge for a moment in the daylight of that spot,

SHAFT IN KILSBY TUNNEL.

and then quickly disappear in the gloom of the opposite direction, with its red tail-lamps burning a sickly defiance to all behind.

Overhead, a novel spectacle is witnessed. The long shaft towers far aloft, its dark sides sweating with the moisture from the hill which has forced its way between the bricks; while far up the fleecy clouds pass over the face of the sky, or, intervening between the observer and the sun, send their long shadows down into the hollow cavern where he stands. These shafts seem as oases of light in the long and dreary pilgrimage of the dark tunnel.

When a tunnel has been completed, it is usual for several of the shafts to be closed, a few being sufficient for ventilation. At Bletchingly tunnel all but one were left open, and at Saltwood five were preserved; the others were closed from just above the arch of the tunnel, and filled up with earth to the surface. The brickwork of the shafts is usually carried some height above the level of the ground, and is covered with a flat or domed iron grating, to prevent anything falling down, through carelessness or mischief.

In carrying a tunnel through a hill, considerable expense has sometimes been saved by making horizontal galleries from the side of the tunnel to the face of the hill, and then by removing the excavated earth through them. The double tunnel through Shakespeare's Cliff, near Dover, on the South Eastern Railway, was constructed in this manner. Seven vertical shafts from the top of the hill were first sunk to the level of the line, and seven horizontal galleries were run from the face of the cliff to the "verticals." The two tunnels were then excavated parallel to the sea, from which they are distant four or five hundred feet. A road was previously formed along the front of the cliff to afford means of access for the workmen. The galleries were each about six feet wide, and seven high; and the excavated chalk was conveyed along them in small tram-wagons, and tipped into the ocean. During the construction of the tunnel, the public were courteously permitted to visit the scene of operations, and the spectacle was impressive. On entering the bore, a lantern was furnished to the visitor, and he ventured as far within as his courage, or his lack of it, allowed. A slight glimmering of daylight tempted some onwards, but the darkness seemed only to be rendered "more visible" by the lantern. On reaching the first shaft daylight was enjoyed, though it came down an aperture nearly equal in height to the Monument of London. Seven times through the tunnel did the sun's beams thus break on the gloom of the long cavern; and then the visitors whose perseverance was not exhausted, might see the extensive preparations that were then being made for continuing the line along the base of the cliffs near the sea-shore to Folkestone.

It is here worthy of remark that all tunnels are not bored. Some are made on what is called the "cut and cover" principle —by first making a cutting, and having this afterwards arched over and filled in. These are sometimes denominated *open tunnels*, an example of them may be found at Kensal Green, Haddon Hall, the Archway tunnel near Leicester, and under Camden Square, London. They are usually made where it is desired to avoid the permanent severance of valuable lands, or to conceal the line from observation. When formed, the sides of the cutting are made nearly vertical, and are kept in their place by timbers till the brick-work is finished.

The cost of tunnels varies greatly. Those made for the old canals were less than £4 per lineal yard; and for railways of the ordinary dimensions, they vary from £20 per yard in sandstone rock—when it does not require a lining—up to £100 and £160 per yard in loose ground, such as a quicksand, which may render it necessary to have brickwork lining of great thickness. The Kilsby tunnel cost about £125 per yard. If they are freely worked, rocky strata are usually the cheapest for tunnelling, as gunpowder may be used, and masonry may be unnecessary. In the blastings at Bishopton, on the Glasgow, Paisley, and Greenock Railway, 314 tons of gunpowder were employed in a length of 2,300 yards in whinstone, some veins of which were so difficult to work, that the rate of progress at each face of the excavation varied from three feet six inches to six inches only a day.

Tunnelling in clay is often expensive and difficult. When tough it is difficult to work; blasting is of no avail, and spades and pickaxes are almost useless. Lecount states that hatchets may be employed to advantage, but that cross-cut saws best answer the purpose. The difficulties which the working of this material presents were illustrated in the case of the Primrose Hill tunnel, which is in the London clay. The engineers adopted the precaution of excavating only nine feet in advance of the brickwork, and supporting the clay by very strong timbering till the arching was completed. The mobility and pressure of the moist clay, however, was such as actually to squeeze the mortar out of the joints, and to bring the inner edges of the bricks in contact. The result was, that the bricks were, by degrees, ground to dust, and the dimensions of the tunnel were insensibly but irresistibly contracted. The only remedy was the use of very hard bricks laid in Roman cement, which set before the pressure became great enough to force them into contact, and enabled the whole surface to resist the pressure. The thickness of the brickwork was increased almost throughout to twenty-seven inches.

Danger arises in the making of tunnels from slips. In the construction of the Fareham tunnel on the Gosport branch, a fall of the earth carried away about forty yards in length of the brick arching, though it was three feet thick. In tunnels made through chalk, it is necessary to act with great caution, as it sometimes contains large holes filled with gravel, which, on being opened pours like water upon the unsuspecting miner. Thus in the Watford tunnel, which passes through the upper chalk formation, covered with a thick irregular bed of gravel, such breakings-in occasioned great inconvenience and one serious accident. In the chalk were fissures, sometimes a hundred feet in depth, filled with gravel, which when worked into, "rushed down with such violence as to plough the sides of the tunnel as if bullets had been shot against it." Such a fall took place at the foot of one of the working shafts, overwhelmed ten men, and led to the construction of the large ventilating shaft near the centre of the tunnel.

The vicissitudes with which engineers have to deal in tunnel making are varied, unexpected and interesting. "When you gentlemen have an easy job and all your own way," we remarked to the Midland "Resident" at Kirkby Stephen, on the Settle and Carlisle, "you are rather dull, but when you get into a mess and have to get out of it, you are delightful. What is the greatest mess you ever were in on this railway?" "Well," he replied, after a pause, "the greatest mess I ever was in was when we were making Birkett tunnel. The rock was so hard and firm that we thought it would stand without lining; but suddenly the roof in one place came down and made a hole sixty feet high." "Sixty feet high," we said contemplatively, "how high is that ash tree by the pond?" "About thirty," he answered, "the hole in the roof of the tunnel was about twice as big as that ash tree. And we had to fill it up." "Fill it up!" we exclaimed. "It is easy to fill up a hole that is down in the ground, but how could you fill one that is up in a mountain over your head?" "We pût timbers—sleepers and what not—across from rock to rock, beginning at the highest part of the hole and working downwards, so that no more rock should fall; then we arched the roof round; bedded the top of the arch with *débris* of all sorts, so that if anything fell it should not injure it. We left nothing overhead but a hole in the crown of the arch big enough for the last workman to crawl through; and then we filled that up also."

In making tunnels the drainage must be good. A drain with the joints slightly open, so as to admit the water from the ballasting, is laid along the centre of the road, and the water that percolates through the brickwork is conducted into it by the various contrivances that have been adopted to prevent the inroads of water into tunnels. At the Cheviot tunnel near Wakefield, it has been necessary to line the roof with sheet lead; and in the Beechwood tunnel of the London and Birmingham line, an interior lining of brickwork nine inches thick has been made, behind which is a system of drainage.

The firmness of the native material, has, in some instances, allowed lining to tunnels to be dispensed with. This is the case with the Penmaenbach tunnel on the Chester and Holyhead line. The excavation is through basaltic rock, and has upright sides and a semicircular top. The Bangor tunnel was also at first considered to be sufficiently solid, but having subsequently shown signs of instability, Mr. Stephenson ordered it to be lined with brick. So matured has been the experience of engineers in the work of tunnel making, that in the formation of the Caledonian Railway, the tunnel under the hill to the north of Glasgow was safely conducted *over* the Edinburgh and Glasgow Railway and *under* the Monkland canal, and within a few feet of both. Several years after the opening of the Midland lines to Manchester, and also to Carlisle, it was found necessary to line the stone tunnels with brickwork. It was a very troublesome task, having to be carried on while the full service of trains was running.

To gain an adequate idea of the peculiarities of tunnel making, the scene should be visited; and it will then be found that operations are going on in what may be called the bowels of mountains full of striking interest. At the mouth of the shaft will be seen the ponderous engine and pumping-gear, and an immense mound of rock or earth-spoil, from the tunnelling below. Here are also temporary buildings for the use of the contractors and their men, and other indications of the magnitude of the undertaking. Permission having been duly obtained of the authorities, and the assistance of a guide secured, the visitor takes a candle stuck in a lump of clay, and prepares for his subterranean journey. Having deposited himself in a tub, and overcome the giddiness which the descent may induce, he observes the lining of the shaft, and the straining of the pumps essaying to lift the volume of water continually pouring down from the crevices and fissures of the earth or rock. This creates a sort of Scotch mist, sufficient to wet a "Southern man" to the skin; but, what is remarkable, it does not extinguish the fragile candles, which burn with singular brilliancy. Having descended to the level of the tunnel itself, this may be explored in either direction. The scene presented fills the stranger with wonder and awe. A great number of men are at work, dimly lighted by innumerable "dips," stuck in all directions. Some men are at the driftways; others are picking the earth from the sides, others, with barrows, are wheeling the stuff out of the way of the miners; while ever and anon the blasting of the rock with gunpowder or dynamite, the crash of the solid material riven in pieces, the fall of the masses, and the reverberation echoing through the gloomy caverns, are sufficient to fill those unused to such scenes with awe or alarm, and to leave an impression not easily effaced. Nor should the undertaking be recommended to those who are not prepared to encounter some risks, and who have not a strong inclination for the adventurous.

On one occasion some of the directors of the Great Western Railway were inspecting the works at the Box tunnel, and several of them resolved to descend a shaft with Mr. Brunel and one or two other engineers, who mentioned the incident to the writer. Accordingly all but one ensconced themselves in the tub provided for that purpose,—he declined to accompany them. His friends rallied him for his want of courage, and one slyly suggested—"Did your wife forbid you before you started?" A quiet nod in response intimated that the right nail had been struck, and the revelation was received with a merry laugh. But as the pilgrims found themselves slipping about a greasy, muddy tub, jolting and shaking as the horses stopped—by whose aid they were lowered,—and how at length they were suspended some hundred and fifty feet from the bottom, till the blastings that had been prepared roared and reverberated through the "long-drawn caverns," more than one of the party who had laughed before, wished that they had received a similar prohibition to that of their friend above, and that they had manifested an equal amount of marital docility.

The Box tunnel, between Chippenham and Bath, was long regarded as one of the most remarkable railway works. It is some 3,200 yards in length, and part of it is 400 feet below the surface of the hill through which it passes. Thirteen shafts were required in its construction for the work and for ventilation; the material excavated amounted to 414,000 cubic yards, and the brickwork and masonry was more than 54,000 yards. The number of bricks used was 30,000,000; a ton of gunpowder and a ton of candles were consumed every week for two years and a half in blasting and lighting, and 1,100 men and 250 horses were constantly employed. For a considerable distance the tunnel passes through freestone rock, from the fissures of which water flowed so freely that, in November, 1837, the steam-engine used to pump it out proved insufficient, one division of the tunnel was filled, the water rose fifty-six feet high in the shaft, and it was found necessary to suspend operations till the following midsummer, when a second engine of fifty-horse power was brought to the assistance of its brother leviathan, and the works were cleared. Another irruption took place, and the water was then pumped out at the rate of thirty-two thousand hogsheads a day.

The Summit tunnel of the Manchester, Sheffield, and Lincolnshire railway, although, in capacity, one of the smallest, is one of the longest tunnels in England. It is more than three miles in length. It is near the point where Cheshire, Yorkshire, and Derbyshire unite,—one end is near the village of Woodhead, in Cheshire, and the other in Yorkshire, and it passes under a bleak hilly moor, covered chiefly with dark heath and bog, barren and dreary in the extreme. The tunnel was formed by the aid of five vertical shafts sunk from the surface of the moor, averaging nearly 600 feet in depth. Around these and the two ends were clustered the huts that served as the temporary homes of the workmen—a sort of scattered encampment between two and three miles long. The tunnel was about six years in progress, and during that time the number of men employed underwent considerable fluctuations: at one time there were as many as 1,500. As the tunnel passes chiefly through sandstone and millstone grit, the enormous quantity of 3,485 barrels, or upwards of 157 tons of gunpowder, were employed in blasting; and nearly 8,000,000 tons of water had to be pumped out during the progress of the work. Most of the excavated rock had to be hoisted by steam engines a height of about 600 feet to the top of the shaft.

The Kilsby tunnel, through the Kilsby ridge and south ot Rugby, was another of the earliest and most difficult tunnelling works. The hill had been tested by trial shafts; was found to consist of oolite shale; and was let as such to the contractor. But between the shafts, under a bed of clay forty feet thick, lay a quicksand, and when the men pierced it a deluge of water burst down upon them through which they had to struggle and swim for their lives. Steam engines of 160 horse-power had to be erected; eventually they pumped it out at the rate of 1,800 gallons a minute for eight months, a quantity estimated to be equal to the Thames at high water between London and Woolwich; and 157 tons of gunpowder had been consumed in blasting before the tunnel was finished. The number of bricks required for that tunnel alone was 36,000,000—enough to make a footpath a yard wide from London to Aberdeen. Meanwhile the expense rose, from the original estimate of £99,000 to an actual outlay of £100 a lineal yard forwards, or a total sum of nearly £300,000. The contractor was so overwhelmed by the difficulties of the work that he took to his bed; and, though released by the company from his obligations, he died.

The deepest tunnel in England is that which passes through the range of hills between Great Malvern and Herefordshire. It is 600 feet from floor to surface, and is 1,560 yards in length; it is wide enough for only a single pair of rails. The geological strata through which it runs are 163 yards of marl, 700 yards of syenite, and nearly 700 of limestone. The marl beds at the entrance are overlaid by a considerable thickness of *débris* from the chain of the Malverns, and above this is a strong, tenacious clay, containing bones and teeth of the rhinoceros and mammoth. In another tunnel in the same district are remarkable geological formations. It is not far from Ledbury station, and is 1,660 yards long. "Nowhere in the world," says Symonds, "is there exhibited such a view of the passage rocks between the Silurian and Old Red systems as at the entrance to this tunnel. The fossils are abundant."

The longest tunnel in England is on the London and North Western. It passes through a range of hills—bearing the name of Stand Edge—separating Marsden on the Yorkshire side and Diggle on the Lancashire side. It has three tunnels running through it—one belonging to a canal, and the other two for the purposes of the railway. The first was completed in 1818; its length being three miles and 171 yards. The first of the two railway tunnels was completed in November, 1848; and its cost was £200,000. The new tunnel was commenced in 1868, and was completed in 1870. Its length is 5,435 yards, one yard less than its twin tunnel. The height of the tunnel inside the brick-work is twenty feet, and the width fifteen feet. The bricks used were nearly 17,000,000, the weight of them was 68,000 tons; 6,000 tons of coal, 170,000 pounds of powder, 100,000 pounds of candles, 6,000 gallons of oil, and vast quantities of timber were consumed. For the conveyance of the material used in the construction of the tunnels twenty-five boats and four steam-boats were constantly plying, and an immense expense had to be incurred in erecting huts, providing business offices, and putting down plant for economising labour.

But perhaps the most noteworthy of all tunnels is the Metropolitan or Underground Railway. When it was first proposed, the idea of a railway for human beings to travel along under the streets and among the sewers was regarded with amusement if not contempt. The omnibus and cab interests, as represented by their drivers, forgetting what their predecessors the stage coachmen had done under similar circumstances, were eminently facetious on the various aspects of the subject, and many jokes, good and bad, were made thereon.

Railway work in the open has difficulties enough, but the bed of a London thoroughfare has been compared to the human body—full of veins and arteries which it is death to cut. No sooner is the ground opened than these channels of gas and water, of sewers and telegraphs are seen "as close together as the pipes of a church organ." The engineers of the Metropolitan Railway had, to begin with, to remove these old channels to the sides of the roadway, and then to cut their way between, "with the delicacy of a surgical operation."

Near King's Cross a special difficulty presented itself in the form of the old Fleet Ditch—a stream of sewage flowing from 50,000 houses from Highgate to the Thames. This "black Styx of London" often in stormy weather rises six feet in an hour, and its force is particularly felt at King's Cross, which lies at the bottom of the Highgate slope. When the Metropolitan line was afterwards enlarged for the accommodation of the Midland and Great Northern lines, the Fleet sewer was carried along a huge boiler-like tube without the spilling

DIVERTING THE FLEET SEWER.

of "one drop of Christian" sewage; but the Metropolitan in its earlier experiences was not so fortunate.

The work of constructing this remarkable railway eventually became, as it must be allowed, somewhat wearisome to the inhabitants of the New Road. A few wooden houses on wheels first made their appearance, and planted themselves by the gutter; then came some wagons loaded with timber, and accompanied by sundry gravel-coloured men with picks and shovels. A day or two afterwards a few hundred yards of roadway were enclosed, the ordinary traffic being, of course, driven into the side streets; then followed troops of navvies, horses, and engines arrived, who soon disappeared within the enclosure and down the shafts. The exact operations could be but dimly seen or heard from the street by the curious observer who gazed between the tall boards that shut him out; but paterfamilias, from his house hard by, could look down on an infinite chaos of timber, shaft holes, ascending and descending chains and iron buckets which brought rubbish from below to be carted away; or perhaps one morning he found workmen had been kindly shoring up his family abode with huge timbers to make it safer. "A wet week comes, and the gravel in his front garden turns to clay; the tradespeople tread it backwards and forwards to and from the street door; he can hardly get out to business or home to supper without slipping, and he strongly objects to a temporary way of wet planks, erected for his use and the use of the passers-by, over a yawning cavern underneath the pavement." Meanwhile Mr. Jay, the contractor, was pushing on with the works as fast as he could, but he was a busy gentleman who was also building government fortifications at Portland, and a railroad in Wales, besides other undertakings elsewhere; but at last, after much labour and many vicissitudes, even the Underground Railway was completed.

When the extension of the Metropolitan was made to Aldgate, some special difficulties occurred at one spot. It was thus described by Sir E. W. Watkin in 1875: "I will give you," he said, "only one illustration of the cost and time occupied by some of these works. It was in carrying the line under the Roman Catholic chapel in Moorfields. By an Act of Parliament, with which the present board had nothing to do, there was a series of clauses under which we were bound to maintain the structure of this Catholic chapel exactly as it stood; we were not to be permitted to pull it down, but up it must remain, under all possible circumstances which might arise in the construction of our works. The chapel had been built upon Moorfields when it was a moor, with the usual amount of bog, and had been constructed on piles, and in process of time these piles got of less service in their position. Some few years ago the architect put upon the roof a tremendously heavy concrete roof, which made the building top-heavy; and, having no secure foundation, we had to under-pin the whole of the chapel some thirty feet deep down to the London clay before we could construct an inch of the railway. In doing that to a large structure it got cracked in various places, and two or three valuable fresco pictures were damaged. In addition to that, every effort was made by the good people to get as good a church, at your expense, out of that transaction as possible. I don't exactly blame them, but I am able to say that the worthy gentlemen and ladies worshipping there have a brand new edifice at the entire cost of the Metropolitan Railway, and I hope you will be well prayed for, for, I assure you, you deserve it. We paid the Rev. Dr. Gilbert, for the reinstatement of the interior of the chapel, £4,000; the engineer's estimate of the cost of underpinning the works is £8,000; we have had to provide for this congregation in the interim a temporary church at a cost of £1,023; we have had to pay to the arbitrator £540 for his services; 100 guineas to the solicitor; and there is a claim made by the architect for £900 for his charges, which we have not yet disbursed. Altogether we have to spend £14,500 for dealing with one structure only in the completion of this short piece of railway of about 600 or 700 yards between Moorgate Street and Bishopgate Street stations. I won't say anything about another cost in reference to Finsbury chapel, for, in comparison, it is moderate, about £1,000."

But if the Metropolitan tunnel line under the streets of London is a striking, though familiar, fact; more remarkable still is it to find a tunnel under a tunnel under the streets of London. Yet so it is. When the traveller by the Midland Railway arrives at Kentish Town and proceeds to Moorgate Street, he passes under two railways at St. Pancras—one above the other—and soon finds himself at the King's Cross station, on the north side of the Metropolitan line. The train again starts, runs for a few minutes, and emerging from a tunnel, the traveller is now on the south side of the Metropolitan; in that short distance he has passed under the Underground. Our engraving on the next page indicates the arrangements. It shows the double line of the Midland, which extends from Camden Town station, and the single line tunnels of the Great Northern, about half a mile long, that come from the King's Cross terminus. Between the Midland and the Great Northern lines are several cross tunnels—"a perfect rabbit warren of them," as an engineer remarked to us—but they are little used. The Midland, the Great Northern, and the Dover and Chatham trains run from

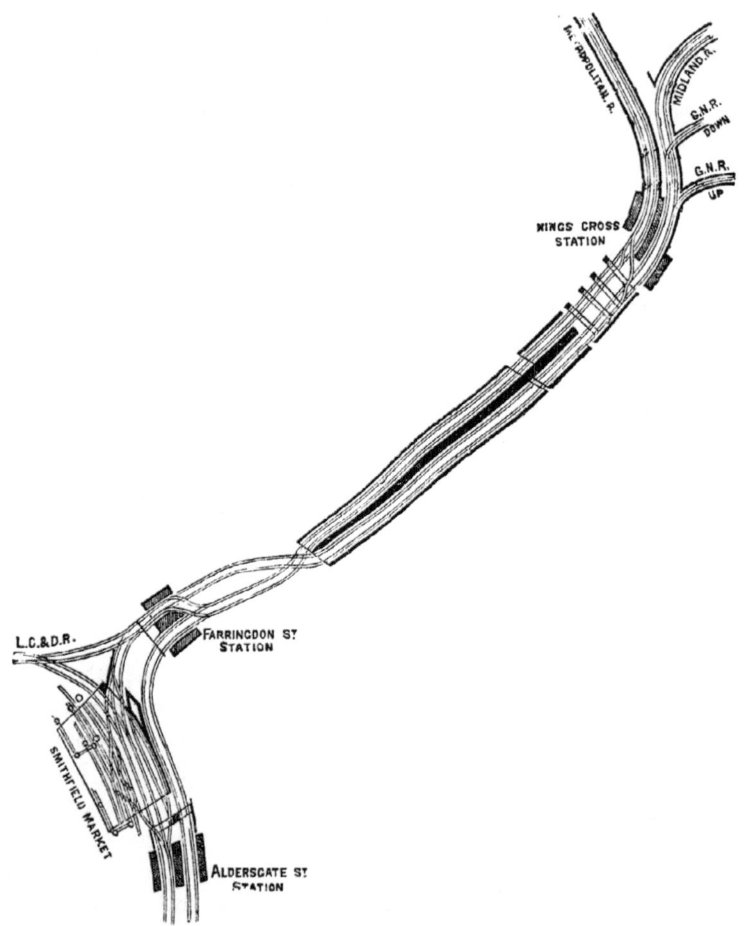

THE UNDERGROUND UNDER THE UNDERGROUND LINE.

the King's Cross (Metropolitan) station, parallel with the original Metropolitan line proper for a distance of about 1,000 yards; they then descend by an incline of 1 in 100 until they have passed through a tunnel under the Metropolitan, and then they rise by a steep slope 230 yards long of 1 in 40* up to Farringdon station; or, rather, three feet below the level of the Farringdon station of the Metropolitan proper. The difference between the rails of the two lines at the bottom of the dip is sixteen feet and a few inches.

Under the Smithfield Market, too, there is a most intricate arrangement of tunnel works. Here, in pitch darkness, except for the light of the lamps, are three main lines and three goods stations on each side of the line; and all with curves, points, cranes, signals, and sidings.

Another railway tunnel in the metropolis is of special interest. It belongs to the East London Railway. In the early part of this century complaints were made of the want of means of communication between the north-eastern and south-eastern parts of the metropolis; and, to diminish this inconvenience, it was determined to make a tunnel under the Thames, from Rotherhithe to Wapping. The tunnel was begun; more than nine hundred feet were completed, and only one hundred and fifty feet remained to be bored, when, meeting with quicksands, the engineer gave up the work in despair. The experience, however, that had been acquired enabled Mr. Brunel to overcome the final difficulties; and in 1843, at a cost of nearly £470,000, the Thames tunnel was finished. For thirty years it was visited as a curiosity; but commercially it was a failure. At length it was proposed that a railway—the East London—should be carried through it, and that, thereby, a connection should be established between the Great Eastern system and the South London lines near New Cross, and after enormous difficulties the work was done.

The construction of a railway tunnel under the Severn was sanctioned by Parliament in 1872. When Mr. Brunel carried the Great Western Railway system to Bristol, he proposed to connect it with that in South Wales by means of a steam ferry of such dimensions, and with such approaches, that loaded railway trucks could be run on board a boat and conveyed across the river without delay. Mr. Brunel died before his plans could be carried out. Subsequently it became evident that the original scheme was untenable; that passenger traffic only could

---

* At one spot it is 1 in 39.

be provided for by ferry; that heavy goods, if carried at all, must go by a bridge or a tunnel. Bridges over the channel have been provided ; and it has been ascertained that the conditions are favourable for a tunnel. The bottom of the river consists of a well-known series of rocks, in great part horizontal, and practically homogeneous. But the magnitude of the work and of the cost long prevented its being undertaken. In the year 1864, plans for the tunnel were deposited, and other preliminary steps were taken to obtain an Act, but want of funds stopped the way, and the Bill fell through. A second and similar attempt was made in 1870, with a like result. Two years later the necessary powers were granted to the Great Western Company.

In the first instance a "heading" has been driven throughout, a long and toilsome seven years' task, during which Mr. C. Richardson earned for himself the name of "the Father of the Severn Tunnel." The width of the stream where the crossing takes place is rather more than two miles and a quarter. It is intended that the tunnel shall be quite level beneath the "Shoots," a length of about twelve chains. The gradient of approach from the Welsh side will be one in ninety feet, and from the English side one in a hundred feet. The length of the tunnel, including approaches, is four miles and a half. The length of the contract for tunnel and open cuttings is seven miles and five furlongs. The tunnel under the river will be perfectly straight, and the curve in the approaches will be simple. The whole of the tunnel will be lined with brickwork, varying from twenty-seven inches to three feet in thickness. Some 200,000 bricks per week are being made out of clay shale extracted from the shafts, and many of the hard blue Staffordshire "clinkers" are also used. About 60,000,000 will be required, and all are to be laid in Portland cement. The roof is semicircular. The side walls are segmental, the invert also, and both of twenty-one feet six inches radius. The dimensions of the tunnel are: extreme width inside, twenty-six feet; extreme height inside, twenty-four feet six inches; height of roof above the rails, twenty feet. The line will be double, and manholes will be inserted every twenty-two yards.*

* The *Railway News.*

On Oct. 6th, 1879, a serious difficulty was encountered. "In a part of the approach to the tunnel," says Dr. Yeats, "400 yards from the river's edge on the Monmouthshire side, a small subterranean watercourse had to be crossed. The discharge, fully 5,000 gallons per minute, could not be controlled by the force at hand; and in about twenty-eight hours the labour of seven years was seemingly lost. The shaft and the whole of the excavation under the Severn were flooded, as far as advanced, and progress was stopped from Oct., 1879, to Feb., 1881. But, though disappointed, the directors of the Great Western Railway Company were not disheartened. The rush of water was from the open country; probably a part of the concealed drainage of Wentwood Forest, and might be diverted in its course. Sir John Hawkshaw was consulted, and induced to take up the matter. Two brick dams of great thickness and strength were built across the heading down which the water had flowed, so shutting off further approach to the shafts and the works under the Severn. Pumping engines of enormous power were applied; the outthrow was soon greater than the infall; gradually the shafts and the works under the Severn were cleared, and excavating could be resumed. It was while clearing these last, that Fleuss's diving apparatus was employed. Provided withal, the contractor's chief diver, Mr. Lambert, descended the Sudbrook shaft, carrying a crowbar, etc., and made his way alone along the flooded heading and the floating timber until he reached a door that required closing. It was more than 1,000 feet distant, and could not be moved on its hinges without great exertion, and without first tearing up tne tub-tramway on the floor. But he accomplished the task, coolly and courageously, to the admiration of all who were aware of the difficulties, and who knew how much depended on his success or failure."

If to walk through an ordinary tunnel without proper precautions is dangerous, we are not surprised at the painful experiences of one who, in November, 1876, was lost in the Underground Railway. Halfway through the tunnel that extends from King's Cross to Gower Street station is a signal box. About nine o'clock one night the signalman observed the form of an old man tottering towards him. He was wet to the skin with water that had run down the walls of the tunnel, against which he had squeezed himself to escape the passing trains. The King's Cross inspector was sent for, and Jones, for that was his name, was taken to the station, and thence to St. Pancras workhouse, to which he belonged. He had, it appears, obtained special leave to visit some friends at Irongate Wharf, and had booked from King's Cross and back. On the return journey a gentleman in the compartment appeared to take an interest in him, and just after they had passed Gower Street station asked where he was going. On saying that he was going to St. Pancras workhouse, the gentleman said, "Oh, you ought to have got out at Gower Street; it is much nearer." On reaching the King's Cross station and getting out, the old man asked the gentleman which was the way to Gower Street, and the latter, pointing the way of the tunnel through which the train had just come, said "That way." Jones went in that direction, and finding there was an incline leading under the arch, went down it, and though he found it getting darker and darker, yet seeing what he thought were lights in the distance, he proceeded, as he knew there were railway arches in the Pancras Road. As he went on, finding there were trains running backwards and forwards, he became bewildered; but, for safety, he crouched close to the wall of the tunnel, and frequently had the greatest difficulty in escaping, as he felt that many of the trains touched him as they rushed by. He believes there must have been as many as two hundred trains pass and re-pass him during the time he was in the tunnel; but in this, of course, he was mistaken. Feeling that his end was certain, he prayed and sang to allay his fears. At the intervals when there was no train coming, he kept groping his way along, and when he saw one advancing he screwed himself up as close as possible to the wall. He did not know where he was going, but presently he saw a man with a lantern, and he felt his deliverance was at hand. He hastened towards the man with all the speed his exhausted state allowed, and, fortunately, at the same time, the man saw him. He was perfectly sober, and could not account for getting into the tunnel except that he took it for a railway arch leading to Gower Street.

The ventilation of tunnels is becoming a matter of practical moment, and various schemes have been devised to supply pure air instead of foul in, for instance, the tunnels under the Alps and under London. The means hitherto proposed have generally been mechanical; Dr. Neale has urged that others should be adopted that are chemical. The human lung absorbs oxygen and gives off carbonic acid gas; let us, it has been said, create a chemical "lung" which would reverse that process and purify the air. The principal deleterious gases in railway tunnels are carbonic acid, sulphurous gases, and carbonic oxide. Into a flask filled with this mixture Dr. Neale poured a small quantity of solution of caustic soda, and after shaking the flask briskly for a few seconds the offensive smell was found to have disappeared. "Into the same flask a current of carbonic acid gas was next passed, so that a lighted taper introduced into the flask was at once extinguished. After a few shakings a lighted taper was again introduced, and burnt with a bright, steady flame, showing that the soda had taken up the acid." It is suggested that locomotive engines might be supplied with a tank containing a strong solution of caustic soda or lime, through which the smoke would be made to pass before being discharged into the outer air, and that by this means the carbonic acid gas and the sulphur would be eliminated. Each train might also be furnished with a truck open at both ends, fitted with trays or other contrivances for holding solutions of lime or soda. As the train advanced, air would rush through the trays, and be robbed of its carbonic acid and sulphur. Of the practicability of the scheme the *Lancet* says it is as happy as it is ingenious, and at once simple and cheap.

The following are some of the tunnels in England over 1,000 yards in length:—

		YARDS.
Box, near Bath	(Great Western)	3,203
Sapperton, near Swindon	(ditto)	2,200
Clayton	(London and Brighton)	2,252
Merstham	(ditto)	1,830
Balcombe	(ditto)	1,133
Rotherfield	(ditto)	1,020
Sevenoaks, near Folkestone	(South Eastern)	3,451
Abbot's Cliff, near Dover	(ditto)	1,933
Shakespeare Cliff	(ditto)	1,342
Shepherd's Well, near Dover	(London, Chatham, and Dover)	2,376
Sydenham Hill	(ditto)	2,200
Ramsgate	(ditto)	1,630
Stand Edge	(London and North Western)	5,435

		YARDS.
Honiton . .	(London and South Western) .	1,881
Midford	(ditto) . . .	1,813
Guildford	(ditto) . . .	1,045
Summit, near Rochdale	(Lancashire and Yorkshire) .	2,968
Lough, near Bolton . . .	(ditto) . . .	2,018
Woolley, near Wakefield . .	(ditto) . . .	1,685
Dove Holes . . .	(Midland) . .	3,000
Blea Moor	(ditto) . . .	2,600
Clay Cross	(ditto) . . .	1,826
Belsize	(ditto) . . .	1,800
Haddon	(ditto) . . .	1,210
Elstree	(ditto) . . .	1,100
Bramhope, near Leeds . .	(North Eastern) . .	3,670

Having now referred to the tunnels in England, we might describe that which it is proposed shall lead out of it—under the Straits of Dover to the Continent itself. We might dwell upon many geological, practical, commercial, and even military considerations concerning the Channel tunnel, that have lately occupied a large share of public attention; but as the undertaking is at present in abeyance, we may content ourselves with only a brief reference to the subject. The circular entrance shaft to the experimental tunnel is sunk in the chalk cliff at the foot of the "Shakespeare Cliff," between Folkestone and Dover, is about 150 feet in depth, and is boarded round. The descending apparatus is a rope and a cage capable of holding four or five persons, worked by a steam engine. At the bottom is a square chamber in the grey chalk, the sides of which are protected by heavy beams, and in front is the experimental boring, a low-roofed circular tunnel about seven feet in diameter, on the floor of which is a double line of tram-rails. This tunnel is admirably ventilated on the pumping system; and on visiting days is lighted with Swann's electric lamps. The *stratum* through which the experimental borings have been made is the lower grey chalk, looks like "Fuller's earth," nearly half clay and the other half chalk. "This material, while perfectly water-tight, is not harder than tolerably hard cheese, and the steam-driven boring knives work in it like cheese-tasters in an uncut Stilton. The stuff taken out is not 'waste,' but material easily converted into cement to line the walls of the tunnel when completed to its full diameter of fourteen feet, and the nature of the working renders it impossible and unnecessary to employ a large amount of physical labour." The excavation was carried on at the rate of 100 yards a-week, or three miles a-year. Simultaneous borings from the French side at the same rate would give six miles a-year, or a tunnel underneath the Channel in three years and a half. A great bed of grey chalk stretches in an irregular curve from England to France, starting from the foot of the Shakespeare Cliff, and reaching to a point on the French coast a little to the east of Cape Grisnez.

We may now avail ourselves of existing agencies for crossing over the "silver streak of sea," and notice some railway tunnels on the continent of Europe and elsewhere.

The first tunnel that pierced the Alps was the Mont Cenis. When it was proposed, where was the engineer who did not smile at the notion of cutting through a mountain nearly 3,000 metres in height, and more than 12,000 in thickness? Where, it was asked, can you get air for workmen, 2,000 metres under earth? Half a century would not suffice for the task. Objections were plentiful, but the dream has become a reality after only thirteen years' labour. The tunnel was begun at the end of 1857, and was finished in 1871.

Here the question may naturally arise: How can a tunnel, if commenced simultaneously at the sides of a range of mountains, be made to meet in the middle? It is obvious that to avoid mistake on so vital a matter most careful scientific methods have to be adopted. In the first instance the centre line beneath which the tunnel will run, has, by the aid of a trigonometrical survey of the district to be fixed above ground. In the Mont Cenis work observatories were erected, at some distance from the entrance of the future tunnel, and marks were placed along the line—the accuracy of which was verified astronomically.

"The transit instrument set up on Mont Cenis was first directed on the mark opposite to it on the mountains, and shining like a bright star; its telescope was then tilted downwards until the flame of a lamp set up in the tunnel itself was accurately bisected by the cross hairs. This operation is repeated three more times, the instrument being re-levelled on each occasion, until the mean of the four observations formed what is called a 'series.' A second 'series' is then made by an independent observer, and should the mean of the two agree to within a small fraction of an inch, the point denoted by the flame is correctly fixed, and a fresh one is sought for; but if there is much discrepancy in the observations, further 'series' are made until the mean of all the various positions of the lamp warrants the adoption of the point as a station." Such was the accuracy of the methods adopted, first for determining the axis of the tunnel laid out above ground; and, secondly, for transferring this axis underground, that the two tunnels pierced from opposite sides of the Alps, duly met.

The agencies by which the actual excavation of the tunnel was accomplished were remarkable in many respects, and especially with regard to perforating machines, and the power employed to bring them into operation. The use of steam would have caused smoke and vapour, which would have been intolerable in a long closed gallery. The power of mountain torrents was therefore brought into service; and, by means of water-wheels, air was compressed into tubes which drove the perforating engines that pierced into the rock the holes necessary for blasting, and it also, after the explosion, cleared the foul atmosphere away. The compressing engines were outside the tunnel, the air from them being driven along flexible pipes; and the perforating engine with its nine or ten perforators itself rested upon a tramway, so that it could be moved forwards or backwards as required. The perforators were similar in appearance to large gun barrels, and out of each of them a boreing bar, or jumper,—by the admission behind it of a blast of compressed air,—was rapidly shot at the rock; the return stroke being made by similar means. At the end of about three-quarters of an hour each perforator had pierced a hole from two feet to two feet six inches in depth into the hard calcareous and crystallized schist traversed by quartz. Another ten holes were then commenced; and so on till about eighty had been made. The perforating machine was now drawn backwards on its truck, and sheltered behind two massive doors. Miners then advanced, charged the holes, adjusted the matches, lit them, retired behind folding doors which were at once closed, and the explosion followed. Air was injected, and gangs of men proceeded to clear the *debris* into little wagons that ran on a tram line beside the main tramway. These three operations occupied altogether from ten to fourteen hours, and it is easy with these data to calculate the rate at which the work advanced.

The St. Gothard tunnel is another of the most remarkable works of engineering science. The line itself is carried 4,000 feet above the sea, along what was an entirely unlevel route, up steep gradients, and along sharp curves, exposed to the dangers of snow and avalanche, and then through a tunnel nine miles and a quarter long, under a mountain range that rises above to the height of 8,000 to 11,000 feet.

No route in the world, we are assured, in the early summer, is more picturesque than that over which the cumbrous diligence

ST. GOTHARD TUNNEL.

daily carried its freight of tourists from the lovely shores of Lake Lucerne to the still lovelier banks of Maggiore. "But when winter comes, and the snowdrifts accumulate in mighty and impassable masses, communication between the Switzers on the two sides of the St. Gothard and the whole populations of the neighbour States is practically cut off." The St. Gothard tunnel and the line of which it forms a part supplies a remedy for these evils, and links together the railway system ending at Lucerne with that which runs to the Italian lakes from Milan.

It begins at Goeschenen, burrows through the mountain to Airolo, and descends with ease towards the pleasant lakes and valleys of Northern Italy. The scenery, wherever a glimpse can be obtained of it, is of the most magnificent description. But the admiration excited by the works of nature is, perhaps, not greater than that aroused by the engineering marvels with which the St. Gothard line is studded from beginning to end. "It not only has the longest tunnel in the world, but twenty-four miles, or more than one-fifth of the whole line, consists of tunnels. Many of these have had to be constructed in spiral or corkscrew fashion, whereby, while making the necessarily rapid ascent from the valleys to a higher elevation, the line is perfectly protected against the avalanches which are frequent at those spots." There are also the lofty viaducts, the bridges, the sheltering galleries, and other works, all of themselves sufficient to make the St. Gothard line one of the most remarkable achievements of modern engineering. The time occupied in passing through the great St. Gothard tunnel is about forty minutes.

We may here quote the words of one who regards this latest achievement of the engineers not without misgiving. "At last," he says, "the great sub-Alpine tunnel is complete. Everybody, of course, deserves to be congratulated upon this mighty engineering achievement, which casts into the shade all the other tunnelling works the world has yet seen accomplished. People, too, who are always in a hurry to get to the end of their journey will rejoice to think that instead of spending twelve hours in toiling up the bleak northern slope of the mountain and descending the smiling valley on the other side, the passage of the St. Gothard may now be made in just forty minutes. To save eleven hours and twenty minutes in a journey of this kind is no doubt something worth achieving. And yet those who know what it was to cross the St. Gothard before ever a workman had struck his pickaxe into the side of the mountain at Goeschinen, and when the awful splendour of the Devil's Bridge and the rich loveliness of the Ticino valley were free from the remotest suspicion of such intrusion, must think sadly of the sorry substitute that is now offered for the glorious climb by carriage or diligence, or still better on foot, that they have enjoyed in former days. Forty minutes in a tunnel, against twelve hours on the open mountain-side!" With fine weather and summer seasons guaranteed all the year round, we shall heartily agree with the graphic writer whose words we have quoted.

The practical results of the opening of the line are of the greatest interest, not only commercially but politically. When first projected it was regarded with jealousy and opposition in Switzerland, and with something more than coldness by France; and had it not been for the new chapters in European history entered upon in the years 1870 and 1871, it is morally certain that it would never have been carried out. The Mont Cenis tunnel was opened in September, 1871; the St. Gothard tunnel was commenced in October, 1872. "The Unification both of Italy and of Germany must be associated with the inception and the conclusion of the work." The St. Gothard tunnel must be regarded not only as a triumph of engineering skill, but as a monument of the political progress of nations. Its object, according to the terms of the official programme, is "to promote intercourse between Switzerland, Germany, and Italy; to invigorate the maritime and commercial power of Italy; to give new life to the old commercial highway of the Rhine; and to reduce the distance between Germany and the Mediterranean coasts." The new St. Gothard route will establish the same relations between Germany and Genoa as the Semmering and Brenner Railway have established between Germany on the one hand and Venice and Trieste on the other. At the same time, "there is no reason why France should not participate in many of its benefits. Eastern France is prolific in manufactures and industries." The St. Gothard tunnel will afford a more direct road for their exportation to other parts of the Continent than any before existing; while for passenger traffic, the St. Gothard route will be shorter for travellers from the French and English capitals to Northern and Southern Italy than the Mont Cenis route or the Brenner.

The Spruce Creek tunnel is remarkable for the singular picturesqueness of its approaches at either end. It is named after the river and village near its eastern end. It is on the Pennsylvanian Railroad, 215 miles from Philadelphia.

The entrances to tunnels are various in style, they should be consistent as entrances to works of solidity, solitariness, and

SPRUCE CREEK TUNNEL.

gloom. Some are thrown into relief by well wooded hills that rise behind them. Red Hill tunnel, as seen from near Trent junction, and Shugborough tunnel, on the Trent Valley line, may be cited as examples. The north face of the latter has a noble archway, deeply moulded, flanked by square towers, and is surmounted by a battlemented parapet.

SHUGBOROUGH TUNNEL.

CHAPTER VII.

Viaducts.—Construction of Viaducts.—Arten Gill Viaduct.—Smardale Viaduct.—Materials for Construction of Viaducts.—Stone and Timber Viaducts.—Alderbottom Viaduct.—Sankey Viaduct.—Tarentine Viaduct.—Dutton Viaduct.—Dryfe Sands Viaduct.—Avon Viaduct.—Dinting Viaduct.—Çongleton Viaduct.—Foord Viaduct.—Ouse Viaduct.—Llangollen Viaduct.—Skelton Viaduct.—Bugsworth Viaduct.—Ribblehead Viaduct.—Dent Head Viaduct.—New Holland Ferry.—Vicenza and Venice Railway.—Conewago Viaduct.—Trenton Viaduct.—Bridges.—Skew Bridges.—Winkwell Skew Bridge.—Rugby Road Bridge.—Maidenhead Bridge.—Drawbridge over the Arun.—Floating Bridge on the Forth.—High Level Bridge at Newcastle.—Royal Border Bridge.—Runcorn Bridge.—Conway Tubular Bridge.—Chepstow Bridge.—Sinking the Cylinders.—Britannia Tubular Bridge.—Severn Bridge.—Saltash Bridge.—Charing Cross Bridge.—Battersea Bridge.—Forth Bridge.—Elevated Railways.—Suspension Bridge over Niagara River.—Conemaugh Bridge.—Level Crossings.

HE viaduct is an important element in railway construction. In passing, for instance, through a town it is desirable to avoid interference with the traffic of the streets it may be necessary to intersect; and though this is sometimes effected by a tunnel, as at Liverpool; or by an open cutting connected by short tunnels, and traversed by bridges, as is the case near the Euston station, or by an embankment, as at Manchester, Birmingham, and many other places, yet it is frequently accomplished by means of a viaduct, or by embankments in which short viaducts are formed. The lines from the City to Blackwall, and from London Bridge to Greenwich, may indeed be styled viaduct lines; and the continuation of the South Western Railway from near Nine Elms to Waterloo is constructed as a viaduct for the entire distance of about two miles. By these means a great saving of land also is effected, it being necessary to purchase only a little more than the actual width of the line, and the spaces between the arches may be used by the Company or let.

The appearance of stone viaducts when in course of construction is striking. A timber stage, called a "gantry," is constructed on each side of the work, sufficiently wide to allow of the piers and abutments being built between. A jenny, or crane, is then placed on a movable platform extending from one stage to the other. The materials are wound up either by hand or steam power, and are then moved slowly along till they can be lowered to the exact position they are to occupy. As soon as the masonry is built up to the level of the gantry, a fresh lift of timber is put on, the crane is raised to the new height, and so the work is continued to another stage. By these means stones of great size can be used.

ARTEN GILL VIADUCT IN COURSE OF CONSTRUCTION.

The engravings of Arten Gill viaduct, in the Vale of Dent, and of Smardale viaduct, near Kirkby Stephen, present a vivid idea of such works in course of construction. Arten Gill viaduct is 660 feet long, of eleven arches, each of 45 feet span, and the rails are 117 feet above the water.

In the erection of Smardale viaduct more than 60,000 tons

of stone were used. It is the highest viaduct on the Midland system, being 130 feet from the stream to the rails, and its length is 710 feet.

Viaducts are of great value in traversing rivers or deep valleys. As an illustration of the contingencies which have to be dealt with in the construction of such works, it may be mentioned that a viaduct having on one occasion been planned across a wide and deep valley on a series of lofty arches, it was found in the execution of the work, that the precise spot on which it was

SMARDALE VIADUCT IN COURSE OF CONSTRUCTION.

intended to rear one of the central piers came exactly over the mouth of an ancient coal pit.

In the building of viaducts, stone, brick, iron and wood are employed, separately or together; the local materials being preferred. In the earlier railways timber was frequently resorted to, the beams being trussed with iron; and the expense of coffer-damming in crossing water was avoided. One of these structures was built on the Derby and Birmingham line, which crosses the Thame and Trent rivers, its length being more than twelve hundred feet, and its mean height thirty-three feet; but its cost per cubic yard was little less than that of many stone structures. On the North Union line a timber viaduct of great length was erected; and on some of the Scotch railways the system of trussed-beam viaducts was applied to very large spans. Another timber viaduct, which combined great lightness of appearance, economy of materials, and smallness of cost, compared with that of an embankment or brickwork arcade, connected the Bricklayer's Arms Station with the main line of the Brighton and the South Eastern Railways. The wood was previously submitted to an anti-dry-rot process, by which it was protected from vegetable decomposition, and from liability to take fire from the burning coals of passing engines.

THE TARENTIN VIADUCT.

When the South Eastern Railway was constructed, it was decided to erect a timber viaduct to carry the line between the Shakspeare tunnel and the Arch Cliff Fort at Dover, the piles being driven into the rock. A light open framework supported an elevated platform, on which the rails were laid, while the sea beats on the "unnumbered idle pebbles" that lie below. A sea-wall, it was believed, would have been washed away. (*Vide* Frontispiece.)

Timber has frequently been employed with stone in the formation of viaducts. One of the largest works of this kind is known as Green's laminated bridge, on the Newcastle and North Shields

Railway. The piers are of stone, and there are five arches of a hundred and twenty-six feet span, besides two others of smaller dimensions; altogether more than a thousand feet in length. Its cost is stated at £24,000; it is estimated that £7,000 more would have sufficed to have built it entirely of stone. Another stone and timber viaduct was built on the Paris and Rouen line, at Bezons. The stone piers were raised on artificial

THE VIADUCT AS IT WAS (MIDLAND RAILWAY). NIPHANY, NEAR SKIPTON.

THE VIADUCT AS IT IS (MIDLAND RAILWAY). NIPHANY, NEAR SKIPTON.

foundations, brought up to the level of the water by means of concrete inclosed within a sheeting of oak piles, driven as closely together as possible, and secured by iron straps and bolts.

In many instances the original timber structures have been superseded by stone. An excellent illustration of this is depicted in the accompanying woodcuts, and they indicate the progress of railway construction and its actual improvement under the name of repair of railway plant. The one represents the timber viaduct that formerly crossed the valley of the river Aire, on the Midland line near Skipton; the other depicts its stone and iron viaduct that has superseded it.

There is another timber and stone viaduct on the East Lancashire line, where it crosses the River Irwell at Alderbottom. It consists of bays or openings, composed of timber framing resting on stone piers. The bridge carrying the old line of railway is nearly adjoining it, but at a lower elevation; the new route being selected because increased power of locomotives allowed the use of steeper gradients than were at first admissible.

The Sankey viaduct is also a "composite" building; its ten arches are supported on about two hundred piles, varying from thirty to forty feet in length. It crosses the Sankey Valley, at the bottom of which runs a canal; and is made of brick, with stone facings.

The Dutton viaduct, across the vale of Dutton and the river Weaver, on the Grand Junction, is considered the best piece of masonry on that line, and is perhaps the finest of George Stephenson's viaducts. It consists of twenty red sandstone arches of 60 feet span and 60 feet high, and it is more than a quarter of a mile long. The foundations of the piers stand on piles driven 20 feet deep. An extensive view is obtained from it; and the traveller looks down also on the vessels that are pursuing their way along the intricacies of the Weaver navigation.

The Dryfe Sands viaduct, on the Caledonian line, is a good illustration of plainness of style combined with strength and beauty.

In the formation of viaducts brick is often used. At Stockport is a structure of this kind, consisting of twenty-six semicircular arches: its extreme length is nearly 1800 feet; its mean height, 90 feet. The Dane Valley viaduct, on the North Staffordshire line, is built almost entirely of brick. The Midland Railway viaduct across the valley of the Avon, near Rugby, is of the same material. It has eleven semi-elliptical arches, each of fifty feet span. It is thought by some to have an excess of masonry in the haunches of the arches, and that the span of the openings is out of proportion to their height. The Congleton viaduct, on the North Staffordshire line, is also of brick. It has ten arches of fifty feet span, and two central ones, which are among the highest in the kingdom. The rails are 114 feet above the bed of the river.

The form and construction of viaducts depend on the exigencies of the case and the preferences of the engineer. The Dinting viaduct, on the Sheffield and Manchester line, has seven

DRYFE SANDS VIADUCT.

stone and five timber arches, the latter being of 125 feet span, and more than 120 feet high. On the same line is the Etherton viaduct, of stone and iron. The foundations of the piers and abutments were laid on the solid rock, and 200,000 cubic feet of millstone grit were employed in its erection. More than 30,000 cubic feet of timber, which by a chemical process had previously

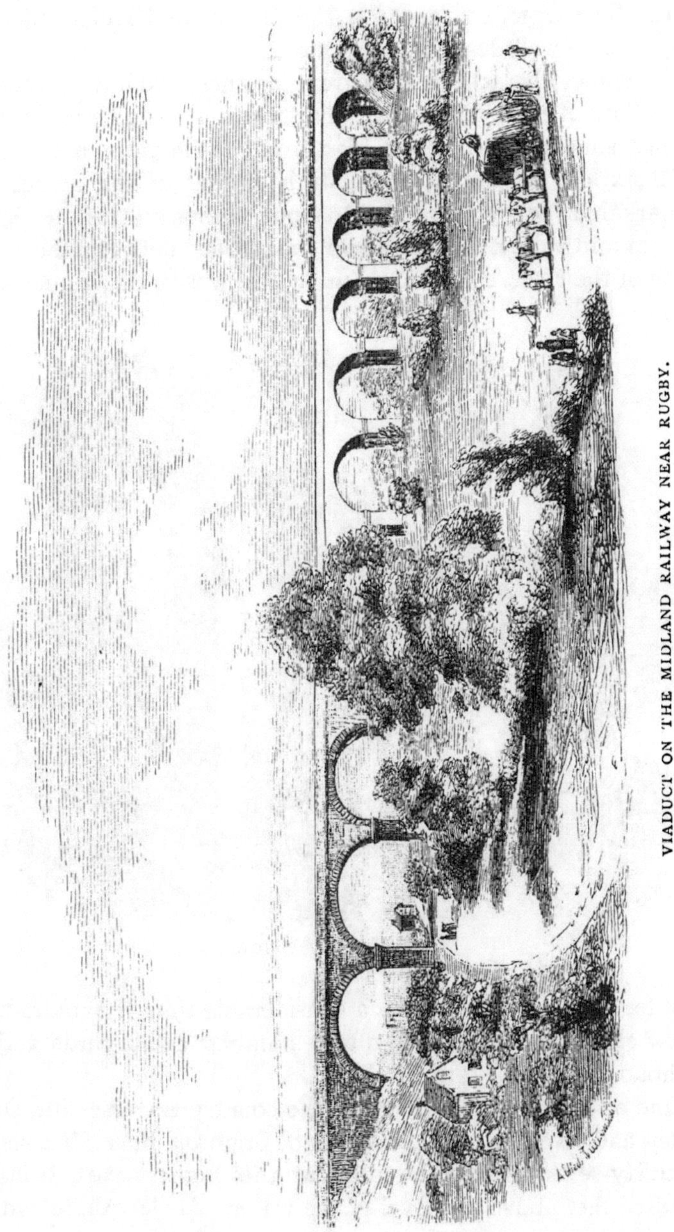

VIADUCT ON THE MIDLAND RAILWAY NEAR RUGBY.

been rendered impervious to dry rot and the attacks of insects, were used. The iron employed amounted to more than eighty tons. The Ogwen viaduct, on the Chester and Holyhead Railway, is also well deserving of notice.

A viaduct characterized by great lightness and loftiness crosses the valley of the Foord near Folkestone. It consists of nineteen arches, some a hundred feet high, and yet the piers are not more than six feet in breadth, or one-fifth of that of the arches. A remarkable skew viaduct of thirty-one arches crosses the Ogden stream and valley. It traverses the chasm between the rocky sides of the river, close to which, in the works, was a quicksand

CONGLETON VIADUCT.

fifty feet deep. Into this for a considerable time the contractors threw earth, at the rate of fifteen hundred cubic yards a day, without any satisfactory result.

One of the largest viaducts in the country traverses the Ouse valley and river, on the London and Brighton line. It consists of thirty-seven arches, the rails, at the highest part, being a hundred feet above the level of the water. Its length, including the abutments is 1,437 feet.

One of the most stupendous efforts of skill and art to which railways have given rise is the viaduct across the valley of the

Dee, near Chirk, in the Vale of Llangollen (see Vignette). It is upwards of a hundred and fifty feet above the river, and is supported by nineteen arches of ninety feet span, and its length is nearly a third of a mile. The boldness of its style and the chasteness of its finish are exceedingly effective. Such architecture imparts grace and beauty to the structure, without impairing its strength. It has an inclination from end to end of ten feet, and connects that part of the Shrewsbury and Chester Railway between Rhos-y-Medre and Chirk. Viewed from beneath, the vast structure presents a noble appearance.

The Skelton viaduct, which carries the Doncaster and Hull

BUGSWORTH VIADUCTS, NEAR MANCHESTER.

line of the North Eastern over the Ouse is one of the greatest engineering achievements of the day. Not only did the foundations present extraordinary difficulties, but the superstucture has some remarkable features. The comparatively low level of the new line required an opening bridge, and the moveable portion so provided for the accommodation of the river traffic is the longest of any work of the kind in England. At the point of crossing the Ouse it is about 800 feet wide, and the moveable part of the over-channel bridge is not less than 232 feet. This part crosses the river where it is deepest ; it turns on a stupendous mid-river pier, and is opened and closed by hydraulic power.

Complete signals have been provided to guard against the possibility of accident to trains while the bridge is open for the passage of ships. The entire structure is carried by seven spans of solid fish-backed girders, resting upon massive iron piers, forced to a great depth into the river bed through various layers of silt, peat, and clay. The structure is one of imposing appearance, and is a great triumph of engineering skill. The line is double.,

The engraving of Bugsworth viaducts represents the old stone one to the right, which, with sixteen acres of land, slipped, and

RIBBLEHEAD VIADUCT, BLEA MOOR.

the new one of timber which had to be erected in its stead, and is still in use.

One of the finest viaducts, and also one of the most impressive views near a viaduct that can be obtained in this country, is that known as Ribblehead viaduct, on the Settle and Carlisle line of the Midland Company. It stands on the watershed of the Ribble, and consists of twenty-four arches, the loftiest, from the bottom of the foundation to the level of the rails, being no less than 165 feet. Behind it, and apparently lying directly athwart the course of the line, is the mighty range of Whernside, nearly

2,500 feet high ; and to avoid it, the railway bears to the right, and before long enters Blea Moor tunnel.

Another of the loftiest viaducts on the Midland line is that at Dent Head, a little to the north of Blea Moor tunnel. It is

DENT HEAD VIADUCT.

near the magnificent Dent Valley. This viaduct is 200 yards long, of ten semicircular arches, rising 100 feet above the public road, and also over a little mountain torrent that falls into the Dent, which runs hard by.

NEW HOLLAND FERRY.

The New Holland ferry, represented in the engraving, may be regarded as a viaduct-pier. It extends 1,500 feet into the

Humber, and along it the trains pass till they approach the steamboats which are to convey the passengers and goods across the river. Instead of stumbling over wet stones, slipping along greasy landing places, and getting in and out of boats, the trans-shipment is easily and securely effected.

Among continental railways, one of the most interesting viaducts is that on the Vicenza and Venice line. It crosses the Laguna Veneta, and required much engineering skill to complete. The base is of the stone of Istria, secured together with

VICENZA AND VENICE VIADUCT.

Roman cement; the upper parts are of brick. The bridge consists of 222 arches, and is 12,000 feet in length. A thousand men were employed on the work, and they were engaged during four years. Thus is Venice—the ocean city—chained to the mainland. No future Rogers will be able to describe the approach to it as he did:—

> "There is a glorious city in the sea.
> The sea is in the broad and narrow streets,
> Ebbing and flowing, and the salt sea-weed
> Clings to the marble of the palaces.
> No track of men, no footsteps to and fro
> Lead to her gates. The path lies o'er the sea

Invisible ; and from the land we went
As to a floating city—steering in
And gliding up her streets, as in a dream,
So smoothly, silently—by many a dome,
Mosque-like, and many a stately portico,
The statues ranged along the azure sky ;
By many a pile in more than Eastern-pride
Of old the residence of merchant kings."

CONEWAGO VIADUCT.

Two more interesting examples of this kind of work may be referred to. One is the Conewago viaduct on the Pennsylvania railway, of which we give an illustration; and the other is the viaduct at Trenton, on the Delaware River.

Bridges are an important class of railway works. The number

of those erected over or under local roads, and for field communications, on English railways alone, is surprising. Sometimes "cattle arches" are also constructed, under which farmers may drive their flocks and herds, instead of running the risk of

TRENTON VIADUCT.

attempting to take them across a cutting or embankment. There are no fewer than 63 bridges under or over the railway on the 30 miles between Liverpool and Manchester. There are 160 bridges over and 110 under the London and Birmingham line ; on the Dover line there are 141 ; and between London and Gosport, on the South Western line, there are 188 ; making a total of nearly 600 bridges on 287 miles of railway. Between Brentford and Colchester, on the Great Eastern line, a distance of 34 miles, are no fewer than 64 bridges and viaducts, and 37 culverts and drains, besides 18 level crossings.

The foundations of large bridges are frequently laid by means of cofferdams, which consist of inclosures made by "piling" round the space that is to be occupied by the pier, so as to render it watertight. The water is then pumped out, and the pier is built inside up to the required height ; or an iron cylinder is driven down within the piles, and inside the cylinder the pier is erected.*

In many cases railways cross roads or canals in an oblique direction. If a common square bridge were here employed the road intersected by the railway would have to be diverted (fig. 1), so as to cross at right angles ; or the arch would have its top and its abutments needlessly extended (fig. 2). To avoid

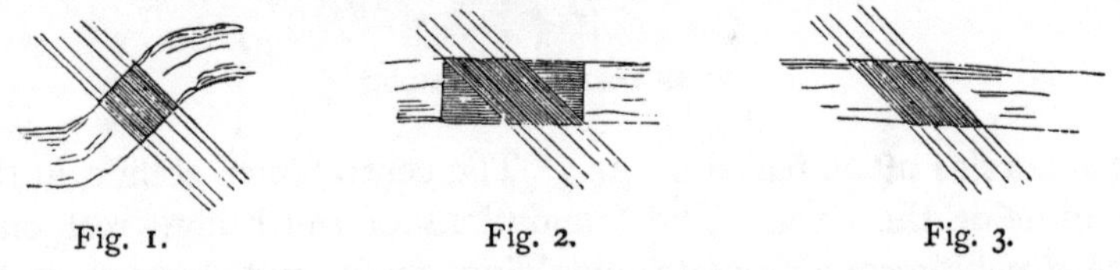

Fig. 1. Fig. 2. Fig. 3.

these evils a skew bridge (fig. 3) is built. Of this there is a good example in the Winkwell bridge, and there are multitudes besides.

The larger bridges on our railways usually cross rivers or canals ; small ones are over common roads. They are sometimes ornate erections. One of the best of the early ones is near Rugby, and is an adaptation of the castellated style. As seen from one side, some of the arches of the great Midland viaduct appear in the distance. Bridges with iron girders are now frequently preferred, as in the case of several which cross the streets of the metropolis.

One of the most remarkable structures of the kind in the country is the bridge which carries the Great Western line over

* The process is minutely described in "The Midland Railway, its Rise and Progress."

the Thames at Maidenhead. It is composed of a central pier and two main arches, flanked at either end by four openings, for the passage of the flood water. The main arches are elliptical, 130 feet span, and 24 feet rise. The land arches are

WINKWELL SKEW BRIDGE.

semicircles of 28 feet diameter. The central pier stands in the middle of the river. The foundations of the bridge rest on a hard pebble conglomerate, overlying chalk, and covered up by

RUGBY ROAD BRIDGE.

loose gravel and alluvial mud. The body of the work is executed in brick; the cornice, cap-stones, and coping are from the quarries of Bramley Whitehurst, near Leeds. The bridge has this peculiarity—it consists of two arches only, probably the largest and flattest, in proportion to their span, that have been executed in brick. Its structure was minutely criticised at the time, and many doubts were expressed as to its stability. It was constructed with only two arches because in the middle of the river was a shoal which provided a good foundation, and because it was important to keep the deep water free for the navigation. It was also necessary to preserve the gradients of the railway uniform, and this depended upon the height of the arches.

A bridge on the South Coast Railway is worthy of special notice. It is over the Arun, near Arundel, and was the first of its kind. The Company was bound to provide a clear water-

MAIDENHEAD BRIDGE.

way of sixty feet for the passage of shipping, and this had to be accomplished by a contrivance called a *telescope bridge.* The rails, for a length of 144 feet, are laid upon a massive timber platform, strengthened with iron, and trussed with rods, extending from its extremities to the top of a strong framework of timber, and rising thirty-four feet above the level of the roadway in the middle of the platform. The framework is ornamented so as to appear like an arch. Under this central framework and under one-half of the platform are eighteen wheels, upon which the whole structure can be moved backwards and forwards, so as either to be clear of the river, or to project its unsupported half across it, and so to form a bridge for the passage of the trains. Two men and a boy are able to open the bridge in about five minutes, the work being done by means of toothed wheels and racks, moved by winches.

A steam bridge, or floating railway, crosses the Forth between Granton and Burntisland. The difficulties that had to be overcome to obtain the necessary communication were considerable; for as the tide rises about twenty feet, a vessel on a level with the quay at high water would be a long way below it at low water. Accordingly alongside the piers at Granton and Burntisland an incline of masonry was built, upon which were laid two lines of rails; on the incline was placed a moveable platform resting on sixteen wheels. Four girders span the distance

DRAWBRIDGE OVER THE ARUN.

between the platform and the vessel; and these are elevated or depressed by means of a winch on each side of a staging, eighteen feet high, erected across the platform.

The high-level bridge over the deep ravine through which the Tyne flows between Newcastle and Gateshead, is a very remarkable structure. It forms the junction between the York and Newcastle and the Newcastle and Berwick Railways. It was proposed by Mr. Hudson, and designed by Mr. Robert Stephenson.

The first difficulty in building it was to secure good foundations for the piers. The piles to be driven were so large that Nasmyth's Titanic steam-hammer had to be used to drive

FLOATING RAILWAY ACROSS THE FORTH.

them. By the common pile a comparatively small mass of iron fell with great velocity for a considerable height—"the velocity being in excess and the mass deficient, and calculated, like the momentum of a cannon ball, rather for destructive than impulsive action. In the case of the steam pile-driver, on the contrary, the whole weight of a bearing mass is delivered rapidly upon a driving-block of several tons weight placed directly over the head of the pile, the weight never ceasing, and the blows being repeated at the rate of a blow a second, until the pile is driven home. It is a curious fact, that the rapid strokes of the steam hammer evolved so much heat that on many occasions the pile head burst into flame." The first pile was driven to a depth of 32 feet in four minutes; and as soon as one was placed, the traveller, hovering overhead, presented another, and down it went, like a pin into a pincushion.

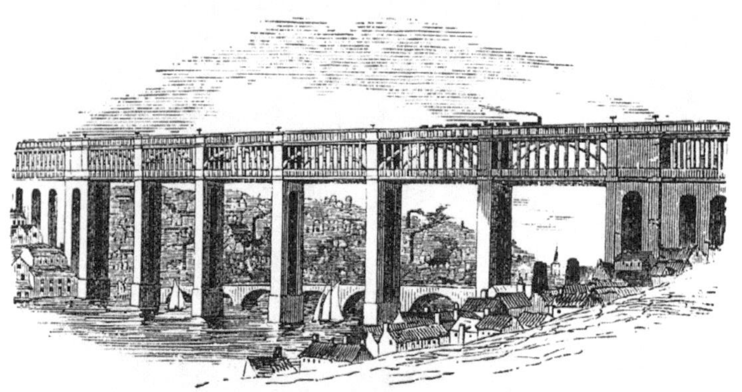

THE HIGH-LEVEL BRIDGE AT NEWCASTLE.

When the piles had been driven and the cofferdams completed the water was pumped out. But though powerful engines were employed, it forced itself through the bed of quicksand as fast as it was removed. Every effort was made for months to overcome it, but without success; until, at last, cement concrete was put in, which set, a foundation was made, and the piers were securely built.

There are two roadways, one level with the Castle-garth, for carriages and foot-passengers, and the other 22 feet above it. The carriage-road is 1,380 feet in length. The bridge is $112\frac{1}{2}$ feet from high-water line to the top of the parapet, and the roadway is 80 feet above the water. Six arches, each of 125 feet span, form the bridge,—the piers upon which they rest being of masonry, and the arches, pillars, braces, and transverse girders of iron. The bridge-piers are nearly 50 feet by 16 in thickness; and in height are 131 feet from the foundation, having an opening in the centre through each. The land arches of the bridge diminish in altitude corresponding with the steep bank of the river basin.

The roadway for vehicles beneath the line forms one of the most striking peculiarities of the work. This roadway is suspended from the great arches which carry the line. The pillars

ROYAL BORDER BRIDGE.

which carry the road add greatly to the picturesque effect; and the multiplicity of column-ribs, transverse and vertical braces, produces a combination of beautiful lines seldom seen.

Two bridges cross the river Tweed at Berwick: one of fifteen arches, built in the reigns of James I. and Charles I., at a cost of £15,000, occupying twenty-four years in the building, and paid out of the national resources; the other, the Royal Border bridge, built by the railway company. It stretches from Castle Hill to Tweedmouth, at a height of 26 feet, and cost £120,000. It is 667 yards long, and was finished in a little over three years. The foundations of the piers were laid on bearing-piles, each capable of carrying 70 tons. The whole is built of ashlar, with a "hearting" of rubble, except the river parts of the arches, which are constructed with bricks laid in cement.

Another viaduct is that at Runcorn. The vast estuary of the Mersey, as it bends south and eastward and separates the counties of Cheshire and Lancashire, long rendered it impossible to secure direct communication between Crewe and Chester and Liverpool; and the traveller was compelled to take a

RUNCORN BRIDGE

circuitous route, first north and then west, or to leave his train and cross the river by steamboat from Birkenhead. At length, to quote the "Tourist Guide" of Messrs. Morton & Co., for whose cheap and beautiful productions innumerable readers are greatly indebted, "the London and North-Western Company resolved to overcome every obstacle and to carry their main line right over the Mersey, and at such an elevation as not to interrupt the busy navigation of the river. Runcorn viaduct consists of thirty-three arches: one of 20 feet span, twenty-nine of 40 feet span, and three of 61 feet." The central part of the bridge that stretches over the navigable channel rests on four massive castellated piers, 300 feet apart, that sink into the bed of the river, and carry the girders 80 feet above the water. "Ten other arches form the west bank viaduct; this leads to an embankment; and the line is now continued upon the Ditton viaduct of forty-nine arches. The appearance of the Viaduct, as it carries the passenger over the river, is very striking. A footway on each side of the viaduct supersedes the old and tedious ferry."

The Conway tubular bridge, in North Wales, has deservedly attracted much attention. Passengers accustomed to travelling by the magnificent service of the London and North Western may remember with interest how people used sometimes to fare at this spot: "On Christmas Day, 1806," says the *Annual*

BRIDGE OVER THE AVON, NEAR BATH.

Register, "owing to a heavy swell in the river Conway, the boat conveying the Irish mail, with eight passengers, the coachman, guard, and a youth about fifteen years of age (in all fifteen in number, including the boatman), was upset, and only two persons saved."

The present bridge is in effect a rectangular tunnel, or hollow square box, the sides of which carry the load. The Conway end of the tube is immovable, being fixed on the pier, and made to rest on two beds of creosoted timber, with intermediate cast-iron bed-plates; but the Chester end is free, so that it may expand by heat and contract by cold. Here the tube rests on cast-iron rollers, which give play, so as to allow twelve inches of motion. The whole mass weighs 1,140 tons.

A tubular bridge has been constructed over the Wye, at

Chepstow, on the South Wales Railway, to which allusion must be made. It consists of four spans, three of about a hundred feet each, and one of 290 feet, extending altogether from bank to bank for 610 feet. The chief span is a modification of the suspension principle, the great length of the girders requiring more support than that afforded by the piers alone at each extremity. Mr. Brunel accordingly contrived that this should be given by means of a tube 309 feet in length, and nine in diameter, which, having been raised to the summit of piers erected on the east bank, and in the centre of the river, is strengthened by massive chains secured to the girders. These girders are fifty feet above high-water mark at spring tides, which here rise from fifty to sixty feet, being more than any other river in the kingdom.

In sinking the cylinders to form the piers of the bridge, the workmen had first to pass through twenty-nine feet of blue clay and sand, below which they met with a thin bed of peat containing timber, some solid oak, hazel nuts, and other similar substances. They next came to several feet of fine blue gravel, and then they reached a bed of boulders, upon which the cylinders were originally intended to rest. After this was a bed of red marl, beneath which there was solid rock, like millstone grit, and into this the cylinders were sunk. The mode in which this part of the work was performed was curious. The cylinders were placed on planks to prevent their cutting into the soft mud. One by one cylinders were added until they had reached the top of the stage (about forty feet in height) which had been erected for the purpose of sinking them. The weight of the column now cut through the planks, and the cylinder sank about six feet into the mud. Two or three men then descended into it, and as they removed the contents, the cylinder continued to sink, and as it descended fresh cylinders were added at the top. This process continued, without interruption, till a depth of about seventeen feet was attained, and then a spring was tapped, and without a moment's notice the water broke in from below in such force as to require the constant action of two thirteen-inch pumps worked by an engine. A remarkable fact attending this occurrence was, that the spring-water invariably rose in the cylinder exactly at that height to which the tube was standing in the river at the moment. That it was not an irruption from

BRITANNIA TUBULAR BRIDGE.

the Wye was considered to be beyond dispute, inasmuch as the river at this point, from the action of the tide, was always heavily tainted with mud, while the water which rushed into the cylinder from below was of exceeding purity, and did not contain a particle of salt.

The problem with which Robert Stephenson had to deal in the construction of the Britannia bridge over the Menai Straits was, How is it possible to hang a hollow iron tunnel across an arm of the ocean, capable of supporting the heaviest burdens that trains could impose, and of bidding defiance to the storms which eddy and whirl along the straits? A long series of laborious and costly experiments had now to be made. Cylindrical tubes were found to fail by collapsing at the top, and they were inferior in strength to those of an elliptical form. Rectangular tubes were next put to the test, and they had so decidedly the advantage in strength, that only the precise form and dimensions remained to be determined. A model was accordingly constructed of one sixth of the proposed Britannia bridge, and the final experiments having terminated most satisfactorily, arrangements were made for the erection of the colossal structure itself.

The Britannia bridge is supported on three piers; two on the Carnarvon and Anglesea shores, and one on a rock in the centre of the straits. The "Britannia tower" rose gradually and majestically from the surface of the water to the height of 230 feet; the piles of masonry on land are each more than 160 feet. The tower was constructed of nearly 150,000 cubic feet of Anglesea marble for the exterior, and nearly 150,000 feet of sandstone for the interior, strengthened by nearly 400 tons of cast-iron beams and girders, and having a total weight of upwards of 20,000 tons. It was originally intended that the pier should be crowned with a colossal figure of Science; but the depreciation of railway property induced the directors to abandon the design. The land abutments on each side of the strait are terminated by two couchant lions of Egyptian character, each weighing eighty tons. No fewer than 8,000 cubic feet of limestone were required for the four.

While the piers and abutments were thus rising, the construction of the tubes was prosecuted with vigour. A timber platform was erected along the side of the water, behind which were the workshops of the artizans, covering three acres and a half of ground. On this platform the boiler-plates were fitted one to another, in a manner similar to that adopted in iron ship-building. The plates varied in their size according to the part of the tubes for which they were intended, being from six to twelve feet in length, about two in width, and from one-half to three-quarters of an inch in thickness. They had, as usual, been forged with the greatest accuracy, each being made to pass between two enormous iron rollers, worked by steam, which squeezed down into perfect uniformity that variety of irregularities to which the workmen have given the term of *buckles*. The plates were then removed to a punching-machine, by which the rivet-holes were made. The lever by which this was done had a pressure of from sixty to eighty tons; and the iron plates were perforated by the steel bolt with apparently as much facility as a child would push his thumb through a piece of blotting-paper. The rivets employed in securing the plates together were no fewer than two millions in number, and in the formation 126 miles of iron rod were used, weighing about 900 tons. As the bolts were heated, a lad snatched one up with a pair of pincers, and flung it to another boy inside the tube, who picked it up, and ran with it to the "holder-up." By an enormous hammer he forced it into the rivet hole till its end protruded the other side, where a couple of stalwart workmen soon moulded it into a head, and the bolt became a rivet. This, gradually cooling, bound the plates of iron together. Practice gave such facility to the work, that a set drove 230 rivets a day. About eighteen were required to a yard.

The spectacle presented during the progress of the works was novel and impressive. Ship-loads of iron were continually arriving from Liverpool, of marble from Penmon, of red sandstone from Runcorn, and forests of timber from a variety of ports, and all were discharging their cargoes at the wharves and platforms. Wagons and carts were incessantly travelling in all directions, on tramways and common roads; vast clouds of dark smoke issued from innumerable chimneys; steam-engines constantly poured forth volumes of steam high into the air; and the whirring of machinery, the explosion of gunpowder, the thunder-like clang of the blacksmiths' hammers at the forges, and the reverberation from the riveters along the tubes, formed an extraordinary chaos of sights and sounds.

The masonry of the piers and abutments being at length

sufficiently advanced towards completion, and one of the tubes being finished, arrangements for "the floating" were made—an operation which attracted an immense concourse of visitors from all parts of Europe, and even from the United States.

Meanwhile the platform which supported the tube to be first removed was partly cut away at each end, and a dock excavated sufficiently large to contain four pontoons. While the tube was unfinished these vessels lay at the bottom of the water, waiting till their gigantic energies were required to bear away the unwieldy burden. The combined power of floatage of the vessels amounted to no less than 3,200 tons; the weight of the tube, with its apparatus, was 1,800. On the day appointed for the floating, the valves in the pontoons, which had previously admitted the water, were closed, and as the tide rose, the vessels rose upon it, and lifted the tube off the platform on which it had been constructed. The capstans on the Anglesea and Carnarvon shores and at the Britannia pier were prepared; cables, six inches in diameter and a league in length, were arranged in their required positions, or fastened to the steamers which were to have the towing of the tremendous freight; a hundred seamen, under Captain Claxton, manned the vessels; nine hundred men assumed their several posts, and the vast and complicated arrangements were complete. The land attachments were severed; the capstans were manned; and then, at the signal of a flag on the Anglesea side, and a shrill strain from the trumpet of Captain Claxton on the top of the tube, "to pipe all hands," a cheer arose from the seamen, who, aided by the steam tugs, told upon the screws and tackle, and upon the hitherto motionless monster; and without injury or jar, it slowly glided away, amid thunders of increasing applause, like a mountain moving on the waves, to the foot of the towers on which it was ultimately to rest.

So complete were the arrangements, and so efficient their execution, that, despite the power of the tide and the shortness of the time in which the work had to be completed, the mass was deposited exactly in its intended position, leaving a clear space of only about three-quarters of an inch. The valves of the pontoons were now partially opened, and as the vessels sank, the ends of the tubes slowly descended to the temporary resting-places prepared for their support.

The next process in these extraordinary operations was to elevate the tube to its position at the summit of the piers,—a work to be performed by means of Bramah's press. The press was securely fitted in the upper part of the Britannia tower, at a height of about 40 feet above the level to which the tube was to be raised. At the top of the piston of the press was a horizontal iron beam, from the ends of which hung two enormous iron chains, of the weight of a hundred tons, and by these the tube was to be lifted to the place of its destination.

The preparatory arrangements having been completed, and two forty-horse power steam-engines set to work, a lifting force was gained of no less than 2,622 tons; and then the great piston began slowly to emerge from the cylinder, till, in about thirty minutes, the bridge was lifted six feet into the air. The tackle was then secured by "clams" at the foot of the press; the weight was removed from the piston, till, descending by its own gravity to the point from which it started, the lifting operation could be repeated; and thus the whole was gradually elevated to the summit, the final lift of the first tube being made on the 13th of October, 1849.

The Britannia bridge, which has been described as an iron tube hung across an arm of the sea, was opened on the 5th of March, 1850, by the passage of three powerful engines, decorated with the flags of all nations, and conveying the distinguished engineer, with other gentlemen of eminence. The train started from Bangor station; and, at seven o'clock in the morning of that memorable day, swept over the threshold of the stupendous fabric, and was soon lost amid the darkness within. On reaching the centre of each of the great spans, the locomotives, weighing ninety tons, were stopped, and rested with all their weight on the floor of the tube, without occasioning the slightest undue deflection. It required next to be ascertained how far the vast corridor was capable of sustaining the equilibrium of forces; and the result was such as to prove beyond doubt the accuracy of the theoretical conclusions at which Mr. Stephenson and his staff of engineers had arrived. The second experimental train that went through consisted of twenty-four heavily-laden wagons, filled with blocks of Brymbo coal, of an aggregate weight of three hundred tons. This was drawn through the tubes with deliberate speed. During the passage, a breathless silence prevailed; but when it emerged at the opposite end, loud acclamations arose, and the report of pieces of ordnance smote on the ear. The examinations were thus continued for a considerable time, and every test served only to demonstrate the stability of the fabric. A train of two hundred tons weight was next placed in the middle of the Carnarvonshire tube, and remained there for two hours. It was found to occasion a deflection of only four-tenths of an inch—a curvature not greater than would be caused by half an hour's sunshine, whereas it is confidently estimated that the entire structure might be deflected to the extent of thirteen inches, without danger. Another testing-train was subsequently formed, comprising three engines, two hundred tons of coal, and from thirty to forty railway carriages, containing between six and seven hundred passengers. The tube was traversed by these at a speed of thirty-five miles an hour.

The arrangements made for maintaining continuity in the entire length of the tube were also perfectly successful; the strain on any one part was distributed over the whole; and thus, as the engines entered the small land-tubes at either end, the motion due to their progressive weight was detected in every tube, even at the distance of 1,560 feet. According to the estimate of the engineers, the bridge is capable of supporting a series of locomotives following one another along its whole length; it was said that a line-of-battle ship might be suspended from it without danger.

The appearance of the bridge is imposing. In the far distance is the undulating landscape, varied by the rich tints of the woodland, and backed by rising hills; while the sun, approaching the verge of day,—

> " Wearied with sultry toil, declines and falls
> Into the mellow eve ; the west puts on
> Her gorgeous beauties—palaces and halls
> And towers, all carved of the unstable cloud."

Stretching far away to the east and west, and glittering beneath the sun's rays, are the Irish Sea and St. George's Channel, connected by the Menai Straits; while the steam-vessel and the deeply-laden merchantman wend their way below. Towards the Irish Sea is the slender fabric of the suspension bridge, over which some seemingly lilliputian vehicle and horses are passing. The small islands and rock which impede the flow of the water along the straits serve to add interest to the scene. To the northward is the Anglesea column, erected by the inhabitants of the neighbourhood in commemoration of the gallant Marquis, who led the British cavalry at Waterloo; while about a hundred yards distant may be seen a humble but touching monument, built by the workmen of the Britannia tower, as a tribute to the memory of some of their comrades who lost their lives during the construction of the bridge. On the south the view is bounded, at the distance of forty miles, by a range of mountains, the loftiest of which is Snowdon. Between the base of these hills and the straits, the little wooden town was built which served for the accommodation of the artificers and workmen. And now, as we are gazing upon this scene of mingled wonder and beauty, the deep-toned reverberation of a train rushing along the iron corridor of the bridge, falls upon the ear; and thus Science and Nature are mingled in harmonious contrast, and receive the grateful homage of every thoughtful observer.

The Severn-bridge Railway supplies a want that had long been felt, of direct communication across the lower part of the Severn, and avoids the long *détour* by way of Gloucester. It is five miles in length. Since the destruction of the bridge over the Firth of Tay it is the longest in the kingdom. Its length is a little over three-quarters of a mile, and it consists of 21 spans, two of which, crossing the channel of the river, are each 327 feet in length. The girders are made on the bowstring principle, and rest upon iron cylinders sunk deep into the rock in the bed of the river, and filled with concrete. Considerable difficulties were met with in the progress of the work, and the erection of the bridge is regarded as a triumph of engineering skill. Twelve of the cylinders were sunk in sand averaging about 28 feet in depth. Driving piles for the staging was found to be impracticable, and Mr. Brunlees' plan was adopted, namely, forcing a jet of water through a pipe to the feet of the piles, thus scouring away the sand as the piles descended. In deep water the cylinders were kept dry by the use of compressed air. Those in the channel of the river were the most difficult to erect. The water varied in depth from 30 feet to 70 feet; at spring tides the water rose 30 feet in a little over two hours, and the current ran at the rate of ten knots an hour. The sandbanks in the river and the strength of the current induced the engineers not to attempt to build the girders on shore, and then to float them to the site and to hoist them into position.

The Saltash bridge is one of the most remarkable in the world. The noble Tamar river, as its waters approach the little village of Saltash, narrows, and soon afterwards widens out into as fine a sheet of water as any of its kind in the kingdom, its distant banks decked with cottages and fringed with undulating woodlands down to the water's edge. Across this narrow part of the channel the viaduct hangs high in air. It consists of 19 spans, seventeen of which are wider than the widest arches of Westminster bridge, and two, resting on a single cast-iron pier of four columns in the centre of the river, span the whole stream, a longer distance than the breadth of the Thames at Westminster. The structure from end to end is 2,240 feet—ily half a mile in length.

"The greatest width is only 30 feet at basement, its height from foundation to summit no less than 260 feet, or 50 feet higher than the summit of the Monument. The Britannia bridge, in size, purpose, and engineering importance, seems to offer the best comparison with that at Saltash, but the Britannia tube is smaller, and cost nearly four times the price of the Saltash viaduct, though its engineers had natural facilities not possessed by Mr. Brunel for his Cornish bridge. The Menai tube is a suspension bridge, and the main tower had a ready-made foundation in the Britannia rock, from which the whole structure now derives its name. To cross the Tamar with one unsupported span nearly a quarter of a mile in length was of course impossible, and Mr. Brunel had not only to make his pier in the centre of the river, but, having no place to which to secure the tension chains on which the roadway hung, had also to contrive to make them in a manner self-supporting." For this the suspension chains hang down from the piers in a segment of a circle, and are bolted to the roadway, while above the roadway, so as to form the other segment of the circle, are two monster tubes of arched wrought iron, connected with the ends of the chains, which precisely answer the purpose of metal bows.

On the great main pier, in the centre of the river, all the strain and pressure come, and nothing short of the solid rock would suffice for its foundation. "To reach this, however, was a matter of no ordinary difficulty, as some 70 feet of water, with 20 feet of mud and concrete gravel, lay between Mr. Brunel and the stone on which he wished to build. An immense wrought iron cylinder, 37 feet in diameter, 100 feet high, and weighing 300 tons, was made and sunk exactly in the spot where the masonry was to rise. From this the water was pumped out and air forced in; the men descended, and, working as in a huge diving-bell at the bottom of the river, cleared away the mud and gravel till the rock was reached. Steam air-pumps were necessary to keep the men supplied, and, as a matter of course, they worked at a pressure of upwards of 38lb. to the inch. At first this affected them severely; many were seized with cramps, faintness, and insensibility, and one died. But after a time forty labourers could remain at work with little inconvenience. All, however, were glad when the solid column of granite built inside the cylinder rose at last above the water's edge."

On this pile of stone, springing many feet below the river's bed, the iron columns for the centre pier were raised. Until these ponderous masses were cast, metal columns of such gigantic dimensions were never dreamt of. There are four of them, octagon in shape, 10 feet in diameter, and 100 feet high. The weight of these columns is about 150 tons each. The metal is two inches thick, and each column is stayed and supported inside with massive ribs. "When all the pieces of the four columns had been cast, each was planed down and fitted together with the neatness of joiner's work. Thus finished, all were sent off piecemeal to the centre pier, though not erected, as they could only be built up under the centre spans as the latter were gradually lifted to their places by hydraulic pressure in one gigantic piece weighing some 1,200 tons. These were put together at the river's bank, were floated out to their place, and then raised in one mass." The chains are similar in principle to those of an ordinary suspension bridge, except that, instead of being made with links of seven bars, each link consists of fourteen bars of iron, an inch thick and six inches wide. The pressure on the centre pier foundation is upwards of eight tons to the foot, or double the pressure of the whole mass of the Victoria tower on the basement. Six inches have been allowed for expansion and contraction to each tube, but the greatest difference yet observed between the hottest and the coldest day has only made a difference of two inches in the length of the bridge. "The fame of Saltash and its magnificent viaduct is likely to be still more widely known than even the colossal work which spans the Straits of Menai."

Among the most remarkable railway bridges are those that traverse the Thames. The Charing Cross bridge consists of nine spans—six of 154 feet, and three of 100 feet. The level of the rails is 31 feet above high-water mark, and the river here is 1,350 feet wide. The superstructure rests upon cylinders sunk through mud and gravel into the London clay to depths of 50, 60, and in one instance of more than 70 feet below high-water mark. They are filled with Portland cement, concrete, or brickwork. To test the strength of the foundations, the two cylinders in the pier nearest to the Surrey side, after being completed up to the level of high water, and filled with concrete and brickwork, were each weighted with 700 tons—an amount equal to the greatest burden they could have to sustain, supposing the four lines of rails on the bridge were loaded with locomotives. This weight thus applied caused the cylinders to sink permanently four inches. To bring the other cylinders to a bearing, so as to prevent any subsequent settlement, each was weighted with 450 tons, whereupon they each sank permanently about three inches. The pairs of cylinders forming a pier are connected transversely by a wrought-iron box girder, 4 feet deep; it also serves as a cross-girder for supporting the roadway. If the four lines of way on the bridge were to be loaded with locomotives, the pressure on the base of the cylinders would amount to eight tons a square foot.

The roadway platform over the 150 feet openings consists of four-inch planking spiked to longitudinal timbers, 15 inches by 15, placed underneath the rails and bolted to the cross-girders. The footpath platforms are of planking, 6 inches thick.

The first cylinder of this bridge was pitched June 6th, 1860, and its construction occupied three years. Nearly 5,000 tons of wrought iron, and nearly 2,000 tons of cast iron, were required. The result has been a remarkable concentration of strength in the piers and the girders within the smallest compass. "The cylinders," says the report of the proceedings of the Institution of Civil Engineers "obtained, for the column of brickwork built inside them afterwards, a foundation as solid as rock itself, and one not likely to be disturbed by any changes which may occur in the bed of the river by the scour caused by the Thames embankment, the scour being a source of evil which has hitherto proved fatal to the foundations of nearly all our metropolitan bridges. Again, with the superstructure, although the space is moderate—154 feet—yet the quantity of metal required in each of these girders amounts to 200 tons, and the skilful way it has been massed together to afford the requisite strength, and yet give little indication of it in its light and almost elegant appearance, is certainly unsurpassed."

The railway bridge over the Thames at Battersea is the widest railway bridge in the world, being 132 feet wide, as well as more than 900 long. It consists of four river spans of 175 feet in the clear, and two land spans of 65 feet and 70 feet respectively. It forms the key to the intricate network of high level lines at Battersea, and it provides ten separate means of access to the Victoria Station. In the tests applied, equal to the weight of the rails fully occupied by engines, the greatest settlement in any place was less than an inch.

The Forth railway bridge will be a remarkable structure. Hitherto the largest railway bridge in this country is the Britannia, with a span of 465 feet. The Forth bridge has a span of 1,700 feet, a ratio of 1 to 3·65. Now, as it is calculated that the average stature of a new-born infant is 19·34 inches, whilst the average height of the Guardsmen sent out to Egypt has been officially given at 5 feet 10½ inches, these figures also have a ratio of 1 to 3·65. Hence, to appreciate the size of the Forth bridge, we have merely to suggest the following simple rule of three sum:—As a Grenadier Guardsman is to a new-born infant, so is the Forth bridge to the largest railway bridge yet built in this country. Bridges a few feet wider in span than the Britannia have been built elsewhere, but they are baby bridges after all.

At the point where this bridge is to be built, the Firth of Forth is divided by the island of Inchgarvie into two unequal channels, but the depth of water in each is such that a smaller span than 1,700 feet could not be economically adopted for either channel. North of Inchgarvie the maximum depth of water is 218 feet, and south of the same 197 feet. In the former channel the bottom is of hard trap rock, and in the latter partly of rock and partly of extremely stiff boulder clay. It is not the treacherous character of the bed of the Forth, therefore, but the depth of water which precludes the construction of intermediate piers. Pneumatic apparatus, say the authorities, is inapplicable to such depths as 200 feet, and no responsible engineer would care to found the piers of an important structure upon a bottom which he had no means of examining by diving apparatus or otherwise. Hence it was resolved to erect, as the Act passed this year, 1882, expresses it: "a continuous girder bridge, having two spans of 1,700 feet, two of 675 feet, fourteen of 168 feet, and six of 50 feet, and giving a clear headway for navigation purposes of 150 feet above high-water spring tides."

When the proposal was submitted for the consideration of Parliament, a model of the central portion was exhibited, on a scale of 40 feet to the inch, showing the two main spans in their entirety, and half of each of the two side or subsidiary spans, leaving the shore ends out of view. These two main spans are 1,750 feet in length, with a headway of 150 feet. The two side spans have the same height of headway, but are only 650 feet in length. The breadth of the bridge itself is about 25 feet, but it appears narrow in contrast with its length. The central pier rests upon a small island named Inchgarvie, and is formed ot four columns, 350 feet in height, laid together laterally, with lattice work in the form of a St. Andrew's cross. These pillars rise 200 feet above the level of the roadway, just as in Brunel's bridge, at Charing Cross, the old red brick towers used to rise above the footway. Similarly bands descend from the height on either side in a graceful slope towards the roadway, where they meet two corresponding curves springing from the bottom of the pier, the point of their meeting being about 600 feet from the centre of that portion of the railway which lies within the pier. "As a similar system of lattice work, both from above and from beneath, springs from the piers on either side of this central pier, a space of 500 feet in the centre is left clear of the cantilered system of support above described. This interval is spanned by a bridge like Sir John Hawkshaw's bridge at Charing Cross, the support being entirely from above." This 500 feet is the free space in the centre of each span which will be available for high-masted vessels. The framework is knit together within by a combination of transverse girders, and it is upon these that the roadway is so carried at a height of 150 feet above high-water mark. The bridge, which is to be throughout constructed of steel, is to carry a double line of rails, will be exactly one mile in length, and is calculated to bear a strain up to the full requirement of the Board of Trade. The principle of construction resorted to is that of continuous girders placed on canting levers and resting upon a central lever.

In some interesting particulars mentioned by Mr. B. Baker, one of the engineers, to the British Association at Southampton, he says it would probably be conceded by every one that a girder bridge would prove stiffer than a suspension bridge; in the case of the Forth bridge, it will also be cheaper. In a long span bridge the weight of the structure itself constitutes the chiet portion of the load, whilst the pressure of the wind is at least as important an element as the rolling load itself, to carry which is the sole useful mission of the bridge. In a properly designed continuous girder for a long span bridge the mass of metal will be concentrated near the piers, where it will act with the smallest leverage and produce the least bending movement. In an ordinary suspension bridge, with stiffening girder vertically to provide for the rolling load, and horizontally to meet wind stresses, the mass of metal will be somewhat greater towards the centre of the bridge than at the piers, and consequently for a given mass the movement will be much less in the continuous girder than in the suspension bridge. Thus the Forth bridge superstructure weighs but two tons per foot run at the centre of the 1,700 feet span, and thirteen and a half tons per foot run at the piers; whilst in a suspension bridge, as already stated, the weight of superstructure per lineal foot would be somewhat greater at the centre than at the piers. This consideration, coupled with the facts that suspension links are more costly than girder work, that a suspension bridge requires a very costly anchorage, and that the contingencies and risks during erection in a stormy estuary are very great, explains why, in such a case as the Forth bridge, well-designed continuous girders form a cheaper, as well as a far stiffer, structure than a suspension bridge with stiffening girder.

Mr. Baker tells us that the width for the superstructure was determined after very careful consideration. Since the fall of the Tay bridge, engineers generally, and the Board of Trade in particular, have vividly realized the fact that the severest wrench to which a railway viaduct is subject arises, not from the vertical stress due to the loading of both lines of rails with locomotives throughout, but to the diagonal stress, due to the combined action of the ordinary rolling load and a violent hurricane. In the case of the Forth bridge this stress would act at an angle of about 45 degrees, so that, were it not for the dead weight of the structure, the required strength would be the same horizontally as vertically, and the economical width would be the same as the economical depth. Although the dead weight modifies this conclusion, it was obvious that the bridge should be a continuous girder of varying depth on plan as well as on elevation, and investigation showed the economical width of superstructure to be about 32 feet at the centre and 132 feet at the piers.

It was open to consideration whether the wind stresses should be resisted by bracing together both the top and bottom members of the girder, or the bottom members alone. The author, however, never had any doubt that, as stresses must sooner or later be brought down to the masonry piers, they had better be brought down at once by the shortest route along the bottom members only. The top members are therefore spaced at the distance of from 33 feet to 27 feet apart, centre to centre, and are unconnected by wind bracing. Each of the main vertical and diagonal struts consists of a pair of tubes spread out at the base like a bridge pier, and the wind stresses on the bracing between the tubes are much reduced thereby. In like manner are the wind stresses on the bracing of the bottom member reduced by the spreading out of the legs of the cantilevers, and the general stresses on the web members by the tapering depth from the piers towards the ends of the cantilevers.

Mr. Baker tells us that, though the works will be on an unusually large scale, no special difficulty will arise with respect to the foundations. The island of Inchgarvie is of trap rock, and the central pier at that spot will consist of four cylindrical masses of concrete and rubble-work faced with granite, and having a diameter of 45 feet at the top and 70 feet at the bottom. The height above water will be 18 feet, and the depth below the same will vary from 24 feet to 70 feet. After the sloping face of the rock foundations has been cut into steps, wrought-iron caissons will be floated out, lowered into place, and filled with concrete, lowered through the water in hopper-bottomed skips. Queensferry pier will be founded on boulder clay. Open-topped cylindrical caissons, 70 feet diameter, with an external and internal skin 7 feet 6 inches apart, will be floated out and lowered into place. The piers will be carried down at least 10 feet into the boulder clay, which will give depths ranging from 68 feet to 88 feet below high water, and 18 feet less at low water in the respective cylinders. The weight of one of the cylindrical piers at Queensferry will be 16,000 tons, and the combined vertical pressure on the top of the pier from the dead weight of superstructure, rolling load, and wind pressure will be 8,000 tons; so the load on the clay will average about 6 tons per square foot over the area of the foundation.

The total length of the great continuous girder will be 5,330 feet, or say a mile, and of the viaduct approaches 2,754 feet, or rather over half a mile. The piers will be of rubble masonry, faced with granite, and the superstructure of iron lattice girders. There will be a strong parapet and wind screen to protect the trains.

About 42,000 tons of steel will be used in the superstructure of the main spans, and 3,000 tons of wrought iron in that of the viaduct approach. The total quantity of masonry in the piers and foundations will be about 125,000 cubic yards, and the estimated cost of the entire work, upon the basis of the prices at which the original suspension bridge was contracted for, is about £1,500,000. Dr. Siemens has said—"The Firth of Forth is about to be spanned by a bridge exceeding in grandeur anything as yet attempted by the engineer."

Before closing this chapter we may refer to what in some sense may be regarded as a continuous viaduct—the proposed "overhead" railway at Liverpool. Railways of this sort have for some time been in operation in New York. The first experiment was tried in 1867, with half a mile of line, what was called the "One-legged" line, from its being carried on a single row of central columns placed between the kerb of the footway and roadway, and supported from the columns on radiating wrought-iron brackets. This was first worked by a fixed engine and cable. It was, however, a failure. A new Company, under the title of the New York Elevated Railway Company, purchased the interest of the original promoters for a small sum, and extended the line a distance of about five miles, working by small locomotives. "The Gilbert Elevated Railway, which was planned to administer the greater part of the elevated railway system of New York, was incorporated June 17, 1872. Though obviously the offspring of the original Greenwich Street line, its first conception by Dr. Gilbert, its promoter, embodied much originality in construction, mainly in the employment of a double row of supporting columns tied together by cross girders, a high longitudinal suspending girder for carrying the line, and elegant arched girders from column to column over the line tying the whole structure together at intervals of 4 feet to 50 feet."

The foundations are composed of from 4 feet to 5 feet of brickwork; into it iron sockets 4 feet long are built, and into these the supporting columns are dropped, and the intervening space rammed tight with iron shavings and turnings, which rust into a cohesive cement-like mass. The *minimum* clear height of the structure, says Mr. George Maw, is 14 feet and of the rail level 20 feet; but as the line does not follow the smaller undulations of the streets, the rail level is occasionally raised 30 feet above the roadway. The longitudinal wrought-iron girders, lightly constructed of angle and "T" iron about 3½ feet deep, and extending from column to column, directly support the permanent way, which consists of "ties" or sleepers 6 inches deep and 7 inches wide, upon which the rail, weighing 56 lb. to the yard, is fixed to the standard gauge of 4 feet 8½ inches. The stations at intervals of about half a mile at the intersections of all the main avenues and streets, are approached by easy flights of stairs at each end of the platforms, which are 140 feet in length, covered with corrugated iron, and provided with waiting-rooms and ticket offices. The motor cars, in the centre of which are placed the boiler and engine, weigh about 30,000 lbs. each, and cost about £1,000; they are enclosed all round and provided with plate-glass windows at sides and ends. All the four wheels of the car are coupled together and directly connected with the engine power. The streets and avenues in New York being mostly at right angles, the curves in the railway in passing from one to the other are necessarily sudden, but they are accomplished with a radius of 90 feet and 103 feet for the inner and outer lines respectively. The position of the columns at these points has to be varied and modified to suit the widths of the intersecting streets, but no difficulty is found in so placing them as to interfere but little with the traffic. The speed of train is thirty miles an hour; but with stops at stations the average train speed of travelling is not above fifteen miles an hour.

A similar work in England has been approved by Parliament. The Liverpool docks stretch along the frontage of the river Mersey, from north to south, for seven miles, and the intended railway will run parallel with the docks, on a high level above

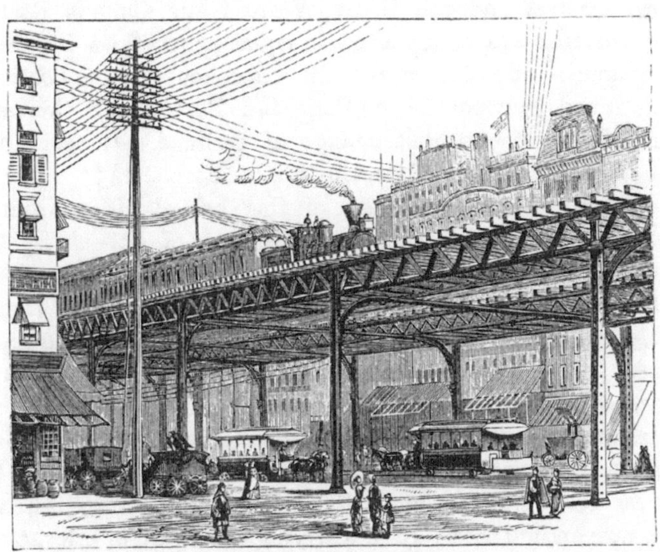

ELEVATED RAILWAY, NEW YORK.

the ground. The line will commence near the northern boundary of the Mersey Dock Board's Liverpool estate, in the adjoining borough of Bootle, and terminate at the Herculaneum Dock, in Toxteth Park. There will be stations at different points close to the line of docks. The line will be carried chiefly on piers and columns at an elevation of from 15 to 20 feet above the roadway, and will pass over several thoroughfares leading from the interior of the city to the river. The Dock Board has agreed to erect twelve bridges at different points, the spans of which are to be 50 feet and 60 feet in width. The railway will, at several points, cross over the Lancashire and Yorkshire, and the London and North Western lines. The railway, which is to be a double line throughout, will cost £650,000 for construction only, no purchase of land or compensation being required. The fares to be charged are threepence a mile for first-class passengers, twopence a mile for second-class, and a penny a mile for third-class. Passengers only are to be carried. The line is to be leased and worked by the London and North Western, or the Lancashire and Yorkshire Company.

The Great International Railway suspension bridge over the Niagara river was erected for the purpose of connecting the New York Central and the Great Western and Canada Railways, and the cost was contributed in equal proportions by the two companies. By its means an unbroken communication is maintained between New York and Boston and the western part of Canada without change of carriage. It cost 400,000 dollars, and was opened on the 8th of March, 1855. The plan adopted in the construction of this bridge differs from that usually followed in England. Instead of flat wrought-iron plate links, connected together by pins passing through their extremities, a simple wire cable is employed, or rather iron wire cables, each 10 inches in diameter and composed of 3,640 separate wires. These cables are capable of carrying a weight of 12,000 tons, while the actual load never exceeds 1,000 tons. The wire ropes are securely anchored in the solid rock, 30 feet below the surface, and they pass over the summits of four solid stone towers 80 feet in height. Besides the wire cables, there are 624 suspending rods, of a carrying strength of 18,720 tons; these support the roadway at different parts, and are connected with the roadway above. The space between the towers is 800 feet, and the "railway track," as it is called in America, is 250 feet above the surface of the river. Absolute rigidity is not secured, which cannot be attained in suspension bridges, but the Niagara Railway suspension bridge is sufficiently rigid to allow of laden trains to pass over it at a speed of five miles an hour.

A picturesque railway bridge on the Pennsylvania line is that at Conemaugh, over a river of the same name.

Before leaving this part of the subject, a word must be said in reference to level-crossing stations. It frequently occurs in the construction of railways that they have to intersect existing roads, which it would be difficult to cross except at the same level. Sometimes by a modification of the gradient of the line or of the road, the one may be taken over or under the other, but where railroads traverse great extents of level country, as in

CONEMAUGH BRIDGE.

Lincolnshire and Cambridge, it would be impossible to take the one class of roads above the other except by a constant series of embankments, along which either the line or the road must pass. To overcome these difficulties, level crossings are provided, and attendants are put in charge of the gates. Such gates are of several kinds and sizes; sometimes four are employed; and sometimes it is considered that two large ones are sufficient. The sketch represents a pair of such as are commonly used on the Great Northern Railway. They are massive, strengthened with iron, and hung on stout timbers deeply imbedded in the earth. They are twenty-six feet and a half in length, and cost about £50. There are small wickets for foot-passengers. In the middle of each gate is a large round board, painted red, by means of which an approaching train may see the gates closed across the line. At night a red light is substituted.

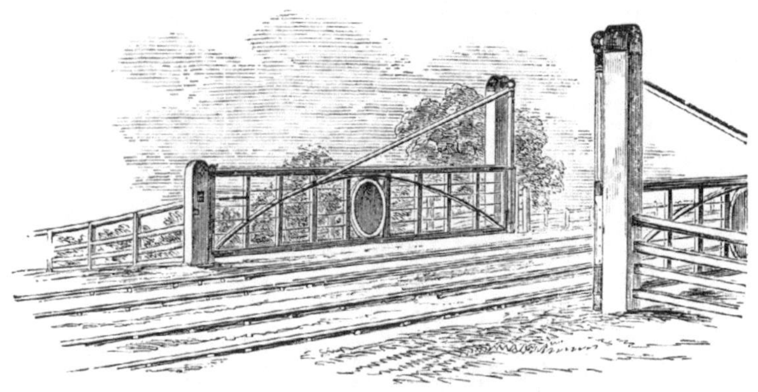

LEVEL CROSSINGS.

In some instances safety gates for level-crossings have been adopted. They can be opened by the movement of a hand-lever, connected with distance signals, and also with signals at the crossing. By throwing the lever over, danger signals are raised, and the gates are unlocked and closed across the railway: the reverse operation frees the line and again locks the gates upon the highroad. As it is impossible for the gates to be opened without the signals being simultaneously raised, and as the latter cannot be released until the gates are again closed and locked, safety is ensured. One man can work both the signals and gates.

CHAPTER VIII.

Temporary and Permanent Way.—Broad and Narrow Gauge.—Break of Gauge.—" Clever but Theoretical."—Broad Gauge Changed to Narrow. —Formation of the Line.—The Road Laid.—Rigidness or Elasticity of Roads.—Ballast.—Burnt Clay.—Stone Sleepers.—Wooden Sleepers.—Creosoting Sleepers.—Longitudinal Sleepers.—Chairs.—Keys.—Rails.—Controversies.—Smoothness of Track.—Rails Kept Warm.—Fish Plates. —Cast-iron Rails.—Wrought-iron Rails.—Steel Rails.—" Creeping " of Rails.—Repair of Permanent Way.—Plate-layers.—Duties of Plate-layers.—Enemies of the Permanent Way.—Water Troughs on Permanent Way.—Opening of a Line.—Opening of London and Bedford Line.

HAVING described the chief works in the construction of a railway, the permanent way, as it is called, comes under consideration. The term is, as a matter of fact, applied to that portion of a line that is the *least* permanent of the whole, and it requires continual repairs and replacement to maintain it in proper condition. The word, however, is employed in contradistinction from the *temporary* way laid down for the use of the contractor in the construction of the line.

Here at the outset we may deal with the question of gauge. This subject has involved a large expenditure of time, discussion, and money. The original width of the coal tramroads in the North of England, which virtually determined the British gauge, was not fixed on any scientific theory ; it was adopted simply because of its practical convenience, five feet being the customary width of the gates through which the "way-leaves" led. When the Liverpool and Manchester line was projected, Mr. George Stephenson, the engineer, saw no reason to depart from the

Initial letter represents Conway Castle and part of its Tubular and Suspension Bridges.

gauge generally established, and the Liverpool and Manchester Railway was laid down with the gauge of four feet eight inches and a half. The branch lines were necessarily constructed in the same way, since the engines and carriages would otherwise have been unable to pass from one to the other ; and when the great main lines were planned to lead southwards to the metropolis, uniformity of gauge was indispensable.

Some engineers were of opinion that the narrowness of the gauge thus selected involved a crowding of the machinery of the engines that was inconvenient both to the builder and the cleaner ; and regret was expressed that the gauge had not been fixed a few inches wider. Further experience, however, showed that these difficulties might be surmounted, and the requisite means for the prevention of the evils referred to were, to a great extent, provided.

The question was under discussion when a great change took place. Mr. Brunel, who had been appointed the engineer of the Great Western Railway, suggested that a gauge of seven feet would be preferable. The proposal was startling. When laid before Mr. Robert Stephenson, the engineer of the London and Birmingham line, he reported unfavourably upon it, and a divergence of opinion arose between the two Boards, which eventually led them to abandon the idea which had till then been entertained of having a common metropolitan terminus for the two lines.

An elaborate exposition of his views upon the subject was made by Mr. Brunel, in several reports he addressed to the Directors. He admitted that in a continuous line of traffic a departure from the established gauge would occasion inconvenience, and that in the case of the Great Western Railway it would almost amount to a prohibition of communication with another line running north from London. But he considered that as the new line was to be carried through a district in which no railways existed, it could have no connection with any other of the main lines, and that as the branches would complete the communication with the districts through which the line would pass, the Great Western system would be independent of other railways for its traffic. He even maintained that the want of connection with other railways would be advantageous, inasmuch as it would be a means of securing a monopoly of railway communication in the West of England and South Wales in the hands of the Great Western Company. The Directors were satisfied, and Parliament was induced to sanction the rescinding of a Standing Order which had prescribed the narrow gauge for general adoption.

Other gauges were adopted for some other lines. Mr. Braithwaite first chose five feet for the Eastern Counties and Blackwall lines, and five feet six was used in Scotland. The Ulster Company made twenty-five miles of the railway from Belfast to Dublin on the six feet two inches scale ; while the Drogheda Company, which set out from Dublin to meet the Ulster line, adopted a gauge of five feet two inches. When the discrepancy was complained of by the Directors of the Ulster line, they were answered by the Irish Board of Works, that though it looked a little awkward, and although the two ends were completed, there was so little chance of the intervening part ever being finished, that therefore no harm was likely to be done. The subject, however, was referred to General Pasley: he consulted the leading authorities, and finally adopted five feet three inches as the national gauge for Ireland, being the mean of all their opinions.

Into the theoretical advantages of the two systems we need not enter: practical considerations were predominant. "The traffic of the West of England," said Mr. Sidney at the time, "requires not huge, unwieldy carriages and trucks, but handy wagons, which may, without inordinate trouble or expense, be run into small road-stations and sidings, to which a farmer may send his couple of fat oxen, or his score of sheep, or his load of corn, in conjunction with one or two more neighbours." But of such traffic there was little on the Great Western Railway, though it traversed rich agricultural districts, because, he remarked, "the whole machinery is on too vast, costly, and magnificent a scale."

The difference in the original outlay between the broad and narrow gauge railways was of great importance. Two lines of rails of the broad gauge were fourteen feet wide, and two of the narrow-gauge are nine feet five inches wide, the difference being within an inch of another track of narrow-gauge railway. Mr. Brunel also made his tunnels six feet wider than those on the narrow gauge ; but of this, only four feet seven inches could strictly be chargeable to the gauge. The increased cost of land

—three-quarters of an acre per mile—was an item of moment. The line was carried through towns and buildings, and where the works were of magnitude, the difference of four feet seven inches in width to every embankment, viaduct, and bridge above ground, and every cutting and tunnel below, involved an outlay of considerable importance, and demanded a proportionate return in the shape of interest on the capital expended. In short, it is estimated that where a narrow-gauge line would require £6,000 per mile, £7,000 would be necessary for the broad; and where the works cost, as on the Manchester and Leeds Railway, more than £40,000 a mile, the broad gauge would *per se* require an augmented expenditure of from £6,000 to £8,000 per mile.

The practical evils resulting from the break of gauge formed the chief consideration that determined the issue. The inconvenience to passengers was great, and the difficulties as respects the goods traffic were greater. The removal involved loss, pilferage, detention, besides a money tax, estimated at from 1*s.* 6*d.* to 2*s.* 6*d.* per ton. At Gloucester it occupied about an hour to remove the contents of a wagon, full of miscellaneous merchandise, from one gauge to another. An ordinary train might contain "loose commodities, such as bricks, slates, lime or limestone, and chalk, flags, clay, manure, salt, coal or coke, timber and deals, dye-woods, iron, iron-ore, lead and metals, cast-iron pots, grates and ovens, grindstones, brimstone, bones and hoofs, bark, hides and sealskins, oil-cake, potatoes, onions, and other vegetables; cheese, chairs, and furniture; hardware, earthenware, dry salteries, groceries, provisions, cotton wool, oils, wines, spirits, and other liquids; manufactured goods, fish and eggs, ripe fruit, etc. Now let us contemplate the loss by damage done to the goods on this line alone, by reason of the break of gauge causing the removal of every article. In the hurry the bricks are miscounted, the slates chipped at the edges, the cheeses cracked, the ripe fruit and vegetables crushed and spoiled; the chairs, furniture, and oil-cakes, cast-iron pots, grates, and ovens, all more or less broken; the coals turned into slack, the salt short of weight, sundry bottles of wine deficient, and the fish too late for market. Whereas, if there had not been any interruption of gauge, the whole train would, in all probability, have been at its destination long before the transfer of the last article, and without any damage or delay." It was estimated that the expense of each interchange of traffic was equivalent to the cost of its conveyance over one hundred miles of railway. No wonder that a Royal Commission declared its opinion that "the continued existence of the double gauge is a national evil."

The experiment of the great engineer—"clever, but theoretical," as he has been called—came to a costly conclusion. In 1846 it had been enacted that all the railways in Great Britain, except the Great Western, should henceforth be of the gauge of four feet eight and a half, and in Ireland of five feet three. In 1867 there were 1,456 miles of the broad gauge existing, and there were twenty-six places where the two gauges met, and where a transfer of traffic had to take place. A mixed or double gauge had been introduced in various directions, but at length it was resolved that the broad gauge should be altered to the narrow, in, at first, some portions, and then on the remainder of the Great Western system. The undertaking had to be carried out in a comprehensive and also an energetic manner, so as to lay as brief an arrest as possible on the through traffic of the respective lines. The plan adopted between Gloucester and Hereford in 1869 has been described by an observer whose narrative we abridge.

The work was commenced first by mixing the gauges in the extensive Gloucester station-yard—a matter of peculiar difficulty, that station being a single platform one; secondly, by mixing the gauges from Gloucester to Grange Court, where the Gloucester and Hereford Railway branches off. This having been completed, the Gloucester and Hereford was closed for a fortnight between Grange Court and Hereford, passengers being conveyed by ten first-class coaches put on the road. A force of 450 men was selected from the gangs regularly at work on the Hereford division of the Great Western Railway, and they were to lodge during the execution of the work in a broad-gauge train of 40 covered wagons, carefully whitewashed, and supplied with an abundance of clean straw and new sacks; the staff occupying a first-class carriage for the night. "At four o'clock on Sunday morning the sleeping train was in motion, and an engineer had gone ahead setting up a flag-pole at the end of each gang's length of work for the day. The train stopped at each flag-pole, and a ganger and gang of 22 men, furnished with a day's provisions, jumped out with all the necessary tools, also a cask of water, 'devil,' iron crock, and fuel. This process was continued throughout the whole length of line 450 men could be spread over. Soon a line of smoke was to be seen ascending, and the work of getting breakfast was actively going on. The men brought their own food—a week's supply—as it was arranged that should the work extend beyond that time through bad weather or any unforeseen circumstance, they were to be allowed to stop for a day to get fresh supplies. Cocoa seemed the favourite beverage, the food various—cold bacon, meat, or bread and cheese." The men were not long over breakfast, and soon the work of narrowing was going on. The first night's halt was called at Fawley. It now became evident that Ross would be reached on Tuesday, and bills were issued announcing the commencement of traffic by rail between Hereford and Ross on Wednesday. Ross was actually reached on Tuesday, and the sleeping train was put into a loop line at that station for the night. "By Thursday night the whole work was accomplished, and the narrow-gauge trains, worked by the proper platforms, at Grange Court Junction, taking throughout the proper lines for Gloucester." In five days the whole line, 22 miles long, was commenced and finished.

Great astonishment has recently been occasioned by an announcement that American engineers had changed the gauge of 200 miles of American railway in 12 hours. Bearing in mind that this involved only moving a nailed-down rail two or three inches, it will be seen that the narrowing of the Gloucester and Hereford Railway as above described in five days was a much more surprising engineering feat. Of the conduct of the 450 men employed it would be difficult to speak too highly during these five days of incessant toil. Not a single instance of disobedience, intoxication, or display of bad temper occurred; on every side the engineers directing the work met with most cheerful obedience.

We now come to the subject of the formation of the line itself. No excellence of superstructure can compensate for insufficient earthworks. For double lines of the ordinary gauge the formation width on embankments is from 30 to 36 feet; in cuttings it varies from 26 to 30 feet. Between the two lines is the "six foot," as it is called, and for it there should be 6 feet to 6 feet 6 inches allowed, and 7 feet to 8 feet 6 inches for the sides.

The width of the side spaces in cuttings leaves room for a shelf between the edge of the ballast and the ditch, so that any wash from the surface of the road-bed is prevented from passing into and choking the ditches; a similar level space is usually left between the outside of the ditch and the foot of the slope itself, to catch the wash from the upper surfaces.

When the earthwork has been formed, the drainage completed, and the shrinking allowed for, the ballast, or at least part of it, has to be laid. Its uses are various: it distributes the weight of the load from the sleepers on to the larger bearing surface of the road; it helps to fix the sleepers in their places; it drains away the surface water; and, being in its own nature intermediate between the rigidity of rock and the softness of common earth, it gives a certain uniform elasticity to the road. It may seem strange to speak of a line of railway as elastic, and it may be thought that the more rigid foundation a road of iron can rest on, the better. In America the problem of deflection and looseness of rail-joints, *versus* anvil-like rigidity of joint-fastenings, has been the basis of permanent-way discussion ever since improvement began. But this arose from the peculiar nature of the climate, where, at a particular time of the year, hardened roads prevail. "Elasticity is defined to be a compromise between smoothness and hardness—that is, the construction may ensure a regular and even movement, and yet there may be something not perfectly unyielding—that is, not harsh like a pavement; for it is obvious that although timber may be perfectly solid and hard, yet with a great pressure, like the weight of a railway train, there may be a certain degree of 'give' which avoids that grating, crashing sensation which is inseparable from a stone-based way." When the Manchester and Leeds line was made, the bottom of a rock cutting was dressed to a surface, and the rails were spiked directly to it. But a few weeks experience was sufficient to show that such rigidity was undesirable; the rails were taken up, and the line was relaid in the usual way. It is a curious fact that if there is not an absolute break in the line of rails, a train may proceed safely upon a very undulating and shaky surface; although, of course, this is not advisable. Firmness, without rigidity, is wanted in a railway road-bed, and this is best secured by ballast.

The materials that are used for ballasting a line are various, the engineer being in part dependent on the resources of the country through which he has to pass. Very hard materials give rigidity to the road, and cause it to "batter out." On the other hand, sand hardly deserves the name of ballast. It is not firm under pressure; it will not drain well; it rapidly washes out; by being blown about by the trains, it gets into the bearings of the machinery; by lying on the tread of the rail it greatly increases resistance, and thereby adds to the consumption of fuel and oil; it also injures the upholstery of the carriages, and is a nuisance to the passengers. It cannot be depended on for a smooth track, least of all in winter. Gravel dredged from some river bottom like that of the Trent, and broken stone are the best, especially where the gravel has a mixture of clean sand; but burned clay, cinder, shells, broken bricks and culm or small coal are all employed. Stone, when broken for ballast, should not exceed 2½ inches in any diameter. Limestone rock is durable, but is of so binding a character as to pack too readily when used as ballast. Gneiss rock answers well for ballast, and breaks easily. On the Great Eastern, broken sandstone, though soft, gives an easy road. Slate rock is the poorest kind of stone ballast, being rapidly decomposed in wet weather. "Hard stone ballast should never be used in cuttings. Gravel, if too fine, will not drain well; if too coarse it will not pack sufficiently to prevent the sleepers from sinking into it. It must be carefully selected also as to its quality. If from the sea-shore, it will hardly bind at all; if mixed with loam, it will never drain well." If it has a natural mixture of clean sand, it will be best quality.

Burned clay is often used for ballast, especially on the lines near the metropolis that run over the London clay field. In burning it a wood fire is first lighted; on this some bituminous coal is placed, and when this is well kindled, a thin layer of clay is put round and on it. "Clay and coal are then placed alternately—the clay in lumps, never so thickly as to choke the fire. In this way, a bank or kiln of clay, up to any size, may be made up and burned. On the Great Northern, these banks are laid up, about 200 feet long, 60 feet wide, and 20 feet high." Care must be taken that it is burned uniformly. If vitrified, it is best; if under-burned, it will dissolve in wet weather. A ton of coal will burn 20 or 25 yards of clay, and with coal at 16*s.* a ton the ballast will cost about 1*s.* 3*d.* a yard.

Twelve inches of ballast are usually laid before the sleepers are placed. These are then placed at their proper levels and distances, and when bedded as firmly as possible, more ballast is deposited around and upon them. If broken stone is used, the larger pieces are spread at the bottom, and they will so wedge into each other as not to be likely to come to the surface. With gravel, the coarser is laid at the bottom. In spreading the ballast, provision is made for the escape of water from its surface. If this is done well, it may be safely said that "the best railways in the world—those which do the most business at the least cost—are the best ballasted."

We have thus dealt with some parts of what is called "the permanent way." But, as we have seen and shall further see, all its conditions contradict its idea of permanence. The foundations of a permanent building are placed at a depth which insures uniform support at all seasons, and, convulsions of nature excepted, for centuries; as, for instance, with cathedral towers, which have not moved in a thousand years as much as an ordinary rail-joint deflects at the passage of a train. A railway is on the top of the ground, and is at the mercy of frost and thaw, of rain and sun, of cold and heat. Each change of the weather alters its resistance, strength, and support. And all this is unavoidable.

We now come to the question of sleepers. Originally it was supposed that nothing less solid and durable than blocks of stone could carry the iron rails and could stand the hard work to which the permanent way would be subjected. These blocks were two feet square and a foot thick. On the London and Greenwich Railway, and on several other of the early railways, granite was used. On the London and Birmingham line no fewer than 152,000 tons weight of stone blocks were laid as sleepers, costing about £180,000. This expense was divisible into three nearly equal parts: one-third for the stone, one-third for the freight from the quarries to the Thames, and the remainder for delivery on the different parts of the works.

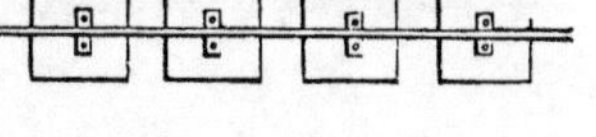

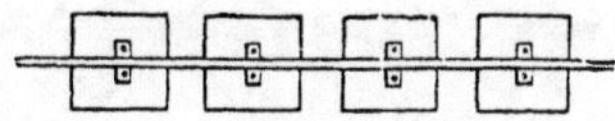

The setting of the sleepers on which the rails rest is a matter of great importance: upon it depends the permanent stability of the road. The old method was, after having spread the bottom of the excavation, or the top of the embankment, with a layer of ashes, small stones, or gravel, to place the blocks upon this, with the chairs and rails attached to them; workmen with narrow shovels pushed the ashes or sand underneath the blocks, and at the same time beat upon the upper side of the block with heavy mallets, till the rails were at the proper level. But by such a method, only a very imperfect solidity could be given to the foundation, and when the trains ran upon the rails the blocks sank, and workmen were required to push more ashes or sand underneath to restore them to their proper level, until the seats of the blocks became sufficiently firm to resist the weight of the passing vehicles.

When George Stephenson was laying down the Liverpool and Manchester line, he compressed and consolidated the foundation so that the weight of the trains could not make the blocks yield. This was done by the impact of the blocks themselves, which were successively lifted up, and allowed to fall upon the seat on which they were intended permanently to rest. The block was dropped from such a height that the effect was greater than the direct weight or pressure of the passing trains.

For the success of this plan, it was necessary that the material on which the coating was laid should be firm and solid; for the least subsiding of the foundation would render all the work useless. Hence, though it succeeded upon well drained and consolidated works, yet in clay, and other yielding soils, other means had to be resorted to. In some cases the blocks were laid diagonally, instead of vertically, as seen in the accompanying diagram, which was thought to have the effect of steadying the rails; while it gave to the workmen access to the four sides, to set them right if they became displaced. The difficulties, however, which attended the use of stone blocks at length led to the substitution of wooden sleepers; and piles of stone blocks might for years be seen at roadside stations on the London and Birmingham line, whence they were sold for about eighteen-pence apiece; or they may to-day be found on

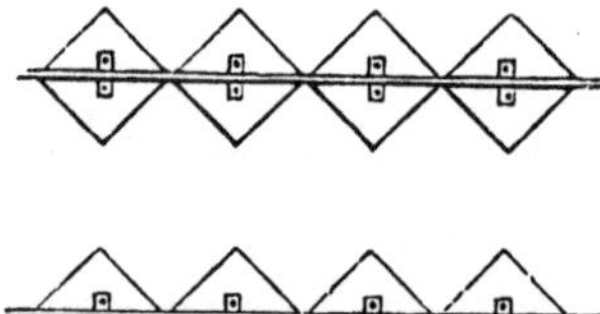

railway platforms doing duty as paving kerbstones, the holes pierced in them for the pins, and the square hollows cut for the chairs, plainly indicating the use to which they were formerly devoted.

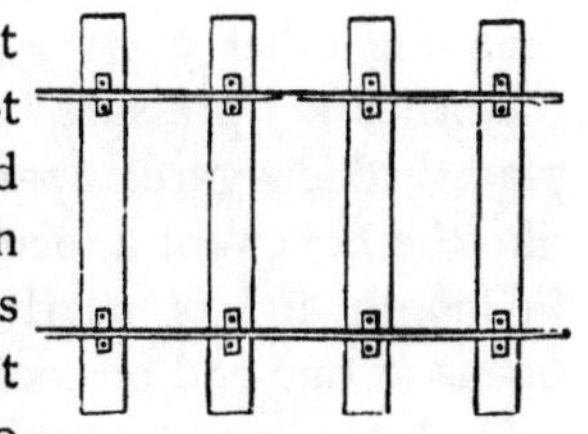

Wooden sleepers are now almost universally employed. They serve not only as a support for the chair and rails, but as ties for keeping the line in gauge. The material first selected was larch, this being considered the most durable wood for the purpose, next to oak. The trunk of the tree was split in two, and placed with the convex side downwards. Timber of larger size is now employed for sleepers. They are in general 9 feet long, 10 inches wide, and 5 thick. These dimensions help to give a large bearing surface on the ballast, and their length especially tends to maintain the steadiness of the track, and to prevent rolling. Deal is usually employed, because, although it is not so close or hard as some other woods, still when properly prepared is very durable, owing probably to the resin with which it is impregnated. In America that kind of pine known as "Hemlock," or "Hemlock Spruce," has been found the best, although white oak, chestnut, and all sorts of wood are used. Sleepers must always be straight, and of an uniform size; otherwise the running would be "poor," as it is called.

For some years past railway sleepers have been subjected to chemical treatment, which enables them better to resist moisture and consequent decay. The Midland Railway thus deals with all its sleepers at some works established for the purpose at Beeston Sidings, near Nottingham. Probably few travellers who have passed this spot have failed to notice the enormous stacks of sleepers piled here. In each stack there are from 1,200 to 1,700; and, as there are some 150 stacks, the number of sleepers on the ground will be over 200,000. They are all Memel timber or deal, and they are all "in the white"; though, before they leave these sidings, they will be as black as if they had been dipped in ink. They will, in fact, not only be placed in creosote, but creosote will be soaked into them—a process which will make them comparatively impervious to moisture and to decay. By means of steam pumps the air is first sucked out of the sleepers, and then creosote is forced into them.

We enter a little house. It contains an engine of 10 horse-power, the force of which can be made to work first one and then the other of two pumps. The one is a "vacuum" pump, the other a "pressure" pump. Just outside the engine-room, placed a few yards apart, are two large iron cylinders, in form like the boilers of a locomotive, only much larger, being 54 feet in length and of nearly 6 feet diameter. A great iron door opens at one end of each, and looking within we see two lines of rails 3 feet apart running along the bottom from the furthest end towards the door, and there they are connected with a line of railway of the same gauge that leads up the yard to the stacks of sleepers. Along these rails, drawn by a horse, come some "lorries" or "trams" with little low wheels, just high enough to clear the rails, and each tram loaded with nearly 50 sleepers, piled in such a form that the tram and its load just fits the shape of the cylinder. One after another several trams are brought to the mouth of the cylinder, and then are pushed along the line of rails inside. Including some 30, previously laid upon the floor to fill up interstices, there are now some 300 sleepers in all to be treated. The door of the cylinder is closed; the engine-man starts his vacuum engine, which will suck the air out of the cylinder, and he will continue this process till there is a vacuum equal to 16 pounds on the square inch. When this has been done, he opens a cock which communicates with a tank of creosote underneath, and thereupon the cylinder sucks up the creosote, so that, in about ten minutes, the cylinder of sleepers which, a few minutes before, was, so far as possible, a vacuum, has filled itself with creosote. But with this the engine-man is not content. He now gets his pressure pump to work, and forces creosote into the cylinder, and into the timber contained therein. The cylinder was, as we have already said, full; but the pump continues to force the fluid in until the pressure is as high as 110 pounds on the square inch, and no less than 750 gallons of the creosote have been forced not only into the cylinder but into the sleepers. This being accomplished, a valve is opened, and the surplus creosote—that is, all that has not soaked into the wood—is allowed to run out. The door of the cylinder is then opened; and the trollies, with their loads of sleepers, are drawn out. The whole process has occupied about two hours. Telegraph poles varying from 22 to 54 feet in length, are similarly treated.

What creosote is may perhaps be known to some through the painful lessons taught by the dentist in the treatment of teeth, when a single drop has a palpable effect. The treatment at Beeston Sidings is not, however, by drops, but by gallons, averaging from perhaps 1½ to 2½ gallons each sleeper, the best close-grained timber taking the least, and the open-grained "woolly" wood taking the most. The work is best done in dry weather. If the sleepers to be operated upon are very wet or are frozen hard, the results are only partially successful; ordinarily the timber is soaked "to the heart" with the creosote. The sleeper when well done should continue sound for 21 years. All the sleepers now and henceforth laid upon the Midland system have to come to Beeston Sidings for treatment. The creosote is brought in iron tanks built for the purpose from various chemical and gas works, each tank containing some 2,000 gallons. Ten or a dozen of these may be standing on a siding ready to deliver up their contents. The part of Beeston Sidings occupied by the creosote works, sleeper stacks, and so forth, is nearly a third of a mile in length.

The distance the sleepers are laid from one another depends upon the weight of the rails. On the South Western line they were originally laid 5 feet apart, and there were portions long remaining where the distance was 4 feet, giving 1⅛ square feet of bearing per running foot. The usual distance at which they are now laid is 3 feet from centre to centre. This gives 2½ square feet of bearing surface for each running foot of road. The lines of heavier traffic, as the Midland and North Western, have a distance of 2 feet 6 inches to 2 feet 9 inches between the centres of sleepers, giving in the first case 3 square feet, and in the second, 2·73 square feet of bearing per running foot. It has been remarked that, with a comparatively wide distance between sleepers, the ballast is more likely to be well packed than where they are close together.

The rails are secured to the sleepers by means of *chairs.* Chairs were formerly fixed to the stone blocks by wooden pegs; they are now held to the wooden sleepers by wooden trenails and iron spikes. The Midland Company use two of wood and two of iron for each chair; the wood giving the tighter grasp in holding the road to gauge, and the iron giving permanent strength and security. So firmly do the trenails hold, that, once inserted, they cannot be drawn out again; if it is necessary to release them, they must be cut off with a plug cutter.

RAILWAY CHAIR.

Chairs are of cast iron, the size and shape of the cavity corresponding with the form and dimensions of the rail; and though depending for their exact shape on the opinion of the engineer, their usual appearance is very similar. The first rails on the London and Birmingham line required a considerable elevation of the chair, which involved the danger of its being wrung from the block—an effect likely to follow in exact proportion to its height. The block was also more loosened in the ground by a high chair, and the cost of the continual repair thus arising, amounted at one time to half the wages expended in maintaining the way in general. The weight of the best chairs is 40 pounds each.

When the rail is laid in the chair, it is secured in its position by a wooden *key*. A key is a small piece of thoroughly seasoned oak, that fits into the cavity left between one side of the rail and one side of the chair. In order to give to the whole greater firmness, the key-wood is steamed, and then subjected to a pressure from a hydraulic machine. Its dimensions are thereby considerably reduced; and the key being retained in a drying-house till required, it is easily forced into the chair when necessary, while the moisture of the atmosphere, and the weather, make it expand so as to hold the rail with great tenacity. So great has been the expansive power of keys, that they have, in a few instances, been known to burst asunder the iron chairs in which they were secured.

CHAIR, KEY, AND RAIL.

On some of the earlier lines the wooden keys were found not to last more than about five years; and as they cost from £8 to £10 per thousand,—and upwards of seven thousand were used in a mile of railway with double track and sleepers of three feet apart,—the expense of renewal became an important item. To provide something more permanent, Mr. W. H. Barlow invented a kind of hollow or tubular key of wrought iron, which was made to press equally against the chair and the rail.

On the Great Western Railway a peculiar plan was for a long while adopted in laying down the sleepers and rails. The rails were bridge-shaped, with wide flanges or wings, and were secured to continuous bearings of wood, instead of across the usual transverse sleepers. It was considered that less noise, greater steadiness of motion, and diminished wear and tear, resulted. The longitudinal sleepers were of American pine, and were connected by transverse pieces.

At first the longitudinal sleepers were kept in their position by a novel contrivance. Piles of great size and length were driven into the road, and the transverse timbers were bolted to them. The piles were also regarded as holding the road firmly down. The timber used in a mile of this road was about 420 loads of pine, and 40 loads of hard-wood ; six tons of iron bolts and 30,000 wood screws were also required. The cost of the first portion, extending from London to Maidenhead, including laying, ballasting, sidings, driving, and all such work, amounted to £9,200 per mile.

Experience, however, proved that the piles, instead of affording support to the road, prevented it from settling into its natural bed, and the cross timbers had to be detached, and the road left to consolidate itself in the usual way, by the weights passing over it.

Various disadvantages were connected with the use of the longitudinal system. The bridge rail used with it was deficient in vertical stiffness ; and, as the timber could not make up for this want, the line sprang on the passage of a train. If the rail "gave," the timber of the sleeper must give too, and crush at the same time ; and cross-pieces of hard board had to be interposed between the rail and the sill, so as to secure a continuous floor for the rail. It was also thought that the *bite* of the engine-wheels on the rails of the longitudinal timbers was not so great as on the cross sleepers. On making a trial one frosty morning, Mr. Gray found that the engine slipped so much on a level piece of ground that the train could scarcely ascend an incline of 16 feet a mile ; but on reaching an incline laid with cross-sleepers, the "engine went up like an arrow." The slipping re-commenced on reaching another portion of the road laid with longitudinal timbers, and again ceased at the cross-laid road.

An important advantage secured by the cross sleeper road is that it gives a wider base of support to a passing train. The longitudinal road is only between five and six feet wide, whereas the cross sleepers are nine feet in length. The general results of experience have led to the longitudinal system being gradually abandoned, even on the Great Western, and the line is replaced, where required, by the cross-sleeper road. Eventually the same plan will be extended over the whole of that system. The rail now used by the Great Western is of steel, double-headed, eighty pounds weight to the yard. The alteration of the gauge of the Great Western has practically involved the alteration of almost everything else. It is said that "at the present day there is not left upon the line a single construction —either engine, carriage, wagon, wheel, or spring—as originally designed."

We may add that on the questions touching the details of the permanent way, there has been, and is, the keenest controversy among practical men. The differences have been as lively as between opinions on ecclesiastical questions. A gentleman in authority playfully remarked to us the other day: "Yes, on this subject we quarrel splendidly. We are quite ready to burn one another at the stake in our disputes about the permanent way."

The earthwork being made firm by its own ample width and by good drainage, "the ballast being deep, clean, and moderately binding, and the sleepers resting uniformly over a broad surface, we have a strong and permanent foundation, on which, if the rails are well fastened, the whole must inevitably lie smoothly and quietly. It is by permanent smoothness in a track that we avoid constant crushing and churning of the ballast; avoid crushing and rotting the sleepers; avoid breaking the chairs or other joint fastenings; avoid crushing and breaking rails; and that we also avoid the great increase of resistance and the largely increased wear and tear of machinery always accompanying a bad track."

How little was known and how much had to be learned with regard to rails may be shown by a single fact. At one time considerable anxiety was cherished as to the effect that frosty weather might produce in glazing the rails with ice. To avert this evil, the idea was seriously proposed, and in 1831 was protected by patent, of making the rails hollow, and, during the winter, filling them with hot water!

The weight and form of the rails employed on railroads have necessarily been a subject of increasing interest. How great the progress that has been made is seen by the fact that the Stockton and Darlington line was "laid with rails of cast iron joined at every four feet," and that the traveller found in passing over them "the jerks and jolts were frequent, audible, and sensible, resembling exactly the clicking of a mill-hopper."

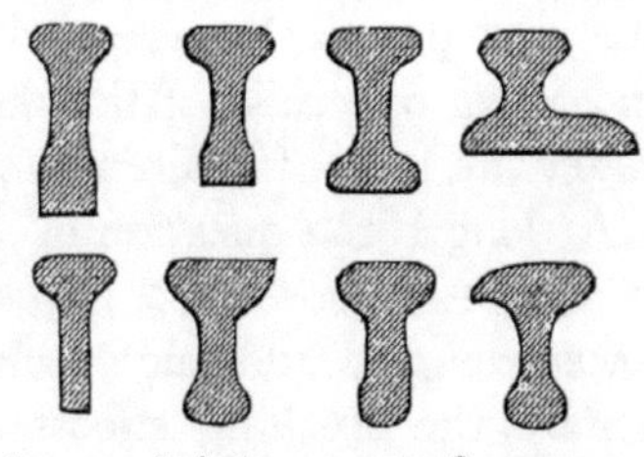

With regard to the shape of a rail, it should be such that the pressure of the passing wheel is as perpendicular downwards as possible; for, if directed sideways, there is not only a loss of power, but a tendency to throw the rails out of gauge and to throw the trains off the road.

An increase in the weight of the rails inevitably followed the increase of the weights they have had to carry. The rails first employed on the Liverpool and Manchester line weighed only thirty-five pounds a yard. But in the report of the directors, in 1834, it was stated that at particular parts of the road the rails were too weak for the heavy engines, and the speed at which they moved; and from the breakages that had taken place, the directors were of opinion that it was necessary to substitute rails weighing sixty pounds to the yard—a change which for a while was found perfectly satisfactory.

One of the most simple and effective improvements with regard to rails was the introduction of the fish-plate. It joins together the two ends of two rails. The word "fish" is probably employed here in the nautical sense. When a mast has been shot through or sprung, it is common to lay a piece of timber on each side of it, and to tie a rope firmly round; and this, in sailors' phraseology, is to "fish" the mast. So with the rails. A strong short plate of iron is placed on each side the two ends of the two rails, and

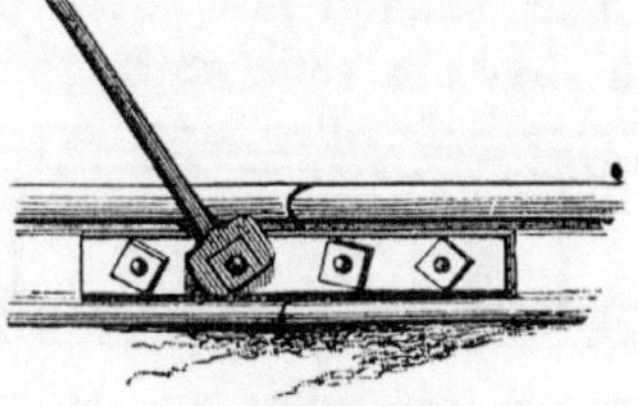

FISH-PLATES.

four bolts are passed through holes prepared for them in the plates and the rails. These bolts have a head at one end, and a nut is screwed on at the other, and the effect is that the two rails are now practically one, and that the line of rails from end to end is as one rail. Allowance has to be made for expansion under the heat of a summer sun, and contraction from frost.

At length the question of the use of wrought iron, and then of steel rails, rose into importance. It was seen that the enormous weights and high velocities which our railways had to sustain, the crushing effects of heavy mineral and merchandise trains, and also of monster locomotive expresses which weighed fifty or sixty tons, necessitated renewals of road of far greater strength than formerly sufficed. Deflection, lamination, splitting, and transverse fractures of rails were of frequent occurrence; and the difficulty of maintaining the gauge of the line not only increased, but created much of the oscillating motion which is so unpleasant to the traveller, and so destructive to the rolling stock. Not only were the rails worn and torn; they were literally ground by the application of the ponderous breaks required to check the trains on approaching stations, in descending inclines, and whenever needed. Hence, more than thirty years ago, Mr. Peter Barlow proposed the use of a cast-iron road, and he laid down sixty-two miles of it on the South Eastern Railway; and his brother, Mr. W. H. Barlow, recommended the adoption of self-supporting broad-flanged wrought-iron rails. This method at the time was regarded as superior to every other; greater evenness of the joints diminishing the wear and tear of the rolling stock. A section of these rails, showing also the way in which they were laid, is shown in the diagrams.

The demand now arose for steel rails. Some of these were laid down in 1862 at Rugby, Stafford, and Crewe stations, and they wore well. In May of that year some steel rails were placed at Camden, parallel with the best descriptions of iron rails; and so severe was the test that the latter soon gave way, while the former continue to show little appearance of wear. "We have found," said the chairman of the London and North Western, "the steel rails wearing actually

as long as thirty iron ones." Steel rails, made by the Bessemer process, have now almost everywhere superseded iron ones.

A curious fact with regard to rails has lately been observed. It is called the "creeping" of rails. It is said that on lines running north and south, the western rail "creeps" and wears out faster than the eastern rail; and the explanation is given in the motion of the earth as it turns from the west towards the east. Everything that has free motion is dragged after the whirling globe; every wind that blows and every tide that moves feels the influence, and the train going north or south is pulled over, and presses the one rail more heavily than the other. It ought, says the *Scientific American*, to be the stronger.

It is not enough that a railway should be made in all respects perfectly good, but it must also be kept good, and known to be kept good. Hundreds of miles of artificial roadway, carried through deep valleys and over mountain heights, spanning swift mountain streams and broad flooding rivers, and piercing ranges of hills, resting on the shifting sands of estuaries and oceans, and exposed to all the changes of night and day, of summer and winter, of rain and storm, of snow and drought, cannot but lay the so-called "permanent way" open to numerous and strange contingencies which must vitally concern the comfort, and even the safety, of everything that passes over it. The road may be slowly undermined by springs, or suddenly washed away by floods; the piers of bridges may be loosened or disturbed; the roofs of tunnels may cave in; or, if nothing worse, culverts and drains may get choked; the sleepers may be rotting; the keys may be loosened from the chairs; the road may become unsteady; and the carriages may move restlessly and uncomfortably forwards.

To avoid all this, or to repair any damage as it occurs, the permanent way of every line is divided into portions—according to the nature of the works—of from seventeen to thirty miles; is placed under the charge of an "overlooker," and is subdivided into "lengths," over each of which is a foreman and a gang of men. The duty of the foreman is to visit his portion of the line every morning before the first train passes, to see that the keys which hold the rails in the chairs are driven home; that the rails are properly in gauge; and carefully to inspect the line, the fences, and the works. The rules are thus expressed: "Each foreman or ganger must walk over his length of line every morning and evening on week-days, and, where passenger trains are run, once on Sundays, and tighten up all keys and other fastenings that may be loose; and he must examine the line, level, and gauge of the road, and the state of the joints, marking, and, if necessary, repairing such as are defective. Each foreman or ganger is required, in the event of a flood, to examine carefully the action of the water through the culverts and bridges on his length of line; and should he see any cause to apprehend danger to the works, he must immediately exhibit the proper signals for the trains to proceed cautiously, or to stop, as necessity may require, and inform the inspector thereof; and until the inspector arrives, he must take all the precautionary measures necessary for securing the stability of the line."

In case of serious repair being required, and one set of men being unable speedily to complete the work, a "relaying party," or the "break-down gang," is summoned.

All this work has, if possible, to be done without impeding the traffic, and so skilfully is this arranged that many miles of rails can be relaid in a very short space of time, and without public inconvenience. This is often extremely difficult, since it is the roads that are most used that most need repair. "On the Nottingham and Lincoln line," recently remarked a Midland Railway inspector, "we have lifted a mile of road in a day; but what are you to do with a line over which a train passes every quarter of an hour?" In all such cases, however, every precaution is adopted. "While the men are engaged in this work they are protected by the red flag, and attended by an official who informs them of the approach of a train, when, if any piece of rail has been taken up, it is immediately laid down again, and temporarily secured in its place for the train to pass over." In like manner the driver of the engine is warned before he starts on his journey, and, if necessary, by fog-signals, of the proximity of the workmen, and he slackens speed before he reaches the spot. The men stand clear of the rails, and on the outside of the line, and the train passes on its way, probably without any of the passengers being aware of what had been going on, or of the break that had happened in the line but a few minutes before.

Among the minor enemies of the permanent way are the

mouse, the mole, and the toad—the foes, as Virgil told us eighteen centuries ago, of the threshing floor; and to prevent the burrowing up of the ballast, and the choking of drains, men are employed in some districts, who emblazon over their cottage doors the important title of "Ratcatcher to the London and North Western Railway."

One special addition has been made by the London and North Western Railway to the furniture of its permanent way, by means of which, at certain points, the engines are able to feed themselves while at full speed. The plan is as follows: "An open trough, about 440 feet long, is laid longitudinally between the rails. Into this trough, which is filled with water, a dip-pipe or scoop attached to the bottom of the tender of the running train is lowered; and, at a speed of fifty miles an hour, as much as 1,070 gallons of water are scooped up in the course of a few minutes. The first of such troughs was laid down between Chester and Holyhead, to enable the express mail to run the distance of 84¾ miles in two hours and five minutes without stopping; and similar troughs have since been laid down at Bushey, near London, at Castlethorpe, near Wolverton, and at Parkside, near Liverpool. At these four troughs about 130,000 gallons of water are scooped up daily."

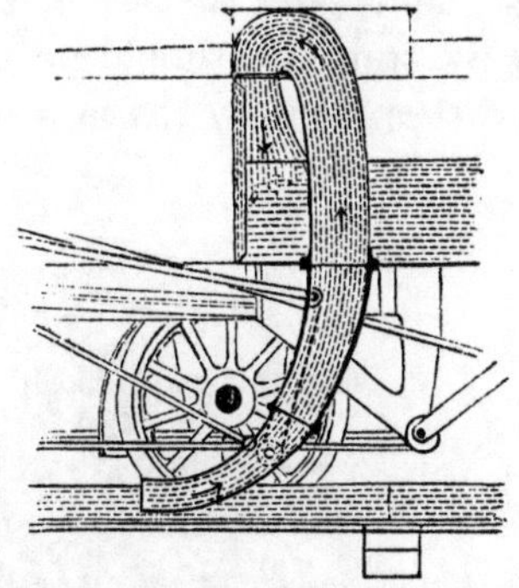

PICKING UP WATER FROM FEED TROUGH.

A railway being completed, and about to be devoted to public use, is opened. How this is sometimes done we are able to tell from our own experience.

"All right, sir," said the engine-driver, as his eye rested on a brief official order we had handed to him, and which bore a signature which has talismanic powers with all Midland Railway people. "All right, sir; we shall be off directly." The train, spic and span new—the lot worth perhaps £5,000—was standing one Monday morning on the new rails by the new platform, under the new glass and iron shed of the recently enlarged station at Bedford, and was about to take its first run to London; in fact, to open the line for passenger traffic. Being afflicted with what Mr. Cobden would have called "a craze" for railways, we had been seized with a passion somewhat akin to that which animated the breasts of those little boys who, on the opening of the new Westminster Bridge, ran a neck-and-neck race that they might achieve the distinction of being the first to cross, and we had resolved to be the first of that great army of the British public who would pass and repass upon this new railway between the Midlands and the metropolis. The authorities, with we suppose an amiable consideration for the eccentricities of literary men, gave the requisite consent; and so we mounted the engine with a sense of satisfaction that by our very position on the train we should be the first unofficials by the first train that ever went by the new route from Bedford to London.

ELSTOW.

The superintendent of the company, Mr. Needham, and Mr. Vaughan, from the locomotive department, had joined us. The time was up. The driver's hand was on the lever, and the signal to start had just been given, when the stout lady—the inevitable stout lady who generally appears on railway platforms at the last moment—hove in sight. The fireman growled, the guard shouted, we were all delayed; but eventually, perhaps somewhat hurriedly, the lady was stowed away somewhere—nobody cared where—and the train was off.

We crossed the sluggish Ouse near the great engineering establishment of Messrs. Howard; went by a bridge over the London and North Western line from Bletchley to Bedford;

saw on our left the historic village of Elstow, the birthplace of "the immortal tinker"; and were soon on the long straight bank that leads to Ampthill tunnel and station. At Ampthill all the little world of curiosity or of idleness has gathered to be spectators of our triumph. The driver looks at his watch; the fireman at the time-table; and it is announced that though we left Bedford two minutes late (it was the stout lady who detained us), we are now in time. "Ah," says the driver with a knowing smile, "I'd sooner pick up one minute than drop two." The passengers are in; Mr. Needham reports progress; and again we start. Soon we are running on the

LUTON.

summit of another long embankment, from which we can see the line far before us, and the country far around us. Occasionally a group of platelayers part to the right and left for us to pass; the village girls pause upon the country road, and shade their bright faces from the sun as they gaze upon the first train that has ever run that way; the old farmer rests his arms upon the top of his homestead gate, and thinks perhaps how things have changed since he "wur a boy"; the larks fly off with long and quivering wing; and now and then a partridge rises and whirrs away. A short cutting, and we are at the pretty village of Harlington. "Very good time," remarks our friend of the loco. department; "three minutes to spare."

We have scarcely left Harlington when right and left we see the long line of breezy chalk hills which tell us we are approaching "the backbone of England." The Great Northern crosses it at Hitchen, the North Western at Tring; but there is a dip in the range before us, and we seem, as we run round a hill artificially scarped and terraced, called Wanlud's Bank, as if we should slip between them. But though the engineers have doubtless done their best, they have had to make two deep

ST. ALBANS.

cuttings in the chalk, a lesser and a larger, to let us through; and at the southern end of the latter we see the signals and buildings of Leagrave. We now cross the ancient Icknield Way, which Roman soldiers built, and which Roman feet have trodden. We see on the right the Great Northern branch from Dunstable and Luton to Hatfield, and in a few minutes we descry the suburban villas that climb the hills that rise around the thriving town of Luton. Here a large number of people have come to bid us welcome, and to hail our departure.

We are just starting, when some one rushes up to the engine-driver and exclaims: "There goes the Great Northern train, and they say they'll be in London first." We looked, and certainly the Great Northern train was in full cry. Our driver smiled as he turned on the steam, evidently not much affected by the challenge; but our less responsible stoker pulls back the fiery jaws of the furnace, and on to the seething sea of flame he flings fresh coals with undissembled satisfaction. Not far from us for a considerable distance runs the single line of the Great Northern branch; there we could observe its train hotly pursuing its onward course, and then we lost sight of it, and at length reached St. Albans.

We are descending a long incline of 1 in 176; and, though the steam is only half on, and the lever is sometimes at "SHUT," we go faster than before. At Radlett we pause, partly to take in water—"Just a sup," says the driver, "to make sure," though there is plenty in the tender; we meet the first down passenger train, and then Elstree station is before us. We enter Elstree tunnel, 1,060 yards in length, and soon after are under the green glass roof of the Mill Hill station. Here the fireman wiles away the momentary delay by opening wide the furnace door, inserting therein a long iron hoe, and raking to and fro the seething mass of white-hot coals and red eddying flames. He then moistens his arid clay from a tin can which he has kept warm upon a little shelf near the fire—a vessel to which he and the driver have frequently repaired during the journey up, and the ownership of which seems to be held in a sort of joint stock coffee company (limited).

Fifteen minutes more, and we are in Belsize tunnel, and overhead spreads the ancient demesne of Belsize. Haverstock Hill and Kentish Town stations come next, and at last we pause for a moment to change our engine for one that consumes most of its own smoke and steam, and is intended for special use on the Metropolitan. At Moorgate Street we say good-bye to our companions in travel. "If the historian of the future," we tell them, "asks you who opened the London and Bedford Railway, mind you tell them the truth. It was not you, gentlemen, you are only the officers of the Midland Company. We represent the great British public. We pay for everything. There are lots of the great British public in those carriages behind; but we are first, and we opened the line from Bedford to London." And so, with cheery words, we parted.

CHAPTER IX.

Paddington Terminus.—"A Certain Field."—Preamble of the Act.—Station and Staff.—Euston.—St. Pancras.—Lost Luggage Office.—Variety of Articles Lost.—The Hat Shelf.—Curiosities of Lost Luggage.—The Departing Train.—Passengers.—Intermediate Stations.—Woburn.—A Lonely Station.—The Station Master and the Keeper.—York Station.—Names of Stations.—Station Notices.—A Passing Train.—Strange Movements of Engines.—A Group on the Platform.—Arrival of Train and Departure.—Maintaining the British Constitution.—Refreshment Rooms.—Wolverton.—Swindon.—Rugby Junction.—Good Digestion.—Wagon Loading Gauge.—Strange Visitors at Stations.—Points.—Crossings and Sidings.—A Railway Siding.—Toton Sidings.—Ingenuity of Inventors.—Home Signals.—Distant Signals.—Junction Signals.—A Country Signal Box.—A Station Signal Box.—Interlocking Signals.—Cannon Street Station.—Cannon Street Interlocking Signals.—Cannon Street Signal Platform.—Messrs. Saxby and Farmer's Instruments.—Seeing Through a Brick Bridge.—Block System.—Block System on Metropolitan Line.—Cost of Block Signal Machines.—The Lamp Room.—Fogmen.—Fog Signalling.—Fog Signals.—Construction of Railway Signals.—Railway Telegraphy.

ERE you are, sir!" is the somewhat self-contradictory declaration of the London cabman, who, at his stand, by a preternatural quickness and accuracy of intuition, divines that we need his services. He snatches away the piece of sacking that is supposed to retain the caloric in the loins of his horse, goes through a series of evolutions in order to bring his cab alongside the kerb-stone, a process which could not be adequately described without the aid of diagrams, and which the uninitiated might consider was for the purpose of driving the horse in at the open door of the vehicle, instead of putting the passenger there. "Paddington terminus" is our only remark, and in a few minutes we are at our destination. Railway stations are of all sorts and sizes, from the little summer-house of one private station on the Brecon and Swansea line, to the stately proportions, vast (and yet, generally, insufficient) area, and enormously costly structures of the metropolitan termini.

Paddington station is one of the earliest of these. Paddington itself is described by Mistress Priscilla Wakefield, in 1814, as "a village situated on the Edgeware Road, about a mile from London." In 1801, when the Grand Junction Canal was opened, and the first barge, full of passengers, arrived from Uxbridge at the Paddington basin, bells were rung, flags were hung, and cannon were fired. But Charles Knight mentions that even so recently as at that time "only one stage coach ran from the then suburban village of Paddington to the city, and it was never filled," and that, to beguile the travellers at the several resting places on their journey, "Miles's Boy" told tales and played on the fiddle. How great the change from all this, when, in 1853, William Robins, the historian of Paddington, wrote that "a city of palaces has sprung up in twenty years," and that "a road of iron with steeds of steam" was in use.

For, meanwhile, important events had occurred. Among these an Act of Parliament had passed, the preamble of which is worth reading: "Whereas the making of a railway from Bristol, to join the London and Birmingham Railway near London, and also branches to Trowbridge and Bradford, in the county of Wilts, would be of great public advantage, not only by opening an additional certain and expeditious communication between the cities and towns aforesaid, but also by improving the existing communication between the metropolis and the western districts of England, the south of Ireland and Wales, and whence, etc." *

But the junction with the London and Birmingham Railway, which was proposed "in a certain field lying between the Paddington Canal and the turnpike-road leading from London to Harrow on the western side of the General Cemetery," was never made. The directors of the London and Birmingham did not see their way to unite in a joint station for the two lines, and so each Company took an independent course,

* Act of Incorporation of Great Western Railway, 5 and 6 William IV., c. 14, section 107.

and as one result the two termini at Paddington and at Euston were erected.

The original cost of the Paddington passenger terminus was £650,000; but for many years the accommodation provided was only "make shift." Not till 1854 was the present terminus built. The style is a mixture of Italian and Arabesque; it stands in an area of seventy acres; it has an extreme length of nearly 800 feet; and it is spanned by three semi-elliptical roofs and three transepts. Between the end of the passenger station and the West London junction—a distance of about a mile and a-half—there are twelve miles of running lines and thirty-eight miles of sidings. A staff of more than 3,000 officers and men is stationed at Paddington, including the chiefs of the service. Nearly 300 trains pass in or out of the station every day, and about 11,000,000 of passengers use it every year.

We might describe other metropolitan stations: that at Euston Square, with its Grecian propyleum and stately vestibule; and the Midland at St. Pancras, with its gigantic roof of two and a half acres of glass, 240 feet across, rising 100 feet above the rail level; a station in the construction of which 60,000,000 of bricks, 9,000 tons of iron, and 80,000 cubic feet of dressed stone were employed. There is the enlarged station of the London and South Western Company at Waterloo; and the new Liverpool Street terminus of the Great Eastern, that covers ten acres of ground, and has an extreme length of 2,000 feet. There are also the stations at the provincial cities of the great railway companies, where enormous outlay has been incurred. At Manchester, for instancc, the London and North Western Company has spent £2,000,000, at Liverpool probably £4,000,000, and at Birmingham £1,500,000, and yet further enlargement has become necessary.

Among the various departments of a principal station, there is one which has special interest for the curious—the Lost Luggage Office. "Gentlemen who *will* look out of the windows of railway carriages to see 'what's the matter,' and get their hats knocked off and left behind at the rate of fifty miles an hour; young ladies who *will* have the windows open and allow their parasols to go ballooning down the line; dandies who won't look after their own luggage, but leave it to 'those fellows, the porters, you know,' and so lose it; wives who *will* terminate their journeys at the terminus in their husbands' arms," regardless of the treasures and the trifles they brought with them; commercial travellers who forget their samples; in short, everybody who misses, or forgets, or leaves behind, or loses anything on a railway, has to have it taken care of for him in what may be called the "waif and stray" department of a railway company.

The variety of articles thus left in the temporary or permanent possession of the railway authorities is surprising. There is the satchel of a young lady—a young lady, we presume, of the period. She had been accustomed, it appears, to travel by herself to the south of France and Italy, and her friends sometimes wondered at her courage: the contents of her satchel, perhaps, explained the problem. They consisted of some biscuits, a bunch of keys, some Eau de Cologne, and a loaded revolver. Not long ago, chancing to wait in the clerks' offices of the general manager's department of a great railway company, we overheard a letter read that told the sorrows of a lady whose pork pie had, on a journey, been lost. Perhaps some sisterly hand had raised the crust to its perilous height, had filled it with the savoury contents, and had adorned the superstructure. She suffered keenly a double wrong: her larder had been robbed and her love had been wounded; and her righteous indignation found adequate expression. What right had the railway company to lose her pie, and to rend the bonds of family affection? No right at all. And though the general manager might have even more momentous affairs to determine, the errant pie was searched for and was brought back from its wanderings, and we hope ample compensation was made for its staleness, to say nothing of "consequential damages."

Other articles in the Lost Luggage Office tell a tale of the idiosyncrasies and eccentricities of their owners. A shawl, a handkerchief, or an umbrella may easily be left behind; but how is it that one gentleman has forgotten a pair of leather hunting breeches, another his bootjack, one soldier his kit, another his regimental coat, a Scotchman his bagpipes? Had the owner of "a very superior astronomical telescope, in mahogany case complete" abandoned the study of the heavens? How many children must have had a defective toilet when so many pinafores, frocks, bibs, and petticoats were left behind.

Other toilets, too, seem to have suffered, since pairs of stockings, and odd ones, skirts and stays in abundance have been lost, and unasked for. What a strange conglomeration of other articles have at other times been unclaimed: "feather beds and casks of cement, galvanized iron coppers and childrens' chairs, registered stoves and oil paintings, spurs and crutches, spades and pomade, books and cradles, perambulators and trowsers, enough in their variety to furnish a house and to fill a shop." Some years ago, an announcement was made in the papers that at Swindon station "a pair of bright bay carriage horses, about sixteen hands high, with black switch tails and manes," had been left by some one of the name of Hibbert; and that unless they were claimed and expenses paid on or before the 12th day of May following, the horses "would be sold to pay expenses." And when the day came they *were* sold.

"But for strangeness of variety," said Sir Francis Head, years ago, when he had visited a Lost Luggage Office, "commend me to the hat-shelf, for nothing can exceed the heterogenous jumble of rank, station, character, and indicative morality which that conglomeration suggests. Here a dissipated-looking four-and-nine leans its battered side against the prim shovel of a church dignitary; there a highly polished Parisian upper-crust is smashed under the weight of a carter's slouch. On one side the torn brim of a broad straw strays into the open crown of a brand new beaver. Some bear the crushing marks of the wheels of a luggage train, or the impression of the moistened clay of an embankment; others are neat, trimly brushed, and show how carefully they have been hung up in the first-class carriage, while the owner inducted his caput into an elegant templar, or fascinating foraging cap, and how he carelessly left it behind. Boys' and mens', quakers' and soldiers', carters' and lords', clergymen's and sporting men's, are all ranged side by side, or thrown together higgledy-piggledy, hurly-burly, topsy-turvy, in a confused conglomeration. There are first-class hats, consisting of sporting, clerical, military, and best beavers; second-class, all neat and well-brushed; and third-class, composed of carters', carpenters', valets', and haymakers'."

Whatever may have been the observations of Sir Francis Head, affairs have altered since his day. "Perhaps," as our attendant sceptically remarked, "the hats he saw were in his imagination. We've only very common-place things here," he remarked; "umbrellas, sticks, wrappers, and such sort of things. Whatever is found in the carriages at Euston, and whatever the other stations can't find an owner for, they are all sent up here. Everything we have is entered in this register. This column tells the 'date when found,' the next 'where found,' 'station no.' (which means the number of articles sent here from that station), 'depôt no.' (that is, the number of articles received in this depôt, which is 5,376 this year. Last year we had 18,000). They're all common-place things," he said, passing his finger down the columns. "Here is a white cashmere muffler, a small roll of letters, specs in case, leather purse containing two postage stamps, *2d.*, and a first-class ticket from Chester to Dublin, a string of beads used by Roman Catholics. Do we ever have anything strange?" he continued. "Once I had. I opened a square box sent from Preston, lifted up some straw, and found a dead child. When I touched it, it sent a cold thrill through me. It was naked—a little child with golden curls. Yes, we sent to the coroner. The mother had poisoned it with laudanum; mother was found out and convicted."

But matters concerning lost luggage are not confined to a particular station, or even to a particular company. The lost article may have passed on to one, or even on to several "foreign" lines, may have to be searched for far and wide, and the assistance of the Clearing House may have to be invoked. The number of articles here reported upon as missing are about 1,000 a day. "Statisticians," says a pleasant writer, "anxious to analyse the varieties of human blundering, will be interested to know that the most fertile cause of the miscarriage of luggage is that which brought Lady Audley to grief in Miss Braddon's famous story. It is the habit of leaving old labels on trunks and portmanteaus. Terrible mistakes are brought about by this practice, such as that which took a Cabinet Minister's luggage to Belfast, while he landed at Killarney. Mr. Childers recovered his property through the Clearing House, but it is often difficult to track a brown leather portmanteau, especially if it have neither conspicuous mark nor initials. Both of the latter, however, are made, for the moment, useless by an old label which misleads the porters at an important junction. Judicious travellers not only have their initials and some device in red or white painted on their trunks, but are very particular to tear or wash off old labels. Those who have not yet commenced that sensible practice should begin at once."

"I don't know how it is," recently remarked a London station-master, "but there is comparatively little luggage lost now-a-days, or if it is lost, it is usually soon recovered. I suppose that it is because passengers are more intelligent or more careful than they used to be." "Or, perhaps," we replied, "it is because railway companies take better care of luggage, and put it in vans or lockers for its special destination; instead of, as formerly, piling it up on the roofs of carriages, covering it over with tarpaulin, and letting it take its chance of being sorted right." But whether it is to be put to the credit of the public or of the company, the reassuring fact remains.

But let us now go down to the platform of the terminus, and see what always has some degree of interest—a departing train. It is filling; let us glance at the passengers who are seated. The first-class carriage has a characteristic assortment of inmates. The middle seats are occupied by two stout gentlemen, one of whom is nearly hidden behind a copy of a morning paper he is reading. Their travelling companions are a young member of an old family in the north, a lady and her daughter. The second-class or third-class passengers are of a somewhat different genus. One, a commercial traveller, puts on a red cap while the train is alongside the platform, and will be nearly asleep before he is out of the yard, for he is an old stager, and economises his strength. The young people here are more communicative, and sometimes facetious. They will perhaps joke about the engine; say that they prefer having their backs to the "horses"; or talk about a "feed of coke"; and when the engine whistles, will exclaim pathetically, "Poor creature!" These puns, mild as they are, are laughed at by the good-tempered passengers as if they had never been heard before. Others of the travellers, having a turn of mind for the agreeably tragic, will talk about some dreadful railway accident, or tell of the disaster to the mail train which left York for London on the night of the 31st of February last, and has never since been heard of. These allusions, of course, produce a gratifying effect on the mind of the anxious lady, who is always to be found in one of the carriages of every train. She was recently in distress about her box, and afraid that if left for a moment unguarded on the platform, it might be pocketed by some one, though it weighs a good half-hundredweight; and now it is a source of solicitude to her because it cannot be put under the seat. Finally it is put in a remote van, where the lady would like to go too.

The train is about to start. The "five minutes" bell has rung; the last places are occupied; friends prepare for their adieus; and the last parcels are hastily deposited in the train. The guards take their places at the beginning and end of the train, and—if it is a long one—at the middle. The station-master sees that all the passengers are accommodated, and that

WOBURN STATION.

the luggage is deposited, before he gives the signal to start. The engine-driver stands with his hand upon the "regulator," and the fireman leans over and watches for the final order. The whistle shrieks; the train is in motion; and with increasing speed it rolls away, and is soon out of sight.

Intermediate stations are of all sorts and sizes, and their accommodation and architectural pretensions also vary. Sometimes they are handsome or heavy, sometimes neat or pretty, and sometimes the characteristics or materials of the neighbourhood have determined their structure and style. The Woburn station, on the Bletchley and Bedford line, was one of the earliest that might be called picturesque.

"Yes, this station is lonely, as you say, very," remarked a station-master to us in a beautiful but solitary valley, in a mountain district. "It is sometimes difficult to get anything even to eat or drink. The farmers kill their own sheep and divide it among them, and I have sometimes to ask one of the guards to

YORK STATION.

bring me something all the way from —— ; and I perhaps give them a rabbit in return for their trouble." "A rabbit!" we exclaimed; "how do you get rabbits?" "Oh, we often get them, and game too," he replied. "The dook preserves the game on both sides of the line; but it gets caught by passing trains, and birds fly against the telegraph wires and lame themselves. We sometimes find wounded or dead birds on the line." "And do the keepers consent to your having them?" we asked. "Well, he returned, "I did have a little bother with one of them some time ago. I had been down to the distant signal, and found a hare on the line, and was carrying it home, when I saw the keeper over the hedge. 'You've no business with that there hare,' he shouted to me; 'it's the dook's.' 'Then,' I said, 'if it's the dook's, the dook had better come and fetch it.' He threatened me a bit, but he didn't come on to the line for it. I paid him out for his interference; for a few days afterwards I saw him coming along the line out at the southern end of the tunnel. 'You're on trespass,' I called. 'You can't come this way.' And I made him go all the way back again, out at the other end of the long tunnel. Since then we have been on better terms. I let him cross the line over a fence when he wants, and he lets me have what game I find without *his* interference. We live and let live, and we had need."

Of intermediate stations, one of the latest and the handsomest is that of the North Eastern Company at York. It is near the city walls. Here, having completed the first portion of its journey of 189 miles in three hours and fifty-five minutes, the "Scotchman" stops for half an hour to dine.

The work of intermediate stations has characteristics of its own, and they are, by one at all interested in railways, worth noticing. It is pleasant to watch the different trains come sweeping up to the platform, or rushing through the station with a *rrh-oar* that makes the ground tremble beneath their iron tread.

"First the shrill whistle, then the distant roar
The ascending cloud of steam, the gleaming brass,
The mighty moving arm; and on amain
The mass comes thundering like an avalanche o'er
The quaking earth; a thousand faces pass—
A moment, and are gone, like whirlwind sprites,
Scarce seen; so much the roaring speed benights
All sense and recognition for a while;
A little space, a minute, and a mile.
Then look again, how swift it journeys on;
Away, away, along the horizon
Like drifted cloud, to its determined place;
Power, speed, and distance melting into space."

Now come long luggage trains, pursuing their heavy way with a business-like stolidity of demeanour perfectly compatible with their great weight and respectability; and then short dapper trains emerge from some out-of-the-way part of the establishment, and take a spurt up or down the line, as if to try their wind and limbs. Occasionally a mysterious looking engine will make its appearance, squealing, hissing, and roaring—now enveloping itself in a cloud of steam, and then rattling away as if ashamed of itself; now advancing a few yards, as if pawing the ground and wanting to start somewhere in great haste; now backing again under the curbing hand of the driver, who restrains its hot breath and life; then, with a succession of curious puffs and pantings, running backwards down the course, or turning into a siding, evidently with something very distressing upon its mind; and at last finishing its evolutions by spluttering and dashing out of sight, as if in search of something which it had dropped on the road, or as if madly intent upon suicide.

Some travellers are dropping in at this intermediate station, for a train is nearly due. They beguile the interval by strolling up and down the platform, perhaps pausing now and then to study an advertisement on the wall, possibly the map, as Anthony Trollope says, "of some new Eden—some Eden in which an irregular pond and a church are surrounded by a multiplicity of regular villas and shrubs—till the student feels that no considerations, even of health or economy, could induce him to live there." Glance round at that group of travellers. There is a country-woman, with a bandbox slung on her arm by an ancient looking silk handkerchief of gaudy colours. A porter is wheeling her luggage to the point where the break-van will stand when the train arrives; and, seated on a hamper, is her grandson, a chubby-faced baby, who stares fixedly at everybody and everything, and who kicks his approbation of the scene, so far as the marvellous swaddling of shawls in which he is enveloped will admit. There is also a stout, business looking, middle-aged gentleman, who has driven up with a well-bred horse. He is the squire of a neighbouring village, a rural potentate, who is going to a large town, where, instead of being regarded with reverence, he will be nobody. A few tradespeople, a papa and his two boys whom he is taking to school, a governess going home for a holiday, and some farmers and cattle-jobbers, complete the picture.

But the train is in sight. It has just passed the curve, and in the extreme distance a white line of cloud appears to rise from the ground, and gradually passes away into the atmosphere.

Soon a light murmur falls upon the ear; the murmur gradually becomes louder; the cloud rises to a more fleecy whiteness, or, as it is tossed aside by the wind, reveals part of the train. The steam is shut off, and the train, with slackened speed, approaches the platform. The doors are opened for those who are coming out or getting in; the baby is handed to a kind-hearted gentleman, who proffers his services as an extempore nursemaid; the seats are taken; and very soon all is ready again for the start.

Meanwhile, the engine has to take in a supply of water; and accordingly the fireman mounts the tender, pulls round the funnel of the water-crane, and, directing it over the tender, turns on the water and obtains the necessary allowance. The engine-driver is also performing a series of gymnastic evolutions under and around the locomotive, using what looks like an oil teapot with a long spout, pouring the lubricating fluid into secret joints and out-of-the-way holes; and then, mounting his engine in a free-and-easy style, he stands ready for his journey.

While these processes are going on, one of the men passes along the line of carriages, in order to supply the axles of the wheels with the well-known yellow grease. This is composed of tallow, palm-oil, soda, and water—the proportions of the combination varying with the season of the year.

The train starts. The platforms are soon deserted, and in the contrast of the recent bustle with the present solitude we think of Campbell's "Last Man." From the station-yard "the arrivals" are also disappearing. The old omnibus is just off. The little baker is briskly trudging along the turnpike; the horse-dealer, who lives near the Blue Lion, is talking confidentially with a neighbour about a certain party who has been bidding for the bay mare; and the large-bodied one-horse fly, with its corpulent rat-tailed steed, which trotted so briskly to the station for its master, who was expected but has not arrived, now lags homeward with the peculiar slowness of gait characteristic of a disappointed vehicle.

Some of the names of railway stations are odd, but more so in America than in England. Stinking Wells is the cheerful title of a station upon a new railway in Nevada; and, it is said, that the brakemen take pleasure in shouting it out "distinkly." And it is necessary to be distinct, especially in some parts of the States. Anywhere, and especially in those wide latitudes, a mistake in a name may lead to inconvenience. Thus, we are told, "An old lady was going from Brookfield to Stamford, and took a seat in the train for the first and last time in her life. During the ride the train was thrown down an embankment. Crawling from beneath the *débris* unhurt, she spied a man sitting down, but with his legs held down by some heavy timber. 'Is this Stamford?' she anxiously inquired. 'No, madam,' was the reply, 'this is a catastrophe.' 'Oh!' she cried, 'then I hadn't oughter got off here.'"

The walls of stations are often occupied by official instructions for travellers, but sometimes they are more useful than interesting. Railway companies are required to set forth the fares to and from all stations to which tickets may be taken. These are generally sufficiently explicit, but we have known them to be elevated so greatly that no one, unless he was very long sighted or eight feet high, could read them. The following notice errs in another respect. It is quoted from the *North Wales Chronicle*, in 1875, and is a copy of a notice put over a booking office at a station on a Welsh railway:—"List of booking.—You passengers must be careful. For have them level money for ticket and to apply at once for asking tickets when will booking window open. No tickets to have after departure of the train."

At many intermediate stations, as well as termini, there is a department of great importance devoted to the proper maintenance of the British constitution. It has been said by those who have studied the noble character of John Bull, that the only certain way in which to keep him in perfectly good humour is to keep him *quite full*. This operation is delicately denominated "taking refreshment;" and our railway managers, having observed that nature thus abhors a vacuum, and that the doctrine of the plenum is, in England, generally accepted, have taken care to promote the good temper of their travellers by the establishment of those most characteristic railway institutions—"refreshment rooms."

In the earlier days of railway enterprise, when it was considered to be a serious matter to undertake a journey as far as from London to Birmingham, the refreshment room at Wolverton achieved renown. Who, then, had not talked about Wolverton's hot coffee, with the five minutes allowed for its consumption, and the various contrivances necessary for drinking it within the time? Who had not laughed at the way in which, when he asked for milk with which to cool the scalding beverage, the amiable attendant remorselessly filled up his cup with *boiling* milk? Who had not heard of the visit of Sir Francis Head, who described the row of youthful handmaidens, who stood behind bright silver urns, silver coffee-pots, silver teapots, piles of sandwiches, heaps of buns and pies and cakes; and who, though they had only seven right hands, with but very little fingers at the end of each, managed, with such slender assistance, in the short space of a few minutes, to extend those hands and withdraw them so often, sometimes to give a cup of tea, sometimes to receive half a crown, then to give an old gentleman a plate of soup, then to drop another lump of sugar into his nephew's coffee cup, and then to receive change out of sixpence for four "ladies' fingers"? The wonderful consumption at Wolverton of all things eatable and drinkable was also recorded, including 45,000 bottles of stout—sometimes for extra stout consumers,—56,000 queen cakes, and 182,000 Banbury cakes, and 85 pigs and piglings who, having been tenderly treated from their infancy, "were impartially promoted, by seniority, one after another, into an indefinite number of pork pies." It has indeed been whispered that the lively narrative of the baronet was perused with special interest by the potentates of the London and North Western Company at Euston Square, and that the rent of the tenant at Wolverton was, at the earliest moment, considerably augmented. We have no doubt, however, that the rumour is a slander, and that personages so august as railway directors would be incapable of availing themselves of what can only be regarded as a literary indiscretion!

But perhaps one of the most remarkable facts anent such establishments is that the rent paid by the tenant of the Swindon refreshment rooms to the Great Western Railway Company is just *one penny a year.* The place was built by the original tenant when the company was short of money, and these were the terms agreed upon. All trains are required to stop here ten minutes. Fortune after fortune has been made by the successive owners.

The writer of "Mugby Junction" was good enough to inform

us that it was to the extirpation of the tyranny under which the British traveller had groaned at the railway refreshment room that that publication was especially devoted. "The pork and veal pies, with their bumps of delusive promise, and their little cubes of gristle and bad fat; the scalding infusion satirically called tea; the stale bath buns, with their veneering of furniture polish; the sawdusty sandwiches, so frequently and so energetically condemned,"—all these were as the outcome of the critic's irony effectually doomed. How the management of refreshment rooms came about in former days he also tells us. The last time, he says, we were behind the scenes at a railway refreshment bar, we were initiated into the story of the sorrows of the broken-down coachman of an esteemed friend. More than seventy years of age, rheumatic, and past work, interest was obtained with certain railway directors, and when, eventually, the post of purveyor of the station was charitably secured for "old Robert," there was sincere rejoicing. "None of us ever thought of his fitness for the post. Neither I nor my fellow townsmen thought of the railway station as a place at which eating and drinking was a possibility for ourselves, or of the ordinary travellers who passed through and lunched or dined there. But the kindly face and venerable figure of old Robert were local institutions; and if, by selling muddy beer, fiery sherry, and stale buns to strangers, his last days could be made easy, who would be churlish enough to cavil at his appointment." Yet charity to old Robert meant cruelty to the public, and the results were painful to many and unsatisfactory to all. So it must be confessed by all who are not endowed with digestive powers like those of a solicitor from St. Neots with whom we once travelled. During a pause of the train at Leicester station, he alighted, and brought back into the carriage a "hunch" of pork pie, and a small flask of sherry. "Can you digest that?" sceptically inquired a fellow traveller. "Digest it!" was the reply. "Do you think, sir, that I allow my stomach to dictate to me what I think proper to put into it?"

Among the minor appurtenances of a railway station is the wagon loading gauge. It is employed to prevent trucks being loaded so high as to touch the arch of a bridge or of a tunnel under which it may have to run. It consists simply of a frame, with a bell attached to it: if the loaded wagon passes freely underneath without touching the bell, it will run safely under any arch or through any tunnel on the line.

Other visitors besides travellers sometimes visit railway stations. Not long ago a wagon of coals had been standing in the station at Kirkby Moorside, and in the wagon a wagtail had built her nest, in which again a cuckoo laid an egg. The wagtail brought off her strange brood, and the cuckoo—a fine bird—came into the possession of one of the company's officials. The fact that a wagon of coals would remain at the station long enough for a bird to build and hatch therein showed the dulness of trade in the district.

WATER CRANE.

We may here mention that a writer in a German engineering journal contrasts the behaviour of different animals towards railways and steam machinery. The ox stands composedly on the rails without having any idea of the danger that threatens him; dogs run among the wheels of a departing train without suffering any injury; and birds seem to have a peculiar delight in the steam engine. Larks will build their nests and rear their young under the switches of a railway over which heavy trains are constantly rolling, and swallows make their homes in engine houses. A fox-terrier named Pincher, at Hawkesbury station, on the Coventry and Nuneaton Railway, for a long time distinguished himself by ringing the bell on the approach of stopping trains, much to the passengers' amusement. One day, after performing this feat, he ran from the signal-box on to the line, and was cut to pieces.

At all stations, intermediate or terminal, ample arrangements have to be made so that trains, whether passenger or goods, may stand, or run, or cross over. The old way in which crossing was effected was homely enough, and such "points" were used as are indicated in the engraving. These have long since been superseded by "points" proper, of excellent construction, temper, and efficiency; and crossings and sidings are now sometimes multiplied into extraordinary number and intricacy. The first principle to be observed is to have, on the main lines, no "facing points," except at junctions. If a train has to be moved from a down to an up line, it must not be done directly. Let *a* be the down, and *b* the up rails. If it is necessary for an engine or for carriages to be removed from the one set of rails to the other, it must be done by the following means: The engine must be brought along the down rails till it has passed the points at *e*; the points must then be altered, and the engine being reversed, it will pass by the crossing on to the up rails *b*,—the wheels passing the points provided for this purpose. This process has only to be reversed, in order to take an engine from the up to the down line. Only in the case of branch lines diverging directly from a main line it is necessary to have what are called "facing points," like that at *g*, which run to and past *d*. There should also be others provided about *f*. But at all facing points accidents are possible, and they can be averted only by special signalling arrangements.

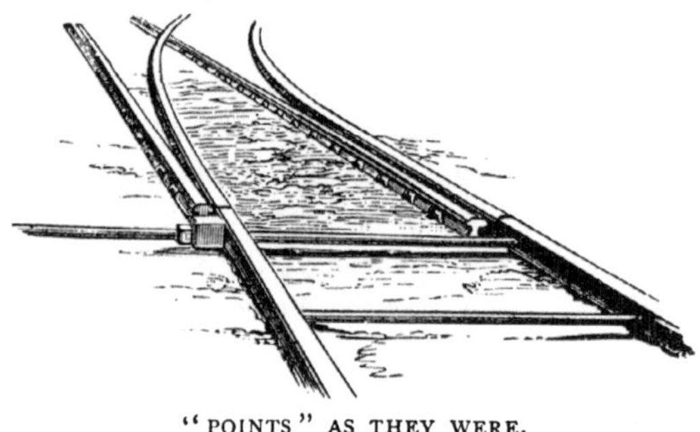

"POINTS" AS THEY WERE.

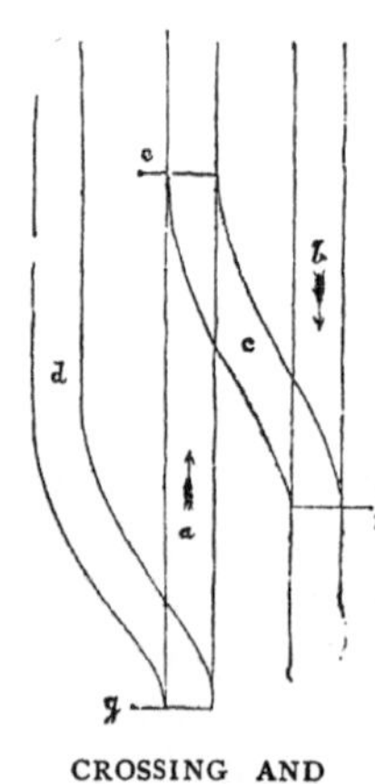

CROSSING AND SIDING.

In the neighbourhood of goods' stations the sidings are frequently extensive; at some places, where the whole work is the sorting and remarshalling of goods or mineral trains, it is not too much to say that the whole station is sidings. On the Midland Railway, for instance, Chaddesden sidings, near Derby, and Toton sidings, near Trent, are wholly devoted to these uses, and there are similar establishments on other lines. Let us visit one of these sidings.

The traveller who, on a wintry or foggy night, flashes along in an express train through the railway sidings at Toton on the Erewash Valley line may well regard the scene as one of bewildering confusion. As he sees the clouds of fire-lit steam, the glancing lights, the white, green, and red signals, the moving forms of engines, trains, and men; and as he overhears, perchance, the bumpings of trucks, the shouts of men, and the squeal of whistles from locomotives and from shunters, he may well consider it a spot from which he ought to be thankful to be quickly and safely extricated. Happily, cosmos reigns amidst this seeming chaos; and the multifarious and apparently bewildering transactions are carried on with order, precision, and security.

"Yours are the model railway sidings!" we playfully remarked to the administrator of this little province of the Midland Railway Company's widespread dominions. "Well," he replied, "they do say we manage pretty well. We had a gentleman here from a great southern railway company for a week, who made drawings of everything. We have had an engineer from the United States, another from Russia, several others from various parts of the world; and it is certain that we get safely through a deal of business. Yes," he continued, "the place has developed wonderfully; twenty years ago it was nearly all fields. There was just the up and down passenger line, one siding, and a weighing machine, over which a mineral train could be passed, and the wagons could one by one he weighed, so that we might check the 'declarations' of weight handed in by the colliery people. As the mineral business increased, fresh sidings were added, and a night as well as a day staff of men was provided."

The characteristic excellence of these sidings is that safety is secured for the main line traffic by keeping all the business of the reception, sorting, and marshalling of the empty coal trains and trucks on one side (for these are coal sidings), and the reception, sorting, and marshalling of the loaded trains and trucks on the other side. "We never," said the superintendent, "'foul' the main line. An empty train arrives from the south by the down goods line. The train is broken up and deposited into one or all of five 'reception' lines, two of which are for wagons going to collieries on the Erewash Valley district; the third is for wagons belonging to the collieries between Masborough and Normanton; the fourth for wagons for collieries between Clay Cross and Masborough; and the fifth for those on the South Yorkshire system. The wagons put into the Erewash reception line are drawn by a shunting engine out at the opposite end from that at which they were put in, and after being 'chalked' with the number of the line to which the horsemen are now to take them, they are drawn to the sorting sidings, of which there are seventeen, according to the particular collieries for which the trucks are destined. They are then marshalled in what is called 'station order.' The guard of the train will have only to unhook the trucks at the particular station, to give them a 'kick' back into the siding, and then to resume his journey."

We now go over and see the working of the loaded trucks and trains on the other side of the line. These arrive on the "up" goods line entirely clear of the passenger. In fact they left the passenger line at Ilkeston junction, 4½ miles north of Toton sidings. They run on the up goods line to Toton, and are delivered on to one of nine "reception," or, as they are called, "bank" lines. "Why we call them 'bank' lines," said the superintendent, "I can't say. It is a common name for such sidings at Chaddesden and elsewhere, as well as here. These 'bank' sidings are the source from whence we draw the traffic with which to make up our trains; so, perhaps, that is the reason for the name." When the engine has brought its loaded train so far, it is detached, it picks up its break, crosses the main line (the only time it touches the main line at Toton) on to the down goods line, then goes with a load of empties back to the place from which it has brought its loaded train, or to some other point to fetch another train of coal. Meanwhile the full train it left at the bank is composed of wagons for three or more different destinations, some for the Midland, others for the Great Eastern, Great Northern, Great Western, and South Western. A "chalker" met the train as it came slowly in, read the "destination label" on each wagon, and chalked upon the truck the particular shunting line to which it should go; a shunting engine, guided by a signal from the foreman at the centre of the sidings, now pushes the train forwards, and then horses draw the wagons into their various sorting sidings. Of these there are sixteen, and they hold in all something like seven hundred wagons, each siding containing wagons intended for a separate district.

At night the same work is carried on by a duplicate staff. The whole place is lit up with gas. The amount of business done at Toton day and night is enormous, but it varies with the season. In a summer month 18,000 wagons will be received and despatched; in winter as many as six and twenty thousand. The staff required also depends on the season and the work. In summer perhaps thirty or forty shunting horses would suffice, but in a severe winter the grease in the axle box will freeze hard, the wheels instead of turning round will skid along the rails, and two or three horses will be required to move a wagon.

"Your horses here," we remarked, "have to be as intelligent as men seem to be in some places." "Yes," replied the superintendent, "it is very interesting to see their sagacity, and to watch them picking their way among the moving wagons, especially at night. After being suddenly unhooked from a wagon they will be perfectly still where there is only just room for them to stand between two lines of rails, while a squealing engine and a shunt of wagons passes perhaps on each side of them."

"But how," we inquire, "with such a fluctuating traffic and amid such a multitude of trains arriving from all sorts of collieries, do you manage to get them away in so orderly and rapid a manner?" "Well, the traffic comes in here from all the collieries on the Midland lying between Stanton Gate and as far north as Normanton in Yorkshire. It comes at stated times, but in constantly varying quantities. We cannot tell how much we shall receive on any one day from any one colliery. But in order to ensure its prompt despatch we arrange, on 'spec,' for a proper supply of engine power, being guided, however, by long experience. When we have not a loaded wagon in the sidings, we order perhaps ten or a dozen engines several hours ahead to be ready at certain times; and, meanwhile, the wagons they are to take accumulate. We never send an engine away south without a full train. Our busiest time is between four o'clock and nine in the evening; and, in winter, until midnight. At the sorting sidings at the south end six or seven engines may be seen at a time attached to, or waiting to be attached to, six or seven loaded trains; and these, when ready, will be following one another out and away. In an hour five or six loaded trains will thus go, perhaps thirty in five hours. We have sorted and sent away north and south one hundred and twenty trains in a day."

"But how," we ask, "do you manage all this intricate work in foggy weather?" "We have for our sidings," he replied, a system of our own. Instead of shouting, we whistle. Thus: when we want a driver to push his train back, a long whistle is given by the man at the tail of the train; the second man, at about the middle of the train, repeats the whistle; and the third man, who is generally in sight of the driver, again repeats it, and also gives a hand signal. If the driver is wanted to stop his train, the first man—who stands in sight of the shunting signal—gives three short sharp whistles; the next man repeats them; and the third man repeats them, and gives the hand signal to the driver. Usually all this is done by shouting; we do it by whistling."

"You said just now that you did your business here with despatch *and safety*. It used to be said you had a great many accidents. Sir Beckett Denison, in one of his kind speeches, called Toton sidings the Midland Company's 'slaughter house'—didn't he?" "Yes, I believe he did," was the reply; "but it isn't correct. The safety of the shunting here has been increased by the men using a long pole of iron or wood for uncoupling the wagons instead of getting between them. We have not had a fatal accident for a considerable time, not a man even seriously injured in shunting for two or three years." "How long are the sidings?" we inquired. "From south to north a distance of about two miles. Where they are thickest it is for about a mile and a quarter."

Perhaps our reader, when he passes by day or night through Toton sidings, or some similar spot on some other company's lines, may cherish some thankfulness for the pains that are taken to ensure his safety and comfort.

Having thus dealt with the subject of stations and sidings, we may refer to the signalling arrangements necessary for their protection.

In doing so we may make the somewhat paradoxical assertion, that one of the greatest hindrances to improvement in the mechanical details of railways, is the preternatural and abnormal genius of English inventors. Every few weeks or days some correspondent writes to a railway manager or engineer, to assure him in the strictest confidence, and with the utmost prolixity, that the writer has made an astounding discovery, or has devised some wonderful apparatus, which is certain to revolutionize that particular department of the railway world. Two inventions were recently recommended for the adoption of the Midland Railway Company. One inventor stated that the worst injuries received by passengers in collisions were caused by the hardness of the wood and iron of which the carriages were built; and he accordingly urged that for the future carriages should be built of leather or other soft and elastic materials, so that passengers should be only squeezed and not cut. Another proposed to guarantee against one train ever running into another. To do this he wished a pair of rails to be fixed at and up the end of every train, so that if a train overtook it, it would run *up* and *on* to, but never *into*, the preceding one. Each inventor sent most elaborate drawings and estimates of the proposed project. Our railway authorities are ever and anon bored with a multitude of schemes from crack-brained theorists on the high road to the lunatic asylum, and eagerly supported by hungry patentees, until we sometimes fancy that the dreams of railway people must be haunted with ludicrous nightmares of railway mechanism in chaotic confusion and conflict, electric and hydraulic machines of every sort and size engaged in murderous internecine battle. And then, at last, when all faith in inventors has fled, some day somebody shows that he has really made a valuable discovery; and eventually, after months of inquiry, experiments, and improvements, it is adopted.

There is no subject in which railway managers feel so deep an interest as the safety of their trains. Enormous sums of money are devoted to this end, and one result has been that the signalling arrangements that were at one time deemed sufficient, have long since been superseded by methods ingenious, elaborate, and costly, to some of which we have now to refer.

The very simplest kind of railway signalling of which we have heard was mentioned to us the other day by one who is now an inspector of permanent way on the Midland Railway. "Forty years ago," he said, "I was on duty at Whitwood Junction on the North-Eastern, between Castleford and Normanton—now a great junction and signalling station; but all

HOME SIGNAL.

my signalling apparatus by day consisted of a board which I had to turn to let either the Leeds or the Normanton train go by; and, at night, I had simply a bonfire of coals burning, which, by the light it gave, told the driver of an approaching train whereabout on the line he was. It wasn't really a signal at all, but simply a fire. There was no back signal of any kind."

For several years the only signal on the Stockton and Hartlepool was a candle placed in a window of the station, its presence indicating to the driver that he was to stop, and its absence that he might go on. On the Stockton and Darlington and the Newcastle and Carlisle lines there were no signals, and there were none on the Liverpool and Manchester Railway when it was opened. "It was not until the year 1834 that the first attempt towards establishing signals was made on the Liverpool and Manchester, in the simple expedient of fixing an ordinary lamp to the top of a post approachable by a ladder. The signal showing a red or white light, was for night use only. Four years later, in 1838, Sir John Hawkshaw devoted his attention to signalling, designing some new disc signals, and through his influence they were introduced on several lines."

Similarly elsewhere. "I was firing," a Midland locomotive superintendent at Rugby remarked, "in '41 on the Liverpool and Manchester line. The only signal used at the stations was a flag that was run up and down a mast by a rope through a pulley. When the wind happened to blow in the right direction, we saw it well; but frequently it hung straight down the pole, and we had to get very near before we could see it at all. This was the only signal they had. There was no distant signal." Arrangements so elementary as these could not suffice, and, in the earliest days of railways, coloured objects were used—a white signal, whether by flag, board, or light, signifying safety, green meant that "caution" should be exercised, while red was the sign of "danger." A station signal was provided for both the up and the down line, one at each end of the station, and of the kind represented in the engraving. On a train stopping, or travelling slowly through an intermediate station, the signal which was painted red on one side was shown for five minutes in the direction from which the train had come, so as to stop any following train; the green signal, on the shorter post, was then turned on for five minutes, to complete the ten minutes' precautionary signal. Exception was made on the Liverpool and Manchester line, where the red signal was shown for three minutes, and the green for five; and also when an express train or a special engine had passed, the green signal only was shown for five minutes. As the lamps and the boards were connected together, the lamp had only to be lighted at night or in a fog, and then the arrangement was complete. When the vane was presented edgewise to the driver of an approaching train, as seen in the engraving, it showed that all was right.

Besides these there were auxiliary signals at most of the principal stations, worked by means of wires, which permitted their being regulated at almost any distance from the signal box. These auxiliaries were especially valuable in thick weather; for, as they were placed several hundred yards from the station, the drivers of engines could obey them when it would be impossible to see the station signals with distinctness. They were constructed with only the green or "caution," and the "all right" signals: the former intimating that the red signal was turned on at the station. In the engraving of the home signal, the reader may observe the lever by which the auxiliary signal was worked.

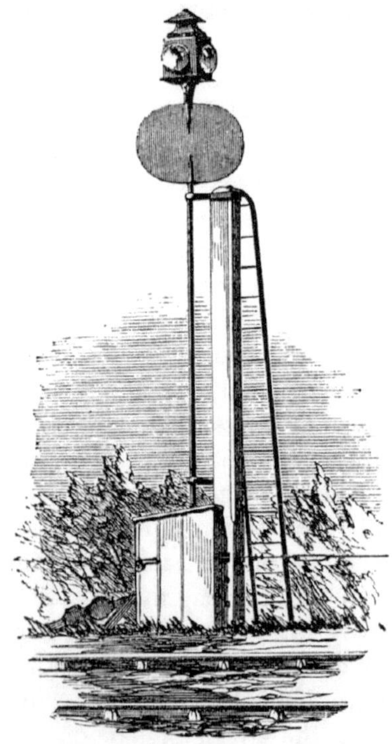

AUXILIARY OR DISTANT SIGNAL.

Where junction lines unite, or lines cross one another at the same level, a more complete system of signalling had to be adopted. A junction or double-signal station had two masts, near the tops of which were arms and lamps. When the arm, which is painted red, and is always on the left of the engine-driver, is at right angles to the mast, it signifies *danger;* if it be at an angle of forty-five degrees, *caution* must be observed; and if the arm be parallel with the post, it is *all right.*

These arrangements still in part exist, but they have been

enormously and scientifically developed. In former times a station-master, or porter, put signals at safety or danger, as the case might be, while some one else worked the points. Or it might be that the pointsman ran from his point to the signal lever, or back again. Or it might be, and too often it was the case, that the signals were not properly worked at all ; " the pointsman, perhaps, was fully occupied in pulling the one lever, and could not get at the other ; or the signalman might vainly

JUNCTION SIGNALS.

trust to the pointsman doing his duty and give the signal of safety when danger was imminent. Points and signals might thus be, and too often were, in direct contradiction, and the driver, relying on the safety which the lowered arm or the white light falsely bespoke, rushed confidently on his headlong way, to wake—if he ever woke at all—amid the crash of shattered carriages and the shrieks and groans of the wounded and the dying." Now what with home and starting signals ;

distance, or, as they are called, distant signals, sometimes at enormous distances; speaking instruments; repeating signals; intermediate repeaters; light indicators with which, in effect, the signalmen can see along curved cuttings, and through brick walls; with fog signals—10,000 of which are exploded by a single Company in less than one foggy month—and with an electric system which anticipates and follows the movements of every train in every part of its career, we have a completeness of control which surpasses anything originally contemplated.

Signal-houses are of various sorts and sizes, but in some respects they are essentially different from what they used to be. Instead of the cottage formerly provided merely for the shelter of the signalman, and from which he went out to change his signal or to pull his lever, the levers and the machinery that works them are, like himself, under cover. Some signal-boxes stand on viaducts that look down upon the crowded suburbs of great towns; some are in deep, dull cuttings; from some we see far away over cultivated cornfields, pleasant hamlets, and woods; while others are in cold, high mountain districts like the Ais-Gill box, on the Settle and Carlisle line of the Midland Company, 1,200 feet above the sea. We enter one by permission of the authorities. It is on a bank in a beautiful ravine in Derbyshire. The hills are covered with trees, in which the light spring green of the young wood contrasts with the deep umbrageous foliage of the pines. Ivy and ferns grow over or around the limestone rocks. Rooks settle on the ballast. Jackdaws whirl high overhead. The Wye brawls along the hollow, where one lonely fisherman is casting his line. Up and down the valley are signals, sidings, lines, junctions, and a tunnel mouth. The box itself is a picture of neatness. The floor is cleanly washed; the signal flags are folded together in the corner; the twelve levers are as bright as steel can be; the various telegraph instruments are by turns silent and anon noisily doing their work; the petroleum lamp can at any moment be lighted; the Company's books, with their broad yellow leaves on which the signalman makes his entries of everything that happens, lie open on the desk; sundry notices and instructions hang upon the walls; the row of twelve signal lamps for the semaphores are in their places; and, even in that lonely spot, scarcely a minute passes without there being some work to be quickly and accurately done or some record to be entered.

In important intermediate stations like that, for instance, at Nottingham, having several junctions and sidings, platforms and cross-over roads, all need special protection from signals. Here, in addition to the signal-boxes outside the station, there is a central or station signal-box that communicates with and controls the rest. A train is coming, we will say, from London. The driver has been allowed to pass the last station before reaching Nottingham, at Edwalton, and is approaching the distant signal of the Trent Bridge signal-box. We will suppose, however, that another train has been detained at the station platform to which the driver of the London train has usually come; and the station signalman will not only have his signal against the train, but will have wired to the London Road signal-box: "Train in platform." Accordingly the London Road signalman will keep his distance signal "against" the train, allowing it, however, to come slowly on until it arrives at his Home Signal. On reaching it the signalman will wire to the station signal-box, "Train waiting"; and thereupon the station signalman will allow the driver to approach at "caution." As he does so he will find, by the signals, to which platform he may come, and he will also know that as are the signals so are the points, and so is the road; signals and points being in their action "locked" together. We may add that, within the station itself, the "cross-over roads" are also protected by signals called "discs," which act simultaneously with the respective points, showing whether these by-paths are clear or "foul," and that all are under the direct control of the station signal-box.

A pleasant writer in the *Daily News* once cheerily described his experiences "in a signal-box." "I have been trying," he says, "to qualify myself for a signalman. One never knows what may happen; as an old fellow said to me the other day, 'A guinea a-week ain't to be picked up under every lamp-post,' and I know that signalmen rarely or never make less than that, and may attain to as much as thirty shillings. I have heard indeed of as much as thirty-four shillings falling to the lot of some lucky dogs, where the chances of distinction before a coroner's jury are exceptionally great; but I have no personal knowledge of such cases, and for the present my ambition does not soar beyond a thirty-shilling box, and the annual bonus which most or all of the companies give for a 'clean book' throughout the year—a book, that is to say, showing no fault-finding by superiors on account of errors or neglect."

He accordingly visited several boxes. In one he felt pretty confident that a week's practice would enable him to do the work without necessitating his appearance before the coroner more frequently than about once a month. In another his heart went into his boots, more particularly when, after inspecting a formidable array of scientific instruments, he was invited to try his hand at a lever, and found he could only get the provoking thing over after a determined struggle, which left him in a state of collapse. "I have no doubt," he playfully adds, "that the rogues picked out Number Thirty-two because they knew it to be an exceptionally stiff one, and knew that it wanted oiling; and I am pretty sure that they were as merry as old Father Christmas behind my back while the struggle was going on." He thus found that the work of signalling demanded very considerable muscular wear and tear; and that in some of the boxes brain and body must be pretty much on the work incessantly.

He entered another box, where there were gongs and bells of various sorts and sizes which rarely were silent for many seconds together, and which kept the operator incessantly on the move answering their demands or heaving to and fro some of those thirty or forty levers apparently in the most promiscuous and haphazard fashion. "My guide, philosopher, and friend, who is steeped to the lips in signalling lore, and has at his tongue's end a language in which 'back-locking,' 'slotters,' and 'replungers' are important factors, dives at once into the midst of things, and I of course look as wise and acute as I know how. The fact that a man feels himself to be a fool is, I hold, no good reason why he should look one if he can help it; and I assumed my most sapient aspect. I hope I impressed the signalman as I intended, but I do not much think I did. It took, I am afraid he thought, a deal of explanation to get a very simple idea into my head, but it began at length to dawn upon me that all this complication was more apparent than real, and that this intricate piece of mechanism, a large signal-box, was after all only the combination of several small ones of the simple character already described."

In the modern interlocking of signals the principle aimed at is, so far as possible, to supersede the man by the machine, to make him merely the motive power of the machine, and to render the machine as nearly as possible automatic. If the safety of the trains were dependent on the signalman, and he were dependent on his memory or his discretion, the conduct of the traffic of some lines, where, for instance, fifty trains an hour pass the signal-boxes, would be impossible. "And when you have an accident here," the inquiry was put to a signalman, "how do you expect to be able to manage it?" "Upon my word," he replied, "I don't know. I never in my life saw such mechanism until I came here; and if I tried to run two trains into one another I couldn't do it." How completely the interlocking is arranged may be inferred from the fact that, in some instances, in order to pass a train from one point of a station to another, some fourteen movements or more of levers are required. "Supposing in some freak of folly I attempted to lower that distance signal for a second train before I had duly passed a first, and given 'Line clear' to the man in the rear box —I should find my lever locked fast, and the distance signal unaffected by my foolish attempt to lower it. It is in fact under the control of the man in the next box as well as myself, and we must both be of one mind before it can be 'taken off.' The mechanism of the thing was explained to me by an officer of the Company, who held up two fingers perpendicularly and put another horizontally across the top of them. That top one, he said, is the signal arm, and it is kept up by two bars underneath. One bar is connected with a lever in this box, and the other with a lever in that, and both must be moved before the signal arm will fall. It takes two careless or foolish men, therefore, to let one train run into another on either side of this station, one man being actually at the station, and the other at the next signal-box along the line."

Besides the signal levers there are those that act upon the points, and it may be thought that a very little carelessness or want of skill would enable a pointsman to shunt one train with one lever, while he arranged his signals so as to let another train smash into it. But here again the mechanism absolutely pro-

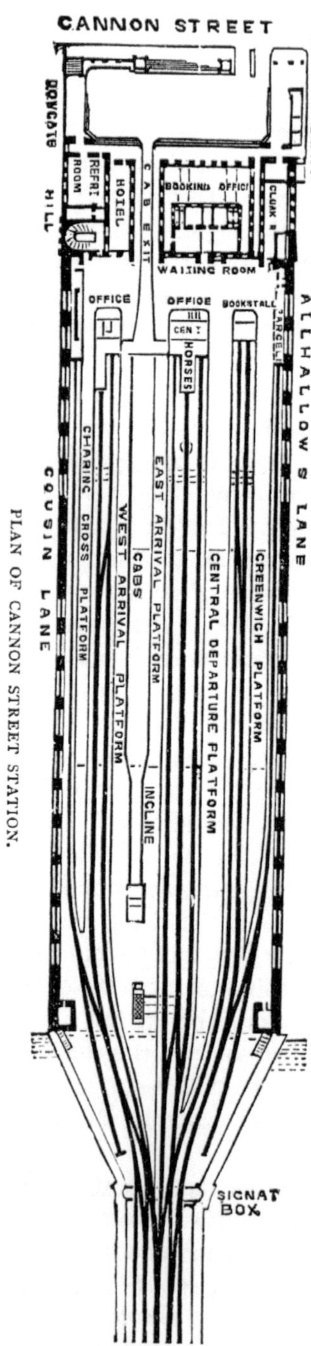

PLAN OF CANNON STREET STATION.

hibits such conduct. It is not only that the book of instructions forbids it, but the levers refuse to be parties to it. The points and the signals are interlocked in such a manner, that until the signal arms all stand at danger, and therefore forbid any train to approach, the lever which works the points is a fixture which cannot be moved. Trains may run away, signal gear may be out of order, engine-drivers may not see the warning or may disregard it, or breaks may refuse to act; but the signal-box is, as nearly as human skill can make it, practically infallible.

The most remarkable illustration of the interlocking system is supplied at the Cannon Street terminus in London. Here the difficulties to be dealt with, in the highest degree complicated, have been overcome by the skill of Messrs. Saxby & Farmer. Four main lines and one engine line, with five pairs of rails, cross towards the station from the bridge over the Thames, bringing with them trains that have converged from the stations at London Bridge and Charing Cross. Between and among the five pairs of straight lines several curved crossing lines meander, touching one pair of rails, cutting across another pair, and effecting junctions each with all, so that trains can run from any one line to any other. The five principal lines, as they approach the station, spread out, eight going to the eight platforms;

and the ninth is for the accommodation of locomotives. The operations which the points and signals have to conduct may be understood from the fact that at the most crowded time of the day eighteen trains arrive and eighteen depart within the hour; and for every arrival and departure there are required two movements of locomotives; and that 108 operations of shifting points and signals have to be performed every hour, or, on the average, one in every thirty-three seconds.

How, we may inquire, is all this done? And we will answer the question with the aid of an excellent description from *The Engineer*.

About fifty yards in front of the Cannon Street station, a platform spans all the lines, high enough to clear the chimneys of the locomotives. "On this platform stands a glass house surmounted by four tall poles, from either side of which project semaphore arms to the number of twenty-four. These arms generally remain in their horizontal attitude to signify danger, and are only occasionally lowered, and that but for a few seconds, to signify that the passage is clear. They command the lines and sidings on the bridge and in the station, and every driver of a locomotive arriving, departing, or changing line, has to keep his eye steadily upon some of them, stopping without fail when their warning blocks his way, and moving without fear when they promise safety." He easily distinguishes which of the signals belong to the line he occupies. If, then, the engine-driver does his duty, and if the signals properly point it out, no accident can happen.

Climb by an iron ladder to the signal platform, and enter the glass house. It is about 50 feet long and a few wide. Half the width is occupied by a row of strong iron levers standing nearly upright from the floor, and placed at equal distances along the apartment; the rest of the width forms a gangway from end to end in which two stalwart men can work, whose time is entirely occupied in looking through the glass sides of their cell, and in pulling this way or pushing that way some of the levers which are arranged before them. These levers work all the 32 point and 35 signal levers; 67 in all. Every lever is numbered, and on the floor beside it there is fixed a brass plate engraved with its name and use. All the point levers are black, the up signals are red, the down signals blue, and the distant signals yellow.

Many of them, too, have numbers, sometimes half a dozen or more, painted on their sides, and these numbers involve the whole secret of the safety which is secured by the mechanism, as will be readily understood if we examine the principles on which it is devised.

The keys and pedals of an organ, as is well-known, command numerous valves admitting air from a wind-chest to the pipes which it is desired to sound. "The key-boards are sometimes double or triple, and are occasionally arranged so that the performer sits with his back to the instrument. The pipes are

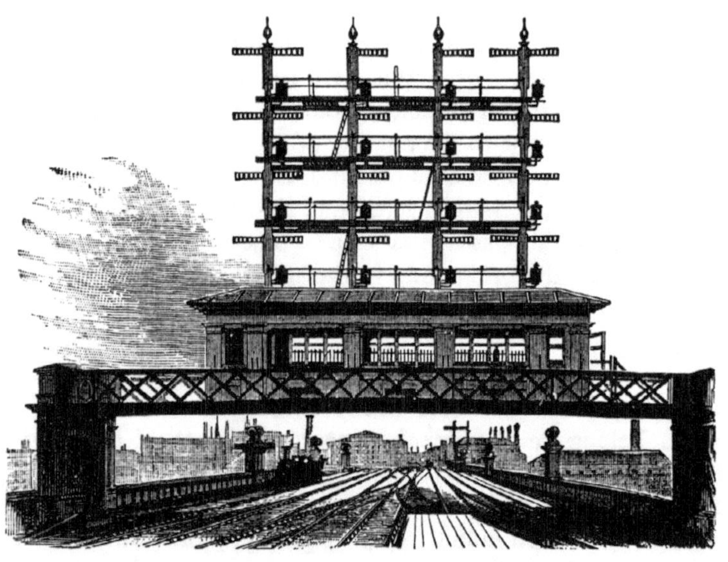

CANNON STREET STATION SIGNALS.

generally spread over a large space, and sets of them are sometimes enclosed in separate chambers. There thus arises considerable complexity in the mechanism by which the several keys are made to operate on their respective air valves. Nevertheless, by means of rods, cranks, and levers, such a connection is effected, that on depressing a C key, not one C pipe only, but it may be twenty C pipes are made to sound, in whatever part of the instrument those pipes may be situated. And so it is with the points and signal levers of the Cannon Street platform. The whole row may be considered to form a key-board of five and a-half octaves, every key of which is connected by suitable cranks and rods to some one of the sixty-seven points and semaphores which have to be played upon. In the organ a touch of the finger serves to depress a key, for the movement has only to admit a puff of air to certain pipes—but here the keys require a strong and steady pull, for they have to move ponderous point bars, or broad semaphore arms, and their movements have to be conveyed round many corners and over considerable distances. In both cases the mode of communicating motion is the same, the two mechanisms differing only in size and strength ; and thus far the organ and the signal instrument exactly correspond."

We may now compare the working of a complicated system of signals with that of an organ. But there is one essential difference : an organist can touch any keys he pleases, and can, if he should be so minded, produce not only concord but discord. "Not so the signalist. Discord is utterly beyond his powers. He cannot open the points to one line and at the same time give a safety signal to a line which crosses it. When he gives a clear signal for a main line, he cannot open a point crossing to it ; when he gives a clear signal for a crossing, he must show danger for all the lines which it crosses. And this is the meaning of the numbers marked on the different levers. No. 10, let us suppose, has 5, 7, and 23 marked on its side. He may pull at No. 10 as long as he pleases, but he cannot move it till Nos. 5, 7, and 23 have first been moved—and so throughout the whole system. No signal lever can be moved to safety unless the point levers corresponding with it have first been moved, and no point lever can be moved while there stands at safety any signal lever that ought to stand at danger. Every lever is under lock and key, each being a part of the key which unlocks some of the others, and each forming a part of the lock which secures some of the others against possible movement, while each is at the same time subject to the control of all those which are related to it."

This result, complex and difficult as it seems, is achieved by mechanism of great simplicity and beauty. Immediately under the floor of the platform, and just in front of the levers, are arranged several series of vibrating and sliding bars, somewhat like the tumblers of a lock placed horizontally. These bars have projections here which stand in front of certain levers as obstacles to their motion, or notches there which permit certain levers to travel. "Some of them have sloping faces such that, when a lever moves along them, it edges them to one side, and this transverse motion being communicated to others of the series brings the proper projections or notches in front of those other levers to which the moving lever is related. Thus, by the movement of one lever, some others are stopped and some are left free, and this simple principle carefully applied to all, works them into a system incapable of discord."

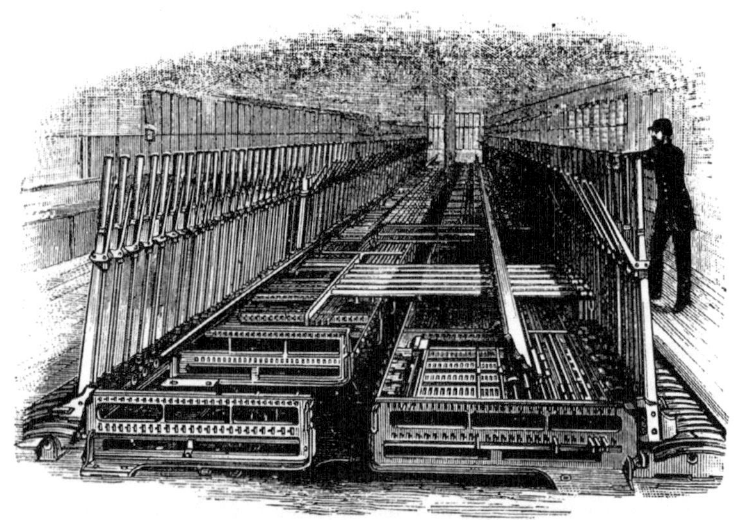

INTERIOR OF LONDON BRIDGE SIGNAL BOX.

The locking apparatus of points and signals is not excepted from the general law of degradation. But since the normal position of all the signals indicates danger, if, through slackness or wear, the lever which works a signal should become partly inoperative, the worst that can happen is to leave the signal at danger. So throughout the whole mechanism—let cranks or slides wear, rods stretch or break, delay may ensue, but danger never.

Let us now explain the system which guides the signalists in their operations. At each end of the glass house a lad is seated, with note-book and pencil, in front of an electric telegraph. "The apparatus on the right rings a bell, the lad looks at its index and immediately exclaims, 'North-Kent,' 'Charing Cross,' or whatever else the needle may direct him to say. An observer looking along the bridge perceives the steam cloud of a locomotive advancing, and presently catches the bright sheen of its steam chest as it sweeps with a train round the curve on the Surrey side. Before he can turn round the signalmen have drawn some three, four, or it may be half a dozen levers, the proper junctions have been effected, and the due signals are set: the train glides safely into its allotted platform. And not one train only, for several trains may be coming up their several lines, and others may be simultaneously sweeping out from the station. The telegraph passes the word from afar, the lad who watches it repeats the word aloud, and the men calmly, quietly, yet rapidly turn it into the practical work of guiding the train to its destination."

Our readers will agree with us that the inventors of such agencies, so economical to the Companies, and so safe to the public, are entitled to the gratitude of mankind.

We have already referred to the ordinary signals of a station —the "home," and the "distance" or "distant" signals—with arms by day, and lamps at night. But suppose that a bridge or a tunnel happens to be so situated at the end of a station, that the signalman who uses the signal cannot see whether it acts properly; and suppose that, though it has worked with perfect accuracy for years, some tempestuous night the oil or the wick of the lamp is defective, or a stone breaks the glass, and the light goes out; may not a train, unwarned of danger, come careering onwards through the gloom and the storm to destruction? The contingency may be remote, but it is possible; and the results—if they followed—would be disastrous. This subject engaged the anxious consideration of Mr. Needham, the Superintendent of the Midland Railway, and he conferred with the Company's electrician about it. "Can't you make us an apparatus," he said, "by which we can see round a corner—see whether a lamp is burning half a mile off and out of sight?" The electrician set his wits to work, and at length was successful. Just over the place where the flame of the signal-lamp burns he placed a thin brass tube, which, as soon as heat is applied, expands. This "expanding piece," as it is called, presses against the short end of a lever, the long end of which is so arranged as to press against a "stop" made of some conducting material, and so placed that the electric circuit is complete. The electric current immediately passes to the signal-house, and indicates that the lamp is burning. No sooner is the lamp extinguished than the "expanding piece" begins to contract, the contact is broken between it and the stop, the circuit is interrupted, and the signal current ceases to flow. "There," said Mr. Needham, as we stood in one of these signal-houses, at the west end of the Derby Station, "the lamp is just lit, and in thirty seconds the brass tube will expand, the current will flow, and on that little box on the shelf you will see the words move up, 'Lamp in.'" We stood, watch in hand; and it was so. Subsequently the lamp was by order extinguished; and in thirty seconds more the words "Lamp in" disappeared, the words "Lamp out" leaped up in their place, and the loud ring of an alarum bell proclaimed the fact. That sound and those words would arouse the attention of the signalman in the stormiest winter night, would tell him that his signal-lamp had gone out, and would warn him immediately to adopt other means for stopping any approaching train, and averting any threatened disaster. Many such signals are in use.

The reader has doubtless heard of the block system; we may state precisely the way in which it is worked on, for instance, the Midland Railway. At certain distances, determined by the amount of traffic, signal-boxes are erected, each of which is supplied with telegraph instruments communicating with the next signal-station up and the next that is down the line. For simplicity, however, we will now deal with only one, the down line; and we will call the stations to which we have to refer A, B, and C. In front of the signalman is the dial of his telegraphic instrument, which also is supplied with a clear-sounding bell, and it is by the aid of both bell signals and dial signals that the work is done. When the instrument is not in use, the handle which works the needle hangs down below the instrument, and is in an upright position. It is also ordered that each beat of the bell must be made slowly and distinctly; and that under no circumstances can a signal be considered to be understood "until it has been correctly repeated back to the station from which it was received, and the acknowledgment given that such repetition is correct." If the reader will now glance over the list of "bell signals" and "dial signals" given below, he will see how ample are the resources placed at the disposal of the signalmen for fulfilling the duties that follow.

Bell Signals.

To call attention	1 beat of the bell.
Be ready for passenger train	2 beats " "
Be ready for goods, cattle, mineral, or ballast train, or light engine	3 " " "
Train on line	4 " " "
Shunt train for passenger train to pass	5 " " "
Signal given in error, train last signalled not coming	6 " " "
Stop and examine train	7 " " "
Shunt train for goods or mineral train to pass	8 " " "
Testing signal	9 " " "
Withdraw, 'Be ready,' and 'Train approaching' signals last sent	10 " " "
Train divided	11 " " "
Train or vehicles running away on wrong line	12 " " "
Time signal	13 " " "
Train or vehicles running away on right line	14 " " "
Lampman required	15 " " "
Fog-signalman required	16 " " "
Opening of signal post	18 " " "
Closing of signal post	20 " " "

Dial Signals.

Signal correctly repeated	1 beat of needle to right.
Passenger train approaching	3 beats " "
Express goods or cattle train approaching	4 " " "
Through goods or mineral train approaching	5 " " "
Stopping goods, mineral, or ballast train, or light engine approaching	6 " " "
Testing signal	9 " " "
Signal incorrectly repeated	1 beat of needle to left.
Fast passenger train on line	2 beats " "
Slow passenger train on line	3 " " "
Express goods or cattle train on line	4 " " "
Through goods or mineral train on line	5 " " "
Stopping goods, mineral, or ballast train, or light engine on line	6 " " "
Train passed without tail lamp	7 " " "
Stop train and instruct driver to come forward cautiously	8 " " "
Testing signal	9 " " "
Line clear of train or engine	2 " " right.

We will suppose that a passenger train is approaching the signal-station that we call A; and thereupon, by one beat of the bell, the signalman calls the attention of station B; and then, by two other beats, he tells B to "Be ready." The signalman at B, having ascertained that the line is clear for the approaching train to run on, repeats to A the signal he has received. Station A now indicates to B the kind of train—viz., passenger train—that is coming forward, by giving the three beats of the "Passenger train approaching" dial signal; and when station B has duly acknowledged the same, and has received the required intimation from station A that his acknowledgment is correct, B must, by the insertion of a little peg into the right-hand hole on the dial, keep the needle to "Line clear." As soon as the train has passed station A, the signalman must give the bell signal "Train on line;" upon hearing which, station B must acknowledge the signal and unpeg the needle. Station A must then give to station B the proper "Train on line" dial signal; and (when station B has acknowledged, and received the necessary intimation from station A that his acknowledgment is correct) he must peg the needle over to "Line blocked," and then call the attention of, and give the signal "Be ready" to station C. So will it be through the series of block stations. Supplementary instructions are given in the event of fogs or snowstorms or other contingencies. In the event of a second train arriving at a signal-station before the preceding train has been telegraphed as clear from the station in advance, the train must be brought to a stand, and the driver must then draw the tail of his train within the signals, and await the signal being given. At night, when trains are ordinarily fewer and further between, it is not necessary to keep all these signal-houses in service. A "switch," as it is called, is then put on, for instance, at B, so that the electric current flows direct from A to C, and then the signalling is carried on as if the B station did not exist. The safety of the line is equally secured, but the blocks are longer, and of course a smaller number of trains can run.

By means of the bell other signals also are given, as, for instance: "Shunt goods train for passenger train to pass;" "Shunt slow goods train for fast goods train to pass;" "Shunt slow passenger train for fast passenger train to pass." In the event of a signalman observing anything the matter with a train as it passes his box, he signals to the next station to "Stop and examine train;" thereupon the signalman puts his signals against the train as it approaches, and the train is pulled up for examination.

The advantages of the block system are great, and none are more conscious of this than the drivers themselves. They run with a sense of security, and the traveller may pass over long distances without hearing the whistle, except at the junctions. Arrangements are also in progress by which even this may be obviated, messages being sent forward to the junction both as to the kind of train that is coming and the line on which it will have to travel, so that the signals and the points will be ready before it arrives.

This system perhaps reaches its most remarkable development on the Metropolitan line. "Suppose," we said to the engineer "London goes on increasing, and more people want to travel by your line, how will you carry them? Trains as near together as every three minutes were recently considered to be your maximum?" "We have already," was the reply, "shifted the block stations and signalled our line for a two minutes' service, and we can begin at any time to carry this into effect when they make more room at Aldgate to receive and to re-start the trains. There, at present, at one point, the trains have to cross one another's path; but as soon as the circle is completed this difficulty will disappear. Aldgate will then be a roadside instead of a terminal station; the trains will pass through one after another, and a minute's interval will be ample." "It is the improvements in the brakes—the use of continuous brakes, also," we suggested, "that aid you in this multiplication of trains." "Yes," said the engineer; "we can now, if we like, pull up our trains, when running at a speed of 25 miles an hour, in their own length—120 yards. But we are not often in such a hurry as that; for we don't allow a train to start till the next length of line is clear. We work the absolute block, and there are never two trains on one section."

Thus does the telegraph supplement the railway; and, anticipating and following the course of the innumerable trains that pass up and down the line, acts like a nervous system, sensitively responding to what may be called the potent energies and activities of the muscular system of the railway itself.

The expense of these signalling arrangements is great. Every lever in a blocking machine costs £8, besides the expense of adapting the signals to it, and in addition to the necessity frequently arising of purchasing additional land at the points where the machines have been brought into action. In the locking machine at Charing Cross there are as many as 100 levers, so that the price paid for it on delivery was £800, besides the cost of fitting it up and putting it into action. The Midland Railway, alone, for some time expended not less than £60,000 a year on the block and interlocking systems.

In close connection with the signalling arrangements of a railway is the lamp department. When we enter a lamp-room of a station we are ready to exclaim, "Can a clean thing come out of an unclean?" but the problem is solved in the affirmative. Here, unless we accept Lord Palmerston's definition of dirt, that it is only "a good thing in the wrong place," everything is dirty, at any rate is oily. The lamps, cleaned and not cleaned, are oily; the benches are oily, the floor is oily, the "waste" is oily, the men are oily; yet from all this come the clear lights of the bright lamps, and the comfort and safety of travellers. The lamp-room is a land of lamps. Rows of lamps hang right across and along the roof; there are upright rows or racks of lamps at the side and ends; there are lamp-barrows on the floor; there are lamps in the adjoining rooms, lamps in hundreds in all.

At the lamp-benches the lamp-cleaners are at work. The lamp is half sunk into a hole in the bench, so that it can be easily held and rubbed and scrubbed. "One man," says the foreman, "can clean thirty lamp-glasses in an hour, but he couldn't do this for long. Another does the burners; he also fills the 'cistern' of the lamp. Each has a pint, and it will burn for twenty-four hours if the wick is properly trimmed."

A lamp-barrow stands ready with its perhaps forty lamps; a train is nearly due that will have to be "lamped"; so the barrow is wheeled off along the platform. "Is it safe," we inquire, "to throw the lamps on and off the carriage roofs, as those men are doing?" "It is the safest way of all," is the reply. "We very seldom have any accident in throwing them. If a man when just going to catch a lamp were to see that the glass was broken, he perhaps would let it drop. It might cut his hands all in pieces if he didn't. They weigh fifteen to eighteen pounds apiece, so their force is great. Sometimes the glass gets cracked; and then, if the valve, by any chance, should feed the flame too freely, the surplus will collect in the glass, and by the oscillation of the train may leak through the crack and drop on the floor."

"The greatest stations for lamping business," remarks the foreman, "are where the most trains start from. Some start from here. Through trains that arrive in an evening when it is getting dark we also have to lamp; and when an express stops we have to see that every lamp in every carriage is burning brightly. If it isn't, it might go out before the train reached the next station at which it stopped, perhaps sixty or seventy miles away; so we shift it. When the Lefroy job was on, we had orders to lamp some trains by day that go through some short tunnels—trains we had never lamped before—and we have lamped them ever since. It costs a lot of money, I expect, to do it. The tank overhead will hold 750 gallons of rape oil, and a gauge affixed shows at a glance how full it is. Though the days are long now," adds the foreman, "every lamp in the service will be in use next week with the excursions; they come home late."

"Semaphore signals are cleaned by a man on purpose for the job. They burn petroleum. He cleans his lamps at the signals; for the junctions lie wide apart. He has to go over a deal of ground—four or five miles, I should say—to do them. At roadside stations the lamps are all brought into the station to be cleaned."

"Yes," said the superintendent of the lamp department at Derby, "we have lately made great improvements in our lamps. Each roof-lamp now has its own cover; and so well is every part adjusted, that I can take this lamp and swing it when it is burning" (and he suited the action to the word) "over my head without disturbing the oil or the light." By the substitution of petroleum oil for rape oil in many of their lamps the Midland Company alone have recently effected a saving of £10,000 a year.

We may add that the lamps that light our trains have, like everything else in railway matters, undergone great changes. "On the Bolton and Kenyon Junction line, one of the earliest that carried passengers," an engineer remarked to us, "the lamp in front of the engine used to be a coal-fire. A sort of crane, with a hook at the end of it, stuck out from the buffer-plank, and from the hook hung a fire-grate, about a foot in diameter, filled with burning coal, the same sort as we used for the engine. The draught created by the engine as it ran forward, and as it oscillated from side to side, kept the fire bright, and the ashes dropped on the road. We could see the line well before us. I have ridden on such an engine many a time."

Before leaving the subject of signalling, we may refer to an important class of services rendered in connection with this department. "Bang, bang, bang," noisily went the knocker on the door of a cottage in a quiet street one night last winter. It was pitch dark; and though the lamp-post stood at the corner of the street, it gave but the faintest glimmer to the gloom. "Bang, bang, bang," again the knocker sounded, and it effected its purpose, for the bedroom window was opened for a minute, and a gruff voice cheerily said, "All right." If we ask what it was that disturbed the deep slumbers of the tired platelayer, the answer would be given in the one short, simple word, "Fog." In that cottage lives a "fogman," and he was wanted for his duties. A quarter of a mile away is the signal-house of the "North Junction"; a quarter of an hour ago the signalman there observed that the mists had suddenly and heavily settled, and that help must be obtained. Accordingly, along his "speaking telegraph"—a special wire with which, in addition to his ordinary signalling wires, he is furnished—he flashed to the "Platform Inspector" on night duty at the station the expressive order, "Send fog-signalmen." On the wall of the station-master's office hangs a list headed: "Arrangement of fog-signalmen, and their respective addresses and posts of duty," and also the names and addresses of the two "gangers" of the said fog-signalmen. A porter is immediately despatched to one of the "gangers," who will at once proceed to summon the men under his command, each of whom knows the exact spot where his duty lies, and thither he will hie himself.

Our fogman is not long in coming to his senses. He buttons up the overcoat with which he is specially supplied by the company for this service; and, though the night is so dark and the fog so dense that he cannot see his hand a foot from his nose, he knows the way he has to go, and soon "reports himself" at the signal-box at the North Junction. The signalman looks him over with a glance to see that he is in all respects fit for his work, and he then "signs on duty," is supplied with a lamp and a couple of dozen fog-signals, and goes to his accustomed post—the distance-signal of the up line half a mile away, as duly recorded on the card in the station-master's office. Meanwhile the other fogmen have hastened to their respective stations; in a short time every one will be at his place; and, as soon as practicable, each will have kindled a fire which will give himself light and warmth.

The duty now devolving upon the fog-signalman is this: He is to place himself as far beyond the distance-signal as he can, so as still to see it—fifteen or twenty yards, perhaps—nearer, if the fog is very thick; as often and as long as the distance-signal stands at "danger," he is to keep two "fogs" on the rail; and as soon as the distance-signal turns to white, meaning "clear," he is to take the two "fogs" off again. The advantage of standing beyond the signal is that there will be more time for the driver of the coming train, after he has heard the "fogs," to glance up at the signal itself, and to verify by his sight what his ear has already told him.

From time to time during the night the men are visited by the foreman signalman, to see that they are vigilantly discharging their responsible duties; and also, at intervals of six hours, to take them refreshments. These consist of a pint of hot coffee for each man, and also a quartern loaf and half a pound of cheese between every four men. These provisions are supplied to the foreman by a woman, who is allowed tenpence a meal a man; and as these fog-signalmen at their ordinary work have to work twelve hours for a day's work, but at signalling earn a day's wage in eight hours, it is a service they are willing enough to perform. As they are relieved by other men every twelve hours, "they would not mind," remarked an officer to us, "if the fog lasted for a month." The relief men are obtained from what are called the "extra gang" of the platelayers in the engineer's department of the neighbouring station.

A fog-signal is somewhat of the shape of a large thick penny-piece. It is about two and a half inches in diameter, half an inch thick, and has two flexible pieces of lead across, which may be so bent as to clasp both sides of the rail. It contains three gun-caps and perhaps half an ounce of gunpowder. It is said that when a "fog" was first used for experimental purposes, a driver reported that he had been shot at by a man who had, to take aim, laid himself down on the ballast. The Midland Company use a large number of these signals. Last winter but one, at Nottingham station alone, forty gross (they are ordered in grosses) were required. They were going night and day as long as the fogs lasted. Fogmen are, during fogs, stationed at many of the home signal-boxes also. If a fog comes on during the day, the men do not wait to be summoned, but proceed at once to their respective stations.

FOG-SIGNAL.

We may conclude this chapter with a brief reference to the telegraphic arrangements of a railway company—arrangements familiar yet wonderful. Some idea may be formed of the extent and multitude of these operations when we mention that on, for instance, the Midland Railway, for the private use of that Company, there are no fewer than 8,000 miles of telegraph wire in almost constant employment; there are more than 9,000 telegraph instruments, employing 15,000 batteries—most of them Daniell's. Including signal-boxes, there are 800 telegraphic stations. The mere "battery power" necessary for such a set of instruments has been emphatically affirmed to be "something enormous." The battery plates, if put end to end, would stretch twelve miles in length; and their power would be sufficient to lift one of Her Majesty's 81-ton guns a foot high in a second of time.

The outdoor staff of the telegraph department sometimes includes as many as 400 men, who carry on the work of the construction and maintenance of the telegraphs. The indoor staff consists of nearly as many clerks, all under the charge of the telegraph superintendent. Candidates for employment under him are of the age of 14 or 16, are first admitted to a preliminary or educational examination, and afterwards to one that tests their competence in telegraphy. Having passed the latter, they receive a certificate to that effect, and are employed as vacancies arise.

The amount of service rendered in the telegraph department

of a great railway company is enormous. The messages on "company's business" number on the Midland Railway alone some 5,000,000 annually, and they increase at the rate of perhaps 500,000 a year. Besides these there are the messages known as "train reports." When, for instance, a train leaves Normanton for the south, a "train report" to that effect is despatched to all the stations within a certain distance ahead, say as far as Sheffield. It is in such brief form as the following: "Number 84 left at 2.5;" and as the train passes in succession the other stations further south, similar "train reports" are forwarded, so that it is known for perhaps half an hour ahead "how she is running." The various signalmen are thus enabled to keep the line clear for the coming passenger trains. These "train reports" on the Midland line alone are not fewer than the amazing number of 10,000,000 a year.

The greatest enemies of telegraphic communication are thunderstorms, hurricanes of wind, and snowstorms. In thunderstorms the electric fluid has been known to flash along the telegraph wires, and to fling the telegraphic instrument across the office at the heads of clerks yards away. In frosty weather rain that falls upon the wires will become frozen thereon, till sometimes around it is a solid mass of pure ice, as clear as glass, in the midst of which the wire looks like "a fly in amber." At such times the force of the wind pressing on so broad a surface is irresistible; the wires and posts go, or the wires are torn in rags that dangle at the posts. In the latter end of 1872 the telegraphic system was thus interrupted over large districts of the country. In March, 1881, the Settle and Carlisle section of the Midland line was visited by a succession of snowstorms—of which we shall have to speak hereafter—which at length seriously interrupted the whole telegraphic system. The wires became a mass of ice, and after a night-storm of rain, snow, hail, and frost that followed as the weather broke, the wires went by the run. The rain, however, in a few hours helped to clear the line; before daylight on the following day a train with a gang of telegraph men got through; by 10 o'clock defects were temporarily adjusted, and the traffic resumed its course. It is at such times when the railway communication is interrupted that the special value of the telegraph makes itself felt. The traffic becomes congested, and the pressure is only relieved by the strenuous efforts of those at headquarters, who by the telegraph can learn the facts of the case and can help to deal with them. Without the telegraph the difficulties attending the re-organization would be tenfold what they now often are. To show the eagerness with which the telegraph is used at such times, we may mention that after the snowstorm of January, 1881, which affected the whole of the Midland lines south of Leeds, the number of telegraph messages passing through the Derby office alone rose in one week from 13,782 to nearly 20,000.

The construction and maintenance of the signals of a great railway company form an interesting department of service. That of the Midland Company at Derby had a small beginning—at first perhaps a dozen carpenters, fitters, and smiths; but gradually the work expanded till the Midland system had to be arranged for signalling purposes into some twenty districts, over each of which is an inspector, with 15 to 25 assistants; and there are now some 800 men in this department—500 at Derby and 300 outside.

The loftiest signals made by the Company are 65 feet high, six feet of which are fixed below ground, and are strutted with cross timbers; if necessary, they are also stayed with wires from the top. The wood of which these semaphores are constructed is resinous Memel pine, a single tree of the right size being selected, and then squared and tapered, so as to be about 14 inches square at the bottom and 8 inches at the top. The usual height of a signal, however, is 45 or 50 feet, and hundreds of this size are used for one of the maximum height. Piles of signal-posts, with all the subordinate but necessary appliances, are always in readiness, so that, in case of need, they can, in a few hours, be despatched to any destination. Some 1,200 or 1,300 signals are sent out from Derby in the course of a year, consuming in their preparation and appliances some 900 tons of iron, and perhaps 15,000 cubic feet of timber.

Much of the apparatus of signals is made of wood; and everything connected, not only with signals proper, but with their manifold appliances, and with the cabins for the signalmen, are provided from the signal department at Derby. Wooden planks, grooved and tongued for flooring, and also—though somewhat lighter—for the roofing of signal-boxes; flights of steps, with step plates ; window sashes and windows ; "benches" on which the "point rollers" and "angles" are fixed ; "crosses" for strutting the semaphores below ground ; lockers and locks—one for each box of each signalman who works in that cabin ; fans; indicator boards for single lines; facing points; "brackets" upon which two signals are erected on one post when there is insufficient room on the ground for two posts ; weights to hold the signals to "danger" when they are "pulled off" by the signalman,—all are made here; and, in addition, there are in readiness, "in stores," lamps, gongs, and a hundred other matters required in this department.

Passing the painting shops we come to the smiths' shops, where the iron work is done. Here all kinds of machines, for planing, boring, drilling, slotting, and shaping, are busily and noisily at work. Groups of men are building locking frames in all stages of progress, and containing perhaps 40, 50, or even 60 levers. Other men are at the forges, and here have just been finished five or six hundred "road gauges" for the gangers to measure and maintain the precise gauge of the "road." Here are "angle pulleys" innumerable : they are required to shift the direction of the wires or rods that pull over the signals or points ; here are some new and handsome metal "staffs" for the use of drivers on single lines ; and near at hand are stores of galvanised wire—"No. 8," nearly $\frac{3}{16}$ of an inch in diameter, made by the firm of Richard Johnson, of Manchester, all for signalling purposes.

MONSAL DALE FOOTBRIDGE AND VIADUCT.

CHAPTER X.

Station Masters.—Duties of Station Masters.—Working Single Line Traffic. — Exceptional Duties. — Perplexities. — Names of Station Masters. — Booking Clerks.—The Booking Office.—Thomas Edmondson.—Ticket-making Machines.—The Dating Press.—The Cash Counter.—Train Books.—Audit Office.—The Clearing House.—Experiences of Booking Clerks. — Involuntary Travellers.—The Parcels Office.—All Sorts of Parcels.—Work of Parcel Clerks.—Signalmen.—Duties of Signalmen.—Guards.—Duties of Guards.—A Polite Guard.—Porters.—Complaints about Luggage.—A Valise of Dynamite.—Baggage Smashers and Bees.—What is Personal Luggage ?—" Checking the Baggage."

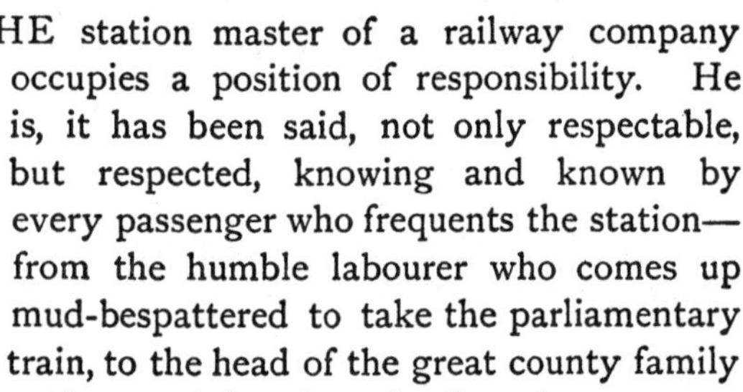

HE station master of a railway company occupies a position of responsibility. He is, it has been said, not only respectable, but respected, knowing and known by every passenger who frequents the station—from the humble labourer who comes up mud-bespattered to take the parliamentary train, to the head of the great county family who steps from his carriage and four into the first-class express. The station master is not only what his name indicates: he is much more. " He is the captain in command of all the human and steam forces that aggregate round that little world—microcosm in the railway cosmos—called a station, and within his own sphere holds the same place as the commander-in-chief—the general manager—does in the more exalted position. Of course the importance of the station master is as the importance of the station of which he has charge." The station master of Euston or St. Pancras holds a different position, and must be differently qualified, from the station master of Auchtermuchty ; still the duties of these officers differ less in nature than in ex-

The initial letter is from a sketch of the Malvern Link station.

tent. Many station masters, too, can count up a quarter of a century and more of railway service.

The station master is answerable for the care of the company's property; for the faithful discharge of the duties of the staff whether permanently or temporarily employed within the limits of his station; for the signalling and the safe working of the trains; and for the security of all moneys received. On him primarily devolves the duty of starting the trains at the right time, and of seeing that there is a sufficient interval to make a collision between them impossible. It is within his discretion to start or to delay trains that may be out of time; his decisions on these points may demand cool judgment and quick resolution. For example, as a general rule, "passenger trains take precedence of all goods, cattle, and coal trains, the regulation being that the latter must not be started from any station when passenger trains are due. But this rule, like most others that guide the difficult and intricate work of the railway, is subject to modifications, according to the circumstances under which trains arrive, the state of the weather, the weight of the loads of goods trains, and the class of engine drawing them. Thus a light 'through' goods or cattle train may be started from a station on a clear day or night before a slow, frequently-stopping passenger train. It may be done at the station master's discretion—but at his responsibility. Again, it is the rule that no goods train is to leave a station if there is a passenger train to arrive, due before, but delayed on the road. But this rule, too, like many others, not only may be broken, but *must* be broken should the efficient working of the service require it. It may happen that, from facts which come to his knowledge, either by telegraph, signals, or otherwise, the station master has reason to think that a passenger train which is due may not come for some time; and he is then justified promptly to despatch the goods train, but taking care to inform the driver of the coming passenger train of the existence of the goods train in front and its next shunting place." Innumerable, indeed, are the circumstances under which a station master has to act with quick judgment, sound discretion, and courtesy, and the various qualities required for the due discharge of all these functions are by no means common.

Such services can be discharged only by the effective co-operation of an adequate staff. At a station like Nottingham, for instance, there are some twenty clerks, twenty guards, thirty porters, forty-five signalmen, a dozen men and boys in connection with the parcel office, besides lamp-men, carriage-cleaners, ticket-examiners, shunters, fish-porters, and others, about 170 in all, upon each of whom devolves duties which require constant attention, practical experience, and good conduct.

Station masters usually consist of two classes, arranged according to the importance of the stations. To speak more precisely, there are two ranks of station masters: the first-class station master, and another—another being a rank widely comprehensive. The appointment of all the staff is made from the superintendent's office; but the local station master may introduce and commend the applicant, and he is frequently officially invited to do so. If the station master has any fault to find with a member of his staff, he reports it with particulars to the superintendent; and, if the offence should be of sufficient gravity, the delinquent may be suspended by the station master, pending the matter being dealt with at headquarters.

Station masters are appointed from those who have had experience in, and who show aptitude for, the duties of the office. As a rule, they come from the superintendent's departments, but sometimes from the goods'. A knowledge of only the goods' would not give the requisite qualifications: there must be a thorough familiarity with signalling, and with the working of trains. Sometimes a man begins as a porter, is then a porter-guard, and through his practical efficiency wins promotion to the office of a station master at a small station. But ordinarily they have begun as booking clerks, have gradually learned the working of all the details of the station, and have thus become qualified for the higher position.

The salary of station masters is progressive. A second-class officer begins with perhaps £95; it will be increased next year to £120, and will rise for a few years at the rate of £20 a year. Some of the great companies make £120 or £130 the minimum for a first-class station master; the boundary line signifying also whether they are entitled to a first or second-class pass in travelling. The salary may steadily rise to a maximum of about £350. If a house is also provided, rent is charged; but £20 is the maximum rent demanded. Sometimes a company has to buy house property near its station in order to avoid paying "compensation" to a former owner: such houses may be eligible for the residence of their servants.

One of the most critical duties of station masters is that of working through the traffic of a great main line on a single line. An accident has occurred, blocking one road, and until it is cleared, a safe passage for both up and down trains must be provided. Not long ago we had the opportunity of learning how these are performed. We were one night travelling by express from King's Cross, when, by the slower speed of the train, and by its stopping at various stations unauthorized by the time-table, we inferred that something was amiss; and, at length, at a roadside station we ascertained that a serious accident had occurred, that several persons had been injured, that the down line was blocked, and that it would be at least midnight before we could get through. After a long time we were allowed cautiously and slowly to start. We went a few miles along the down line, and then, once more, were stopped. It was as dark as pitch; and, save the blowing off of the steam of the engine, and a low conversation between the guard, the engine-driver, and a man who emerged with his lamp from the gloom, we could see and hear nothing. At length we could catch the long whistle, and then the roar of an approaching up train. Louder and louder it came; and with a flash and a scream, it passed us, and was gone. A few minutes more, and another up train came by with a crash; and yet a third, and a fourth; and once more we were left to ourselves. "Now," said a signalman to our engine-driver, "back by the cross-over on to the up rails, run down to Welwyn crossing, back again on to the down line, and go ahead!" Accordingly we were slowly shunted on to the very rails on which, a few minutes before, those up trains had been running with such terrible speed. Then our engine was reversed, and away we ran; we passed the workmen who, by torch and firelight, were clearing the down line, where precious blood had so recently been spilt, and precious limbs had so recently been shattered; and we were thankful when, after a pause, we crossed over by what was to us a facing point to our own down rails, and eventually reached in safety our destination.

It is, however, of interest to know that all the arrangements necessary for the working of single line traffic, day or night, can be carried out with precision and safety. The Great Northern Company, for instance, requires that, under such circumstances, "the following rule shall be rigidly put in force." A pilot or goods or coal engine must be obtained; and "written orders" must be "given at both ends of the single line by the chief officer on the spot, that no engine or train be allowed to go on it without the pilot engine is at the end from which the train is about to start; the district agent will then proceed to pass the traffic on one line, accompanying the pilot engine backwards and forwards." If a pilot cannot be procured, "one man, whose name must be given to the person" in charge of the arrangements at each end, "must be appointed, in writing, to act as pilot man, and he must ride on every train or engine in both directions, and this one man must continue riding to and fro between the aforesaid places until relieved."

The financial responsibility of a station master may be considerable. At a first-class country station he may receive from fares and from the district collector as much as £10,000 in cash at a time, and may have to pay £1,000 in wages on the same day. But the £1,000 will not be taken out of the £10,000: the wages will be received in full, and the money received will be sent away in full.

Upon some station masters, not strictly official exceptional duties devolve. It is so, for instance, with the station master at Hawes junction, on the Settle and Carlisle line, who renders valuable services to the Meteorological Society and to the public. On the western slope of the embankment, a little to the north of the station, are placed water-gauges, barometers, and various other appliances, the data of which, collected at various hours, are daily transmitted to London. The following is an exact copy of the message sent on the day we happened to call:—

86032 04235 85532 02431 29000
37270 Slight showers snow during night. Very cold.*

* In the first group of figures, the first three represent the reading of the barometer, the last two refer to the wind, and state that it is north. The second group mentions the force of the wind, weather, and temperature. In the other groups the readings of the barometer, the direction and force of the

Station masters have their perplexities as well as other people. An illustration may be mentioned. A certain station master on a branch line in Leicestershire had given orders to the driver of a goods train to take away with him some empty trucks that stood in a siding. The driver demurred; the station master insisted; the driver flatly refused, and did so with gestures which—as the sequel will show—added, as the station master considered, insult to disobedience. Not long afterwards a passenger train arrived, in one of the carriages of which the chairman of the company was seated—a gentleman distinguished, among other qualities, by his extreme gravity of demeanour and sense of decorum. The station master at once mentioned his grievance. "And what did the driver say?" inquired the chairman, after hearing sundry particulars of the dispute. "He said he wouldn't take the trucks, sir," returned the station master. "He positively refused, did he?" exclaimed the chairman. "Yes, sir, he did." "And what did he do then?" continued the chairman. "He started his engine, sir," added the station master, "and did like this, sir;" and the station master, in too literal imitation of the example of the offending driver, put his thumb to his nose, and stretched out his fingers in a manner like that of certain rude little boys when they take what we believe is popularly designated "a sight." It so happened that several persons from a little distance on the platform were watching this somewhat animated conversation of the station master with his august superior; but though they could not hear what was said, they were surprised—if not scandalized—to observe that just as the train was moving away, the station master was plainly seen apparently most mutinously "taking a sight" at the chairman of the company of which he was a servant.

A playful writer has made the following comments upon the names of sundry station masters engaged in the service of the Midland Railway. "On the Midland system," he said, "there

---

wind at various hours of the day, the rainfall in the twenty-four hours, the temperature at the time, and the maximum and minimum temperature are given. If there is a dead calm, there is no "force" or "direction" of wind to tell, and cyphers are used. Notes are added with regard to the appearance of the sky and the weather.

are only ten station masters who can be represented under their true colours; these are seven Browns, two Whites, and one Green. The naturalist will be surprised to learn that one Eagle, two Martins, two Foxes, and a Dolphin are employed by the company, and may be seen booking passengers and parcels to various parts of the country. The geologist would find Stone at Gargrave, Cliff at Elslack, Hill at Ben Rhydding, and Home at Armley. Botanists would have to go to Rothwell Haigh to find one solitary Fearn, and the florist would be delighted to find at Draycott a full-blown Rose each day, whilst a Marigold is perpetually blooming at Wolverhampton. Timber would appear to be scarce, as there is only one Poplar at Dronfield, one Ash at Bentham, and a solitary Twigg at Unstone. Fruits are anything but abundant, there being only one Cherry at Southwell, a Nutt at Barnt Green, and a good-sized Plumb at King's Norton; though an Orchard exists at Sandiacre, and an Appleyard at King's Cross. It appears absurd to keep Clay at Sutton and Potters at Ketton and Loughton. There is a Furnace at Cromford, a Brook at Ashwell, whilst Bells are kept at Nottingham Road and Hampton. And, oh, how the mighty are fallen! two Kings, one Baron, three Knights, a Marshal, a Herald, a Judge, and a Friar lustily call out the names of their respective stations to thousands who little dream of their former greatness. For all domestic purposes, four Cooks have been deemed sufficient; but only one Carver (though Moore could be had from Oakley if required). Tradesmen would find Turners at Woodlesford and Bugsworth, Smiths at Stanton Gate and Settle, and a Skinner at Duffield, whilst a Master could be had from Apperley Bridge, if required. A Barber is kept constantly at Pinxton, Taylors at Budworth, Kentish Town, and Helpstone, and ready-made Coates sufficient for two companies are always on hand at Barnsley. A Miller is kept at Fishponds, and a Gardiner at Bristol. Historians will be surprised to learn that the Welsh reside at Barrow, and the Scotts at Thorpe. To provide a dinner (unless you could put up with a Fry from Gloucester), Salmon would have to be had from Harpenden, Rice from Hitchen, and Porter from Radford, whilst Salt would have to be procured from Basford, and Pepper from Camp Hill. *Entrées* could be had from Walsall or Berkeley, Jelly being kept at both stations. The Stocks are at

Kilnhurst, as a warning to evil-doers, and *per contra* at Rawmarsh an Organ has been sent for their use. The station master at Great Bridge is said to be Rich; at Belfast, Little; Kegworth, Cross; Thurgaton, Kind; Little Eaton and Haslour, Sharpe; Hazlewood, Swift; and Steeton, Wright. A full-rigged Ship has long been kept at Wisbeach, and a Brigstock may be seen unfinished at Kirby Muxloe. If only a Rivett is lost at Broughton, it may be found at Rolleston. The facilities for recreation are great. You may Read at Willington, Hunt at Wilnecote and Gloucester, Gamble at Water Orton, and admire the Rainbow at Eckington, in a very few hours. English geography has been taken great liberties with, and we are asked to believe that Warwick is in Lincoln, Buckingham in Blackwell, Sunderland in Crouch Hill, Bolton in Terrington, and Buxton in Hassop. We are also told that the East is at Stoke-on-Trent. Yorke is where he is wanted, and the garden of Eden can be seen at St. Albans. Two stations (which shall be nameless) are handed over to the mercy of two living Savages. Finally, to be grave, the Tombs are at Peak Forest, and the Saxton's house at Manningham; and, though truth is sometimes stranger than fiction, it is notorious that only one Christian is to be found amongst the entire number of the company's servants!"

An important class of duties discharged at every station are those of the booking clerk. He has been playfully described as "the young gentleman of pleasing manners, who hands you your ticket through a pigeon-hole, and flings about sovereigns and silver as if coin came as natural to him as mud comes to a hippopotamus." In the early days of railways, passengers, on some lines, were required to give and to spell their names to the clerk, in order that they might be written on a large green paper ticket; and, in other cases, metal tickets were used, on which was engraved the name of the station to which the traveller was going. Their size and shape are indicated in the engraving drawn from a ticket we have seen, formerly in use on the Leicester and Swannington Railway. When the passengers reached their

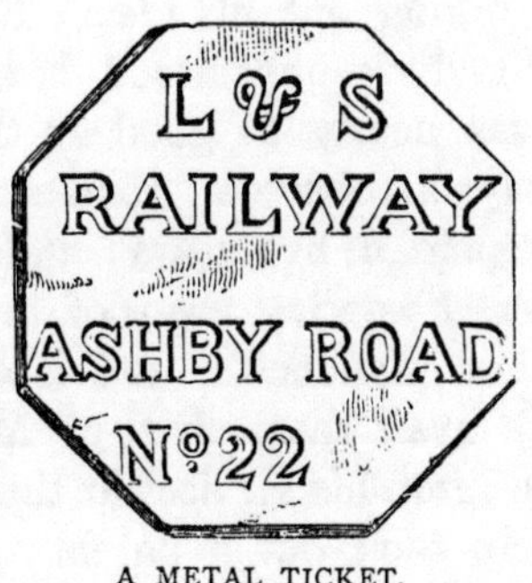

A METAL TICKET.

destination, these tickets were collected by the guard, placed in a leather pouch, and taken back to Leicester to be used again. But improvements came, and came in an interesting way.

A Quaker, in the year 1840, was walking in a field in Northumberland, and he had an idea. Though a man of integrity, he had in business been unsuccessful, and was now a railway clerk at a little station on the Newcastle and Carlisle line. When a passenger came, it was the duty of Thomas Edmondson—for that was the name of the clerk—to tear the bit of paper off from the printed sheet, and, with pen and ink, to fill up the form for the use of the traveller on that journey. On that particular walk on that day in the field he suddenly paused, as an idea struck him how much time, trouble, and liability to mistake would be saved if the work were done by a mechanical process—if tickets were printed with the names of stations, the class of carriages, and the dates, and all on one uniform system by all the railways. "Most inventors accomplish their great deeds by degrees, one thought suggesting another from time to time; but, when Thomas Edmondson showed his family the spot in the field where his invention occurred to him, he used to say that it came into his mind complete, in its whole scope and all its details." And Mr. Edmondson's idea has saved a good deal of trouble to a good many people besides himself.

On the machines thus invented may be seen the name of Blaylock. Blaylock was a watchmaker, an acquaintance of Edmondson's, and a man whom he knew to be capable of working out his idea. Edmondson told him what he wanted; Blaylock understood him; and the third machine they made was nearly as good as those now in use. "The one we saw," says an observer, "had scarcely wanted five shillings' worth of repairs in five years; and when it needs more, it will be from sheer wearing away of the brasswork by constant hard friction. The Manchester and Leeds Railway Company were the first to avail themselves of Mr. Edmondson's invention; and they secured his services at their station at Oldham Road for a time. He took out a patent; and his invention became so widely known and appreciated that he soon withdrew himself from other engagements, to perfect its details and provide tickets to meet the daily growing demand. He let out his patent on profitable terms—ten shillings per mile per annum; that is, a railway of thirty miles long paid him fifteen pounds a year for a licence to print its own tickets by his apparatus; and a railway of sixty miles long paid him thirty pounds, and so on. As his profits began to come in, he began to spend them; and it is not the least interesting part of his history to see how. He had early in life been a bankrupt. The very first use he made of his money was to pay every shilling he had ever owed. He was forty-six when he took that walk in the field in Northumberland. He was fifty-eight when he died, on the twenty-second of June, 1852."

The dating-press, which stands on the counter of every booking-office like a sort of bottle-jack, and with the click of which we are all familiar, was also an invention of Mr. Edmondson's. The only attention it requires is that the clerk the last thing at night changes the type for the next day, and occasionally sees that the ribbon is properly saturated with the ink the type requires.

Among the duties of the booking clerk is to keep an ample supply of tickets for his own station to every other to which passengers are booked, and especially when fairs or other popular gatherings are likely to cause a special demand. Some tickets are rarely used, of others he will receive 10,000 at a time.

Before the booking clerk lifts his hatch to issue tickets for a train, he sees that everything is in order. Before him is a set of five bowls, in which his change is arranged. Over these a lid, A, can, when necessary, be drawn and locked. The bowls, B B, usually contain respectively two-shilling pieces and

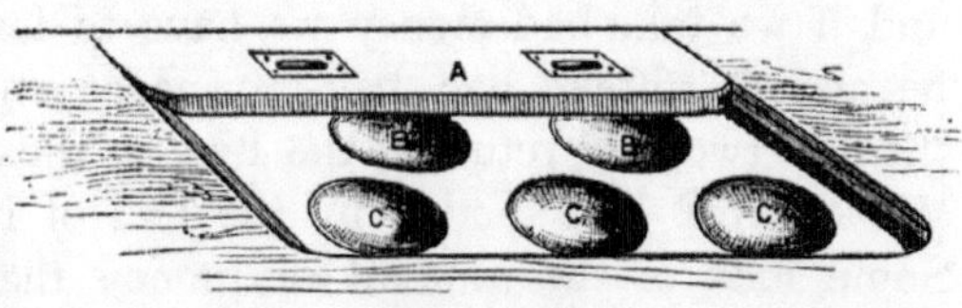

CASH BOWLS.

gold; the other three, CCC, have severally half-crowns, shillings, and sixpences; the whole sum amounting to £1, or, in some instances, to £2; so that, after the passengers have been supplied, and the train has gone, and the clerk has put down his "hatch," he can the more easily "take the tickets off," and balance. Just above the row of tubes that contain the tickets runs a narrow strip of slate, on which, when he issues a ticket, he writes the "commencing number" of the ticket—the number of the first ticket issued for that train to that station; and as the tickets generally stand with the lowest protruding a little forwards, he can tell by a glance at the tubes those from which tickets have been issued, and by pulling out the bottom one, and comparing its number with the number marked on the slate, he knows at once how many for that station have been issued. The clerk now proceeds to enter in a "train-book," printed and ruled for the purpose, the number of tickets he has issued to each station, and the money he has received; and thus he ascertains the amount required to balance with the cash in his bowls, less the £1 or £2 change previously placed there.

The entries in the train-books thus made are at the end of the day all "totalled up," and are recorded in a "summary book." The cash taken through the day has to agree with the total in this book, and with the amount he pays that day into the bank.

At the end of the month the commencing and closing numbers of each set of tickets to each station is entered into the "classification book," and the total amount of money received for ordinary tickets, season tickets, parcels, and telegrams, must agree with the sum paid during the month into the bank. A copy of the "classification sheets" is taken from the book, and forwarded to the audit office of the company, and also a copy of the "foreign proportion sheets" for the use of the Clearing House.

"Everything," said a clerk, "has to balance to a farthing; and if we take bad money we have to lose it. I have taken," he added, "fifteen bad half-crowns at one races, but I broke them in two, and returned the bits to those who offered them. We can tell bad money by the feel of it, without seeing it." Some idea of the amount of money that flows through the narrow wickets of some booking offices may be formed from the fact that the "takings" by the ten booking clerks at Euston station, from passenger tickets alone, amount to upwards of half a million sterling a year, and are gradually rising towards £600,000. Each takes on the average fifty thousand pounds in the twelvemonth.

But when a railway ticket, issued by the booking clerk, has travelled with its purchaser to the journey's end, and has been given up to the collector, it is not yet done with. These used-up bits of pasteboard are tied into bundles; are duly scheduled as to their number, class, and station; are despatched to the audit office, and are checked by the returns sent in from the stations whence the tickets were issued. If the ticket carried the traveller simply over part or all of the line of the issuing company, its career is completed at the audit department of that company; but if the traveller went with it a mile farther on to a foreign line, the ticket also commences a new journey, and is despatched, with sundry data referring to it, to an important institution known as "the Clearing House."

When the first long railway was completed, and when a traveller with one ticket and one payment could take a journey from one end of that line to the other, it was considered a great event; but when several different railways came to be connected together, the question was asked whether one ticket could not be made to clear a passenger, or even a parcel, over the whole journey. Hence the proposal to establish a clearing house for railways. It was not an original idea. There had been clearing houses before there were railroads. Banks had a clearing house, and there had been at Charing Cross a clearing house for coaches. The greater part of mankind, it has been well said, "is naturally averse to putting its hand in its pocket; but when this operation must of necessity be performed, wishes to make short work of the agony, and forget it. Now, this happy oblivion would have been impossible to any traveller who essayed the road between, for instance, London and Holyhead, but for a clearing house. No one person could conveniently have 'horsed' a coach 'through' between those places." Hence the horses of one proprietor ran for forty or fifty miles, then those of another took up the running for a similar distance, and then others had their turn. But though the road was "horsed" by sections, travellers could not think of paying by sections. Hence a coaching clearing house, which enabled passengers to book through and pay their fare at one end of their journey, was founded, and it was a precursor of the organization in Seymour Street, Euston Square, London.

In 1841, Mr. Kenneth Morison, chief auditor of what was then the London and Birmingham Railway, proposed to Lord Wolverton that the clearing house system used in banking and coaching should be extended to railways. In 1842 five companies agreed; in 1846 there were forty-six such companies; and in 1850 the "Railway Clearing Act" was passed, which defined the powers of the new establishment. There were, of course, at that time pessimist "prophets, robed in wet blankets," who did not foresee the issues of the change, but the anticipations of even the most sanguine as to the success of the work undertaken have perhaps been exceeded.

One department of the work of the Clearing House deals with railway tickets. If a ticket carries a traveller, not only over the railway of the issuing company, but on to what is technically called a "foreign" line, that ticket is forwarded to the Clearing House, and instead of each individual company settling its accounts with perhaps five and thirty other companies, the exact amount of money due respectively to each on every ticket is determined by the Clearing House. It has a debtor and creditor account with them one and all, and by it, as the common creditor of all, the balance due to each at the end of every month is paid over.

The arithmetic thus involved is enormous, but it is worked out every day down to such problems as the fourth part of a schoolboy, and to the charges on "horses, carriages, and corpses," which it is directed are not "to be included in the parcels." As the items to be dealt with for passengers—besides goods—on a line of thirty stations amount to thousands, some idea may be gathered of the bewildering character of the business to be dealt with, and the multitude of the items to be accurately determined.

The Clearing House also does much more than this. At every junction in the kingdom where the lines of two companies converge, the Clearing House stations what are called "number-takers." Their duty is to take the number of every carriage, wagon, or other vehicle, and of every sheet that passes from one company's system to another; to make a record of every mile thus travelled over a foreign line, and of every hour in which each vehicle has to be charged "demurrage" for delay or detention. For instance, let it be supposed that a truck laden with fish is sent from Yarmouth to a consignee in Liverpool. The truck arrives by Great Eastern line safely at Peterborough. Its number is taken, and note is made of the company to which it belongs. From Peterborough the truck bound for Liverpool has several courses open to it. It might be sent along the Great Northern to Retford; or by the Midland to Burton-on-Trent, and thence by Crewe; or by Midland, then *via* Manchester, to Liverpool. That truck and its route become perfectly known to the Clearing House. The ownership of the truck is also noted, since companies not unfrequently use the first that comes to hand, to whomsoever it may belong. The knowledge thus acquired is sent in to the Clearing House, and also the amount of charges, and whether paid in advance or not; and the Clearing House decides the proportions in which the sum charged is to be divided.

The fish truck just spoken of might possibly have its earnings divided among four companies. "First and foremost come the 'terminal' charges, as they are called, generally 4*s.* per ton for ordinary goods, 1*s.* 6*d.* for grain, and 9*d.* for minerals. These terminal charges are credited in equal shares to the terminus of collection or reception and the terminus of delivery, and the rest of the sum is divided between the several companies according to mileage. In the instance of the fish truck the terminal charges would be first divided between Yarmouth and Liverpool, the Midland line over which the truck merely runs without lading and sheeting, or unlading and unsheeting, getting no share of these, but only its mileage." Then comes the question of the truck itself, for the owning company is entitled to charge the others for hire of rolling stock, and has to be credited therewith by the Clearing House. Its business thus includes the charging, counter-charging, checking, and settling accounts, even to the damage, for instance, to a cask of spirits stove in, or to a wagon that has broken down, or to a leakage in a whisky barrel which has passed over the lines of several different companies, no one of which thinks itself to blame. When rolling-stock was injured while in the hands of another company than that owning it; whose fault was it? Was the wheel a bad one, or was it badly used?

The money here annually cleared is about £17,500,000; the settlements made yearly by the Merchandise Department number 2,500,000, and passenger settlements are some 2,750,000. The number of miles charged for use of rolling stock is over 500,000,000, the work involving upwards of 30,000,000 of entries yearly.

The number of persons employed at the Clearing House is

necessarily large, and is increasing as through traffic over foreign lines increases. When Mr. Noble, the present General Manager of the Midland Company, was at the head of the Clearing House, the clerks were about 800 in number; there are now 2,100.

The experiences of booking clerks are sometimes amusing.

"Yes," remarked one, "some passengers are odd. They ask for tickets for places they are thinking of, but not going to, and are very angry when we give them one they don't want. Others sometimes come short of money, and they wish us to trust them for the balance. We don't turn them away if we can help it. If they have luggage, we send them and it to our station master's office. He perhaps takes what money they have, and issues a way-bill. So much 'paid on' and so much 'to pay'; their luggage, or their watch, or whatever they have to give us, is handed with this way-bill to the guard of the train they are going by; he gives it to the station master at their destination; and when they have discharged the balance, they get their property again. Yes, sometimes we've been cheated. A sailor's box has been found with bricks in it, instead of clothes; but now, if we have any doubt, we require the owner to open it, and to show us the contents, before we issue the ticket." Another booking clerk had a handsome meerschaum pipe left with him as security for a fare he consented to advance; but it was not reclaimed, and at length the clerk sold it as a curiosity to recoup himself. In a third instance a traveller left a white-handled pocket-knife with the clerk in lieu of a halfpenny of which he was short in purchasing his ticket, and never came for it. "I have often," said a Derbyshire booking clerk, "lent a neighbour who was going to sell butter and eggs at Chesterfield the amount of her fare, and she has paid me when she returned."

Travellers are of all sorts—most of them voluntary, some involuntary. In January, 1877, half a dozen children, each about ten years of age, were charged before the Bristol magistrates with having travelled, without taking their tickets or paying their fares, on the Great Western Railway, in the truck of a goods train, for three days and three nights. It was found that they had been playing in the goods station yard at Plymouth when a guard shouted to them, and they became so frightened that they hid themselves in one of the trucks. Keeping very quiet, so as not to be detected, they all fell asleep. During the night, the truck was attached to a goods train which was being formed for Penzance. The train then started without any one knowing that the stowaways were there. The truck was shunted when the train reached Truro in the night, and there the urchins woke up, and, being much frightened, they stole out of the station and tried to walk back towards Plymouth. They had only gone a short distance when the rain came down in torrents, and so drenched them that they determined to go back to the railway station, where, unobserved, they got into another covered truck, which they thought would take them back to Plymouth. This truck was booked through to Bristol with a load of general goods; it was consequently not shunted at Plymouth, but with numerous delays and shuntings in the course of the goods traffic *en route*, it arrived at Bristol. The urchins slept a good deal of the time, but were so exhausted when discovered that three or four of them could not stand. They soon recovered under the attention they received, but appeared in the most bewildered state of mind. They were taken to the police station and cared for during the night. Their names and addresses were telegraphed to Plymouth, and the Plymouth police discovered that inquiries had been made at the police station for two or three of the little travellers, and their parents were in great distress at their loss. The magistrates expressed their astonishment that the boys' hunger had not caused them to declare themselves. They were eventually dismissed, the bench expressing the opinion that it was hardly a case of fraud.

The parcels office is an important department of every station. Parcels are collected from the parcel offices in the town, and also by "collecting vans" which call at the wholesale houses. Nottingham, for instance, has three receiving houses, and the whole town is mapped out into five divisions, called A, B, C, D, and E, a van being assigned to each. "We have," said the chief clerk, "four such vans collecting every night. They begin at 6.30 and finish at 9.30, or, in a busy season, an hour later. If, when the vans call, the parcels are not ready, they have to be called for again, and meanwhile the vans go for orders elsewhere. There is a regular scrimmage at night. The Midland, the London and North-Western, the Great Northern, and the parcel companies are all eager to obtain goods, and they each do their best to win. As soon as a van has got a load, it comes to the station to discharge, and then hurries off for more."

Various towns have their special classes of parcels, according to the local trade. The lace and millinery trades of Nottingham, for instance, yield large numbers of light and valuable parcels, which perhaps have to be sent off to catch some vessel that may be sailing from Liverpool; and, "four hours after we receive them they are delivered to the consignee at the dock side." Millinery goods are made at Nottingham in tens of thousands of dozens, and as they are despatched in light boxes they are classed in what is called the "frail" trade, for which fifty per cent. additional is charged. The number of parcels "inwards" and "outwards" thus received and despatched is very large. At a station like Nottingham they may average 30,000 a month, while at Christmas time there may be 5,000 a day for three days together.

"Yes," said the chief clerk, "we have everything you can imagine sent by 'parcel'—birds, beasts, live fishes in tins, badgers and foxes; in fact, everything from a live gorilla to a dead baby." "A gorilla!" we exclaimed. "Yes; it was sent to a gentleman at Loughborough who had a fancy for keeping such pets; but when it got there it was found to be loose in the van; and so they sent it, van and all, on to Nottingham. It was bigger than a man. I tried to capture it, but it bit me across the thigh, and then rushed out into the street. Everybody gave chase with sticks and dogs; and at length they ran it into a timber yard, where two dogs tackled it. But it knocked them over time after time with its fists. At last two men got a chain and a rope over it, and it was sent back to Loughborough."

Many curious incidents have occurred in connection with the business of parcels offices. One night, at a certain station in the north of England, a large hamper arrived by the mail, booked as containing a live dog, and addressed to a clergyman in a certain Lincolnshire village. The hamper was taken into the parcels office to await the proper train; and some lads, interested in dogs, resolved to gratify their curiosity by having a sly peep at the visitor, and they gently untied the thick string with which the hamper was secured. But no sooner had they done so than, with a loud snarl and yell of anger and terror, the dog leaped up at the lid, out of the hamper, and rushed out of the office; and though hotly pursued by clerks, porters, and guards, it sped down the platform, and was lost—among darkness, sidings, and carriages.

Blank despair was on the faces of the too curious clerks. What was to be done? What a row there would be. At length a suggestive mind hazarded a proposal: "Why not send Nipper?" Nipper was an old dog, "a thorough-bred mongrel," a disreputable-looking thief, who hung about the station under a kind of law of "toleration." But the case was desperate, and required a desperate remedy. Accordingly, Nipper was found, feasted, decorated with a pink ribbon tied into a festive-looking bow—to show that he was fondly cherished and was in holiday attire. He was then carefully packed in the hamper, securely fastened, and forwarded by the next train. No complaint, we are told, ever reached the railway company; and the hope is cherished that Nipper became a reformed character, that he lived long and peacefully, and ended his days with the respect of the parish as the clergyman's dog.

We enter a parcels office just before a train is starting. Men and boys, porters and clerks are shouting to one another at the top of their voices. A parcel porter seizes a parcel, calls out the name and destination written thereon, and the clerk replies by assigning the route along which it is to travel. "Tomlinson, Falmouth," exclaims the parcel porter; "Bristol and West," replies the clerk. "Aberdeen," bawls another porter; "Edinburgh," answers the clerk. Meanwhile, while the porter shouts the address to the clerk, and he replies, the clerk, with the aid of a "manifold writer," makes out a way-bill in duplicate, with name, address, and amount to be charged. One way-bill is sent with the parcel, the other is filed. At the end of the day the duplicates are placed together, the amounts entered thereon are checked with the cash book; and they are then passed to the "abstract clerk," who abstracts the amounts that will be due from each station to which the parcels have been sent. At the end of the month these abstracts are balanced, summarised, and sent to the audit office, where they are checked with the foreign stations, and then despatched to the Clearing House for the division of the receipts among the different companies over whose lines the parcels have travelled.

The parcels are now handed, with their way-bills, and also with any "despatches" (letters on the company's business), to the guard of the train, who at once begins to sort the parcels and to check them with the way-bills. Sometimes this is sharp work, for it has to be done before the train reaches the first station at which it stops—which may be only a mile or two distant, and here some parcel and bill may have to be delivered.

"Inwards" parcels, when received, are taken into the office, called off to the clerk, checked with the way-bills, and, when all is found correct, sorted for the different deliveries, and distributed by the vans.

At the head of the parcels office is the chief clerk. All the other clerks, except the "abstract clerk," take weekly turns at the different duties of the office, each thus becoming familiar with all the work of the office, and the hours of service also being equalized. The parcel porters interchange their work in a similar way.

The duties of the parcel clerks are, by practice, discharged with great rapidity and accuracy. The work is all done in a noise and a bustle, but the clerks become so used to it that, with two or three sets at work at the same time, they will despatch or receive two or three hundred parcels in half an hour. This is important, because the time is often short between the arrival of the vans and the departure of the trains, and every parcel must leave by the earliest train.

The signalman belongs to an important and responsible class of railway servants. Some of his duties may be described. He has to see that the points and signals are kept in perfect order; and to report to the station master, and to the inspector of the permanent way, any case in which the points, switches, or signals are defective. He must frequently try the working of all his signals to see that they work well. He must know that care is used in putting on a distant signal, and must watch the signal or its repeater to see that it fully obeys the lever. He must ascertain that the signal wires are kept at the proper length by means of the regulating screws, so as to allow for the variations made by the temperature. In the event of a distant signal not working properly, a man with hand signals and detonators must be stationed within sight of the home signal; and, if necessary, other men must be placed at intervals on to the defective signal, for the purpose of repeating to the man stationed at the distant signal the signals exhibited at the home signal. "If, when two or more trains approach a junction at nearly the same time, the signalman should have lowered the signals for a train which should have been kept back for the passage of another, he must not attempt to alter the order of the trains by reversing the signals, but must put all the signals to danger, until all the trains have been brought to a stand, when precedence can be given to the proper train. Signalmen are also required to ascertain how the ordinary and special trains in their respective districts are running, and to give information to guards. The guard in charge of a train which should shunt for another train to pass, must instruct the engine-driver where to shunt, and on arriving at a station, junction, or siding, where he should shunt for another train to pass, must inquire whether the train due to pass him there is late. The guard must be informed as to the whereabouts of the train, and, subject to the order of the station master, must proceed or shunt, as may be necessary. If he goes forward he must take care that there is ample time to reach the place he intends to proceed to, and to get his train shunted off the main line."

Other important rules are also laid down for signalmen. Thus "no engine or vehicle must be shunted or moved from one main line to the other, until the proper signals have been exhibited, as may be required; and care must be taken when the main line is about to be obstructed after a distant signal has been placed at danger for the purpose of protecting it, to allow sufficient time to elapse for any approaching engine or train which may have been near to or within such signal before it was so placed at danger, to pass before the obstruction is allowed."

The signalman must see that each train that passes has a tail lamp on the last vehicle, in order that he may be satisfied that the whole of the train has gone, and that none of the vehicles have broken away. If the signalman observes anything unusual about the train as it runs by, such as a signal of alarm by a passenger, or that a tail lamp is missing, or is not burning, that goods are falling off, or that a vehicle is on fire, or that there is a hot axle-box, he must give the station in advance the signal to stop and examine the train, and that station must immediately exhibit the danger signal. The train, when thus stopped, must be carefully examined and dealt with as occasion may require.

Again, if a portion of a train should be running back in the wrong direction, the signalman must give the prescribed signal to the signalman at the next signal-box towards which the portion of the train is running; and the man who receives this signal must stop any train about to proceed on the same line, and take protective measures, such as turning the runaway train across to the other line or into a siding, as may be most expedient under the circumstances. If a portion of a train has escaped, and is running away in the proper direction on the right line, the section in advance must be signalled accordingly, and this signal must, if necessary, be sent forward, and such other measures be taken as are expedient. If a signalman observes that a train has become divided, the "train divided" signal must be used. If the train is running on a falling gradient, where the stoppage of the first part would risk a collision with the second part following, the signalman must take measures accordingly, with instructions for which he is provided. Each signalman must register in the train-book the time of his arrival on duty and of his leaving and affix his signature.

The duties of guards are perhaps known to our readers. Some, however, of themselves may be unaware how greatly the position of guards has been improved. "In my early days," remarked one of them, "we were called brakesmen; we had no brake-vans; we had to ride on the top of the carriages or on the loaded vans, anywhere we could, and to get on and off anyhow we could. And on a frosty night it *was* getting off. Our limbs were often benumbed with cold; we were sometimes so stiff with cold that we had to be lifted off, and some, when they were lifted off, were found to be frozen to death. When trains were running down an incline, we had to scramble or jump from one wagon to another in order to put on perhaps five or six brakes. When you jumped upon a load of goods sheeted down, you could not possibly tell what you jumped upon, and, in consequence, many men lost their limbs or their lives. When a train stopped for anything, the brakesman had to go back a quarter of a mile ; he was not to return till he was whistled in, and then he had to run in as quick as he could for fear he should be overtaken by a following train. I have run many a pair of shoes off in my time in doing this."

We need not say that the duties of guards are now very different from all this, and that their circumstances are incomparably improved. Their responsibilities are, however, equally great, and the importance of their services is fully admitted. The driver and stoker may be useful, but the guard is "the cynosure of all eyes. 'Where is the guard?' cries the aged dame transfixed among a pile of trunks. 'Where is the guard?' shouts the stout gentleman, vainly seeking his smoking compartment; and 'Where is the guard?' echoes the bewildered young lady, who has lost her lap-dog and her temper. To all and everybody the guard is the leader, the representative of the train. Proudly as Louis XIV. in his royal robes, the British railway guard, standing in full uniform at the side of the winged express preparing to start, may lay his hand on his heart and say, 'Le train, c'est moi.'"

Ten hours is the usual daily work of the guard. But it is found to be best for the service, and for the comfort of the whole body of the guards, that there should be change from day duties to night duties, and from the conduct of one train to another; and these arrangements go by the name of "roadsters"—pronounced "roosters." For example, "the guard of a London and North Western 'through' train will leave Euston for Liverpool on Monday in charge of the 9 a.m. express, which arrives at 2.45 p.m., and start from Liverpool on his return journey with the 4 p.m. train, arriving at Euston at 9.15 p.m. The next day, Tuesday, the same guard will take charge of the train leaving Euston at noon, which, dividing at Shrewsbury, does not arrive at Liverpool till 6.15; but he will not then return to London, but stop at Liverpool for the night. It will be seen that on Monday the guard is on duty, or rather in his van, for just eleven hours, while on the Tuesday his hours on duty are not more than six and a quarter, so that, taking the average of both days, he has less than eight hours and a half per diem." But to this must be added the time before the starting and after the arrival of the trains, during which the guard has to be at his post.

The travelling done by an old guard may be considerable. With an average of 300 miles a day, and counting six working days in the week, it would come to 1,800 miles a week, 93,600 miles a year; and in twenty-five years of service, to no less than 1,330,000 miles—"equal to making three return journeys to the moon."

It is the duty of the guard to be in attendance half an hour before his train starts. While the train is at the station, the guards are under the orders of the station-master; the train itself being under the immediate control of the guard, who instructs the driver as to the general working of the train. The guard must satisfy himself before starting, and during the journey, that the train is properly loaded marshalled, coupled, lamped, greased, and sheeted; and that the brakes are in good working order. He must also carefully examine the loading of any vehicles he may attach on the way, and, if necessary, must have a load readjusted or a vehicle detached.

If the guard wishes to attract the attention of the engine-driver, he may, besides using the communication, apply his brake sharply, and release it suddenly. This operation, when repeated, will call the notice of the driver, to whom any necessary signal can be exhibited. When the driver gives three or more short, sharp whistles, or sounds the brake whistle, or applies the communication, the guard, or guards, must immediately apply the brakes. If from any cause a train is stopped except where it is efficiently protected by fixed signals, the guard, if there be only one, or the rear guard, if there be more than one, must immediately go back 1,200 yards to stop any following train; and must, besides his hand signals, take detonators, which are to be used by day as well as by night, and must place one detonator upon the line of rails on which the stoppage has happened, at a distance of 400 yards from his train, another at a distance of 800 yards, and two, ten yards apart, at a distance of 1,200 yards.

While a guard is in charge of a train, he has to make entries in a book provided for the purpose as to the running of his train, and, at the end of his journey, he transcribes them into a formal "journal," and sends it to the superintendent's office. This journal has some forty-four columns. In these have to be entered the names of the stations stopped at, the published time of departure, the times of actual arrival and departure, the time spent at each station, and the number of vehicles attached and detached. Space is also provided for the guard's explanatory "remarks." On the back of this journal are other spaces to be filled in: the number of the engine, or the numbers of the series of engines successively drawing the train; the names of the drivers and the firemen; the time lost by the engine arriving late to train; or by waiting for "foreign" trains; or waiting for their own Company's trains, or other causes. Particulars have also to be entered of any time lost on the journey, by engine in running, at stations, or by signals, etc.; the time gained; and the total number of minutes of late arrival. The guard has also to make an exact return with regard to the working of the continuous brake in use on his train. At the foot of the document the signature of the head guard has to be placed, and also the names of the under guards.

Some 1,600 of these "journals" are received daily at the superintendent's office of the Midland Company. These data are all carefully considered, and the cause of delay is, if necessary, "taken up" by the traffic inspectors or through the local station masters. We glance over some of these journals. There was a delay by such a train of four minutes through "attaching" a composite carriage; of one minute in "slowing" over a bridge that is being rebuilt, and of two minutes at another place in "excessing" a fare from a passenger who was perhaps too sleepy or too short of change to be more prompt. These guards' reports are "abstracted" into books printed, ruled, and bound for the purpose, so that the minute history of every individual train and the precise cause of any delay is on permanent record, and can be referred to at any time afterwards.

It is thus seen that much intelligence, activity, and watchfulness are required on the part of railway guards, and it is usually found that they are not deficient in these respects. An amusing illustration of the formal politeness of one of them once occurred at the Reigate station. The guard came to the window of a first-class carriage, and said: "Please, sir, will you have the goodness to change your carriage here?" "What for?" was the gruff reply of Mr. Bull within. "Because, sir, if you please, the wheel has been on fire since half-way from the last station!" Mr. B. looked angrily out; but when he saw that the wheel was sending forth a cloud of smoke, he lost no further time in condescending to comply with the request.

With the duties of railway porters our reader is acquainted. In some places they are more onerous than in others. At a London terminus one of them, with perhaps a tinge of exaggeration, thus told his tale: "My gang, as I say, comes on at a quarter to three in the morning,—a gang of twelve men. First of all we 'see up' a market train due about three—we unloads her, and that is pretty stiff work. Then in the fish season there are fish trains that keep arriving between the other trains. By-and-by comes the up limited mail, and there is the getting out of the bags, loading them into the van, shunting, and what not. Then there is a passenger train with fish and parcels; and then comes the six o'clock down, with newspapers—the papers are always very heavy—newspapers, horses, carriages, and such like gear. At 6.25 there is a short train, and then the 'Bristol cheap' at 6.45—milk cans and luggage. A cheap train is always a bothersome thing to start. There are lots of lone women and children, and they get mixed in such a contrairy way, and want an uncommon lot of sorting. More horses and carriages with the 7.45. Stop, I had forgotten the 7.30, a short train. The 8 o'clock West Midland and North train is always very heavy—especially with horses and carriages in the season. After she is out we gets time for a bit of breakfast, but have to be back in time to get the mails in to the 9.15, and load up the luggage. At 10 o'clock there is an 'out' long train that takes mostly a lot of fish, and is always heavy in luggage. Then the work gets warmer still with the 10.15 train, the 11, the 11.15, the 11.45, and the 12 trains. You don't have a minute's respite—on the tear all the time; for we have to 'make' the trains, unload and clean them. After we see out the 12.35, we are supposed to get our dinners, getting back at 1.30 to load for the 2 train, and then comes the 2.20 and the 2.40. After that there is the turning of the mail carriages on the turntables, that their heads may be the right way for the down journey. When this is over there is the 3.40 to load 'down,' and more truck work. When we are through with that we are supposed to be done, except on Saturdays, when we remain on till five o'clock to see the expresses up. But if there is anything extra going on, we stop on till the work is done, no matter how long, and the meal times—short enough they are at the best—are often cut into, so that a man has to get his food down anyhow."

Complaints are sometimes made of the want of due respect paid on the part of porters to passengers' luggage. It appears that occasionally a like lack of caution is manifested by owners to their own property. It is said that on a train lately on a western railroad in America, some passengers were discussing the carriage of explosives. One man contended that it was impossible to prevent or detect this; if people were not allowed to ship nitro-glycerine or dynamite legitimately, they'd smuggle it through in their baggage. This assertion was contradicted emphatically, and the passenger was laughed at, flouted, and ignominiously put to scorn. Rising up in his wrath he drew a capacious leather valise from under the seat, and slapping it emphatically on the cover, said: "Oh, you think they don't, eh? Don't carry explosives in cars? What's this?" and he gave the valise a resounding thump. "Thar's two hundred good dynamite cartridges in that air valise; sixty pounds of deadly material; enough to blow this yar train and the whole township from Cook county to Chimborazo. Thar's dynamite enough," he continued; but he was without an auditor, for the passengers had fled incontinently, and he could have sat down on twenty-two seats if he had wanted to. And the respectful way in which the baggage-men on the out-going trains in the evening handled the trunks and valises was pleasant to see.

The neglect of carefulness appears in one instance at least to have involved inconvenience to the offending official. "An unknown genius," says an American periodical, "the other day entrusted a trunk, with a hive of bees in it, to the tender mercies of a Syracuse 'baggage-smasher.' The company will pay for the bees, and the doctor thinks his patient will be round again in a fortnight or so."

Of railway servants it may be stated that every punishment, whether of fine or reprimand, is entered against the name of the man incurring it; and these records of men who commit themselves in any way are carefully examined and considered in dealing with any matters affecting their position. This fact is perfectly understood by the men, who know that any offences they have committed stand against their names in the company's books so long as they remain in its service; and that a sufficient number of "black marks" would ensure their dismissal or their reduction to less important positions.

But with regard to the conduct of railway servants generally, we agree with the sentiment of cordial respect expressed by Charles Dickens. "I would ask you," he said, in speaking on behalf of the Railway Provident Institution, "to consider what your experience of the railway servant is. I know what mine is. Here he is, in velveteen or in a policeman's dress, scaling cabs, storming carriages, finding lost articles by a kind of instinct, binding up lost umbrellas and walking sticks, wheeling trucks, counselling old ladies, with a wonderful interest in their affairs—mostly very complicated—and sticking labels upon all sorts of articles. I look around me. There he is again in a station master's uniform, directing and overseeing with the head of a general, and the manners of a courteous host. There he is again in a guard's belt and buckle, with a handsome figure, inspiring confidence in timid passengers. He is as gentle to the weak people as he is bold to the strong, and he has not a single hair in his beard that is not up to its work. I glide out of the station, there he is again, with a flag in his hands. There he is again, in the open country, at a level crossing. There he is again at the entrance to the tunnel. At every station that I stop at, there he is again, as alert as usual. There he is again at the arrival platform, getting me out of the carriage as if I was his only charge upon earth. Now, is there not something in the alacrity, in the ready zeal, in the interest of these men, that is not acknowledged, that is not expressed in their mere wages? And if your experience coincides with mine, and enables you to have this good feeling for, and to say a good word in regard of, railway servants, then if we take a human interest in them, they will take a human interest in us. We shall not be merely the 9.30 or the 10.30 rushing by, but we shall be an instalment of the considerate public that is ready to lend a hand to the poor fellows in their risk of their lives."

The question of what is, or is not, "personal luggage" may to some readers be of practical interest. "It may well be imagined," says the *Solicitors' Journal*, "that it is not always easy to decide what is 'personal' or 'ordinary' luggage. In the County Court at Exeter it was held that a photographic apparatus was not 'personal luggage.' In 'Cahill *v.* the London and North Western Railway Company' * it was held that a box containing only merchandise was not personal luggage. In 'The Great Northern Railway Company *v.* Shepherd' † it was decided, on the same ground, that a passenger could not recover for the loss of a number of ivory handles which were packed up with his luggage. And in 'Mytton *v.* the Midland Railway Company' ‡ the sketches of an artist were held not to be his 'ordinary luggage.'" On the other hand, a hamper containing two pairs of shooting boots, a couple of fowls, and apples and vegetables intended for a present were decided to be personal luggage, and, having been lost, the company had to pay the value of it. The dispute was not over the boots, but over the vegetables. Happily most of the railways give a wide interpretation to the law in this matter in favour of their passengers.

There are considerable advantages in the American methods with regard to passengers' luggage, especially for long journeys. "Checking the baggage," is an expressive phrase in the States. "I am going," remarks a traveller, "say from Utica to Toledo, and I have two parcels. Do I direct them carefully on parchment? No! I arrive at the station and get my ticket, followed by a muscular negro, Cuffy by name, who carries my baggage. He goes with me to the luggage van, and cries out:

"'Massa George, gib 'un a check for Toledo for this jebbleman.'

"Massa George looks up from a chaos of luggage, and answers to him:

"'How many?'

"'Two, and all going through.'

"'Two checks for Toledo—right!'

"As he speaks, Massa Jack, the under contractor, selects four brass tickets with leather loops attached to them, which hang with some hundreds of others from his arms, and, looping two on my luggage, hands me the two duplicates.

"'2359,' '2617' are the figures on my tickets, and on producing them at Toledo to-morrow, or to-morrow six months, my black portmanteau and blue hat-box will be handed to me. I shall find them, I know, as well as the brass labels, twins to mine,

---

* 9 W. R. 391. † 21. L J. Ex. 114, 286. ‡ 7 W. R. 737.

upon them. I shall call out to the porter or baggage-master, '2359, 2617,' and out will roll, as in a pantomime trick, my black and red portmanteau and my blue hat-box. Presently, before the train starts, Cuffy will call out the numbers to the luggag man, 'who stands by the van near the blazing red lamp, tha turns his face to currant jelly, and whose business it is to checl all luggage passing from Utica any whither.' You may go a thousand miles, and pass nights on the road, but need nevei give a sight to the luggage till you reach your destination."

CLAY CROSS JUNCTION.

CHAPTER XI.

The Vicar's Alarm.—The First Locomotive in the World.—Trevethick and Jones.—The Trial.—Improvements in Engines.—London and North Western, Midland, and American Locomotives.—Speed and Momentum of Engines and Trains.—Life of a Locomotive.—Cost of Engine Coal.—Locomotive Establishments.—The Metropolitan Railway Locomotives.—Fitters and their ways.—Duties of Drivers and Firemen.—Working of Engines.—Incidents.—A Night Journey on the Dover Night Mail.—Possible Locomotives of the future.—Electric Railways.—Break-Down Train.—Railway Carriages.—The Old Tub and the New Bogie.—A Railway Carriage Building Works.—The Wood Yard, the Shaping Machinery, Carriage Wheels.—Wringing on the Tires.—Furnishing the Carriages.—Painting of Carriages.—Pullmans.—Injuries of Carriages by Travellers.—Cost of Repairs.—The Botany of a Railway Carriage Window.—Sleeping Cars in America.—"One Good Turn Deserves Another."—A Sheet Stores.

ONE dark night in the year 1784, the venerable Vicar of Redruth, in Cornwall, was taking a quiet walk in a lonely lane leading to his church. Suddenly he heard an unearthly noise, and to his horror, he saw approaching him an indescribable creature of legs, arms, and wheels, whose body appeared to be glowing with internal fire, and whose rapid gasps for breath seemed to denote a fierce struggle for existence. The vicar's cries for help brought to his assistance a gentleman of the name of Murdoch, who was able to assure him that this terrible apparition was not an incarnation or a messenger of the Evil One, but only a runaway engine that had escaped from control. This, it is believed, was the first locomotive ever built.

Ten years passed away, and this engine worked on the Merthyr Tydvil Tramway, which has "the honour of being the oldest railway in the world," the Act of Parliament having been granted to it in 1803. The engine had a dwarf body, which, in the roughest style, was secured on a high frame-work built by a hedge-carpenter. Surmounting all was a huge stack, ugly enough when it was new, but in aftertime made uglier by white-wash and rust. Every movement of the engine caused a hideous snorting and clanking, accompanied by the loud noise of the escaping steam.

The Merthyr locomotive was the joint production of Trevethick, a Cornishman, and of Rees Jones, of Pennydarran, who laboured under the direction of Samuel Homfray, the iron-master, and chief proprietor of the Penydarran Works. This gentleman was so pleased with the success that he saw foreshadowed, that he laid a wager of £1,000 with Richard Crawshay, that, by its aid, he would draw a load of iron to the Navigation from Penydarran Works. Richard ridiculed the idea, and accepted the wager. One or two attempts to run the engine had already been made; but in one case it would not move at all, and in another it wanted to imitate Pegasus and to soar into the air, instead of steadily taking the iron way carefully laid for it.

The day fixed for the trial was the 12th of February, 1804, and the track was a tramway lately formed from Penydarran at the back of Plymouth Wall, down to the Navigation. Great was the concourse assembled; "and the rumour of the day's doings even penetrated up the defiles of Taff Fawr and Taff Bach, bringing down old apple-faced farmers and their wives, who were told of a power and a speed that would alter everything, and do away with horses altogether."

On the first engine and train twenty persons clustered, anxious to win immortality. The trams, six in number, were "laden with iron, and, amid a concourse of villagers, including the constable, the 'druggister,' and the class generally dubbed 'shopwrs' by the natives, were Mr. Richard Crawshay and Mr. Samuel Homfray, both as interested as a bet of £1,000 would naturally make them. The driver was one William Richards, and on the engine were perched Trevethick and Rees Jones; their faces black but their eyes bright with the anticipation of victory. Soon the signal was given, and amidst a mighty roar from the people, the wheels turned, and the mass moved downward, going steadily at the rate of five miles an hour until a bridge was reached, a little below the town, that did not admit of the stack going under, and as this was built of bricks there was a great crash and instant stoppage. In a minute or two Richard Crawshay thought his £1,000 were all right, but it was only for a brief time. Trevethick and Jones were of the old-fashioned school of men, who did not believe in impossibilities. The fickle crowd, who had hurrahed like mad, hung back and said, 'It wouldn't do'; but these heroes—the advance guard of a race who have done more to make England famous than battles by land or sea—sprang to the ground and worked like Britons, never ceasing until they had repaired the mischief, and then they rattled on, and finally reached their journey's end." *

The return journey, on account of gradients and curves, was a failure; but from this run on the Merthyr tramway the eventual success of the enterprise—though attended by suspense, delays, accidents, and misadventure—was assured.

To the connection of the locomotive with the success of the Liverpool and Manchester Railway we have already referred Though much more was performed by the early engines of that line than could have been anticipated, it was soon found that their strength was insufficient to sustain the shocks and strains to which they were exposed, and repeated and thorough repairs became indispensable. For many years the locomotive departments of the early companies had to carry on elaborate and expensive improvements, to meet the requirements of an increasingly heavy traffic, and of higher velocities than the imagination of the most sanguine friends of railways had anticipated. These improvements, too, were made amid the bustle and responsibilities of pressing duties. Engines with known imperfections had to be employed in the day, and repairs had to be made during the night, in order that the requisite number of engines might be ready for service. The outer and inner framings were stayed in various parts; iron wheels were substituted for wooden; crank-axles were formed with almost double the amount of metal at first employed; and pistons, piston-rods, connecting-rods, and brasses were strengthened; till, with the exception of the boiler and cylinders, there was about as much left of some of the original engines as there was of the sailor's knife, which, while declared to be "quite an antique," was

* "History of Merthyr."

currently reported to have recently had two new handles and several new blades. Alterations so extensive naturally involved a considerable augmentation of the weight of the engine; and thus the four tons and a half which the *Rocket* weighed, became increased to the ten tons of the *Planet* class.

Other important alterations followed. The cylinders and the machinery by which the working wheels were driven, were originally placed outside the wheels; they were removed to the space under the boiler; the cylinders were now enclosed in the smoke-box, and protected from cold; and the driving power was made to act nearer the centre of *inertia* of the engine and load. There was, however, a serious drawback; for this arrangement required that the axle of the driving-wheels, on which the greater part of the weight of the engine rested, should be constructed with two cranks, so as in fact to be broken and discontinuous in two places. At a more recent period it was found difficult to compress machinery of sufficient power into the narrow space between the wheels; and the cylinders and working-gear were, in some cases, restored to their original position outside the wheels. This plan, in its turn, has been objected to, as giving instability to the engine when in motion; and the former arrangement of the machinery has been again adopted.

The £550 early engine, on four wheels, and of four or five tons weight, has thus been superseded by the six or eight-wheeled engine of £2,500, and of thirty, forty, fifty, and even sixty tons; and though cost and weight are not to be identified with efficiency, yet they are fairly indicative of the extent of the alterations, and, we may safely say, improvements, which have been made. The successful competitor on the Liverpool and Manchester line was required to draw a load of only three times its own weight, or a total of less than twenty tons; before many years had passed an engine was able to draw after it, without difficulty, thirty passenger carriages, each weighing five tons and a half, at thirty miles an hour; the express trains on the Great Western ran at from sixty-five to seventy-five miles an hour; and the goods engines would draw 500 tons at twenty miles an hour.

Even in the early days of railway enterprise engines and trains ran at great speeds on special occasions. "As long ago as '45 or '46," remarked Mr. Allport, to the writer, "when the battle of the gauges was being vigorously carried on, I wished to show what the narrow gauge could do. It was, of course, before the days of telegraphs. The election of George Hudson, as member for Sunderland, had that day taken place, and I availed myself of the event to see how quickly I could get the information up to London, have it printed in the *Times* newspaper, and brought back to Sunderland. The election was over at four o'clock in the afternoon, and by about five o'clock the returns of the voting for every half-hour during the poll were collected from the different booths, and copies were handed to me. I had ordered a series of trains to be in readiness for the journey, and I at once started from Sunderland to York. Another train was in waiting at York to take me to Normanton, and others in their turn to Derby, to Rugby, to Wolverton, and to Euston. Thence I drove to the *Times* office, and handed my manuscript to Mr. Delane, who, according to an arrangement I had previously made with him, had it immediately set up in type, a leader written, both inserted, and a lot of impressions taken. Two hours were thus spent in London, and then I set off on my return journey, and arrived in Sunderland next morning at about ten o'clock, before the announcement of the poll. I there handed over copies I had brought with me of that day's *Times* newspaper, containing the returns of what had happened in Sunderland the afternoon before. Between five o'clock in the evening and ten that morning I had travelled 600 miles, besides spending two hours in London—a clear run of 40 miles an hour."

Thirty years ago the *Lord of the Isles*, shown at the Great Exhibition, was the type of the class of locomotives then being constructed for the Great Western Railway, and it was able to take a passenger train of 120 tons, upon easy gradients, at an average speed of 60 miles an hour. The weight of the engine in working order was 35 tons, besides the tender, which, when laden, weighed nearly 18 tons. It is said that one of these large engines belonging to this company was—we suppose as a delicate compliment—nicknamed "the Emperor of Russia," on account of its extraordinary capacity for the consumption of oil and tallow!

The narrow gauge lines, too, were not behind in the colossal power of their engines. One of the most remarkable of these was the *Liverpool*, built on Crampton's patent, and exhibited at the Crystal Palace. It weighed 32 tons; and the evaporation of the steam when at full work was said to be equal to 1,140 horse power. It was built, in order to ensure steadiness, with

A LONDON AND NORTH WESTERN ENGINE.

a very low boiler. Another narrow-gauge engine of that period is represented in the engraving. It belonged to the London and North Western Company, and was constructed by Robert Stephenson & Co. at Newcastle-on-Tyne.

MIDLAND EXPRESS ENGINE.

The main line passenger engine of the Midland Company is very powerful. It weighs, when loaded, more than 60 tons, and it can draw, on a level, a load of 240 tons at a speed of 45 miles an hour.

Among the latest and best of these wonderful machines are the main line six-wheeled the and eight-wheeled bogie passenger locomotives of the Midland Railway. The former have cylinders of 18 inches diameter and 2 feet 2 inches stroke. The driving wheels are 6 feet 9 inches diameter, and four are coupled. These engines will draw 26 coaches upon a level at the rate of 50 miles an hour, or 19 coaches up a bank of 1 in 100 at the rate of 30 miles an hour. The tender will carry about 3,000 gallons of water and five tons of coal, an amount which enables the engine to run, without stopping for water, a distance of from 100 to 120 miles. The bogie passenger engines are also a very powerful type. One of them is represented in the engraving The exact dimensions are as follows: cylinder 18 inches and 26 inches stroke, wheels 7 feet in diameter; the centre, from trailing to the driving wheel, 8 feet 6 inches; and the driving

NEW MIDLAND BOGIE ENGINE.

wheels to the centre of the bogie 10 feet. The extreme wheel centre over the tender is 43 feet 8 inches; and the total length over all, or the buffers, 52 feet 4 inches. The tender will hold 3,000 gallons of water, and will carry 5 tons of coal, enough for a run of 100 to 120 miles. These engines will draw 24 coaches on a level at 50 miles an hour, and will draw 18 coaches up an incline of 1 in 100 at 30 miles an hour. They are admirably adapted for running at high speeds on railways that have quick and varying curves, as they pass round them smoothly and without oscillation. As a driver of one' of them remarked, "they will bend like a whip." The express engines of the Midland Company will work with a power of from 350 to 1,250 horses.

Engines used on American lines have remarkable characteristics of their own. Some of these are plainly indicated in the accompanying engraving.

It is difficult to understand the speed not only at which colossal structures travel, but at which some of their parts are working. When, for instance, a train is running at 50 miles an hour, the pistons are passing backwards and forwards along the cylinders at the marvellous rate of 800 feet a minute, and the movements of some parts of the machinery are distinctly and regularly dividing even a second into many equal parts. When a train is running at 70 miles an hour, a space is traversed of about 105 feet per second—that is to say, thirty-five yards between the tickings of the clock. If two trains pass one another at this speed, the relative velocity will, of course, be doubled ; so that, if one of them be seventy yards long, it would flash past the other in a second. Now, according to the experiments of Dr. Hutton, the flight of a cannon-ball, having a range

AN AMERICAN LOCOMOTIVE.

of 6,700 feet, takes a quarter of a minute, which is at the rate of five miles a minute, or 300 miles an hour; and hence it follows, that a railway train moving at 75 miles an hour has one-fourth of the velocity of a cannon-ball, and is practically a huge projectile, subject to exactly the same laws as projectiles, and having the same force as projectiles; only that a cannon-ball weighs perhaps 100 pounds, and a train may weigh 100 tons. This force, like that of a cannon-ball, is estimable "as the weight of the body multiplied by the square of its velocity, and the blow which the oscillations of an engine cause to be given to the rails are comparable with the impact of a rifle bolt upon an iron target. In gunnery practice the tests are generally applied direct, in railway battering the blows are indirect. The gun-shot hitting on an incline does not penetrate, but makes a more or less deep scoop, and travels on deflected from its former course. The blow is just as hard whether the thing that gives it has travelled 60 miles, 60 yards, or one-sixtieth of an inch, the actual force of impact is always given by the actual velocity of the moving body at the instant of collision. Every vertical oscillation, every lateral oscillation of a locomotive, then, is calculated to make the engine hit the rails with a terrible force, equalling, or exceeding, the tremendous blows of the largest steam hammers." Happily, in railway accidents, these terrific forces are never fully exerted; the steam has been shut off, suction in the cylinders is induced, and the brakes are put on; or the blow is indirect; or the buffer-springs yield; or in other ways the momentum is diminished before collision takes place.

With regard to swift and sustained speed, it is probable that the best long run ever made was by a special train in July, 1880, on the Great Northern Railway—a train which conveyed the Lord Mayor of London to Scarborough. The distance from London to York, 188 miles, was accomplished in 217 minutes—an average, including a ten minutes' stoppage at Grantham, of 52 miles an hour. The first 53 miles from London were done in an hour, not 10 miles of the road being level; and whereas King's Cross station is 130 feet above the sea, for about 13 miles the line is about 400 feet above the sea, descending at the 53rd mile to about 150 feet. Stoke box, 100 miles from London, was passed in 1 hour and 51 minutes; and between Barkstone and Tuxford, 22¼ miles, the speed was at the rate of 64 miles an hour. The whole run was done in 3 hours and 27 minutes, exclusive of stoppage. The Great Northern Company's *Scotchman*, in its ordinary journeys, occupies 21 minutes more.

As the charges for horsing the old coaches exceeded all others, so the heaviest item in the working expenses of railways is for locomotive power. The average work of an engine is about 20,000 miles a year, or 80 miles a day, allowing for the time during which it is laid up in the "hospital" for repairs; for though the engine does not tire, it wears, and, like the animal frame, is constantly undergoing renewals of parts—tubes, tires, cylinders, crank-axles, and boilers—indeed, in almost everything but its name-plate. "Do not engines wear out?" inquired Mr. Denison of Mr. Allport. "According to our books," he replied, "there never was an engine on the Midland Railway that is not on the books now; but the engines have been renewed over and over again. They are like the Irishman's knife, which he said had been in his family so many years, and which had had so many new blades and so many new handles. So it is with the locomotive. It is renewed from time to time; and all these renewals come out of the working expenses, so that there can be no depreciation. It is included, in fact, in the expenses." The average life of a locomotive boiler is about fifteen years, during which the engine will have run about 300,000 miles.

One of the chief items of cost in working a locomotive is for fuel. "On the South Eastern Railway," says the *Railway News*, "the consumption of fuel per train mile is about forty-nine pounds; on the Midland, forty-six; and North Western, forty-six; on the Great Northern, forty-five; on the Great Eastern, forty-two; and on the London, Brighton, and South Coast, thirty-nine pounds per train mile. The average of these figures is forty-four pounds, which may be taken as that of the railways of the United Kingdom. From the Board of Trade returns for 1881, we find that the total train mileage of our railways for that year was about 248,500,000 miles. This would give, on the basis of forty-four pounds per mile run, a total of 5,467,000 tons for the year, or 600,000 tons short of the whole quantity of coal brought into London by rail and canal last year. Considering the enormous benefit which the railways are to the country, this cannot be regarded as a large proportion of the total coal production of the country. The price paid by the different companies for their coal varies, of course, very much, according to their distance from the pit. Thus, the Brighton Company, for the second half of 1881, paid over 14*s*. a ton, the South Eastern about 12*s*., the Great Eastern, 10*s*., the Great Northern, 7*s*., the North Western, 6*s*., and the Midland about 12*s*. a ton." A fair average for the railways of the United Kingdom would, therefore, be about 10*s*. a ton; and, at this rate, they paid, in 1881, nearly £2,734,000 for coal alone.

In connection with the locomotive department of a railway are not only the central establishments, but also various running and repairing places at convenient parts of the system. These, in many instances, like everything connected with railway work, have grown from little to much. "You manage your engines in Nottingham differently from what they did when I was there," recently remarked an old Midland locomotive superintendent at Peterborough. "When I was there," he continued, "we had only two engines: we ran one one day, and the other the next. We took three trains a day of passengers, goods, and minerals to Long Eaton, and one to Kegworth; and then we came home and put her by to rest and repair, and next day we ran the other engine." Now there are nearly one hundred Midland engines stationed at Nottingham, each of them incomparably more powerful than those of early days.

The locomotive station of a railway company includes two departments—the repairing and the running. The work of the former is done by men called fitters. "I have been a fitter," said an engineer to the writer, "in a running-shed for twelve months. There were about 150 engines stationed there, perhaps 100 of which would run every day. We only did what are called running repairs, by which I mean repairs that could be completed between the time an engine came in from her ordinary run, and the time she was wanted for her next journey; as, for instance, renewing joints that were blown out of the dome of the cylinder covers or steam chest covers." "Blown out?" we inquired. "Yes; a joint is made by putting red lead where the cover touches the cylinder, and then screwing it up tight with the nuts. In time the red lead perishes, and the steam works its way through the joint. The way our work was arranged was as follows: there were ten of us, and we had to finish before we left at night. We were like clerks at a bank; everything had to be cleared up for the day, nothing left for to-morrow."

"How did you know what you had to do to an engine?" "A list of the repairs required was fixed up in the fitters' shop, giving the numbers of the engines in one column, the nature of the repairs in another, as reported by the drivers. To tell the truth, we didn't always do what they asked for, but in some cases only what we believed to be necessary. We used to find that certain drivers thought about their engines as some men do about their bodies, that they wanted a deal of patching and physic; but, somehow, if they didn't get it they did very well without it. Drivers of that sort soon get to be known to the fitters, and are treated accordingly. To the list I have spoken of the fitters would come. Against the number of the engine that stood first, the first fitter would write his name, to show that he would take that job in hand. The next fitter would take the next job; and so on till they were all finished. Suppose there were twenty jobs to be done by the ten men, then as soon as the first had finished his work, he would come back to take another, till all were completed."

Fitters, it appears, have their fun as well as other people. When the cat is away the mice will play; and when the foreman of fitters is absent the humorous propensities of the men sometimes find vent. "I have known," said an engineer to the writer, "a group of three or four fitters, instead of continuing their work, ensconce themselves inside the firebox of an engine that was under repairs, in order by the light of a candle to play at cards. While busily engaged in their game a co-conspirator quietly opened the smoke-box door at the front end of the engine, stuck in one of the tube-ends the nozzle of a two-inch hose-pipe, and then turned on the water at high pressure. The water immediately rushed along the tube, and, flying with great force across the fire-box against the opposite side, splashed over the candle, drenched the card-players, and led to the ridiculous spectacle of four men trying at the same moment to crawl out at the furnace door through an oval hole 18 inches by 15 inches, the fountain being still at full play, and pouring its volume on the retreating forces, who, as one by one they emerged, received the undissembled congratulations of their mischief-loving companions."

Occasionally a joke is practised upon young apprentices. After an engine has had its first trial run, and is brought into the shed, it is carefully examined all over, to ascertain whether any portions have "heated." On such occasions it is not uncommon for apprentices to be full of curiosity and activity in their professional inquiries, and of this some old fitters take advantage. As one part after another is tested by the hand and found to be cool, some one suddenly suggests, "Just feel if the piston-rods have heated." An apprentice eagerly obeys, forgetting that which his monitor remembers, that the piston-rods have been running up and down through the steam in a cylinder of something more than 212 degrees of temperature, and he soon finds that, though the rod has not "heated," it is hot!

"Yes," said an engineer, "I have had other jobs to do—engine work. I once made a new locomotive out of two old ones. The foreman took me to what we called the condemned siding, where old engines were placed till they were broken up. There were two old engines, both of the same class, and the foreman said, 'Now, you can have anything you like out of those two engines, and I will give you a new boiler.' I took the best parts of both—one cylinder from one and another from the other—and so built up a new engine, which, though it is years ago, I happen to know is running still as a good engine up and down a very stiff incline. But engines are now built in a much more business-like way, and beautiful and powerful locomotives are turned out."

"When you went out to test your repaired engines, or to try your new ones, did you ever come to grief?" we inquired.

"Yes," said our friend. "One foggy morning I was on an engine, going from Battersea Park station to Croydon to fetch a train. We could not see fifty yards before us, and we were running along at only about ten miles an hour, when all of a sudden over we went. I found myself in a ditch bottom at the side of the line. Could see nothing, but could hear a tremendous noise of steam blowing off. I sang out to my mate, 'What's up?' 'I don't know,' he answered. We got out of the ditch, went to the engine, and found her lying on her side. Neither of us was hurt, but the tender of the engine, which had been running first, had the wheels on both sides cut off the axles as clean as if it had been done with a knife. We sent to the next station; they 'blocked' the line and telegraphed to the break-down gang, and in about three hours they got the engine on her legs again. The tender had to be taken home on the top of a truck. We had run into a truck loaded with bricks which had come out of a siding, and was standing across the line we had been going on. The bricks were smashed to dust, and our engine looked as if it had been powdered all over with cayenne pepper. Another time I was on the express, and when running about thirty miles an hour, we 'pitched into' a cattle train that was going about ten miles an hour. The passengers were not seriously hurt, but a right reverend prelate suffered from an unfortunate collision of his nose with the padded walls of his carriage. Unhappily, the guard of the cattle train was killed, and so were eight bullocks. The latter were so smashed up, that one of the bullocks was cut in two, and half of his body was actually pitched on to the top of the chimney. The first effect upon myself was that the shock brought down the coals out of the tender on to the footplate, and I was imbedded in them up to my knees."

But the fitters have now finished their work with a particular engine, and it has to be got ready for duty. About two hours before it has to start, a man lights the fire by putting a shovelful of hot coals in at the furnace door. When the fire is fairly lighted, he opens the whistle of the engine, so that, as soon as the boiler begins to make steam, the fact is announced. People

LOCOMOTIVE STATION, WELLINGBOROUGH.

who live near a running-shed sometimes wonder what causes the strange noises they hear. There is a low, faint whistle, which, as the steam is generated, gradually increases in volume, until, in the course of a quarter of an hour it would, if not arrested, become a full-blown shriek. The lighters are, however, by these means informed that the fire is burning, that the water is heating, that the steam is getting up, and that the engine will soon be ready for her work. A ton or more of coals and two or three thousand gallons of water supply her enormous requirements for the first part of her next journey, and "she" is ready to be taken in hand by driver and fireman.

It is the duty of the engine-driver and fireman to be punctually at their posts an hour, or more, according to the previous instructions of the locomotive superintendent, before the time of starting the train. On their arrival at the shed they "sign on duty," by which is meant that they give their names to a clerk at the office, and it is entered, with the hour and moment, in a book provided for the purpose. Driver and fireman also sign their names. They then satisfy themselves that the engine they are to drive is in proper order, and that the distinguishing lamps are in their places, and, if necessary, that they are lighted. It is also the duty of the driver before he leaves the shed with his engine to examine the "Notice Case" that hangs up in the shed, to see if there are any instructions affecting his train or the condition of the road over which he will run. Let us look at these cases. They are large. One is, perhaps, six yards long and four feet high, and is faced with glass. It is divided into three parts: one headed "Latest," another "Permanent," the third is for premiums and fines. Here are notices to the following effect:—"There will not be any water at —— station on Monday next, 2nd October. Drivers must, if necessary, provide themselves at —— station." Here is another: that the "'Distant Signal' at —— station has been moved," and that it is now 1,000 yards from such and such a cabin. Others are to a similar purport, or perhaps they cancel notices previously posted. A printed copy of these notices is also given to the driver, for the receipt of which he gives his acknowledgment in a form provided for the purpose.

The importance of the notice-board may be illustrated. By neglecting to examine it, a driver and his fireman lost their lives. "By incessant rain a river had become so swollen that, by the rush of water, the buttresses of a wooden railway bridge became shifted. The bridge was inspected, and one side of it was pronounced to be dangerous. Arrangements were made to work the traffic 'single road,' and 'notice' of such arrangements was posted in the running-shed. The driver neglected to read the notice; he ran his train past the man appointed to pilot him over, and got off the metals down an embankment. The regular fireman came late on duty, and was sent home again, '*until wanted;*' an extra fireman was sent to do his work, and while the poor fellow, no doubt, was striving to do his best, and probably rejoicing to think that he had come down to the shed in good time to secure a trip, he was suddenly summoned into another world."

In these notice-cases are a list of fines that have been levied in the locomotive department of the company for sundry petty delinquencies; and hard by is a list of gratuities that have been given for special services. Thus we read that a cleaner, whose name and station are mentioned, has been awarded *2s. 6d.* for drawing attention to a defective driving-tire; that another cleaner has had *2s. 6d.* for drawing attention to a defect in engine No. 308; and that an engine-man has had a similar present for calling attention to a coke wagon he observed to be on fire. Then again there are premiums. We read as follows:—A. B., during the first six months of the current year, ran 12,925 miles; burnt 3,449 cwts. of coal, averaging 29·9 lbs. per mile; oil, 625 pounds, averaging 4·8 per 100 miles; average number of carriages per trip, 8; trips in which time was kept, 617; trips in which time was lost, 14 (30 minutes lost in 14 trips); and that to him a premium was given of £1 5*s*. A goods driver for similar services received a premium of £3. These gifts graduate from the above sums down to 10*s*., and are awarded twice a year.

Now these premiums do not come "by luck," but by most careful attention. There are good and bad ways of "firing" an engine. To fire properly, the fireman should stand in such a position as to command the coals in the tender, and to work the shovel without shifting his feet, except when he turns slightly on his heels, first toward the coals, and then towards the fire-hole. The shovel, too, should enter the fire-box as little as possible. It should be stopped dead at the fire-hole ring; and the impetus given to the coals should be sufficient to discharge them, like shot, right into their intended destination, close to the copper. It is a common practice to pick up with the shovel as much coal as it is possible to heap upon it, pushing the shovel into the coal with the knees; but this should not be done. Each shovelful should be put in its place. The first should find a billet in the left-hand front corner; the second in the right-hand front corner; the third in the right-hand back corner; the fourth in the left-hand back corner; the fifth under the brick arch close to the tube-plate; the last, under the door.

To do this, as soon as the shovel enters the fire-box, it should be turned over sharp, to prevent it falling too far forwards.

The secret of good firing is to fire little and often. When fresh fuel is put on, a black cloud of imperfectly consumed carbon rises from the chimney; so that the most suitable spots for the use of the shovel should be selected and habitually used, and no stoking business be in hand "when the engine approaches junctions, signals, or stations. It should be done after passing them. The grand aim of first-rate stoking is to keep the steam at one pressure; that is to say, the needle of the pressure-gauge should, as nearly as possible, point to a full boiler pressure, up hill and down dale. To accomplish this—and it is done on the crack engines every day—firing must be studied. Engines are not alike. Some are robust, others very delicate, but the generality of engines require the exercise of trained skill to jockey them. Some engines steam best with a low fire, and others may carry fuel up to the fire-hole. Nearly all engines are affected by cross winds. The firing should be done when the steam is just on the point of blowing off—a condition which generally happens while the engine is on a rising gradient, for the fierce blast causes a maximum supply of oxygen to pass through the fire and the tubes, which generates great heat and much steam."

It is astonishing what may be done by some drivers and firemen in the economy of fuel. "A case occurred a short time ago," says Mr. Michael Reynolds, "that will just illustrate the point. Driver A. had for a long period been a heavy consumer of coal, compared with other drivers working the same trains. His engine was equal to theirs in condition, and there was no distinction between them in any one point, or in the coals, the loads, or in keeping time. But he always consumed two or three pounds per mile more than other men in his 'link.' Driver B., on the other hand, stood at the top of the premium list month after month. It was decided by the locomotive superintendent to change the firemen of the two drivers who were so wide apart in consumption. This was done for three months. After working a month the change was striking. Both men had felt the electric shock, and figured on the coal-premium list both together, in the centre of eighteen other drivers; but driver B. was still first by fourpence. The next month both men 'went in for it,' and it was in every sense of the word a struggle. Their coal was weighed, and everything they required to be done to their engines was done at once. Well, the long looked-for coal-premium list came out for the second month, and, as was fully anticipated by those who knew anything of the firemen, the formerly heavy consumer beat the man who had so long been top coal-man by 8*s.* 6*d.*! The secret of this change rested with driver B.'s fireman, who studied economy with a vengeance from every point of view. He did what many others did not care about doing, namely, he fired little at a time and often, he studied the road, kept the shovel and the fire-irons out of the fire-box, took advantage of every contingency—as, for instance, the protection of a cutting or of trees—for the opening of the fire-door—to work his engine fully up to the mark with a shovelful of coals less to-day than yesterday."

It is now nearly time to start, and everything being in readiness, the driver and his fireman mount the foot-plate and proceed from the running-shed to the station where their train is being marshalled.

Just, however, as the engine leaves the shed, an incident sometimes occurs that creates surprise. Suddenly an enormous gush of steam pours forth from the cylinders in front of the engine, perhaps envelops even the chimney in a fleecy cloud, and possibly suggests to the timid that an accident had occurred. It is done for an important purpose. When the engine last stopped running there was a certain amount of steam in the cylinders which, as they cooled down, would condense into water. Before the engine begins another journey this water has to be cleared out of the cylinders, otherwise the pistons would not work freely and fully along the cylinders, but would have a cushion of water at each end, which, being incompressible, would cause danger of the cylinder ends (or lids, as they are called) being knocked out. The volume of steam we have seen forces out the water and makes all clear.

The place for the driver, when his engine is under steam, is upon the foot-plate, so that, in an instant, he can command the regulator and the reversing lever. This is especially requisite at night, when it is imperatively necessary that the attention of the driver should be continuously directed to the engine, "listening constantly to the sound of the *beat*, to detect any irregularity that may arise from some defect in the machinery or from priming, frequently casting his eye on the pressure-gauge and on the level of the water in the gauge-glass. As the fireman puts on the coals, the driver should occasionally see that he is placing them next the walls of the fire-box, and not in a heap in the middle. When the rails are slippery, great care is required to prevent the engine from slipping, by closing the regulator in time. By unceasing attention to the action of the engine, a man will soon be enabled to check her in the act of slipping, and to prevent her from flying round at the rate of 800 or 1,000 revolutions per minute."

The instructions given to drivers and firemen are numerous and weighty. When a passenger train is about to start from a station, the driver satisfies himself that the line before him is clear; and when starting, the fireman looks back on the platform side till the last vehicle has drawn clear of the platform, to see that the whole train is following properly, and to receive any signal that may be given. It may seem unnecessary, if not absurd, to say that a driver, when he starts on his journey, should know that his train is following; yet it is a fact that drivers have pulled out of a station without their trains, that they have not found out their mistake until they reached the platform of the next station, and that they have there actually whistled to their guard to put on his brake. Others have lost eight carriages out of twelve, and have observed no difference in the working of the engine.

On the other hand, there are drivers who habitually work their engines according to the load; and they can tell, after knowing the number of coaches in their train, when a guard's brake has been inadvertently left "on." An express engineman one day, says Mr. Reynolds, as soon as his train stopped at Brighton, jumped off his engine, and said to the guard, "Guard, thy brake's been on, I'll swear.' "No it has not," said the guard. "Then thy mate's has," replied Ben; and when the wheels of the rear van were examined, they were found to be black-hot, with a flat place worn on the tire.

In starting, the regulator should be opened gently, especially when there is a full boiler. "If the engine has to wait some time for a train, the steam-pipes and cylinders may be kept warm and free from water of condensation by opening the regulator a very little, with the brake screwed on hard. As the engine comes to feel the load, so the regulator may be opened more, until the engineman and lookers-on can hear what it is likely to do with the train. A few clear, sonorous puffs at the start do good; they rouse the fire into action at once—there is no hesitation in the matter. They also clear the tubes of loose cinders or soot left in them after being swept out. It is cruel, wicked, not to give the noble iron steed a little grace at the start, so as to give him an opportunity of shaking the cold and stiffness out of his iron limbs; and, moreover, it is a loss of time to commence reining in, by extra cutting off the steam, before he is half a dozen yards away."

The driver must endeavour to regulate the running of his engine as nearly as possible according to the "working time-table"—a book from which he learns not only when to stop, but the time when he is due to pass stations and sidings at which he does not stop. He thus avoids extreme speed, or the loss of time through slowness. He has to observe anything wrong on the line of rails opposite to that on which his train is running, he must sound his whistle and exhibit a danger signal to any train or engine he may meet, and stop at the first signal-box or station, and report to the signalman, or person in charge, what he has observed. Should he meet an engine or train too closely following any preceding engine or train, he must sound his whistle and exhibit a caution or danger signal, as occasion may require, to the engine-driver of such following engine or train. Just before entering a tunnel, the sand-valves should be opened, and the sand be allowed to flow until the train emerges from the tunnel. Sand is cheaper than steam.

A great part of the driver's time when on the foot-plate is spent in looking out for signals. The old master drivers, who travel the road at express speed, secure a few seconds in reserve before reaching a busy junction station, so as to reduce speed. This may be required only at exceptional places, where the view of the signals is defective, and where a great traffic is going on, or where there are curves in the line. He will also, as far as possible, not only see that a signal is "off," but that the condition of the road is such that it ought to be "off." Such watchfulness will have its reward in the increased safety of his train.

Opportunities also frequently arise for the special vigilance of a driver. "A few years ago a goods train, having two engines attached, was proceeding south at midnight, and after it had passed a fast express train, a thought struck the driver of the express that, for two engines, it was a *very short* goods train. He stepped over to the fireman's side of the foot-plate for the purpose of seeing whether there were any tail lights on the last vehicle; but, owing to a curve in the line, he could not ascertain that point. He, however, shut off steam, and gave instructions to his mate to have the brake in readiness, 'for,' said he, 'it strikes me very forcibly, mate, all the train is not there.' When they had run about two miles, and were thinking of getting up the speed again, a red light was seen ahead surging violently from right to left. They pulled up at once to it, when a goods guard informed them, as he held his bull's-eye light into their faces, that a wagon-axle had broken in *his* train, and had caused twelve trucks to leave the rails, and that they were across the down-road right in the way of the express. The guard got up on the step of the engine, when they pulled gently down to the scene of the accident, where a sight presented itself which told them that something else besides being able to drive an engine was required to make a man a good railwayman."

Railway service, says Mr. Reynolds, demands eyes that see and heads that think, and are ready at a moment to detect an intimation of anything wrong. "Driver Standiford, in charge of an up midnight mail, running to time, expected to pass driver Coven at or very near the Harrow junction—Coven being also in charge of a mail going down. But as they did not pass each other near the usual spot, driver Standiford became very anxious about the whereabouts of Coven, and he looked with the greatest anxiety at every signal he approached to see whether the latter was signalled. Disappointed, he said to his mate, 'Coven not signalled yet; something is surely wrong; stand handy to thy brake.'

"Such a thing as losing time with the down mails was very rare; so that, when they were late, the first idea about the matter was that a pitch-in had happened, and nine times out of ten this thought was the correct one. 'Ten minutes late,' said Standiford, as he crossed over to the fireman's side of the engine to get a better view of the line in going round a curve, at the same time telling his mate to let the fire alone awhile until they knew or saw something of the down mail. During those anxious moments Standiford never lifted his hand off the regulator handle. For aught he knew, his life and those of others were threatened, and he expected at every chain to be suddenly summoned to shut the regulator and stop quick. With the assistance of the gauge-lamp Standiford once more looked at his watch; the mail was now seventeen minutes overdue. As he returned his watch to his pocket he also stepped over to his own side of the engine foot-plate, and he had scarcely been there fifteen seconds when something was struck by the buffer-beam or guard-iron of the engine. It was neither timber nor stone, but was something much softer. Standiford heard something grating under the ash-pan; he shut off steam, and ordered his mate to stop the train. A spot of oil, as he thought, had settled on his face; but on wiping it off with the back of his hand he observed it was blood! Forty thoughts sped through his brain. A man killed—fogman, signalman, Coven, front guard, or fireman—and on this he urged his fireman to put his brake on tighter if possible; but he had no sooner done so, when, to his astonishment, he heard the mail coming at a tremendous speed; he instantly seized the gauge-lamp with his right hand, and with his left opened the whistle freely to attract the down mail engineman's attention. Coven, as he came round the corner, saw the danger light and shut off steam, put on the brakes, and pulled up as quickly as possible. When he had stopped he jumped down, and discovered, a few yards in the front of his engine, in the four-foot way, two dead steers, and ten living ones wandering about the track. Meanwhile Standiford had stopped also; but after examining his engine, and on being satisfied that it was a beast he had run over, he put on steam again and pursued his way south." His thoughtfulness had prepared him for the emergency.

When the driver has completed the trip or series of trips on which he started, and has brought his train to its destination, he runs his engine to the locomotive yard, and over an ashpit, where his fireman has the engine fire taken out, and the smoke and fire-box emptied of ashes. While this is being done the driver reports himself as "on the ashpit," and the fact is entered in the "ashpit book." He is now allowed half an hour to get his engine into the shed, to have it looked over for any defects, to see if any repairs are necessary. These are entered in a book set apart for that purpose. About the end of the half-hour the driver enters the office, and fills up a certain schedule. This is headed, "Driver's weekly account of materials consumed and duty performed by engine No. ——, stationed at ——, week ending ——." There are spaces for the names of the driver and fireman; the miles run each day of the week, with passenger trains, or goods, or assisting; for running light, piloting, shunting, or ballasting; the hours in steam; the coal stations at which the engine coaled, and the cwts. of coal taken; the oil, tallow, and waste consumed; and any "remarks" thereon. Having filled in these and other particulars, the driver's work is done; he "signs off," and leaves.

In a single long journey the services of several engines may be engaged. It is all a question of practical convenience. Between London and Liverpool, for instance, one engine may take the train from St. Pancras to Leicester; another from Leicester to Trent, and a portion on to Nottingham; a third, that has come from Nottingham to Trent, may run on to Derby; an engine of greater strength, to overcome the inclines—perhaps a bogie engine, that will better deal with the curves—will take it to Manchester; another from Manchester to Liverpool; and possibly, in addition, a pilot engine may be required to assist to Leicester, and another through Derbyshire. In other cases one engine will run to Leicester, another to Manchester, and a third to Liverpool.

In arranging the work of the various engine-drivers at a particular "loco. station," the principle recognised is to endeavour to equalize the labours of the men in their respective grades. For instance, at Nottingham, a week's service may be as follows:—On *Monday* the driver would take the 8.30 a.m. express from Nottingham to London, and would bring back the 1.50 slow, *viâ* Trent, doing 257 miles in 13½ hours. On *Tuesday* he would drive the 10.15 express to London, and return with the 4.20 slow; 248 miles, 13h. 50m. On *Wednesday*, the 12.30 to London, and the 5.30 express back; 248 miles in 9h. 10m. On *Thursday* he would be off duty, and on Friday and Saturday he would repeat Monday and Tuesday's work. On Sunday he would not run. Four men work these trains round. They are very experienced, but not necessarily the oldest drivers in the service: these may perhaps begin to lose nerve for express running. They are paid by miles, 15 miles being reckoned as an hour's work. Another class are the "single-wheel" enginemen, those who run engines the wheels of which are not coupled. The third and fourth classes are the four-wheeled coupled engines which run between Nottingham and Leicester, Derby, Sheffield, Lincoln, and Retford. The fifth class are pilot and excursion men.

We may here remark that an indispensable qualification of drivers and firemen is the excellence of their sight; and on this they are examined not only at the outset, but at intervals, sometimes twice a year afterwards. In doing this a staff of wood is employed. It is (besides the handle) nine inches long by two wide; is painted white, and on each of the four flat sides are painted in three divisions a number of black spots a quarter of an inch square. This staff is held up at a distance from the candidate of fifteen feet, and he is required to count any set of spots on any side. If unable to do so, he is ineligible for the service. Each eye is tested separately. If his "length of vision" is satisfactory, he is examined on the subject of colour. Some men are naturally "colour blind"; others may be better described as "colour ignorant." They may see the colour plainly, but not know its name. The "wool test" is employed. Some forty pieces of coloured wool—all shades of green, red, magenta, scarlet, brown, and bronze—are hung in a row on a stand, and the candidate is required to tell which is which. Bits of wool representing the colours of the danger and the caution signals are also given to him, and he has to match them with those on the stand. On this subject, also, the candidate must satisfy the examiner, or he is ineligible as a fireman. The answers given are entered in a form, and are preserved for future reference.

Sometimes the eyesight of a driver or fireman, after he has been long in service, is found, upon re-examination, to have partially failed. Under these circumstances he has to be "reduced" to an inferior position. Passenger engine-drivers may thus have to be employed in the safer service of shunters. In such matters the safety of the men and of the public is the supreme consideration.

When the local locomotive superintendent requires additional drivers for his work, he communicates the fact to the chief of his department. In reply he perhaps obtains permission to have a certain number—say half a dozen—of firemen examined as to their qualifications. An inspector from headquarters, himself probably an old driver, is sent over; and for two or three days he travels on an engine with the candidate, who takes charge of the engine. At the end of the trial the inspector makes his report. If it is to the effect that the fireman is a fit and proper person to undertake the higher duties of driver, the man goes over to headquarters; and, if approved, is a "passed man," held in reserve for special work, or to fill temporary vacancies, with a view to ultimate promotion to permanent service. A somewhat similar course is adopted when cleaners are advanced to the position of firemen. Sometimes, when trade becomes seriously slack, drivers have to be temporarily reduced to firemen, and firemen to cleaners.

Of the character and work of engine-drivers we have had an opportunity of speaking at length elsewhere; and we believe that, as a rule, they have discharged their gravely responsible duties with great satisfaction to their employers and to the public. Occasionally some have been found who have allowed their ingenuity and enterprise to flow in undesirable channels. "I knew a driver," remarked an engineer to us, "who used to run between London and Rugby, who once showed his professional knowledge in a new direction. Just before leaving Euston, he noticed on the platform near his engine a little toy terrier that seemed to have lost its owner. Tempted beyond measure at such unexpected treasure trove, he beguiled the dog nearer to him, and then seizing a favourable opportunity and the dog at the same moment, put the latter into his tool-box. Soon there was eager inquiry up and down the platform for the lost dog. The train started; but the station-master's suspicions being aroused, he ordered a telegram to be despatched to Rugby, the first stopping-place, directing a search to be made for the dog from the engine of the train back through every carriage to the rear van of the guard. On approaching Rugby platform the driver noticed two policemen waiting to receive the train. 'Get the dog,' said the driver to his fireman, 'and bolt with it the moment you have a chance.' The fireman pocketed the prize, and awaited events. As the engine drew up, a policeman mounted the foot-plate, and was beginning to search, when the driver accidentally (on purpose) with a hammer concealed under his arm smashed the water-gauge glass of his engine. Out rushed, with a loud noise, volumes of steam, and the policeman, thinking the boiler had burst, leaped back on to the platform and ran for dear life. Meanwhile the fireman quietly walked off on the other side with the dog under his jacket, and eventually succeeded in depositing his treasure in a safe place outside the bounds of the station."

The experiences of engineers, officers, and men, are sometimes unpleasant. "The greatest 'funk' I ever was in," said a Midland engineer to the writer, "was many years ago. I wanted to go from Preston to Lancaster, and with that intent got into the van of a goods train. The brakesman was in the front of the train, and I was alone. We soon started; but when we had run a little way into the tunnel the train pulled up, and after a bit proceeded to back. The tunnel was a very old-fashioned one, very narrow all ways, so that if a passenger put his head out of a carriage window he was very likely to strike the wall. We had backed only a little way, when suddenly I saw another train following on our rails into the tunnel. (There was no block system in those days.) A smash was inevitable; and, to escape it, I was just going to get down on to the other line of rails, when at that moment another train on the other line came dashing past us, and all I could do before the collision was to throw myself on my back on the floor of the van. What I felt during those about thirty seconds I cannot describe. The blow came. The engine broke its lamps and buffers against the van I was in, knocked off its own funnel, and made our van tilt itself up on to the smoke-box end of the locomotive, where it was fast taking fire. I was soon on my legs; ran back to tell that the whole place would soon be in a blaze, and we at length managed to extinguish the flames and to remove the trains."

We have already recounted some of our own various experiences in riding on engines: a graphic writer has sketched those through which he passed. Having, as he tells us, ensconced himself in a couple of great-coats and a fur cap, "I stroll," he says, "on the platform at Cannon Street with the assumption of an indifference I blush to record. The mail train lay alongside, '72' blowing off a stream of hot impatience to be away. Her Majesty's mail men were hurling enormous bags of letters from their red carts, and porters frantically hurled these bags into the two mail vans, in which stood clerks ready to begin their task against time *en route* in the sorting of these many missives, portentous with weal or woe, riches or ruin. Huge piles of luggage, disgorged from cabs and carriages, were being stowed away as quickly as the individual anxieties of their owners would permit. The passengers, as they stood around the carriage doors, were a study. Each face had a tale to tell; and not a few of them might have afforded materials for any amount of romance. In nearly every case this night journey would seem to have been taken rather of necessity than choice; '72,' however, screaming a shrill warning for all to stand clear, heeds not these matters. A porter, to whom I take an instant dislike, touches his hat, and tells me, with a sardonic grin, that Mr. Watkin is ready; so I walk nervously up to '72,' which is still hysterical, mount the step, and squeeze through a narrow gangway, and at last am in for it.

"'Right away, sir,' shouts a horrid man on the platform, waving a lantern as if the whole business were rather funny.

"'Right away, sir,' says the stoker.

"'Right away!' echoes Mr. Watkin, who stands with his hand on the regulator.

"Another short squeal from '72,' who 'refuses' for a moment, and the next I am jerked incontinently forward. It seems I have been standing on the foot-plate which covers the play between the engine and tender. This plate has a tendency to 'wobble,' and is positively not fit to stand upon. Having recovered myself, I begin to wish I had thought of making a few simple bequests to friends I never hope to see again, and for the first time think tenderly of my tailor, and wonder how the poor man will get paid. When I venture to open my eyes I find that we have rolled out of the station and are rumbling slowly over the river. Feeling no small astonishment and satisfaction that I am still alive to the appreciation of surrounding objects, I think I will begin to look about. To do this with any effect it is absolutely necessary that I should be able to stand still, and to achieve this it is equally necessary that I should hold on to something. A copper pipe looks tempting, and I grasp it unhesitatingly; it was—well, it was not cold. I smother a wicked word that bubbles up, and, after a more carefully conducted experiment or two, manage to clutch something not absolutely red-hot. My general demeanour all the time is very much that of a figure on wire worked up and down by springs from beneath. We are still moving slowly, as it were picking our course from out the intricacies of lines that cross and recross our path. Before us, high in the air, shine out innumerable signal lamps, each with its own meaning, each terrible if wrongly read or carelessly adjusted. A short stop at London Bridge, and we are away again. And now the feeling of disquiet is leaving me, and in its place comes a deep admiration for the mighty minds that have thought out the wonderful machine upon which I ride, and which, obeying the slightest touch of a practised hand, is beginning to bound, and thunder, and crash into the darkness. Above us, from the funnel, streams a flame-tinted comet-like cloud; in front, beneath us, glistening in the light of the forward lamps, stretch out the weblike lines that alone divide us from annihilation, whilst on either side looms nothing but thick night. Around, above, beneath, below us the very air seems ripped to ribbons as the iron monster rends out its terrible way; then ever and again, as if in anti-climax to some unknown horror, we rush with a wild screech into dark dank tunnels from which it is like resurrection to emerge.

"After somewhere about thirty miles I have got my locomotive legs on, and have ventured to let go my hold of support, and after two attempts at smoking, in which my tobacco entirely disappeared in about three whiffs, I learn how to smoke at a mile a minute and begin to feel better. But do what I will I cannot think steadily; one moment I am ready to invoke Zeus, the fabled owner of Pegasus, and back '72' at long odds against anything that fiery untamed one ever did; the next—well, it's no use trying to write the thoughts of that night, though I am convinced that some of them were really noteworthy, but as they galloped into my mind they got shaken into hopeless jumble by the incessant *vibrato* which my anatomy was undergoing. Nevertheless, zealous for my literary duty, I took out a notebook, and, by the light of the little lamp that shone on the water-gauge, tried to make a few shorthand notes. These are now at the service of any ardent student of Pitmanian lore who likes to call at the office for them.

"It is now horribly cold, and I am suffering from extremes of temperature, a bleak wind such as I never felt before blowing right off the sea, which we had reached, freezing me to my waist, while the heat from the furnace fires bakes my legs. I begin to speculate how much longer I can bear this combination of untoward circumstances, when we plunge madly into the base of a hideous cliff. Then, just as I feel convinced the end of all things is at hand, we are standing quietly at the platform of the Dover station, and five minutes later at the pier. The Calais boat lies heaving beneath us, painfully suggestive of stomachic inversion. Mail bags, luggage, and sleepy passengers are all huddled down a gangway of 45 degrees declension, and all is hurry, confusion, and crush. I turn away and walk to my hotel with the gentleman who has brought the people safely thus far, and wonder if ever there flits across the minds of our travelling millions any sense of gratitude to enginemen, whose exceptional mishaps are duly and justly noted, but whose general vigilance, the only thread upon which hangs the life of the traveller, is unchronicled, unheard of. For myself, I shall never take a night journey without a vivid remembrance of two hours on '*72*.'"

The Metropolitan Railway Company, by reason of the narrow limits to which it was confined, and the enormous cost of land around its original route, long suffered special inconvenience from the insufficiency of its locomotive establishment. This is situated at Edgware station, and every inch is crowded up. Since, however, the opening of the Harrow Extension Railway, new works have been erected at Neasden, for the maintenance of the rolling stock. On this company's lines the fires of the locomotives are drawn only once a week, that the engines may be washed out. "Practically," said the engineer, "we run them a thousand miles without their being stopped."

We may add that the Metropolitan and the District Railway Companies work their trains, so far as the public is concerned, as one main line. This is done by interchange of mileage; that is to say, as the Metropolitan engineer explained to us, "for every mile the District runs over us, we run a mile over them. The trains are practically the same in carrying capacity, and the wear and tear of the road is nearly the same. Our line is about twice as long as theirs, so we run eight trains over them, and they four over us. If one company does more miles working in the half-year than its proportion, it is adjusted in the next half-year. No money passes."

We are told that the locomotive engine as it now appears may some day become a thing of the past. "Nearly thirty years ago," Mr. Fowler, the engineer, has said, "when projecting the present system of underground railways in the metropolis, I foresaw the inconveniences which would necessarily result from the use of an ordinary locomotive, emitting gases in an imperfectly ventilated tunnel, and proposed to guard against them by using a special form of locomotive. When before the Parliamentary Committee in 1854, I stated that I should dispense with firing altogether, and obtain the supply of steam necessary for the performance of the single trip between Paddington and the City from a plain cylindrical, egg-ended boiler, which was to be charged at each end of the line with water and steam at high pressure. In an experimental boiler constructed for me the loss of pressure from radiation proved to be only 30lb. per square inch in five hours, so that practically all the power stored up would be available for useful work. I also found by experiment that an ordinary locomotive with the fire 'dropped' would run the whole length of my railway with a train of the required weight. Owing to a variety of circumstances, however, this hot-water locomotive was not introduced on the Metropolitan Railway, though it has since been successfully used on tramways at New Orleans, Paris, and elsewhere. I am sorry to have to admit that the progress of mechanical science, so far as it affects locomotives for underground railways, has been absolutely *nil* during the past thirty years. Whether a hot water, a compressed air, or a compressed gas locomotive could be contrived to meet the exigencies of metropolitan traffic is a question which, I think, might be usefully discussed."

The recent wonderful developments of electric science have extended even to the domain of railway locomotion. The great cost, it has been urged, of railway construction is caused by the fact that bridges and other works are required to be made strong enough to meet the necessities of the locomotive, which is five or six times heavier than an ordinary carriage of the same size. If it were possible to pull or push the train without the use of a locomotive, a great advance would be made in railway propulsion. "Electricity," says Professor Ayrton, F.R.S., "enables this to be done. Hence the wide future that was open for its practical employment in our great arteries of traffic. But a train could not go of itself, like the witch on the broomstick, and power must be expended to start it, and still more to keep up its motion. Power could not be created. All they could do was simply to make machines and devices for converting one form of power into another. Practically, they would employ the power drawn from coal when electric railways were made. The burning of coal instead of zinc was the secret of the great development of electricity, as the latter was about thirty times as dear as the former. One reason why the electric transmission of power could be made so efficient was because electricity had no mass, and therefore no inertia; and therefore it required no additional force to make electricity go round a corner, as was the case with water or material fluids. In order to work a railway by means of electricity, they must have two wires—one might be in the earth itself, and the other insulated from it, and some contrivance must be used by means of which a continuous connection was kept up between the dynamo machine on the moving train and the two wires. The simples. method of doing this was to use the two rails—one as the going wire and the other as the return wire—and let the current enter the carriage by means of the wheels on one side, and leave it by means of the wheels on the other. The axle, however, must be broken and insulated, otherwise the current would pass through the axles to the carriages, instead of through the dynamo machine." He exhibited a model of an electric railway, devised by himself and Professor Ferry; and he added that within a little while an electric railway on the plan he had explained would be in operation in New York.

An electric railway has been projected to pass under the Thames, and to connect Charing Cross with the Waterloo terminus of the South Western Railway. The Siemens Electric Railway at Berlin has made the public familiar with the fact that the electric current can be rendered subservient to purposes of locomotion, and there are some who indulge in pleasant visions of the time when a properly constructed "accumulator" shall even stow away enough electric energy to give motive power to a bicycle. The proposed electric railway is to commence thirty yards south-east from the base of the statue of King Charles I., and to pass beneath houses and streets, and then under the Thames, to a point beneath the loop-line station of the Waterloo terminus. The South Western Railway Company is to have power to contribute towards the construction of the line, and to enter into agreements with respect to its use, ownership, and management. The promoters ask for authority to provide engine-houses, stations, warehouses, yards, depôts, and works; and to levy tolls, rates, and charges; and to make provision as between themselves and the South Western Company for the appropriation and use of joint and separate stations, the supply of rolling stock and machinery, of officers and servants for the conduct of the traffic, and also the appointment of joint committees. The development of enterprise in these directions will be watched with interest both by the railway world and by the public.

BREAK-DOWN TRAIN.

To the locomotive department of a large station a break-down train and gang are attached, the arrangements of which we may describe. These are maintained in the highest degree of efficiency. Everything is in constant readiness for action at the shortest notice. A telegram flashes into the passenger station that there has been an accident. Two copies are immediately sent, one to the locomotive superintendent, or his foreman in charge at the "locomotive shed," the other to the "traffic inspector" of the district. A list of the names and addresses of the foreman in charge of the break-down vans and of the skilled men, twelve in all, who form the break-down staff, hangs up, framed and glazed, on the wall of the office; these are at once summoned; and, if additional hands are wanted, they are made up, as the circumstances require, from the ordinary staff connected with the locomotive department.

The break-down train itself is soon ready—in fact, always is ready. It consists of seven vehicles : two tool-vans, one riding-van, one laden with wood "packing," the break-down crane, and two "runners" or wagons which act for the protection at either end of the crane, one supporting the "jib," while the other carries the "balance blocks."

We enter the tool-van at one end of the train. Within it are arranged ropes of different lengths and thicknesses, "snatch blocks," small and large-sized pulley blocks, bars, shovels, screw-couplings, "clips" for securing broken axles, and various other kinds of tools. The next is the "riding-van," for the accommodation of the workmen who go with the train. Formerly they used to ride on the trucks, or on the engine, "to hang on where they could." The riding-van will hold forty men. "At the end," says our engineering guide, "you see these cupboards." He opens them and displays flags, fog-signals, signal and roof lamps used for lighting and protecting the train, train signal lamps, all ready trimmed for lighting, and four train lamps. In the centre is a stove with an oven attached, to keep the men warm, and, if necessary, to warm their food. Round the sides of the riding-van are "box-seats," in which are tools of various kinds, wood scotches, small "packing" shovels, hammers, bars of various descriptions, and "sets" for cutting shackles or bolts. "What," we ask, "is a 'set'?" It is a piece of sharpened steel, like the head of an axe without the handle, varying in weight from one pound to three. A piece of hazel, commonly called a "set rod," is wrapped round it, and the two ends form the handle. The "set" is held on anything it is required to cut, and with the blows of a heavy hammer, given by those accustomed to such work, it will quickly sever any bolt or shackle. In this van are also shovels, hammers, chisels, bars of various descriptions, everything of the kind likely to be wanted.

The third is a wagon carrying wood planks, "packing," as it is called, of various lengths, from two to six feet long, and from an inch to six inches in thickness. When, for instance, a screw-jack is employed to lift up the end of a wagon that has gone off the rails, the bottom of the jack must rest upon a flat piece of oak timber, else it would be pressed down into the ballast. There are, perhaps, three tons of packing in this wagon.

The next vehicle carries the crane itself, which is calculated to lift five tons, but when properly secured will lift considerably more. The balance block of the crane is movable, and when in use is heavily weighted with a number of blocks of cast iron; and in addition to this, when a heavy weight is being raised, the crane is secured to the permanent way by means of four clips, which are attached to each corner of the crane and clip the head of the rails. These are tightly screwed down after the crane has been properly arranged in position for any lift that it may have to perform. The jib of the crane, which is about 20 feet long, is also raised into its proper position; and it is now easy even to load one vehicle into another. A powerful brake is attached. The crane itself is usually worked by five men. The frame of the crane is iron, and the wagon which carries it is also iron throughout, weighing altogether about 15 tons

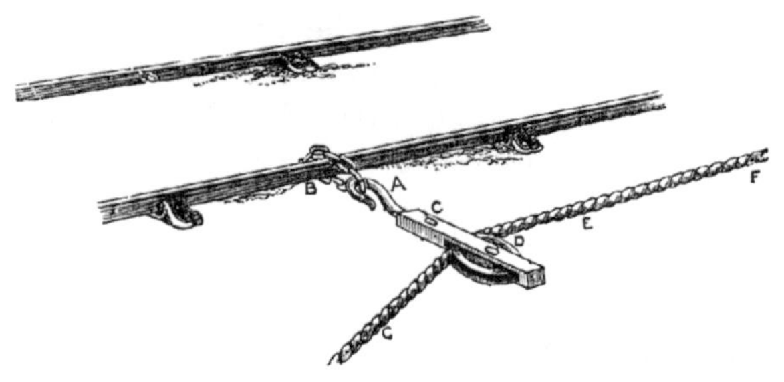

A SNATCH BLOCK.

Next to the crane is another runner, which supports the jib of the crane.

The next vehicle is another tool-van, which contains oil and naphtha lamps, crosscut saws, hand saws, axes, traversing jacks of various sizes, which are used for not only lifting but carrying anything into position, bottle-jacks of various sizes, and hydraulic jacks, each calculated to lift 15 tons, which one man can work with the greatest ease. There is a bench at one end, with a pair of vices and cupboards underneath, and there are also various tools used in connection with break-down work.

When the break-down train is running to the scene of accident it is signalled as if it were an express passenger train, and it takes precedence over all other trains. A good supply of both torch and naphtha lamps are always ready for night use as soon as the train arrives at its destination. These are usually held by bars specially arranged for the purpose, driven into the ground. Fires are also made of coal or broken wood.

There are several useful appliances carried with the vans, which are found to be of very great service. One is a "snatch block." This is used in various ways. In some cases when it is found necessary to turn a wagon over which has been turned upside down, the snatch block ACD is secured to the rails by means of a chain B wrapped round the rail. One end of a rope EFG, of about 2½ inches diameter, is attached to the engine, the other end passes through the snatch block, and over the wagon, which can thereby be turned over with very little trouble. In cases where wagons are down any steep embankment or in fields, they are pulled back to the line in a similar manner; only two blocks are used, and, instead of being attached to the rail, one is fastened to the draw-bar of the crane, and the crane itself is secured to the rails. The other snatch block is secured on the wagon about to be pulled up, and the rope passing through both blocks draws the wagon within reach of the jib of the crane. This takes it up bodily and places it on the rails. It is also frequently used for pulling a wagon on to the road, where, for instance, an engine cannot pass.

The second appliance is called a "ramp." There are right and left hand ramps. These are used for getting wagons on to the rails when they have run off. The ramp is so constructed as to fit the rail at one end, A, and the sleeper at the other, B. The ramp has two spikes or claws at the end which rests on the sleeper, and these are fixed immediately in front of the wheel of the wagon which it is intended to pull on the rails. The ramps are forged out of the solid, having a flange on the right side of C, and a jaw, A, on the top nearest the rail, which guides the wagon wheel into position. Either two or four of these ramps can be used at the same time for a wagon, according as may best suit its position off the road. As soon as the

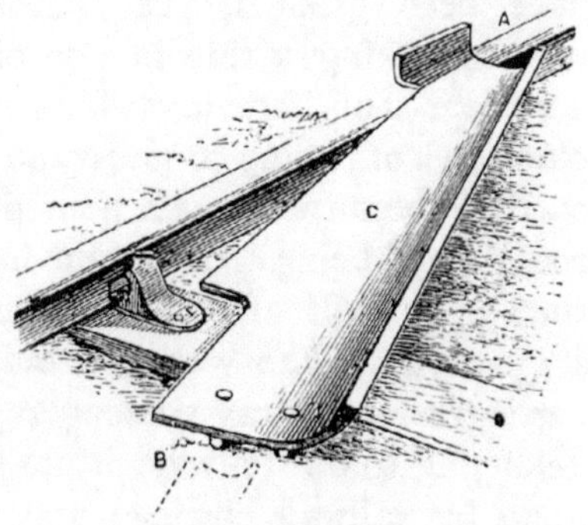

A RAMP.

weight of the vehicle gets upon the lower end of the ramp, it presses the teeth into the sleeper, and this compels it to keep its position.

The third appliance is a catch or "clip." This fits on the rail. The foot rests on the bottom flange of the rail, and is used to prevent a wagon, when lifted by the jacks, and when being forced over, from going too far. The wheel might drop over on the outside were it not prevented by this simple and useful kind of clip. It is used for both engines and wagons.

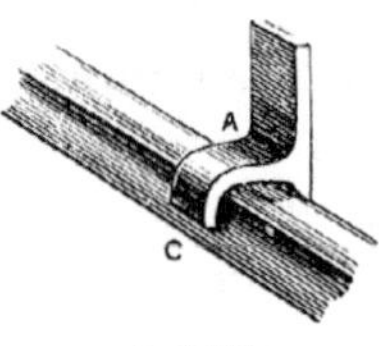

A CLIP.

A top coat is provided for each man of the break-down gang; and, in addition to what "time they may make," a bonus of *2s.* is given to each on every occasion he is called upon to "main line break-down work."

Refreshments are also supplied for the staff by the foreman in charge, which, as a rule, is obtained from the nearest public-house, shop, or farmhouse. In some cases in lonely places, where the work has been heavy, it has happened that refreshments have had to be brought from a considerable distance. "They are always willing," says the engineer, "to help us in a difficulty. Sometimes they make a fresh baking on purpose for us."

The improvements that have been made in railway carriages have been gradual, but unceasing. Some travellers can remember taking a ride in one of the original passenger "tubs," a vehicle that bore a striking resemblance to a modern cattle truck; or of having to put up an umbrella in even a second-class carriage, because the rain poured in through the lamp-hole in the roof; or of being crowded up in the narrow first-class carriages that were built after the fashion of the "inside" of the old stage-coach. The work of building and repairing the 40,000 carriages for railway passengers, and the 400,000 other vehicles belonging to our railways is, no light task; and, beside the work done by railway carriage and wagon building companies, the great railway companies have vast establishments of their own. The Midland Railway Company, for instance, in 1875 and 1876, bought a piece of land at Derby for this department alone, fifty-four acres in extent, whereon they erected more than fourteen acres of buildings, with more than ten miles of sidings, and here they employ some 2,000 men. The works consist of seven large shops, of the same design, and of the uniform height of twenty-one feet to the underside of the principals. The saw-mill, the wagon-shop, the carriage-shop, and the painting and trimming shop are on the west side of the yard, and these are entirely used for the preparation of timber, the putting together of material, and the completion of vehicles. The great ranges of buildings on the east side are for the manipulation of metals. Special precautions are adopted throughout for the prevention of fire. Spaces of at least seventy feet have been left between the blocks of building, and each block is surrounded by a seven-inch water main, always charged with water at a pressure sufficient to throw a jet over any roof of any building; and hose-boxes, with hose, stand-pipes, and everything complete, are fixed conveniently to seventy hydrants in various parts of the yard. Fire-buckets filled with water, and hand-pumps, are ready for use in every shop.

We first approach the timber-yard. Here, being discharged from trucks, or stacked in vast piles, are logs of ash, elm, East Indian teak, Honduras mahogany—worth from £15 to £20 a log—red, white, and yellow deals from the Baltic and Canada; oak from Quebec and Stettin—worth £5 to £50 each; and satin-wood from Kauri, in New Zealand. Seven or eight thousand enormous butts, the lot weighing, perhaps, 10,000 tons, are piled in apparent confusion; but each bears certain mysterious hieroglyphics, which tell to the initiated when and whence it was brought, and what place it had in the stock-taking. Overhead is a travelling crane, or gantry as it is called, by which, aided by a stationary engine, these giant forms can be handled and dandled about like so many gigantic babies, and can be borne away (here we beg permission to drop our simile) to the saw-mills to be cut up.

The first building we enter appears of enormous proportions. It is 320 feet long by 200 wide, while the light and lofty roof, tinged with a soft sky-blue colour, gives it a bright and airy appearance. The whirr of the machinery, and the screaming, with every variety of harshness of note, of innumerable saws, tell us that this is the saw-mill. Here are a hundred machines —for sawing, planing, moulding, shaping, morticing, tenoning, boring, turning, and recessing—all specially designed for the conversion of timber from the log into scantlings of every description for wagon and carriage work.

We approach the vertical frame saw. It has, perhaps, fifty blades, and it saws the wood into fifty slices, with a speed of nearly 100 strokes for an inch of wood, and at the rate of eight feet an hour. "We like forest-grown oak the best," says the foreman. "Hedge-grown is scrubby and full of rubbish—knots, and stones, and nails sometimes two feet inside the wood. But they don't punish us so bad as they do the circulars." We pause for a moment to look at the shaping machines, revolving some 2,000 times a minute; in fact, so rapidly that it is only with the closest scrutiny that we can tell that the keen blades are moving at all—blades that will shape the wood into almost any required form. Here also are the "endless band saws," of various sizes, and from an inch to an eighth of an inch in width, so that they can not only cut continuously (as their name implies), but can work in any direction the governor listeth. The endless saw, it has been remarked, is "a triumph of human ingenuity." It revolves round two wheels, much in the same way as a band revolves round two drums. "The wheels are perhaps three feet in diameter, and two inches in thickness at the circumference. They are placed—one as low as the workman's feet, another rather above his head—six or seven feet apart. Round the wheels there stretches an endless narrow band of blue steel, just as a ribbon might. This band of steel is very thin. Its edge towards the workman is serrated with sharp deep teeth. The wheels revolve by steam rapidly, and carry with them the saw, so that instead of the old up and down motion, the teeth are continually running one way. The band of steel is so extremely flexible that it sustains the state of perpetual curve." The ancient stories of sword blades that could be bent double are here surpassed by a saw that is incessantly curved and incessantly curving. "A more beautiful machine cannot be imagined. Its chief use is to cut out the designs for cornices and similar ornamental work in thin wood; but it is sufficiently strong to cut through a two-inch plank like paper," while it is itself apparently as flexible as indiarubber.

Here are moulding machines, which can at the same time plane, mould, tongue, or groove all four sides of a piece of timber; also moulding machines for moulding short pieces of timber; and dovetailing machines, a very ingenious mechanical arrangement, by which dovetails of boards are at one operation expeditiously cut out and made to fit exactly together. The panel-planing machine reduces the panel boards for carriages to an even thickness and a perfectly true face; and the sand-papering machine smooths the panel so that it is ready to receive the paint. Attached to the sand-papering machine is an exhausting fan, which withdraws the dust, and prevents it injuring either the work or the lungs of the workmen.

We notice in the sawing mill that, despite the work constantly going on and the enormous power required, the main shafting, pulleys, and belting are "conspicuous by their absence." The fact is they are in a cellar, nine feet deep, under our feet. By this arrangement the quick-running and dangerous machinery is kept away from the general workmen; the floor of the mill is clear for carrying or stacking the various lengths of timber; and the sawdust, shavings, and other refuse from the machines can be removed without interfering with the work of the mill. The mill floor, which serves also as the roof of the cellar, is supported by 500 cast-iron columns, and is made specially substantial and stiff, in order to bear the weight and to resist the vibration of the machinery.

The two engines, of 18-inch cylinder, which drive the machinery, are apparently small in size, but they develop an exceedingly high actual horse-power. Their three boilers have a working steam pressure of 140 pounds a square inch. "The engines are provided," says Mr. Clayton, "with a very heavy fly-wheel, and most perfect governor, in order to enable them to overcome any sudden increase or decrease of work to which sawing machinery is liable."

We next enter the wagon shop. It also is 320 feet by 200. Here the timber from the saw-mill, and the metal parts from the machine shop, meet, and are built together into wagons. So complete is the fit that the men here have very little actual mechanical labour, as may be judged by the fact that "one pair of men can build ordinary open goods wagons at the rate of one a day."

The next is the carriage building and finishing shop, where, again, the timber from the saw-mill and the ironwork from the machine shop meet, and are formed into carriage bodies. These are seen in all stages of construction, and in all states of repair. Some are just lifted off their bogies; from others the bogies have been removed for repair. Here are "bodies" "in frame," mere skeletons—like the ribs of a whale without his blubber,—but withal well-formed skeletons of sound English oak, to be covered with panelling, to be sheathed with Honduras mahogany. Here are carriages partly stripped of their panels, the clean bright patch of new wood showing boldly against the deep, dead chocolate of the old painted side. Here are some of the new Midland bogies, fifty-four feet long, some six-wheeled, others four-wheeled; the latter being the type at present principally built by the Midland Company, partly because they are found "handier" to lift. Carriages so heavy as these, and of such a length, necessarily gain immensely in steadiness. The body of the carriage is mounted on a "bogie," or a bogie truck, each having two or three pairs of wheels. Through the centre

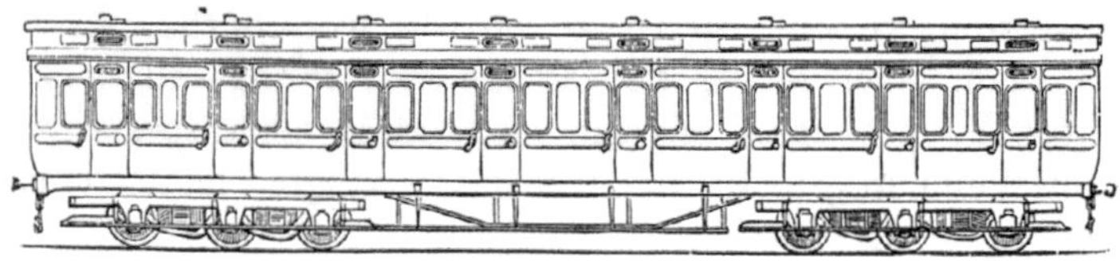

NEW MIDLAND BOGIE CARRIAGE.

of each truck runs a massive pin, which bolts it securely to the body, but allows it to revolve sufficiently to run easily and safely round the greatest curve on any existing railway. The interior of these carriages has all the improvements which have been made from time to time in railway carriages, and several others of its own. One of these is the clerestory roof, sometimes called the "tunnel" roof, which gives an air of lightness and space so pleasant to a railway passenger. The first-class compartments are upholstered in the usual way, with movable arms; the wood-work is of sycamore, divided into panels by maple mouldings, and these carriages are among the finest, if not the finest, upon our English railways. The third-class compartments have also been improved, till they fairly compete in popular esteem with the first class. In the west end of the carriage shop is a space set apart for the "finishing" of carriages. This includes the veneering over the inside panels, the insertion of the window frames and windows, the fixing of the maple and satinwood, and the cabinet work generally. Hard by this shop, and in practical conjunction with it, is the panel shed—a timber building 300 feet long by 100 wide, with walls formed of louvre boards, where is a large stock of mahogany panels, maple boards for moulding, and also dry boards for carriage work. All this remains for two years to season before it is used.*

The last shop on this side is for painting and trimming. It is nearly 400 feet by 300; has seventeen lines of railway, on each of which ten ordinary vehicles can stand. For a carriage to be able effectually to resist the action of the weather, and also to maintain a suitable appearance, it has to receive a succession of coats. Including the lead colour, the "filling up," the rubbing the surface smoothly down, the painting, and the repeated varnishing, there are no fewer than twenty-five operations before a carriage is finished. Meanwhile, in their various stages of painting they present a varied appearance: their dull look in the initiatory stages, the improvement made at each successive stage, until at last they are completed as handsomely as a gentleman's carriage; and a bystander can see his face in the carriage almost as plainly as in a mirror.

At the west end of this block the trimming and upholstery work of the carriages is prepared; indeed, much of it is being done while the carriages are being painted. The cushions are stuffed with horsehair, and are covered on one side with woollen cloth, and on the other with American cloth, the latter being cleaner and cooler for dusty and hot weather. The horsehair is worth from a shilling to eighteenpence a pound, and a single compartment of a first-class carriage will require 100 to 110 pounds—costing, therefore, from £5 to £8 for one compartment. The roof is lined with what is called wax cloth, worth two shillings a square yard and upwards.

On the other, the eastern, side of the yard are the buildings in which metal work is dealt with. There is the foundry, whence, for instance, 2,000 tons of castings are annually turned out; there is the smithy, with its ninety-two rows of hearths; and the bolt and spring makers' shops, which manufacture more

---

* From a paper contributed to the Chesterfield and Derbyshire Institute of Mining, Civil, and Mechanical Engineers, by Mr. T. G. Clayton.

than twenty tons of bolts and nuts every week, and which make and repair springs. Here also is the wheel-tiring shop. The work done by railway carriage wheels is enormous. A wheel of four feet diameter is, of course, twelve feet or four yards in circumference. In running a mile it will have to turn round 440 times, and in ten miles 4,400 times; that is to say, in running from London to Leeds, a distance of about 200 miles, it will turn some 88,000 times. That is a good many turns, and a good deal of wear and tear, for one very moderate journey. It is frequently necessary to remove wheels from, and to force others upon, their axles, to do which a machine, with a pressure of two hundred tons, is applied. Here, also, the various processes are carried on by which wheels are made or repaired—a trade of itself; and of tires alone, remarked Mr. Clayton, "we have 140,000 or 150,000 of our own running every day," a number since largely increased. "Before a carriage begins its journey," he continued, "the train examiner takes what is called 'a pricker' (a piece of iron bent into a suitable shape), with which he opens the grease holes, to know that they are properly lubricated, and also to tell whether there is sufficient brass in the 'journal' against which the axle in running presses, so that it may run with safety and ease. Experience enables him at once to know by the 'feel' of the pricker if all is right."

We may here remark that in the repairing shed of the Metropolitan, at Edgware Road, the tires when put on are heated by gas. The tire is placed on a sort of gridiron, and jets of blue gas are lit. The wheel hangs above by a chain; and when the tire has been sufficiently expanded by the heat, the wheel is quietly lowered into it. As the tire cools, it contracts, and is securely "wrung" on. "By this process," remarked the engineer, "I have never had a tire go wrong."

To the machine and fitting shop—which contains nearly 200 lathes and machines required for finishing the iron-work—is brought nearly all the material made in the foundry and smithy, whence it goes over to the wood shops, to form part of the vehicles under construction or repair. Such are some of the arrangements made at the Midland Railway carriage establishment in order to maintain in efficient order a rolling stock consisting of some 4,000 carriages and 34,000 wagons. To these considerable additions have lately been made by the purchase of what have hitherto been the wagons of private owners.

We may add that in each department there are convenient and comfortable mess-rooms for the workmen. There are several cooks in each room, and each workman brings his victuals of fish, flesh, or fowl, or chops, beef, or steak, and at the meal-time he finds his dish set before him, all excellently cooked, and also hot. This is a great boon to the workmen who live at a distance from the works. At breakfast every day a minister conducts a short service, and delivers a brief address, or if one cannot be obtained there are several of the workmen who are able to suitably address their fellow-workmen on religious topics. On several occasions the workmen here, including those of the locomotive department, have been addressed in the open air by distinguished visitors; and thus, at the recent Church Congress held at Derby, the Rev. Canon Farrar spoke to a delighted auditory of some 2,000 of them.

The cost of the repairs of passenger carriages has been estimated at from 1½*d.* to 2½*d.* per train mile. The cost of repairing goods trucks varies very much, but in general is from 2½*d.* to 3*d.* per train mile. On several lines this is greatly exceeded, and the maximum reaches 6*d.* There appear to be two general causes for this result: one, the large proportional stock required for the mileage run in agricultural districts; the other, the large stock needed for mineral, more especially for coal traffic. For this traffic the number of trucks in a train is large; the trucks are heavily laden, and liable to much rough usage.

In competition with the best bogie carriages are the Pullmans, "fit," as Sir Edward Baines has said, "for the journeyings of monarchs." In the autumn of 1872, Mr. Allport visited the United States, and found how rapid and remarkable had been the success of these carriages. In 1867 there were only thirty-seven of them in America; but five years later there were 700 in remunerative operation; and the company's contracts are with more than 150 different railways, and extend over 30,000 miles of American railway. Careful observation and inquiry led Mr. Allport to the conclusion that these carriages might be of service in this country, especially for long or night journeys. Eventually it was arranged between the Midland board and Mr. Pullman that his cars should be introduced on their lines;

and a contract was entered into for fifteen years, by which the Pullman Company provides the cars in good order and with suitable attendants; and the railway company supplies motive power, warmth, and protection. In payment, the railway company has the ordinary first-class fare, and the Pullman Company a certain very moderate additional sum. That everything has been completed without regard to expense may be

INTERIOR OF PULLMAN CAR.

inferred from the fact that the Pullman parlour car costs no less than £3,000—a sum nearly equal to that spent on the magnificent travelling carriage built by the London and North Western Railway for the use of the Queen.

When the first journey of the Pullman train was run, it was from St. Pancras to Bedford. "Literally nothing," wrote one who then travelled, "seemed left to desire. Entering the train from one end, you were introduced to the parlour car, a luxurious contrivance for short lines and day-travel only. It was a tastefully and richly decorated saloon, over fifty feet long, light, warm, well ventilated, and exquisitely carpeted, upholstered,

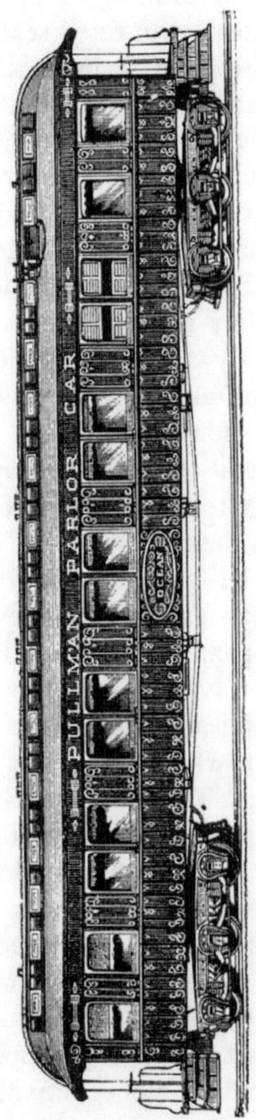

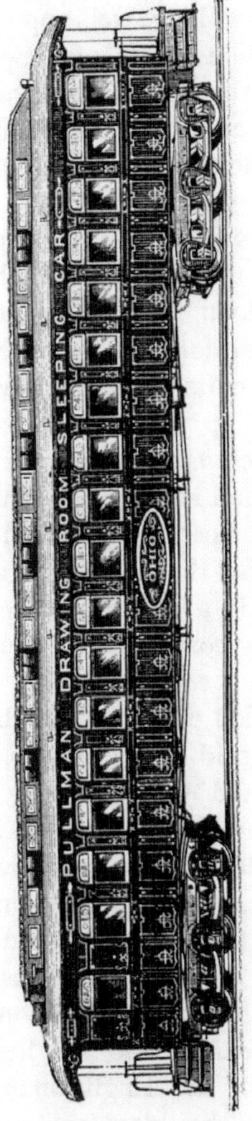

PULLMAN CARS.

and furnished. Along each side, and close to the windows, were crimson-cushioned easy chairs, in which, by means of a pivot, you might swing yourself round to converse with your neighbour, or, by means of one of the thousand ingenious contrivances with which the whole train abounded, you might tilt yourself back to the proper angle of enjoyment. The centre is free for passing to and fro. There are various little saloons of the private box order, in which a family party might make themselves happy. Then you came to the drawing-room sleeping car, another long, well-appointed saloon, with fixed seats at the windows like short sofas, two and two, and facing each other. Between them a firm, convenient table could be planted, and upon one of them we were able, while the train ran at over fifty miles an hour, to write without difficulty. The tables removed, the seats lowered to meet each other became an admirable bedstead, while some beautifully ornamented and finished panels overhead, that appeared to be merely part of the sloping roof of the saloon, were unfastened, and in a moment converted into equally comfortable upper berths. By-and-by the saloon was restored to its normal drawing-room aspect, the tables were again put up, waiters entered with snow-white cloths, pantries and anterooms were brought into operation, and there appeared a dining hall as complete in its requirements as the drawing-room and sleeping-room had been in theirs."

How far the Pullman car will be generally preferred in England is a matter of some doubt. Americans themselves, when they come to this country, appear well content with the matchless speed of English railway travelling and the comfort of half-filled ordinary first-class carriages. When Lord George Bentinck said on an off-day at Newmarket, only a few owners, trainers, and jockeys being present, "This is what I like. I hate a crowd," he expressed a feeling widely distributed among our population, and one adverse to the adoption of long cars. They are, without question, a great boon to ladies and to solitary travellers. Relieved of the custody of her impedimenta, of all fear of insult, and pleased with the handsome surroundings of the Pullman drawing-room, the lady traveller will appreciate the provision made for her comfort; and the more social varieties of the Englishman, if travelling alone, may also take kindly to the long car. A shy and sensitive minority will perhaps prefer the comparative seclusion of the ordinary first-class carriage.

Some of the sleeping cars on American lines appear to have their drawbacks. A traveller tells us of his experiences in one of them. "There was something touching," he says, "in the perfect neatness and comfort of the beds. In the midst of a great, dirty, roaring, selfish city, one could hardly have looked for such domesticity and motherly providence. How cool and fresh the linen looked! How springy the mattresses! How soft the pillows! Surely this must be the happiest way to bridge the two hundred and odd miles between New York and Boston! 'To sleep!' and, by a sleep, to say we end the newsboys and the pop-corn man, urchin with gum-drops, and with Ridley's candies, the long array of 'bound books,' novels, 'Harper's,' 'Leslie's,' 'Fun for Three Months,' and, though last not least, the stench the gloom, the smoke, the dirt, of that foul place, the depôt at New Haven! 'Tis a consummation devoutly to be wished! I little thought that in that sleep there might be dreams!

"After the tedious gentleman had given me my ticket, I suffered myself to be led like a lamb to a bench in an alcove at one side of the car. This bench a youth shared with me, and opposite were two other victims. All four of us were innocent and unsuspecting; we entered into a light and courteous conversation; we played about the subject that lay nearest our thoughts, as though we were utterly indifferent to it; we encouraged each other in a fatuous confidence in the honour and good intentions of those to whom we had blindly intrusted ourselves. We expressed our belief in the beds! Each one told the other that he expected to sleep like a top! We believed we should, or we tried to believe it; and as we really know nothing about tops and how they sleep, perhaps we did sleep like them. In that case, tops are a miserable class of creatures. Conversation soon became confidential. The youth, my neighbour, wound up his watch. He said that he had been told that he must particularly look out for pickpockets in the sleeping-cars! His papa had told him that they looked remarkably like gentlemen. His watch was a valuable one. He had more money with him than he cared to lose. His aunt had advised him to pin it into his fob; but his brother had told him that all such devices were useless against pickpockets.

"Then the man appeared who makes up the beds. He pulled levers up and down, shots bolts, turned windlasses, adjusted screws, and finally we saw our snug alcoves transformed into four beds of such a guileless and prepossessing appearance as might have deceived the very elect! For us, as for the rest, snow-white sheets were spread; crimson blankets—which the chilly August air, and the dreary, pattering rain made seem most comfortable—were cosily tucked in, plumpest pillows invited our heads, and the shadowing curtains enclosed me and the confiding youth in their folds while we undressed for the night. But, reader, I am no poet, and cannot describe that night.

"After a few hours of abortive attempts at sleeping, I at last found myself, in the early grey of morning, as wide awake as if it were broad noon. I leaned out of my coffin and looked about in the dim light to see how it fared with the other dead people. My confiding friend was sitting on a pillow on the floor by the side of his berth, apparently wondering why his maiden-aunt had not included sleeping-cars in her list of dangers he was to avoid."

One good turn deserves another; and we are patriotically happy to read in the Detroit *Tribune* that the Wagner Sleeping Car Company have been fitting up and advertising an "English parlour car," to be put upon the Michigan Central. "It is built," we are told, "in continental style, with compartments, doors at the side, a smoking-room in each end, and a narrow foot platform running along the side. It will be elegantly fitted up, and equipped with sofa chairs."

But while the railway companies are endeavouring to promote the comfort of their travellers, it is to be regretted that there are some passengers who are unworthy of such consideration. A chairman of the London and South Western stated to a meeting of shareholders, that he had been shown a cushion in one of their carriages in the back of which no fewer than one hundred and fifty holes had been cut; and the amount of loss which railway companies sustain from wilful and wanton damage is as great as it is inexcusable. A railway carriage is often so mutilated that it has to be upholstered *de novo;* and brainless fops who wear diamond rings consider it a display at once of their elegance and wit to scrape the glass in such a manner as to interrupt the view, or even to outrage decency, so that the window has to be replaced before the carriage again becomes suitable for public use.

Some travellers, it appears, are careful observers of such scientific *minutiæ* as the botany of the interior of railway carriages. Dr. M'Nab, Professor of Botany in the Royal College of Science, Dublin, says that in a railway carriage on the express between Paddington and Milford, he noticed in the window two tufts of moss, one near each corner of the glass. "There was a little black soil kept moist by the condensation of vapour on the window, and two little bright green patches, consisting of about forty or fifty plants, about one-eighth of an inch in height, and apparently very healthy. The other window had the same moist deposit of soil, but no mosses. I put a small quantity of the soil and moss into my pocket-book, and after my return to the college placed two or three of the little plants under the microscope. The plants have only a few leaves, and probably belong to the genus *tortula;* but along with the moss I could detect an abundance of two species of *oscillatoria* in a very healthy condition, with abundance of *phycochroma* in their cells. On examining the slide with a higher power, I detected a number of diatoms, all belonging to a small species of *navicula.* The soil in which the mosses were growing was very peculiar. It consisted almost exclusively of exceedingly minute black particles, appearing as mere specks with a sixth-inch object glass, and all exhibiting the most active Brownian movements. The moving soil seems a fitting accompaniment to the locomotive habitat of the specimens. I suppose it will be necessary to say the distribution of the plants is remarkable, extending, as it does, from Paddington to Milford and back. You may, therefore, accept this as a small contribution towards the 'Botany of the South Wales Express.'"

Mr. Elliott, the Midland station master at Leeds, has invented an ingenious contrivance for labelling railway carriages. It consists of a wooden framework encasing transparent indicators inscribed with letters about an inch and a half deep. These work in a groove, and by means of an ordinary carriage-key may be concealed behind the frame, or let down so as to indicate to the passengers, by day or by night, the destination of the carriage. Carriages running between London and Leeds and Bradford may be labelled "London" on the upward journey, and on the downward, as may be arranged, "Leeds" or "Bradford."

Near Trent station is a spot often passed by those who are

unaware of the interesting and useful work there carried on. The place is situated just where the two lines from Trent converge, and whence they run on together towards Derby. It is known among railway men as "the sheet stores"; it is not only a store, but a manufactory. At one time the spot was used—it being on the Erewash Canal as well as on the railway —as a coke stores; and the directors of the old Midland Counties Railway Company had offices here for the transaction of business. The basin, formerly used for coaling purposes, now receives barges which bring ballast that has been dredged from the Trent, and which is here trans-shipped into ballast trains for the service of the line.

Our reader has some rainy night stood at a roadside station and watched a goods train pass slowly by. It was a very wet, long, low, solid mass, and over each wagon was some sort of black-looking covering that glistened in the lamp-light, and showed pools of water that had collected in the folds of the sheets—water that otherwise would have soaked into the boxes or bales of merchandise of various kinds underneath. It is to the making and the repair of these sheets that the extensive manufactory near Trent station is devoted.

Sheets were employed for a very curious purpose at one time. The circumstance is little known, but it was mentioned to us on unquestionable authority. When coals were first carried by railway on the then London and Birmingham line, *they were sheeted down, for fear they should be seen,* it being thought beneath the dignity of a railway company to carry minerals! An indignant objection was at first made to their being carried at all, and it was reported to Stephenson that Mr. B——, of the London and Birmingham line, had said: "They will want us to carry dung next." On hearing this, "Old George's" anger was aroused, and he replied, "You tell B—— from me, that when he travels by rail they carry dung now."

The selection by the Midland Company of the present lonely spot for their sheet stores was partly because of the risk of fire consequent on the inflammable nature of some of the materials employed. Formerly the work was carried on at Derby station, over the cheese warehouse; and, within a twelvemonth of the removal to temporary premises near Trent, they were burned down.

The covers are made of a stout canvas, sent here in "bolts," or pieces of 100 feet each, from Dundee, Leeds, or elsewhere, and cut up in lengths 20 feet long. A single sewing-machine will do as much work as half a dozen sewing-men. When the sheet has been made, it is taken to a large shed, laid on the floor, and "dressed"; in other words, it is vigorously scrubbed with a long-handled stiff brush dipped into a combination of boiled linseed oil and vegetable black—the black being the soot of burned cabbage stalks or other vegetable refuse. One coat of this oil is brushed in on each side, then three more are added, and the sheets have now a bright "face" upon them.

Besides the making of new sheets, there is also the mending of old ones. "You can't guarantee a sheet," said Mr. Clatworthy, the superintendent, "after it has had even one journey." The corners of the trucks, the awkward projections of the packages, or the carelessness of those who handle the sheets, will cause them to be pierced or torn; and, if there is one hole, however small, it may let through water enough to spoil a lot of valuable property. A large number of men and boys may be seen squatting about on the floor, in tailor-like positions, darning, patching, and piercing the places that have already been found—perhaps by holding the sheets before a window—to be defective. These darns are subsequently blackened over by boys; or, in bad cases, the whole sheet is re-painted. A sheet will sometimes come in for repairs half a dozen times in a year. A mark placed upon it, and sundry brief but suggestive records in a "sheet-book," enable the clerks to recognise any sheet, and to trace its history.

When a sheet has been painted, it is laid over a pole, and hoisted by a couple of ropes and pulleys over the heads of the workmen, that it may dry. It is then lowered, to be stencilled with the gigantic fourteen-inch letters M R Co. These are put twice on each side of the sheet, so that it may easily be recognised; and, with the same design, the edges of the sheet are painted yellow, so that when folded up and mixed with the sheets of perhaps half a dozen other companies, each may be known without unfolding all. The Great Northern has a white and blue line from corner to corner; and the London and North Western has two red lines running lengthwise over the sheet. These drying rooms are heated by steam, and will hold 600 sheets. Each sheet when finished is worth about £2. It lasts ordinarily four years; though, said Mr. Clatworthy, "we often get rather more out of them." Several thousand new ones are here made every year.

In addition to sheets, various kinds of covers and ropes are made at the Trent sheet stores. The shunting ropes are of six-inch rope, ten yards long, and are intended chiefly for goods yards and collieries. Into one end of the rope a great hook is spliced, and into the other end perhaps a ring. These are so firmly interwoven that not an engine on the line could draw one out: the rope would rather break. "Lashing ropes," for binding wool or timber on wagons, ropes for slings with which to hoist goods into warehouses, and similar appliances, are here prepared. Covers for the horses are also made. Formerly they were of ordinary oil-cloth, which effectually excluded the wet, but as effectually kept in the moisture. Flannel is now preferred, and it supplies a warm jacket for horses in wet or cold weather, and fewer of them now go to the infirmary.

MONSAL DALE.

CHAPTER XII.

"Bradshaw."—The Editorial Department of a Railway.—The Official Time-Table.—The "Working Time-Table."—The "Appendix" to the Working Time-Table.—Excursion Time-Table.—The Staff of a Railway Editor.—Charms of Early Railway Travelling.—Third-Class Passengers.—Improvements in Third-Class Travelling.—"Third Class by all Trains."—Numbers of Third-Class Passengers.—First-Class Passengers.—Workmen's Trains.—Special Trains.—Fox Hunters.—New "Twin Day Saloons" of London and North Western.—Dining Saloon Cars on Midland.—Limited Pullman Express on London and Brighton.—Special Sociability of Certain Railroad Travellers.—The Royal Train.—Odd Ideas of Locomotion.—A Passenger Travelling as Merchandise.—An Exciting Episode.—Carelessness of Travellers.—Foolishness of Travellers.—A New Zealander.—An Iron-Clad Train on Duty.—Railway Travelling in War Time.—A Military Railway.—Private Owners of Railways.—Other Passengers by Railway: Horses, Cattle, etc.—Legal Definition of a Pig.—A Lap Dog.—A Tiger.—Fish Traffic.—Milk Traffic.—A Goods Station at Night.—Coal Traffic.

HE legal historian records a remarkable judicial opinion. It appears that some years ago a witness observed that he had on a certain occasion examined the pages of "Bradshaw's Guide" for some twenty consecutive minutes; whereupon the judge declared that the evidence of such a person must not be relied upon—that he was a fit subject for a commission *de lunatico inquirendo.* We are so unfortunate as to differ from the learned gentleman. We are of opinion that one of the most valuable, if one of the most unconnected, periodicals issued from the monthly press, is that which bears the name of *Bradshaw*, and that it contains data which even the statesman, the philosopher, and the humorist may ponder. The name itself is suggestive. "Some men," it

The initial letter represents a temporary over-bridge.

has been said, "are born to greatness, others achieve greatness, and others have greatness thrust upon them;" and to one of these orders of fame we must assign a position for the author of the work in question. It is something to leave behind us a title which posterity will ponder; it must be more to win contemporaneous renown; what must it not be to write our name upon both the present and the future literature of our country? To insert his name in the almanacks of his empire was an honour Julius Cæsar laboured to deserve, and Augustus intrigued to share. But to make one's name a necessity in the language of our country, and every month to have it proclaimed and re-proclaimed amid the busiest haunts of men, must be a triumph the Cæsars never won. Sneering critics may extinguish ambitious enemies by the mere use of an indefinite article, when they recount that "*a* Mr. So-and-so then addressed the meeting;" but that which is the marring of one man may be the making of another; the insertion of the article may turn a surname into a noun, and be the means of spreading it on every side and of handing it down to coming centuries. Thus our reader may muse, in mood more grave or gay, when he next stands at a railway book-stall and buys "*a Bradshaw.*"

But though month by month tens of thousands peruse the pages of this most popular of all the monthlies, even fame so great is not without alloy. Ill-natured people declare that the volume is as unintelligible as a book of logarithms to a school-girl, and that its study is as exacting a mental toil as the mastery of the integral calculus. Still we venture to think that after all there may be something worth pondering in a sixpenny "Bradshaw," — something that deserves the scrutiny even of gentlemen who can talk by the hour about the currency, who can revel in a "price current" that informs us that bones were "inanimate," and that "calves moved off heavily," and who can grow eloquent over the provincial politics of a town council's balance sheet.

It is not long since our journeyings were regulated, not by a volume that contains nearly half a million items, but by a few coachmen's "way-bills." It is not long since—as Mr. Oliver Heywood remarked at the opening of the Eccles, Tyldesley, and Wigan line—that railway passengers "had to give their names, and spell them, in order to their being written on a large green paper ticket; when between Liverpool and Manchester there was a long stay at Newton in order that passengers might refresh themselves with Eccles cakes; and when 'a guide' to the line to London cost five shillings, with a cheap edition at half a crown." Nor are we aware of any better means by which to give vividness to our conception of the greatness of this peaceful revolution than to hold in our hand a time-table as it was years ago and as it is to-day.

The "Railway Companion," as it was then called, was less than half the size of a page of "Bradshaw," and contained only about six leaves of railway information. Some cab fares, some little plans of towns, and maps of the counties through which the railways ran, were added. The book was enclosed in a cloth cover, upon which was a small gold label, and it was sold for a shilling. Subsequently two editions of the "Guide" were published at threepence and sixpence; these have grown in their proportions with the growth of what is called by courtesy "our railway system," until we have now a volume of hundreds of pages, telling us of the movements of the thousands of passenger trains that daily run along our great iron thoroughfares, or wind their course along the innumerable byeways that cross and re-cross the land.

But besides the "Bradshaw" of the book-stall, there are other railway guides that tell of the working of particular railways: the official productions of the editorial departments of the companies themselves. It is not enough to run trains, and to run them safely and punctually at convenient times; it is also necessary that the public should have adequate and accurate information thereon; and the labour and care thus involved, directly and indirectly, is greater than is generally supposed.

There is, firstly, the official time-table of the passenger trains. In the arrangement of these, various considerations have to be regarded. The seasons, the earnings of the train service already in operation, the growth of trades or of towns, the changes contemplated by neighbouring companies, the suggestions made to or by officers of the company—all are carefully considered, and are embodied in a report that is submitted to the general manager, and afterwards to the directors. This report being sanctioned, the new proof-sheets are prepared, the corrections being marked, sometimes to the number of scores on a page, on one of the current time-tables; and then every item is finally reconsidered, to see that there are no mistakes or omissions, or clashing of arrangements of trains that should meet at junctions or with other companies. Meanwhile, in another department the runnings of goods and mineral trains also are determined; it being understood that, in all cases, the passenger trains have the preference. The manuscripts are now sent to the printer, who, to avoid risk of error by resetting, keeps all his type, as used at the last printing, still standing; the proofs returned by him are carefully checked and corrected, and then a "proof time-table" is printed, and forwarded to the editors of all railway local time-tables. "Foreign" railway companies now send in any alterations they propose, and these have to be compared with and adjusted so that the through traffic of each company concerned may work harmoniously. All being settled, and the necessary corrections being made, the official time-tables are ordered to be printed. For the Midland Railway Company 33,000 to 35,000 are required; more in summer—when they are also larger in size—than in winter; and all are ready about nine days before the end of the month.

Copies are now sent to all the stations on the system for use or sale; and some thousands are despatched by post to principal hotels and to certain business houses in all parts of the kingdom. The price at which they are sold is 1*d.*; their cost of production is at least 4*d.*

Meanwhile other departments of the editing are being actively pushed forward. The times for the running of goods and mineral trains have been considered; the alterations required to suit the changes in the passenger trains have been determined; and, as the outcome of all, the "Working Time-Table," as it is called, for the use of the company's servants, is prepared and completed. This is a remarkable production. The copy that lies before us is a volume of more than 400 octavo pages. It gives particulars of every train—passengers, goods, and minerals—(except excursions and specials) that runs; and it states not only the times at which each train stops at an intermediate station, but also (in smaller figures) the time when it is due to pass other stations. It mentions where shunting engines will work, and when and where express goods will be marshalled; it classifies certain goods and mineral trains; and it gives the maximum dimensions allowed for a wagon-load on "foreign" lines. The page open before us deals with a couple of hours' morning traffic between Nottingham and Clay Cross; and we observe by the figures at the top of the columns that sixty-three trains have already run since the day began; before it ends the number will be 157; the list of which occupies twelve full octavo pages, and from Clay Cross to Nottingham twelve pages more. In some other directions the line is even more busy, and the time-table is more voluminous. From Normanton to Skipton, for instance, in the twenty-four hours of the day 200 trains are run; they fill nearly fourteen pages of the time-table, and there are 200 more trains the other way. This working book is divisible into several sections—the last being "City and Suburbs of London,"—and every driver, guard, signal-man, and platelayer, and every other outdoor member of the staff, is supplied with at least that section that covers the ground to which his duty relates. These books are issued a week before they come into operation, that the men may have time to inform themselves of the changes that are impending. A signalman, for instance, wants to know what goods trains are to be shunted at his post; a guard has to inform himself of the first station at which he must be ready to stop and to deliver his parcels; and a driver learns where, for the future, his train is to be pulled up. An acknowledgment that the men supplied with these books have actually received them is in every case insisted upon, and an official record is preserved of the fact.

Besides the working table, there is also its "Appendix." The instructions in this were formerly included in the previous; but it was found that while much of the information of the latter was liable to changes, there was much that was permanent, and that each might be treated separately. Hence the "Appendix." The Midland appendix contains more than 150 pages octavo. It mentions all the distinctive whistles to be sounded by drivers on approaching the different junctions, particulars which fill forty pages; it states what are the head, tail, and side lamps to be carried; it gives instructions for the use of the continuous brakes; the regulations for the working of the block system; the loads for engines on different gradients; and a thousand other necessary details.

But the editorial work is not yet completed. The working time-table and its appendix deal only with ordinary trains at ordinary times. The excursion trains need specially to be considered, and special instructions have from time to time to be issued concerning them. There are excursions and excursions. Some are run by the company, and are duly announced by advertisement; others are ordered by schools, clubs, societies; and others by private or public bodies. The pages of the working time-table of excursion trains, from May 20th to May 28th inclusive, run from 280 to 317; and each page contains instructions about three or four such trains. The week following is from May 27th to June 3rd, covering Whitsuntide, and its pages continue from 318 to 430; and they describe the working of upwards of 500 special excursion trains on all parts of the Midland system, all of which have to be kept clear of the ordinary passenger trains. Before the year closes this time-table of excursion trains alone will have swollen into a book of 1,300 or 1,400 pages. Besides all these larger books there are, perhaps, a dozen small ones to be provided for local use in the great centres of the system.

The posters, also for the official use of the Company, are prepared in this department. There are great bills with blue lines at the top, representing the running of the main line trains; there are thirty or forty printed on two or three different colours, which state the working of the fast and express trains to and from some one great town and London; and there are those printed on card that mention simply the trains that run to and from particular stations—Derby, Birmingham, or Nottingham, for instance—to every other part of the system and beyond.

The work thus involved in preparing (to say nothing of the printing) and despatching these productions to their destinations is considerable. Most of them travel as parcels; three or four cab-loads may go by post. The editors of some 350 private local time-tables generally send back copies of their productions to the company's office in acknowledgment of the official copy previously received. When critically examined, it must be allowed that these are not always infallible, though many of them are excellent.

At the editorial office of the Midland Company, nearly thirty clerks are employed on these and other duties. "It means at times," said one of them, "a lot of day and night work. The pressure at the last is terrific."

Having referred to the literary aspects of passenger and other railway locomotion, we may turn to the practical. In doing so we may venture to repeat that the worst forms of railway travelling for the poorest third-class passenger are incomparably better than the best methods for even the rich of former days. There is now no clambering over dirty wheels—no hurting one's shins on sharp irons—no wedging of one's self amidst piles of luggage on a lofty unsheltered platform, around which numerous legs hung dangling like a dozen brace of black and brown grouse; no necessity for one's comfort that the drip of our umbrella should be turned into a neighbour's neck. It is at the same time a pleasant thought to many, that, while the train bowls along over the iron road, there is no plying of the whip, there are no foaming mouths, no turgid veins of generous steeds; the giant power that bears us swiftly onwards has bones of brass and iron, and nerves and muscles that cannot tire.

We will, however, frankly allow that some of the charms of our earlier railway travelling have been withdrawn. When the first London railway—that to Greenwich—was opened for traffic, it was exhibited as a show, and special attractions were employed to make it "draw." "A band of musicians in the garb of the Beefeaters was stationed at the London end, and another band at Deptford. For cheapness' sake the Deptford band was shortly superseded by a large barrel-organ, which 'played in' the passengers; but when the traffic became established, the barrel-organ, as well as the Beefeater band at the London end, were both discontinued. The whole length of the line was lit up at night by a row of lamps on either side, like a street, as if to enable the locomotives or the passengers to see their way in the dark; but these lamps also were eventually discontinued as unnecessary. As a show, the Greenwich Railway proved tolerably successful. During the first eleven months it carried 456,750 passengers, or an average of about 1,300 a day."

It may seem paradoxical, but nevertheless it is true, that the most important travellers, those who are the most numerous, and who best support the railways, are the third-class passengers. Only gradually has this fact been learned by the companies and by the public. It is only a few years since the parliamentary trains were run in bare fulfilment of the obligations of Parliament, and when a journey by one of them could never be looked upon as anything better than a necessary evil. To start in the darkness of a winter's morning to catch the only third-class train that ran; to sit, after a slender breakfast, in a vehicle the windows of which were compounded of the largest amount of wood and the smallest amount of glass, carefully adjusted to exactly those positions in which the fewest travellers could see out; to stop at every roadside station, however insignificant; and to accomplish a journey of 200 miles in about ten hours—such were the ordinary conditions which Parliament in its bounty provided for the people. When the first edition of this work was issued, we called attention to what were then regarded as great improvements, then recently provided, for third-class travellers. The London and North Western Company, we remarked, is now running "a train of third-class carriages, covered in, with side-doors and seats, which starts from the metropolis every morning between six and seven o'clock, and arrives at Liverpool, Manchester, and Leeds the same evening—travelling at an average speed of fifteen miles an hour, including stoppages; but when in motion, at twenty-five, to avoid the danger of being overrun by other trains. On its arrival at Blisworth, sixty-three miles from London, it is detained an hour and a half, to allow the mail and three other quick trains to pass, and for the purpose of warming and refreshing the passengers, for whom a large and commodious room is provided. Another half-hour is allowed at Birmingham and Derby. The object of these stoppages is, in fact, chiefly to prevent the use of the train by those for whom it is not intended. A similar arrangement is made by an up train for the people of the north."

In the course of years a few further meagre concessions were made; but still the speed of trains that carried third-class passengers was slow; neither through tickets nor through journeys could be taken; and travellers had to get forward as best they could by a series of fragmentary journeys over the lines of different, rival, and often conflicting companies. Thirty years ago a third-class passenger from London to Liverpool had to spend two days on the journey; and a second-class passenger from London to Liverpool had to stop at Birmingham for the night, or else to proceed by first class at first-class fare. "We remember," says a writer, "once standing on the platform at Darlington when the parliamentary train arrived. It was detained for a considerable time to allow a more favoured train to pass, and on the remonstrance of several of the passengers at the unexpected detention, they were coolly informed, 'Ye mun bide till yer betters gaw past; ye are only the nigger train.'"

At last came a revolution. On the last day of March, 1872, we remarked to a friend: "To-morrow morning the Midland will be the most popular railway in England." Nor did we incur much risk by our prediction. For on that day the Board at Derby had decided that on and after the 1st of April they would run third-class carriages by all trains; the wires had flashed the tidings to the newspapers; the bills were in the hands of the printers, and on the following morning the directors woke to find themselves famous, not perhaps in the estimation of railway competitors, but in the opinions of millions of their fellow-countrymen who felt that a mighty boon had been conferred upon the poor of the land. This step had, we believe, long been in contemplation, and in deciding to adopt it the Board had had to prepare for what some expected would be a serious sacrifice of revenue; but reasons of high policy won the day, and tens of millions of passengers who have since been borne swiftly and comfortably over the land have been grateful that instead of the narrowness and greed so commonly and often so unjustly attributed to railway administration, a statesmanlike and philanthropic temper has prevailed and triumphed.*

"If there is one part of my public life," Mr. Allport has said, "on which I look back with more satisfaction than on anything else, it is with reference to the boon we conferred on third-class passengers. When the rich man travels, or if he lies in bed all day, his capital remains undiminished, and perhaps his income flows in all the same. But when a poor man travels, he has not only to pay his fare but to sink his capital, for his time is his capital; and if he now consumes only five hours instead of ten in making a journey, he has saved five hours of time for useful labour—useful to himself, to his family, and to society. And I think with even more pleasure of the comfort in travelling we have been able to confer upon women and children. But it

* "The Midland Railway: its Rise and Progress."

took," he added, "five-and-twenty years' work to get it done." It is a happy circumstance when the hard realities of railway administration are thus tempered by a spirit so humanitarian and elevated.

That the concessions thus made to the needs of the public have been justified, the following figures will prove. In 1850, passengers of all classes in England were in number 58,000,000, and the receipts were less than £6,000,000; in 1880, the passengers were 540,000,000, and the receipts from them were £20,000,000. The number of passengers had multiplied about nine times, and the receipts had multiplied between three and four times; and the notable fact is that the greater part of all this enormous increase of railway traffic is due to the third-class passengers. In 1850 the third-class passengers were nearly equal in number to the two other classes put together; since then the increase of the two classes has gone on at a slow rate, while that of the third class now numbers five times as many as those of the first and second classes combined. Mr. Allport says: "From 1862 to 1871, or nine years preceding the change of carrying third-class passengers by all trains, the passenger receipts per mile on railways open increased 4·31 per cent., and they increased nine years after the change 15·69 per cent." No wonder that the *Times*, remarking upon these facts, said: "The third-class traffic of railways grows and grows till it overshadows all the rest of their passenger business." The *Railway News* also thus writes: "Take the last decennial period as an illustration. The number of passengers has increased on the railways from 337 millions to 626 millions. But this increase of 289 millions is actually less than the increase in third class alone. These have risen from 228 millions in 1870 to 523 millions last year—an increase of not less than 295 millions."

In 1881 the returns were, on the railways of the United Kingdom, exclusive of season and periodical tickets, as follows:—

	Number of passengers.	Amount received.
1st Class	37,993,944	£3,779,371
2nd "	64,474,717	3,398,806
3rd "	520,579,126	15,266,519
		1,506,332*
Total	623,047,787	£23,951,028

* Holders of season or periodical tickets—an average of a year each.

"One would have thought," said the *Quarterly Review*, "from the pride taken by railway people in their express trains, that it was these that paid the dividend. Everything must give way to them. Coal and goods trains are shunted—parliamentary trains are drawn into sidings—and signals are manned to clear the road and signal it 'all clear' for the 'down' or 'up express.' Chairmen are almost ready to weep when they hear of an accident befalling them. Yet it is even doubtful whether, in many cases, the express defrays the cost of working it, while the speed at which it runs increases all the elements of danger in travelling by railway." These fast trains—to use the words of Mr. Hawkshaw—"run the gauntlet through goods trains, coal trains, and cattle trains." To keep out of the way of the fast trains, the goods and coal trains are run with light loads and at high speeds, thereby occasioning great wear and tear of road and rolling stock, and increase in the working expenses. Passengers in first-class carriages, too, have their costly peculiarities. They expect not only a seat for themselves, but another for their feet. Some regularly fee the porters or guards, "paying the tribute known at railway stations by the name of 'fluff,' to reserve a compartment for themselves. Others, solitarily disposed persons, fill up vacant seats with their wrappers and carpet-bags, so that the first-class compartments are rarely more than half filled." "You will find," remarked Mr. Sheriff, M.P., a railway authority, "if there are half a dozen first-class compartments, half a dozen persons will immediately take a single place in each, and there will be a great outcry if anything like five or six people are put in."

Another source of waste in running fast trains has been described by Mr. Stewart, then Secretary of the London and North Western Company: "When there are only three or four passengers for a place, a through carriage must be provided for them. There must be a carriage put on for the Buckinghamshire line, another for the Bedford line, another for the Northampton line, another for Leamington, and so on; so that, apart altogether from the feeing of porters, there is a great waste." In illustration of this statement, Mr. Stewart stated that on two days selected as a fair average, whilst 4,482 passengers were booked from Euston Square, the trains to accommodate them contained 13,512 seats. "Thousands, nay millions of miles are run," said Professor Gordon some years ago, and it is true to-day, "by locomotives and carriages whilst they are performing an amount of transport preposterously disproportioned to the power and capacity of the trains employed for effecting it." The average number of persons carried per mile at that time by all the trains in the United Kingdom for which the returns were made up was only thirty-two, or four more than the full complement of an omnibus. "Engines of 300 or 400 horse power, weighing thirty to forty tons, with carriages behind them weighing equally as much, are set to draw about half a dozen more passengers than could be taken in an omnibus, and who might be easily, though not so quickly, of course, drawn upon the line with a single horse."

An important class of trains are known as "workmen's trains." In the recent report of the Select Committee of the House of Commons appointed to consider the working of the Acts relating to artisans' and labourers' dwellings, there is a recommendation "that the obligation placed upon the Eastern Counties system of railways out of London to provide trains for artisans at the rate of 1*d.* for each passenger per course of seven or eight miles should be extended to other suburban railways as opportunities may offer." This is, doubtless, in the interest of the class referred to, an excellent suggestion, but for some of the railway companies it might involve serious practical difficulties. Many of the railway companies, besides the Great Eastern, already grant special facilities for working men to live in the suburbs. The Chatham Company, for instance, runs workmen's trains to and from Victoria or Ludgate Hill or any intermediate station on their metropolitan extension line: from Penge three trains, Sydenham Hill three, Dulwich three, and Herne Hill three. The fare by these workmen's trains for a double journey between Victoria and Ludgate is 2*d.*, and a return ticket is 1*s.* a week. Many of these trains carry from 700 to 800 passengers. It is, of course, highly desirable that the home life of the working classes should thus be improved; but while there is no difficulty in running special working-men's trains early in the morning, this involves the necessity of the same number of passengers being carried back to their homes in the evening, at the time when the company's ordinary traffic is at its heaviest. The consequence often is that the workmen, when returning, crowd out of the trains a much more remunerative class of traffic; and that the company is a pecuniary loser thereby. The Parliamentary Committee appointed in 1872 to inquire into the amalgamation of railways recognised the right of the companies to some consideration for their attempts to improve the condition of the lower classes, and suggested that "where the municipality of a town desires the running of workmen's trains, it should be enabled to guarantee to the company a certain amount of traffic."

Special arrangements are made by railway companies for the convenience of other special classes of the community. Social Science and British Association Assemblies, Church Congresses, Wesleyan Conferences, etc., are all considered, and even the sport of fox-hunting is not overlooked. When railways were first proposed, country gentlemen became greatly alarmed about the dangers with which their favourite sports were threatened. It was asserted that, there being no longer any use for horses, they would become extinct, and oats and hay would be rendered unsaleable. "But railroads," says Mr. Anthony Trollope, "have done so much for hunting that they may almost be said to have created the sport anew on a wider and much more thoroughly organized footing than it ever held before." Trains are now arranged to take hunting men from the large cities; and hunters walk in and out of their railway boxes as quietly as though they were holders of season tickets.

The latest developments of railway passenger locomotion are in some respects the best. Many years ago Sir Samuel Morland constructed for himself a coach with a sort of movable kitchen, so fitted with clockwork machinery that he could broil steaks, roast a joint of meat, and make soup as he travelled along the road. This ingenious gentleman was made a baronet by Charles II., and died at a good old age, so that good food by the way did not appear to have shortened his life. "But then it must be remembered that he travelled in his coach and saw what was to be seen as he went along. Flying through a country, arriving only to depart and departing only to arrive, appears to be exactly the course of training to prepare an average man to have said of him what was said of one by Humboldt:—'This man has gone farther and seen less than anybody I ever met.'" Still, to be able to eat and even to sleep on a long journey is, frequently, an enormous boon to the traveller. For such a journey by day, the new twin day saloon of the London and North Western between London and Liverpool is excellent. The two saloons—for ladies and gentlemen—are connected by a covered gangway two feet wide, along which the attendant can pass. The length of each saloon is thirty-four feet; and the height from the rail at the side is ten feet eight inches. There are six wheels to each saloon. The under frame is of oak, and the sides are plated with steel. The total weight of each saloon in running order is about fourteen tons; the passenger accommodation is for eighteen ladies and twenty-one gentlemen. The saloons are fitted with electrical communication, and with hot-water heating apparatus.

The Great Northern, Company, also has recently begun to run a "dining-car" between King's Cross and Leeds, and the comfort of this mode of passing the time appears to be appreciated by passengers. The Midland Company, too, which was the first to place Pullman cars on English lines, runs a "dining saloon car" between Liverpool, Manchester, and London. The first train of this series consisted of three Pullman cars. It left St. Pancras at 2.5 p.m., and was timed to reach Leicester at 4.19 p.m. One of the cars was the ordinary Pullman drawing-room carriage; another the dining-room car; the third was a smaller but handsomely fitted car, run expressly for the occasion. On the middle car was a complete little cooking stove, capable of providing a dinner for forty persons.

The Pullman limited expresses on the London and Brighton seem to provide almost the perfection of travelling arrangements. Instead of their being ordinary trains with one or two or more Pullman cars attached, all the carriages are on the Pullman plan, and they are so coupled that the officials in charge can walk from one end of the train to the other. "Entering it," says a traveller, "you enter a mansion on wheels. You can roam about from parlour to drawing-room, dining-room, and smoking-room. The ladies have also a boudoir. Servants are at your call by electric bell; but you need not call for light or fire. A pleasant and equable temperature is maintained by hot-water pipes, and lighting up is done before there is time to demand it. No sooner do you enter a tunnel than the bright but soft and equal light of the Edison electric lamp is shed all over the compartments.

It noiselessly comes at the moment it is needed, and is as quietly gone when the need for it is over. It beats the good fairy of nursery lore, for it needs no summons. It is with you before you can as much as think of a wishing cap, and it is itself a magic lamp." With this train service Brighton may well come to be more appropriately than ever considered as London-on-Sea.

At night the whole train is lighted by electricity. "The steady soft white light of the incandescent carbon threads in the little sealed glass lamps—these tiny horseshoes, burning but not consumed—were approved, admired, acclaimed. To read by them was a pleasure. There were thirty lights in the train; none gave a less brilliant light than another; and any one light could be put out without the others being affected. The light came from thirty-four of Faure's accumulators in the guard's compartment. These magazines of electricity had been filled at the Strand, but they will hereafter be charged by an engine and dynamo machine at Victoria Station." A proposal has been considered for making the train store up electricity for itself by the working of a dynamo machine attached to the axle of the engine.

Arrangements are now contemplated for the running of sleeping cars from Paris to Vienna and back. There should be no more difficulty in this than in travelling from New York to San Francisco by "lightning express in Pullman cars," carrying all that is wanted with them. And if through traffic with sleeping and eating cars,—so that one literally lives on board,—can be made successful, the plan may be extended beyond Vienna, on one side to Constantinople, and also to Calais, Cologne, and Bologna. For all this, like the perfect river steamer, we are indebted to institutions of purely American growth. When long journeys are to be made without stopping, and eating and drinking are to be done in the train, the long car is indispensable.

One of the effects, we will not say advantages, of travelling in a long car may be to promote sociability. "An American," says a St. Louis paper, in an article on native politeness, "may not be so elegant at a dinner party, but he will not ride half a day in a railway car without speaking to the fellow-passenger at his elbow, as the Englishman will." "No," remarks an

American critic, "indeed he will not: 'fore George he will not. How often, oh, how often, have we wished that he would! But he won't. He will pounce upon a stranger whom he has never seen before in all his life, and talk him deaf, dumb, and blind in fifty miles. Catch an American holding his mouth shut when he has a chance to talk to some man who doesn't want to be talked to."

But sociability in Pullman cars may, especially under certain circumstances, take more demonstrative forms. "I have never," observes another traveller, "got so well acquainted with the passengers on the train as I did the other day on the Milwaukee and St. Paul Railroad. We were going at the rate of about thirty miles an hour, and another train from the other direction telescoped us. We were all thrown into each other's society, and brought into immediate social contact, so to speak. I went over and sat in the lap of a corpulent lady from Manitoba, and a girl from Chicago jumped over nine seats and sat down on the plug hat of a preacher from La Crosse, with so much timid, girlish enthusiasm that it shoved his hat clear down over his shoulders. Everybody seemed to lay aside the usual cool reserve of strangers, and we made ourselves entirely at home. A shy young man, with an emaciated oil-cloth valise, left his own seat and went over and sat down in a lunch basket, where a bridal couple seemed to be wrestling with their first picnic. Do you suppose that reticent young man would have done such a thing on ordinary occasions? Do you think if he had been at a celebration at home that he would have risen impetuously and gone where those people were eating by themselves, and sat down in the cranberry jelly of a total stranger? I should rather think not. Why, one old man, who probably at home led the class-meeting, and who was as dignified as Roscoe Conkling's father, was eating a piece of custard pie when we met the other train, and he left his own seat and went over to the other end of the car and shot that piece of custard pie into the ear of a beautiful widow from Iowa. People travelling somehow forget the austerity of their home lives, and form acquaintances that sometimes last through life."

What may be perhaps regarded as the perfection of railway travelling in the world is attained under the arrangements for the passage of the royal train, when, for instance, the Queen goes to or from Scotland. The train is fitted throughout with continuous brakes, with an electrical communication between the compartments of each saloon and carriage and the guards, and with a communication between the guards and the driver. A pilot engine is run fifteen minutes in advance of the train throughout the journey, and in order to guard against any obstruction or interference with the safe passage of the train, no engine except the pilot, or any train or vehicle, is allowed to proceed upon or cross the main line and stations during an interval of at least thirty minutes before the time at which the royal train is appointed to pass, all shunting operations on the adjoining lines being suspended during the same period; while after the royal train has passed no engine or train is permitted to leave a station or siding upon the same line for at least fifteen minutes. In addition to these regulations, no light engines or trains, except passenger trains, are allowed to travel between any two stations on the opposite line of rails to that on which the royal train is running from the time the pilot is due until the royal train has passed. Every level crossing, farm crossing, and station, is specially guarded, to prevent trespassers; and all facing points over which the pilot and royal train have to travel are securely bolted. Platelayers are also posted along the line to prevent the possibility of any impediment at the occupation road-crossings.

Some passengers, we may add, are eccentric in their ideas of locomotion. Not long ago, on the arrival of the 3.15 Irish mail at Chester platform, a man was found lying underneath a carriage. He was grasping the brake-rod with his legs and hands, and in order to hold the rod securely, he had some flannel in his hands. He had ridden in this way from Holyhead to Chester, nearly ninety miles. How he escaped death was a marvel. He was sentenced to pay twenty shillings, or to have twenty-one days' hard labour.

Another passenger, of an adventurous order of mind, desired a similarly cheap and airy ride from Euston to Liverpool. His name was John Smith, and he was described as "a seafaring man respectably attired." It appeared from the evidence, and indeed from Mr. Smith's own admission, that on the previous night he left the Euston station by an express train at nine p.m., which, travelling at a high rate of speed, does not stop until it reaches Rugby at eleven p.m., a distance of 82½ miles. "Mr. Smith did not take his seat like an ordinary passenger inside any of the carriages, but he travelled underneath one of them, and would, no doubt, have concluded his journey to Liverpool in safety, but that on the arrival of the train at Rugby the wheel-examiner, seeing a man's legs protruding from under one of the carriages, had the curiosity to make further search, and discovered Mr. Smith coiled round the brake-rod, a piece of iron not above three inches broad, in a fantastic position. Mr. Smith was immediately uncoiled, and being technically in error was detained in custody. The bottom of the carriage was only eighteen inches from the ground, and where the engine takes up water as it travels, Mr. Smith was not more than six inches from the trough ; he therefore had not far to fall in case of a casualty ; but the bench, surprised at a railway passenger under any circumstances having survived a journey of eighty-two miles, said 'it was a miracle he was not killed,' and let him off with a fine of *2s. 6d.* and costs, or fourteen days' imprisonment. Mr. Smith stated that his journey 'was not a very comfortable one,'"—a remark the accuracy of which—however on other matters we may differ from him—may be conceded.*

It has usually been understood that the line of demarcation between passenger traffic and goods was in the nature of things sufficiently plain. It has been left to the ingenuity of an American to endeavour to confound these distinctions. An "old and well-known citizen" of Chicago, of "an eccentric and jocular disposition," lately conceived the brilliant idea of boxing himself up, and obtaining transportation to Philadelphia as merchandise. He was informed by the agent of the Adams Express Company, to whom he announced his intention, that no objection would be raised to his travelling to Philadelphia in a box, but that he would have to pay passenger fare. Mr. M'Auley declared, however, that he would go as merchandise, and would pay no more than 2 dols. 50 c. per cwt. Accordingly, he packed himself up in a box with a week's provisions by his side, and was taken by an expressman to the railway office. The box was 18 in. wide, 6 ft. long, hooped with iron bands, and fastened by a padlock. It was addressed to "Miss Kisselman, Philadelphia," and the agent was told that it contained flowers. On the same night

* *Pall Mall Gazette.*

the box was forwarded to its destination, the charges having been prepaid. At an early hour on the following morning the real nature of the contents of the box was discovered by a railway guard, and when the train stopped at Van West, Ohio, Mr. M'Auley was taken out of his box, put into gaol, and in the evening was "shipped home," having had a narrow escape of being shot by the guard as a train robber. He states that on an early occasion he intends to try the question again.

Among the episodes of travelling experiences may be mentioned one from the pen of a lively journalist. "Maybe," he says, "a man feels happy, and proud, and flattered, and envied, and blessed among men when he sees a pretty girl trying to raise a window on a railway car, and he jumps up and gets in ahead of the other boys, and says, 'Allow me?' oh, so courteously. And she says, 'Oh, if you please, I would be so glad,' and the other male passengers turn green with envy, and he leans over the back of the seat and tackles the window in a knowing way with one hand, if peradventure he may toss it airily with a simple turn of the wrist; but it kind of holds on, and he takes hold with both hands, but it sort of doesn't let go to any alarming extent, and then he pounds it with his fist, but it only seems to settle a 'leetle' closer into place, and then he comes around, and she gets out of the seat to give him a fair chance, and he grapples the window and bows up his back, and tugs, and pulls, and sweats, and grunts, and strains, and his hat falls off, and his suspender buttons fetch loose, and his vest-buckle parts, and his face gets red, and his feet slip, and people laugh, and irreverent young men in remote seats grunt and groan every time he lifts, and cry out, 'Now, then, all together!' as if in mockery, and he busts his collar at the forward button; and the pretty young lady, vexed at having been made so conspicuous, says, in her iciest manner, 'Oh, never mind; thank you! It doesn't make any difference,' and then calmly goes away and sits down in another seat; and that wearied man gathers himself together, and tries to read a book upside down."

Passengers are often grievously careless of their own lives or limbs, or of those of others. This is especially the case on the Metropolitan railways. People may be seen jumping out of every train that arrives before it has stopped, and when it is moving at a high rate of speed. This is, of course, done to save time; but were they to reflect how short a time they save, and what risk they run in doing it, we cannot but think they would hesitate before taking the chance of paying so high a price for so small an advantage. Indeed, it frequently happens that they gain nothing at all, for when the exit gate of a station is at the engine end of a train—as at the Mansion House and many other places,—the person who waits in a carriage till the train has come to a stand, as a rule gets to the gate before another who leaves the same carriage when the train is in motion. "A constant, I may say an almost weekly, cause of accident," says the chairman of a railway, "sometimes a daily cause, is that of people falling from getting out of the trains while they are in motion. We do everything we possibly can to caution people against so dangerous a practice. People forget with a body like a train weighing 200 or 300 tons, and with an immense amount of accumulated momentum, that if it is only going at one or two miles an hour, and the foot of the passenger is partly on the platform and partly in the carriage, there must be a serious and dangerous fall; and we find—I hope I shall not be scolded for stating the fact—the fact is, for one man who gets hurt from this unfortunate habit of getting out of the trains while they are in motion, five women get hurt." *

Nor do persons acting thus confine the chance of accident to themselves alone. An approaching train on the Metropolitan has one especially dangerous feature—the array of doors which fly open from the carriages as they emerge from the tunnel, in readiness for one or more of the occupants to jump out. These doors, being open while the train is running, form so many battering-rams, each ready to strike down those who, from want of knowledge or by accident, may be within its reach, and throw them possibly under the train, or, at all events, violently on to the platform. The danger does not cease here, for even if people at the station, aware of the effect of a blow from one of these doors, were to keep well clear of them, they would still be exposed to the unsteady, staggering rush of passengers who, leaping from the moving train, light upon the platform with control over their feet and legs for the moment gone.

Other forms of thoughtlessness on the part of passengers

---

* The *Globe*.

often lead to serious consequences. We are aware of the punishments properly inflicted on lads for throwing stones at running trains; some of the occupants of these trains are almost equally culpable in throwing empty bottles out of trains. This is often done from excursion trains, and even from ordinary trains. "These people," says a correspondent of a London paper, "often starting by an early train before their usual breakfast hour, are in the habit of loading their pockets with sandwiches and bottles of beer or diluted spirits, to eat and drink while they are travelling, and when the bottles are empty they are thrown out of the window to save the trouble of carrying them. Only the other day I was travelling up to London, and at nearly every station at which the train stopped passengers might be seen bringing bottles of spirits or beer into the carriages from the refreshment rooms, and which when empty were pitched out of the window while the train was at full speed. I saw several bottles thus thrown, and while passing a bridge over a highway, a man and child had a narrow escape from being struck by a bottle being thus carelessly thrown, and which fell close behind them with very great force. I am sure that none of these dangerous and formidable missiles are thrown with the intention to do harm; but, in passing along the country at a rapid rate, these bottles have a dangerous velocity given to them which thoughtless passengers have no idea of. Especially over populous routes, where out-door labourers are passing and about, this practice is attended with very great danger, as the bottles do not fall where the passengers suppose they do."

Not long ago, in eight days there were no fewer than three instances reported in which injury had been done by persons throwing bottles from trains in motion. "As the 10.10 a.m. train from Euston was passing Mancetter-crossing box, near Atherstone, a bottle was thrown from the train which broke two panes of glass in the box. The signalman had a narrow escape from injury. On the 19th of May a passenger threw a bottle from the 10 a.m. express train from Liverpool to London, when the 2.45 p.m. train from Euston was passing near Berkhampstead. The bottle came in contact with the fireman's head, almost cutting his eye out, and the train had to be stopped at Berkhampstead to set him down. On the 23rd of

May, the fireman with the 2 p.m. train from Carlisle was struck by a piece of glass which came from a bottle thrown out of the 3.10 p.m. train from Preston. The bottle struck the engine of the 2 p.m. down train, and was shivered to pieces, a piece of glass cutting the fireman's neck." In view of such facts, some of the principal railway companies have found it necessary recently to issue warnings on this subject to their travellers and to the public generally.

The eccentricities of English travellers, however, if dangerous, are not so odd as some "in foreign parts." It is said that not long ago an engine-driver in New Zealand noticed a lady energetically waving her hand at a siding where he was not timed to stop. On pulling up his train she was asked if she wished to "come on board," when she stated that her object in stopping the train was to ascertain whether any passenger could give her change for a £1 note!

The most startling uses to which railways have recently been devoted are military. The first armour-plated train was used for the defenders of Paris in 1871; and latterly our Egyptian correspondents have recounted to us such unusual railway experiences as the following:—"A strange excursion," writes 'One of the Passengers,' "started a few nights ago upon the line which runs between Alexandria and Kafr Dowar. To say our party was not made up of pleasure-seekers would do scant justice to the gallant fellows who belonged to it. It is true that the members of this pleasure party were armed to the teeth, carried cutlasses at their waists, and Martini-Henry rifles in their hands, while some had revolvers in their belts, and all wore jack-knives. But a merrier set could not be found than my companions.

"Grim enough was the train that waited to convey them. In place of cushioned carriages were hard railway trucks, without seats or any other kind of comfort; while the contents of some of the wagons were not precisely of that kind which is usually supposed to be intimately connected with pleasure-taking. First of all was an empty wagon with low sides, on which was laid a lot of railway metal; then came a truck with sides about two feet high, from the front of which peered the muzzle of a 40-pounder Armstrong gun. Round the sides of this wagon were plates of iron fixed, by the care of Captain Fisher, of the *Inflexible*, so that a rifle bullet would hardly be able to penetrate them, while to protect still further anybody that might choose to ride in the vehicle, sand bags were piled on each other, so that the cannon seemed to look out of a nest of them, so thickly were they laid and so high did they stand. Then we saw a truck similarly equipped, from which a Nordenfelt with its fan-like arrangement of barrels peered, and yet another fitted also with sand bags, and carrying a 9-pounder gun. Now came the engine covered up to the funnel with sand bags tied all round it, and then three more trucks all armoured like the preceding three, and carrying two Gatling guns. Such a train had never been sent on a holiday excursion before.

"Yet uninviting as was the conveyance thus placed at our service, the tars jumped into it with more alacrity than they

BRITISH IRON-CLAD TRAIN IN EGYPT.

would have even entered a Pullman saloon. What cared they for easy chairs and lounges, for cushions or carpets? . . . We had companions. Another train, composed of really comfortable carriages, was just behind; and in it were about 700 marines; but the sailors did not care much for the 'jollies,' and wanted to be well in advance and have the fight, if there should be any, to themselves.

"But the trip now really looked like business. Our aim in moving out was a serious one. For some days Arabi's men had been working on the railway line which we were about to advance upon, pulling up the rails and running away with the sleepers. The 40-pounder on the hill above Ramleh had every now and then dropped a shell on to them, driving them away for the nonce, only to return again when they thought the

English gunners were not looking. . . . So that we fairly expected to see a good gap made in the line, and looked forward to having to wait some little while during the repairs, which we quite expected would be the signal for a heavy shell fire from the enemy's lines, not quite a mile from the spot where we were going. Yonder, right ahead of us, lay the station at the junction of the two lines of the Rosetta and the Cairo Railway, and this station we knew to be frequently occupied by Arabi's men. Our people had been in it once, and noted loopholes and other such extremely unpleasant arrangements for annoyance, and we quite thought there would be a party of Arabs there to dislodge, perhaps with a lively little fight.

"At last we got the order to start, and on we steamed, ot course very carefully. Nobody knew where the line might be mined, and although we had an empty truck in front to explode any little device of this kind, it was necessary to move circumspectly, lest we might get into trouble unawares. The night was as still as though we had been the only human beings in the country. The stars shone out as placidly from the sky as if war and desolation had been in some other planet and not near our own. Yet every puff of the engine and every turn of the wheels brought us nearer to the enemy's lines, behind which lay hid any number of men from two to twenty thousand, and any number of guns, say, from ten to a hundred. Still not a shot was fired. . . .

"On we went; sometimes we stopped while an official went forward; then we would go on a little way and stop again. Still no shell came, and still we proceeded. Our work was to protect a party of engineers sent to repair a piece of the line, and to try and get a broken-down engine on that line back to Alexandria, and we knew Arabi or his people could see us. Why did he not blaze away? We reached the place where the work was to be done. No shell was yet sent against us or the train. Out went the engineering party from the carriage in our rear, taking with them the rails and sleepers in the fore part of our train. Away, too, went a company of marines along the line up to the junction station, whence, however, not a shot came. It was evident that we were to have no hand-to-hand fight. The countenances of the tars began to be sorrowful for the first time.

"For an hour or more, perhaps two, the rapping and the picking went on, the line repairing being progressed with pretty rapidity, till, just as it was pronounced on the point of being finished, there flew a shell just over the train, screaming and whistling as it went far past us, right into the lake, sending the water around flying into the air as it burst, but doing no more damage than if it had been fired into the clouds and exploded there. Our men laughed as they got round their weapons and got the order to send a 40-pounder shell into the enemy's camp. With a very little loss of time, for the gun had been trained with great accuracy on the spot which was to be aimed at, the weapon was prepared, the sailors stood by, and away went the big shell right on to the very place which had been indicated. Not a moment to be lost. Now we could see lights dancing about us, heralding a great movement, and then the engineers came in, saying they had done their work, and just then came another shell from Arabi, followed by two from us. Half a moment later and we had the marines all in, and then we began to steam back quicker than we came, for we had no obstacles to fear, and no mines to take notice of were to be apprehended, and of course all the time our guns were loaded once more lest the enemy should fire again. But we looked in vain for another mark of his attention. The dark lines of land which indicated his position had suddenly ceased to give any evidence of life; no more lights were to be seen; no more flashes of guns; all was still."

Again. Among the most spirited incidents of this war, the capture of Zagazig takes a foremost place. It was effected by two officers and five troopers. The rest of the corps had been left behind in the headlong gallop from the battle-field. "The little party dashed through the crowd assembled round the station, and there found four trains laden with soldiers with the steam up, and at the point of departure. They reined up in front of the first engine, and, with levelled pistols, ordered the engineer to dismount. He refused, and was at once shot; the rest bolted, as did the passengers, including some pachas, whose luggage was taken, and thousands of troops fled across the country. Our cavalry came up half an hour later."

But if the military operations of the iron-clad train were thus entirely satisfactory, it cannot be said that ordinary travelling—

if so it could be called—on an Egyptian railway in war time was pleasure without alloy. One who recently passed through these experiences tells us that in an evil hour the spirit of investigation induced him to go to the front by train, instead of on horseback in the usual way. No one, he writes, who has not tried it can possibly conceive the sensation of being roasted through by direct fire from above, by reflected heat from below, aided by furnace blasts across the sandy expanse; and the real way to try it is to ride from Ismailia to Kassassin—the extreme front—on the back of a quadruped. "'Go by train,' kind friends said—'so cool, so expeditious, so convenient. You can take boxes of wine and provisions for your friends in divers regiments, who will straightway receive you with open arms, more widely spread even than usual.' Happy thought. Excursion train! Five minutes for refreshments every now and then. Everybody goes to the Derby by rail now—why not to 'the front'? At six a.m. the train was to start. Twenty miles in, say, three hours. Slower than it should be, but comfortable. Actually a first-class carriage formed part of the convoy, attached to the extreme end, away from the engine. The rest of the train was made up of trucks laden with multifarious stores. True, there were no cushions in the compartments—they had been looted long ago for beds; but the backs were well padded, and the general effect was decidedly promising. We got in—an officer of the 1st Life Guards, two of the Scots Guards, some Indian officers, two artists attached to the illustrated papers, and myself. Taking advantage of the method of transit we had laden ourselves overmuch, perhaps, with small impedimenta, for bundles of sardine boxes peeped from beneath the seats, while loose wine bottles rattled in the nettings. It was dusty and over-warm—of course it must be that,—and the flies were most annoying.

"Away across the desert—past Nefiche, whilom a stronghold of Arabi's, shortly to be the base of operations for the Indian contingent—away towards Mahuta. Certainly we were proceeding very slowly, with too many stoppages, each one longer than the last. Presently an officer of the Grenadiers put his head in at the window. 'I say, you fellows. Do you want to be left behind?' General consternation. 'What!' 'This ramshackle old engine can't drag so heavy a train. They've unshipped all but the first two trucks; the rest will be picked up some other time.' What a scurry! How we tumbled out! What a wild grabbing there was for bottles, bags, boxes! Meanwhile the officer in charge caracoled up and down. 'Never mind waiting for these people; steam ahead!' At this barbarous order there was a wild shriek and general stampede—boxes, bottles were abandoned to their fate, flung anywhere, and we crawled up the fronts of the two tall trucks with a desperate energy begotten of despair.

"Off we started again; more stoppages, with longer and longer intervals of inaction. The only moving thing at last was the officer in charge, who became rabid and foamed at the mouth. The water from the tanks had been allowed to dribble away and waste; there was no fuel, and engines without water or fuel are of no more use for motive purposes than a dressing-table or a hip-bath. Here we were, eight or nine miles out in the desert, and here we were likely to stop. It was presently discovered that, hidden in one of the trucks, was a little water in a barrel; and hard by was a little wood, which, if husbanded, might enable the crazy machine to drag on alone—a greater *trouvaille* than those in charge deserved. So off it crawled, in hopes of being able to reach Mahsuma, where was a supply of water and coal, leaving us perched on the top of the trucks with the full sun of midday blazing on us, and hope vanishing in the distance. Hotter and hotter it grew, and more stifling; the iron bands which fastened the hay bales together, on which we sat enthroned, became so heated that the finger could not rest on them. We had nothing to eat, for everything of that sort had been dropped. The mouth felt like a redhot nutmeg-grater, the tongue like wash-leather. How long was this to last? Would the engine ever return, or must we, in a cooked state, make the best of our way to shelter afoot? Two hours passed. A low whistle—the engine was coming back—fuel and water had been reached, and all was well. By-and-by we struggled up to Mahsuma—marked by the white bell-tents of the Guards, otherwise a bit of desert undistinguishable from the rest—and a little later reached the Life Guards' camp, or rather the Cavalry camp."

Before the war ended a hundred miles of railway were provided as an accessory to the military operations in Egypt. The ships were to land the rails and other plant at Ismailia. The heavy description of the rails, 70 lbs. to the yard, rendered them, it was said, better suited to a permanent line than a merely flying military tram-road ; and the sleepers, which are mostly of broad iron plates, hollowed beneath, were well adapted for resting on the sand of the desert. A railway corps was specially trained for laying and working the railway. It consisted of No. 8 Company Railway Engineers, among whom were platelayers, engine-drivers, and mechanics capable of building a bridge or a pier. This company had previously been exercised for such services on a section of railway at Upnor Castle, on the Medway.

We may here remark that some railways, though used by the public, are in a special sense private property. A line, for instance, that connects the seaside village of Felixstowe with the Great Eastern system is the property of a single owner—Colonel Tomline, formerly M.P. for Grimsby, who has not only constructed it at his sole cost, but for some time worked it himself. It is now worked by the Great Eastern. It is 14½ miles long, and joins the Great Eastern at Westerfield, about ten minutes' run beyond Ipswich. It was completed within twenty months of its commencement. Colonel Tomline, it is said, spent a quarter of a million sterling on the undertaking. The Maenclochog Railway, in the heart of North Pembrokeshire, and terminating at his slate quarries a few miles from Fishguard, is the freehold property of Mr. E. Cropper, and is worked by his servants, his engines, and his rolling stock for both passenger and goods purposes. But while "Colonel Tomline's efforts led him through 14½ miles of dry and easily worked soil to his goal, those of Mr. Cropper were met by deep rock cuttings and valleys, mountain and moorland, river and forest, in the course of nine miles of railway, forming a variety of difficulties and of scenery in such a short distance" said to be "almost unparalleled." The railway from Sunderland to Seaham Harbour is the private property of the Londonderry family.

There are other travellers by passenger trains besides men, women, and children ; namely, horses, dogs, cattle, sheep, and pigs. Cattle, sheep, and pigs, however, usually have the honour of trains to themselves. The Government returns do not now specify the numbers of the animals thus conveyed ; but so long ago as 1864 it was calculated that if the live stock that then became passengers were marshalled in a procession ten abreast and ten feet apart, the line of horses would extend for 6 miles; the phalanx of pigs would be 44 miles in length; there would be 9 miles of dogs, 60 miles of cattle, and 160 miles of sheep. In other words, there would be a procession of horses, pigs, dogs, cattle, and sheep ten abreast, extending so far that, while the rear ranks of the sheep were bleating in London, the front ranks of the horses would be neighing among the hills of Cumberland. We need not add that these numbers have since enormously increased.

The legal status of some of the articles—or, more strictly, some of the passengers—who travel by railway may sometimes be difficult to define. A porter, for instance, is said to have explained to an old lady that her cats and rabbits would have to travel as dogs. "I have been a rector for many years," says a traveller, "and have often heard and read of tithe-pigs, though I have never met with a specimen of them. But I had once a little pig given to me which was of a choice breed, and only just able to leave his mother. I had to convey him by carriage to the X station; from thence, twenty-three miles to Y station, and from thence, eighty-two miles to Z station, and from there, eight miles by carriage. I had a comfortable rabbit-hutch of a box made for him, with a supply of fresh cabbages for his dinner on the road. I started off with my wife, children, and nurse; and of these impedimenta piggy proved to be the most formidable. First, a council of war was held over him at X station by the railway officials, who finally decided that this small porker must travel as 'two dogs.' Two dog tickets were therefore procured for him; and so we journeyed on to Y station. There a second council of war was held, and the officials of the Y said that the officials of X (another line) might be prosecuted for charging my piggy as two dogs, but that he must travel to Z as a horse, and that he must have a huge horse-box entirely to himself for the next eighty-two miles. I declined to pay for the horse-box—they refused to let me have my pig—officials swarmed around me—the station-master advised me to pay for the horse-box and probably the company would return the extra charge. I scorned the probability, having no faith in the company—the train (it was a London express) was already detained ten minutes by this wrangle; and finally I was whirled away bereft of my pig. I felt sure that he would be forwarded by the next train, but as that would not reach Z till a late hour in the evening, and it was Saturday, I had to tell my pig tale to the officials ; and not only so, but to go to the adjacent hotel and hire a pig-stye till the Monday, and fee a porter for seeing to the pig until I could send a cart for him on that day. Of course the pig was sent after me by the next train ; and as the charge for him was less than a halfpenny a mile, I presume he was not considered to be a horse. Yet this fact remains—and it is worth the attention of the Zoological Society, if not of railway officials—that this small porker was never recognised as a pig, but began his railway journey as two dogs, and was then changed into a horse."

Another correspondent of a public journal mentions that at the high-level Crystal Palace line he had been much interested by the wrath of a lady against some of the porters, who had prevented her taking her dog into the carriage. "The lady argued that Parliament had compelled the companies to find separate carriages for smokers, and they ought to be further compelled to have a separate carriage for ladies with lap-dogs, and it was perfectly scandalous that they should be separated, and a valuable dog, worth perhaps thirty or forty guineas, should be put into a dog compartment. I have some of the B stock of this railway, upon which not a penny has ever been paid, and I could not help comparing my experience of this particular line of railway with that of my fellow-traveller, and wondering what sort of a train that would be which would provide accommodation for all the wants and wishes of railway travellers."

Occasionally animals other than domesticated are passengers by railway. We have already referred to the exploits of a gorilla that went to Nottingham ; we find, also, that on the 10th of July, 1877, the station-master at Weedon, on the London and North Western, was informed that a tigress had not only travelled on the line, but, moreover, had made its escape. She was somewhere, he ascertained, between Wolverton and Rugby, and she was prowling about at large. The station master thereupon gathered some friends, and, with some officers from the Weedon garrison, went off on an engine in search. The tigress was discovered near the line, her movements having been watched from a telegraph-box by a porter who had sighted her. A number of country people acted as beaters, and she was at length despatched after receiving no less than eight rifle bullets, besides several charges of small shot. She belonged to Mr. Jamrach, of Ratcliff Highway, and had been forwarded from Broad Street in what is called a "low-sided junction wagon." While at large she had killed and partly eaten two sheep.

It is not surprising that railways were soon brought into use for the removal of live stock. The cattle dealer calculates that for every day a beast is travelling, whether on foot or by train, it loses a stone of eight pounds; not to speak of the suffering to which it is exposed in long journeys by road. The transference of stock is not, however, the easiest or pleasantest part of the duties of railway men, to say nothing of the occasional hazards to the public. "Here," says a writer, "you meet bipeds who, *per force*, fiercely frightened, are pushing onwards; and if you have to run the gauntlet of this road when all is in full play, look not only to the safety of your corns but to that of your life. A charge down this incline of a hundred or two of horned cattle just released from durance vile, and followed closely by sticks and dogs, is not to be treated as you would treat a contemptible enemy. But on this occasion the porcine element—less dangerous by far—prevailed. Some hundreds of pigs, despite an unanimous remonstrance that filled the air far and wide, were being trans-shipped from the railway trucks to vans and carts. This mode of conveyance is adopted when the time for getting them to market is very limited, or they have to pass through some of the crowded streets of the metropolis. Even in an open country road Master Pig is a troublesome customer; but in the midst of London street traffic he gets stark mad, and runs everywhere but in the direction he ought." It often happens, too, both on arrivals and departures, that different lots of cattle, sheep, and pigs get mixed together; but this apparently alarming difficulty is got over by the men, who, by long experience, are familiar with the marks of various breeders and the names of salesmen to whom the stock is consigned.

The scenes presented at the "great cattle market of the world" shortly before Christmas are more striking than pleasant. The curiosity of a visitor led him to witness the spectacle. At one point, when his topographical knowledge was at fault, he was told: "Go on a bit and you'll hear 'em;" and, he adds, "I did 'hear 'em,'—the barking of innumerable dogs, and the hoarse shoutings of men standing out as a duet to a roaring *obbligato* accompaniment from the throats of some thousand cattle. The snorting of a locomotive a little off the road to my right told me that the landing-place was close by, and turning through a gate and wading knee-deep in mud, in the direction of the sound, I soon found myself in the midst of a scene I shall not easily forget. A train, stretching far into the night, apparently interminable, and laden with sheep and beasts, was drawn up alongside a narrow platform, on the near side of which were I should not like to say how many 'pens' for their reception. The doors of most of the trucks being opened, a couple of drovers made their way into each, and then apparently went mad, with a view of inducing the frightened beasts to vacate the trucks for the pens, which they in some cases obstinately refused to do until urged by means more effective than gentle. At length the train is cleared, and I inquire when the next will arrive.

"'You'd better ask at the office,' I'm told.

"The office, I find, is what I had taken to be a stable. I push open a door, and discover a couple of drover boys in fierce combat *re* the ownership of a stick, with which a third boy bolts as I pass in. After a little trouble I am directed by one of the fiery youths to an inner chamber—*the* office—an apartment some nine feet square, in which sundry drovers are baking before a huge fire, and the atmosphere is redolent of mutton hung just a trifle too long.

"'Can you tell me when the next cattle train comes in?' I ask of a muffled man who writes by a lantern at a small table.

"'About three; where do you expect 'em from?' replies the muffled man without looking up.

"I explain with difficulty that I don't expect anything; and, though politely invited to sit down, I am convinced the company think me a little gone in the upper storey for being out at such an hour without any business; besides, the cooking drovers are beginning to brown; so I excuse myself, and promise to look in later on. Once outside, I attached myself to another drover, who seemed very preoccupied and disinclined to fraternize; however, some tobacco made him somewhat more sociable, and he informed me he was going to take some sheep to the 'rails,' and if I wanted to see the market place I had better come along. We went back again to the railway pens, and my friend, with some more dreadful persons, proceeded to eject a lot of sheep into the lane. Out they scampered, as if glad of any place that had not four sides.

"'Ninety-eight,' said one of the dreadful ones.

"'Right,' said my drover, consulting a ticket.

"'How did you know that?' I asked of the dreadful one.

"'Counted 'em,' said he.

"I am sure I looked as if I thought he was lying, for the sheep had rushed out in wild confusion apparently in a heap. I found out afterwards that the thing was possible enough to these men from constant practice, but I had no opportunity of apologising. In a few minutes we were on our way—that is to say, the sheep, the drover, his man, his dog, and myself. As we neared one of the great entrances to the market, symptoms of insanity developed in my three companions, who rushed in amongst the sheep, and I saw them no more. Within the market is 'confusion worse confounded,' for they are driving the beasts in from the lairs in which they have been deposited since their arrival during the two past days. Some of them are as wild as the traditional 'March hare,' and come tearing and bellowing down the alleys followed by frantic drovers' men yelling their war-whoop of 'Turn 'em back.' It is pitch dark, and the long-horned brutes are on you before you can see them. I would not have it known how many times I scrambled over railings barely in time to save the tails of my coat from disgrace."

Besides the multitudes of live stock brought by railway for the feeding of the great towns, there are also innumerable trucks and trains of dead meat. Not long ago the *London Scotsman* referred to this subject as seen from its northern, or departure, end. It appears that the north of Scotland is tapped by two railway systems which converge at Perth. Aberdeenshire and Banffshire are served by the ramifications of the Great North of Scotland, which meets the Caledonian at Aberdeen. Inverness and Moray shires, and the counties still farther north, use the Highland Railway, which, striking inland at Forres, cuts off the angle involved in the Aberdeen route. "From almost every station on these two railways fresh meat is habitually forwarded. Huntly sends eight tons per day along the Great North, from the juicy pastures of the 'Aucht an' forty daugh,' and the bieldy slopes of the Foudlands. Inverurie does a large trade also. The pretty town at the junction of the Don and the Urie averages twelve tons daily, forwarded by four dealers. Then we take a slant along the Buchan and Formartine line, and find Peterhead, which is besides given largely to the herring and whale fishery, with this other iron in the fire besides. The rich meadow-land of Buchan makes glorious beef. At one time Buchan had a breed of cattle of its own—known among our grandfathers by the name of 'Buchan humblies'; long, low, brindled or black polls, with a fine capacity for taking on beef, but with a greater celebrity still as noble milkers. But the 'humblies' took a long time to grow, and were apt to get 'set' and stunted during stirkhood, besides which, when they had attained their full size, that was by no means gigantic. So they have been almost without exception supplanted by the bigger Aberdeenshires, the kindlier shorthorns, and the great-framed, fast-growing crosses, although even now a trace of the 'humblie' still lingers in many a herd." Peterhead sends away an average of twenty tons per day. Minor "roadside" stations contribute over sixty tons per day. Aberdeen, besides sending southward a large number of very large-headed and preternaturally "canny" men, sends likewise an immense quantity of meat to feed them and others.

A carcase destined for the London market is divided into halves; each half is sewn up in canvas, and packed into wagons, the backbone downmost and the shanks up, as closely as possible. A row well packed generally fills a wagon, and weighs from four to six tons.

The Great North of Scotland goods train, which leaves Keith early in the morning, conveys into Aberdeen the dead meat wagons from the stations on the main line. Another, which leaves Peterhead, brings up the dead meat from the Buchan district. "These two trains, during the winter months, bring to Aberdeen on an average twenty-five wagons daily of dead meat. On arrival in Aberdeen the wagons and their contents are turned over to the Caledonian Railway, and by it they are despatched at twelve noon by the express train containing London goods only. This train, which requires two engines, contains on an average thirty-five to forty wagons laden with dead meat. On reaching Perth, the meat from the Inverness district, brought down by the Highland Railway, is in waiting." At Perth the express is split into two trains: one taking the east coast route and picking up meat all along it, the other taking the west coast line and receiving contributions as it rattles southward to Carlisle.

The cargoes of these various trains, in which the commissariat of the metropolis is so deeply concerned, have to be treated on their arrival in the most expeditious manner. "The most important are the two express meat trains from Scotland—trains which may be said to have revolutionised the cattle trade of the Highlands. The first arrival is the daily meat express from Inverness and Aberdeen, and all Scotland north of the Tay, consisting of about forty-four wagons filled entirely with fresh beef and mutton. It performs the journey in about thirty hours, and arrives punctually at Camden at 11.5 p.m. The second Scotch meat express consists of fifty-five wagons, drawn by two powerful engines. As far south as Rugby it is principally filled with fresh butcher's meat from the west of Scotland, and arrives at Camden at 2.40 a.m. These valuable freights are despatched with all celerity to Newgate and Leadenhall Markets, from whence they are distributed by noon all over London; so that the bullock that was grazing under the shadow of Ben Wyvis, may within forty-eight hours be figuring as the principal *pièce de resistance* at a West-end dinner.

"There are numerous other food trains which come in from the midland counties. The Aylesbury meat, butter, and milk train, averaging about twenty wagons, arrives nightly at 1.20 a.m.; the Bletchley train, similarly freighted, averaging twenty-five wagons, arrives at 1.55 a.m.; and the Northampton and Peterborough train, also averaging twenty-five wagons, at 3.5 a.m. About half an hour later a train comes in from Chester, principally freighted with cheese. And thus the arrivals continue all the night through, and the food is rapidly forwarded by the carts and vans which are in waiting to the meat markets, provision shops, and milk and butter dealers in all parts of London. . . . The fish trains are of a more irregular character, the arrivals depending upon the season and the takes of fish at different parts of the coast. When the mackerel fishing is at its height, special trains come in laden with the fish at the rate of ninety tons a day for a month. Then, when the herring season sets in, from ten to twelve wagons a day arrive with herrings from points as remote as Banff, Peterhead, and the north-east coast of Scotland; about a similar quantity coming in from the east of Scotland and the north of Ireland. The station is a busy scene on the arrival of these fish trains."

The fish traffic at many country stations is very large. "At Nottingham," remarked an official, "it is almost the largest we have for money. It arrives by the mail due very early in the morning. This train brings fish from the east coast—from Hull, Berwick, and the whole of Scotland. Hull and Grimsby also send a train here by 'M. S. & L.,' leaving Grimsby at five, and arriving at 10.30. Here it shunts off the trucks that are for Nottingham, and for the Erewash Valley and Mansfield lines; it then goes forward to Bristol. Yes, it supplies Bristol with fish. The other night it came in with forty-eight wagons and two engines, and was late because the catch had been so large that they could not get it all loaded at the usual time. Grimsby is our best fishing port for winter and summer in England, I should think. The London market depends on Grimsby for its crimped cod, much of which comes through Nottingham.

"The fish we get at Nottingham," he continued, "are of all sorts—sometimes very large. We had a fish last week that weighed nearly two hundredweight, and another of more than twenty-one stones, at fourteen pounds a stone. It was halibut." It seems strange, but it is true, that much of the fish that travels by land goes in water. They are in tanks, holding perhaps half a ton of salt water each, and half a ton of live cod. The tank is lifted by a crane on to the railway truck; and when it reaches its destination at St. Pancras, a horse truck is ready; and directly the train arrives, the tank is put on the truck and is taken away to Billingsgate. The empty fish tanks will be returned in the carriages that have taken them up, perhaps by the first down passenger train.

The receipts at a country town station on account of the fish trade are often large. The fried fish men buy a "kit," or barrel, of fresh fish of the merchant, and fry it; and having sold it, perhaps in pennyworths at a time, pay for it in halfpence; so that when the wholesale dealer settles his railway charges, he will perhaps do so with £15 worth of fishy, green-moulded coppers—as much in weight as a man can comfortably carry.

It is, however, at the railway stations on the seaboard itself, in the fishing season, that this business is seen in its magnitude. Then the exportation of herrings to the London market from Peterhead, during the season, amounts to perhaps 80 tons a week, some of the large English towns on the road intercepting a portion. Fraserburgh, last season, says a local authority, forwarded about 80 tons to London; Banff sent 120 tons; Lossiemouth also a considerable quantity. There is a considerable export Londonward of cured herrings also—about 500 tons; but some of these go by steamer. There is a saying that the town of Amsterdam is built on old fish bones, and the fish whose bones are here referred to were not so much caught off the coast of Holland as off the east coast of Scotland, and as far south as Yarmouth on the coast of England. "Fresh fish is now recognised as an important part of the food of people in the populous midland counties of England; and as it is of recognised importance that the fish should go into these markets in a fresh condition, there is every reason to suppose that the traffic will considerably be increased. I don't say but the traffic must be carried on under somewhat onerous conditions, at a fast speed and low rates, but as the necessity of accommodating the needs of those large English districts will be seen here in the north, the traffic is one which we may fairly expect continuously to increase."

The milk traffic by railway during the last few years has developed enormously. As the rate is only a halfpenny a gallon for short distances, and a penny for long ones, farmers find that it pays to send their milk even to distant cities. The rich meadow lands, for instance, near Derby, on the Wirksworth, Duffield, Ripley, and Castle Donington lines, forward their milk to Derby by the earliest morning and the afternoon local trains; and, by six o'clock in the evening, the middle platform at Derby will sometimes be crowded up with cans ready to leave for London by the mail. The morning passenger train from Derby, soon after eight o'clock, generally takes eight or ten vans of milk, each containing more than 40 "churns," each churn holding 15 or 16 gallons.

Again, at Nottingham the milk arrives between seven and eight in the morning, and between five and six in the evening. Perhaps five and twenty milk dealers send their carts to meet these trains. The churns in which it comes are made very strong, of block tin iron-bound; when empty they weigh about two stones, when full about 16 stones, or two hundredweight. "Yes, there are large dealers as well as small. One of them has 350 men in 30 different towns, stretching from South Shields to London, who sell his milk retail. He has 160 men in London alone. In order to obtain the required quantity of milk he makes yearly contracts with large dairies. These men sell 15,000 gallons of milk in London every day, all of which, of course, goes by rail. But the milk brought to Nottingham by rail is consumed here. This trade has all been made in the last ten years. The milk brought is excellent—far superior to what it used to be. If you go into our refreshment room, and look at a glass of milk that has been standing there for two or three hours, you will find the cream thick on the top."

We have elsewhere told of the working of the inward and the outward departments of a great London goods terminus—St. Pancras; we may therefore content ourselves with a description, written some years ago, of a similar scene at Camden station. "The working of a London railway station is one of the busiest night sights of London, for all the outward merchandise traffic is loaded and despatched to the country at night, and nearly all the inwards traffic arrives from the country in the early morning for delivery to the consignees before the usual hours of business begin. Fancy fifteen hundred men nightly occupied in loading and unloading goods in the goods sheds of a single company; vans arriving from all parts of the metropolis, beginning at 6.30 p.m. and ending at 9.30; a little army of men struggling with the bulky packages, which they deposit on their respective platforms, from whence they are loaded into the railway wagons placed alongside, and despatched at once, train by train, to the remotest parts of the kingdom. The scene appears at first one of inextricable confusion—men battling with bales, barrels, crates, and hampers, amidst the noise of voices and clangour of machinery. Yet the whole is proceeding with regularity and despatch, and in the course of a few hours the last train outwards has left, and the station is wrapped in quiet until the time of the early morning arrivals.

"The Camden station occupies about fourteen acres, and is provided with nearly twenty miles of sidings, mostly converging on the great shed itself, as large as a West-end square, being 400 feet long by 250 round. This shed is fitted up throughout with stages and platforms, between which the wagons are ranged, into which the goods are loaded, and every contrivance is adopted which mechanical skill can suggest for facilitating the despatch of business. As the vans come in, the packages are hoisted out of them by hydraulic cranes, and wheeled direct to their respective stages, the names of the places of destination—Liverpool, Glasgow, Manchester, etc.—being conspicuously indicated alongside the wagons about to be loaded with the goods

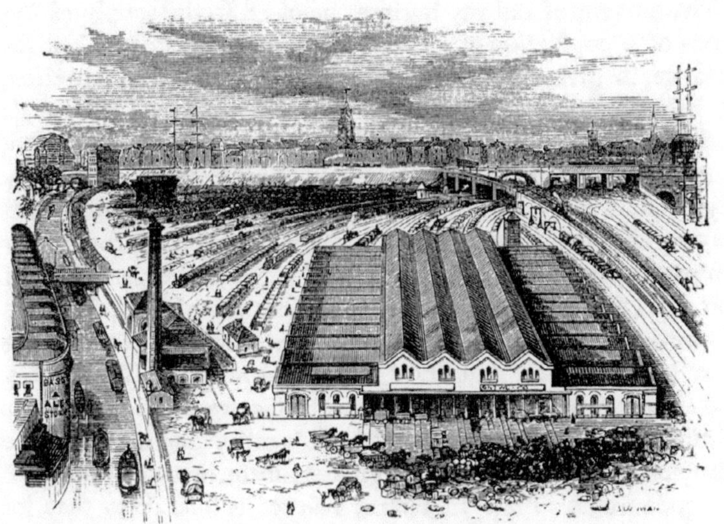

ST. PANCRAS GOODS STATION.

for those places, where they are trucked at once, and packed, corded, and tarpaulined. The wagons, when complete, are then cleverly drawn out of the platform sidings by ropes worked round hydraulic capstans, when they are marshalled on their respective sidings, and despatched train by train, almost with the regularity of clockwork. The number of wagons loaded and despatched from the Camden station nightly is about 670, in 27 trains, averaging about 25 wagons per train. Although there are about 10,000 packages despatched nightly, averaging from 90 to 100 lbs. per package, the quickness with which the work is got through is such that scarcely two hours elapse between the arrival of the goods in the station and their departure by railway to their respective destinations.

"After midnight the goods trains begin to come in from the country. Now the bustle is in unloading and despatching by van to the London customers the articles which have come to hand. The same number of trains, carrying about an equal number of packages, have now to be disposed of. After 3 a.m. the station is again in full work, and the press of vans and carts is as great as on the previous evening, until about 6 a.m., when the business of the night is nearly got through, and the station again reposes in comparative quiet." *

The amount of railway business involved in the supply of the needs of a population of 4,000,000 may be understood when, for instance, in giving evidence before a Parliamentary Committee on behalf of a mid-London railway, Mr. Samuel Morley, M.P., said that "at his place of business in Wood Street, there were usually about 3,000 bales or packages of goods in and out every day." And the expedition with which such work is transacted may be shown by the fact that the goods entrusted to railway companies at 7 o'clock in the evening, at distances of even 200 miles from London, are delivered next morning at the doors of the consignees in the city, and many kinds of goods arrive even by 9 o'clock. But it is not surprising that Mr. Morley added that "the congestion of the traffic from the narrowness of the streets in that locality, and the want of an outlet, put the occupiers of warehouses to the greatest inconvenience."

Goods traffic, in one important respect, is inferior to that for passengers. "Nothing," said Mr. Robert Stephenson,† "is so profitable, because nothing is so cheaply transported, as passenger traffic. Goods traffic, of whatsoever description, must be more or less costly. Every article conveyed by railway requires handling and conveyance beyond the limit of the railway station; but passengers take care of themselves, and find their own way without cost from the terminus at which they are set down. It is true, passengers require carriages of somewhat more expensive construction than those prepared for goods; but this expense is compensated for by the circumstance that they are

* "The Great Railway Monopoly."

† Address to the Institution of Civil Engineers.

capable of running, and do run, a much greater number of miles—that the weight of passengers is small in proportion to the weight of goods—and that consequently the cost for locomotive power is less." Still the carrying of goods and of mineral traffic is, on some lines, the principal source of profit.

In the conduct of the mineral traffic there is an important difference of administration among railway boards. On the North Eastern and Great Northern lines, coal is carried in wagons most of which belong to the companies; hence the uniformity of build and appearance which they present. On the other hand, the London and North Western, and the Midland, have been accustomed to allow coal-owners or merchants to provide their own wagons for their own traffic; hence their endless diversity of shape and size. This system has some advantages. The proprietors feel that they have more control over their own property, and that if they have not wagons enough to do their business, or if they have too many, it is their own affair; and these opinions have been so strongly held that owners have till lately objected to accede to any other arrangement, except under compulsion.

But serious objections have long been urged against the private ownership of railway rolling stock. According to this plan, it is necessary that every empty truck shall be returned empty to its owner; and one man's truck cannot be left at another man's colliery; whereas if all the trucks belonged to one Company, it would be enough to leave the required number—the first that could be most conveniently obtained—for the use of the particular trader. He wants, perhaps, twenty trucks; and, according to existing methods, his twenty must be found for him and brought back to him, though one may have gone to Brighton, two to Exeter, four to Carlisle, and the rest to King's Lynn; whereas by the proposed arrangement all that would be necessary in his case would be to deliver to him the first twenty that could be got hold of. Depôts could be formed every here and there for the collection and distribution of wagons, and the work would be easy; whereas now enormous shunting sidings are required, and an engine may be a whole day picking out the wagons for a particular owner.

Frequently, too, it happens that, while certain collieries are busy, others are comparatively idle; the former are in want of trucks with which to carry their coals, and the latter have empty trucks standing useless in their sidings. In fact, there is scarcely a colliery on the Midland system that has siding accommodation for all its own wagons; and the consequence is, that if, from want of trade, or defects in the mine, or a strike among the men, the colliery is thrown out of work, the company has to find room on its own sidings for the empties. It is believed that such is the increase of economy that would be secured, that three-fourths of the present number of trucks, and three-fourths of the present number of sidings, would be sufficient if the trucks belonged to the companies.

Another, and perhaps the most important, result of a change of system would be the increased safety of the traffic. If trains are delayed or accidents occur on, for instance, the Midland Railway, the common, if not almost invariable, explanation is that some mineral truck has broken down, or has run off the rails, and further inquiry into the subject would reveal the surprising fact, that out of a hundred breakdowns of goods or minerals wagons, ninety-four per cent. are with the wagons of private owners; that is to say, that if the wagons of private owners were made as strong and as safe as the wagons of the railway company, the number of breakdowns would be reduced to about one-tenth of what they are. Now, the breakdown of a mineral truck not only certainly involves delay—delay which may derange the entire traffic of the line for hours, or even days—but it may be one of the most perilous forms of accident.

These and other considerations have led the Board of the Midland Railway Company to arrange for the purchase of the mineral wagons of private owners, and this is now being carried forward on a large scale.

One arrangement of the railway companies with regard to their coal traffic has been freely criticised: it is their practice of allowing the use of their coal depôts to only a limited number of coal agents. "Why," it has been asked, "cannot any person have a truck of coals consigned to him at the station, and be allowed to fetch it away?" This problem was, some years since, practically tested at Nottingham. There had been there only a small coal wharf, and inconvenience had arisen. To remedy it the company bought from fifteen to twenty acres of land for coaling purposes. At once they received innumerable applications from all sorts of persons for coaling space, and the yard became so crowded and confused that it would have been impossible to carry on business. "We were receiving," said Mr. Allport before the Royal Commission, "constant complaints from the consumers, the traders, and the coal-owners; and I went myself to Nottingham, and spent nearly a day there, for the purpose of investigating them; and I found that although we had appropriated so large a space to the coal traffic, the whole yard was so crowded that it was impossible to get rid of the trucks. I found upwards of 500 trucks of coal standing in the Nottingham yard, and it was quite impossible for any of the parties to get at them. I then ascertained that great numbers of them were small dealers, receiving a single truck, and that others were private consumers, receiving perhaps a truck."

To remedy these evils, it was arranged that only a limited number of the largest merchants should be admitted to the ground, and that each should be allowed to stack a certain number of hundreds of tons of coals. If the land had been large enough for a dozen such merchants, a dozen would have been selected; but it was not so, and nine dealers were admitted. The largest were accepted, and they are charged a "terminal" at Nottingham of twopence a ton. The results of this arrangement have been satisfactory. Similar methods have been adopted in every large town on the Midland system, and Mr. Allport subsequently gave evidence—"There is not a single coal-owner now complaining."

HAMPTON STATION.

CHAPTER XIII.

Working of Trains.—"Correspondence" of Trains.—Punctuality of Trains. —Mr. S. Laing.—Sir D. Gooch.—Mr. Allport.—Mr. Paterfamilias and his Opinions.—Snow-storms on Railways.—A Young Lady's Experience.—Other Trains Snowed up.—Snow-storm in Scotland.—Results of Weather on Railway Finance.—Cost of a Snow-storm to a Railway.—Snow Sheds.—Railway Accidents.—A Paradox: is it true?—Safety of Railway Travelling.—Curative Effects of Railway Accidents.—Horse-racing on Railways.—Brake Trials at Newark.—The Trial Trains.—The Westinghouse Brake.—"Mr. Vacuus Smith."—Mr. Clayton's Brake.—A Ride on an Engine with a Vacuum Brake.—Earl de la Warr's Bill.—Communicators.—The Cord System.—Results.—Running Powers of Railways.—"Facility Clauses."—Interchange of Traffic on Metropolitan Lines.—Lines jointly Owned or Worked.—"Compensation."—Curious Cases.—Taxation of Railways.—The Railway Commission.—Alleged Excessive Railway Rates.—Reply of Companies.—Classification of Rates.—Special Rates.—Reasons for Special Rates.—Uniform Mileage Rates Impracticable and Pernicious.

HE working of railway trains now deserves our careful attention. To run a train at all involves a good deal. It means coal, oil, tallow, cotton waste, wages, wear and tear of engines, carriages, rails, sleepers, ballast, bridges, embankments, cuttings, stations, and all the other belongings of railways, not under cover, but in the open air, exposed to the sundry and manifold changes of the weather for which our climate is noted. But there is not merely one train, or one class of trains, but many trains and many classes. On the same lines of railway run express and mail passenger trains, at a rate of perhaps 45 miles an hour; others at 35 miles an hour; and stopping trains, calling at all stations, at 25 or 30 miles an hour. There are also express goods trains, slow or stopping goods,

The initial letter represents a fogman's hut.

shunting or ballast trains, followed by or mixed with through heavy coal trains from the great coal-fields of the country, on their way to the large centres of population; yet one and all have to be run with order, regularity, and punctuality.

When a railway company has successfully completed the arrangements on its own system, and is prepared fully to carry them out, it is reminded that it "does not live unto itself." Provision has to be made for the "correspondence" of some of its trains with those of other great companies with which it is in constant practical alliance and action. A passenger who has come from Peterborough by Melton and Syston to Leicester, complains that his train is late; he perhaps forgets that it was in connection with a train from Yarmouth off the Great Eastern, and that it arrived twenty minutes late at Peterborough. Similarly a passenger from Bristol for Manchester may be detained in starting, because his train is waiting for a Great Western that has not arrived from Torquay or Penzance. Perfect punctuality is, of course, theoretically desirable; and it could be guaranteed. All that would be necessary would be to alter the time-bills of the railway companies, so as to allow an ample margin for all contingencies. But when, on the other hand, we should have in all ordinary journeys to wait at the stations for "time," or to loiter out on the road the time that occasionally was required for dealing with exceptionally heavy traffic, it would be allowed that the remedy was worse than the disease. "Personally," said Mr. S. Laing, in a letter to the President of the Board of Trade, "as a director, I should have no objection to see my responsibility sheltered by the decree of a public authority, extending the time of the express trains between London and Brighton from one hour and a quarter to one hour and a half, of the stopping trains from two hours to two hours and a half, and all other trains in proportion—and less than this would not answer the object. But as a shareholder, I should deprecate it, because I believe it would so inconvenience the public that it would drive away a large amount of traffic. As a resident in Brighton I should deprecate it, because the prosperity of Brighton depends mainly on its being within 50 miles of London, while such a decree would practically increase the distance to 60 or 70 miles; and lastly, as an individual traveller on the railway, I should deprecate it, because I would prefer to travel, as at present, in a time so short that I do not feel it to be irksome, taking my chance of now and then being a little behind time, rather than see an unnecessary quarter of an hour added daily to my journey under the plea of consulting my safety and convenience." The immense majority of travellers would take the same view, and if two railways were running side by side at the same hours and fares, one at 40 miles an hour, the other at 30, with any of the advantages of greater safety and punctuality which the slower speed would give, the great majority of passengers would patronize the faster train.

Nor is it only at a single point or two that one company is in correspondence with another. At Bristol, said Mr. Allport in evidence before the Royal Commission, our trains are placed in connection with the trains from the extreme west—from Cornwall and Devonshire. At Gloucester the Midland comes into connection with the South Wales system, stretching from Milford Haven, Swansea, Cardiff, and Monmouthshire. At Worcester there are lines approaching from another part of the system of the Great Western, and from Hereford and South Wales. At Birmingham the Midland system comes in contact with the main artery of the London and North Western system; and at Burton they are flanked by the North Staffordshire Company. At Eckington they are in connection with the Manchester, Sheffield and Lincolnshire Company; at Normanton with the North Eastern system; and at Oakenshaw with the Lancashire and Yorkshire line. It is easy to see how impossible it is "to fit a train running from south to north with all these various branch connections, the main line having far more important sources of traffic to accommodate than the few passengers who may be brought in by the branch lines of other companies. The principle to be recognised is the accommodation of the greatest number, and this can be accomplished only by the apparent occasional neglect of the few. To attempt to run trains so as to suit all the branches would throw the whole system out of gear—would be impossible."

The uniformity of railway arrangements is constantly being interfered with by the varying conditions of traffic, of weather, and of season. The excursion and summer traffic to the sea-side, to Ireland and Scotland, and the cross Channel service to the Continent, and the consequent complications at junctions, make absolute regularity impossible.

As the British Paterfamilias sits after breakfast, some winter morning, by his warm fireside, toasting his toes and reading his paper, his eye rests upon a paragraph which gently stirs the choleric within his protuberant breast. It is, perhaps, to the following effect: "Snow-storm in Hampshire. Up mail detained several hours." "Bad management again," remarks Mr. P——; and he is evidently under the impression that that part of the railway system would have been far better administered if his had been the presiding mind. Fortunately, however, for Mr. P——, he was safe and warm in bed during the vicissitudes of that night. For what was happening?

A dense sky had been hanging over these grey snow-clad Hampshire hills, and then those hills disappeared under the whirling dance of snow-flakes. "Where usually is a varied landscape of meadow, river, trees, and hedges, is now one unbroken line of white, with an occasional dark object peering through to mark the spot where usually is a fence or a tree. Away it stretches till we reach a dark fir plantation, and then again we are lost amid the snow-clad range of the Purbeck Hills. Now and then drift across the grey expanse small flocks of larks, with their heads turned westward, their slow dreary flight adding a melancholy touch of life to the lifeless scene. The lines were just visible under the snow, which was piled high in the centre of the railway, and crowds of men were employed in sweeping it away; while the wind rendered their task almost endless by blowing it back again almost quicker than they could brush it away, a fine white powder being drifted in a ceaseless shower across everything from the masses on the roads, where the dense white stuff lay wholly between the hedges, level with the tops." When dug out it came out in square blocks like sugar, or still more like starch, for it had the peculiar blue tint that this latter commodity possesses, and none of the brilliant sparkle of a lump of sugar.

The guard of a goods train thus narrated his experiences that night. "I daresay," he said, "it was much the same on all the lines. I can only speak for myself, and I know that I never was out in such a storm in all the winters that I've been guard on the London and South Western. Bad enough we had it, in all conscience, coming up from Salisbury in the dark right against that east wind, driving and howling incessantly, and the snow enough to blind you if you'd only turned your face straight towards it for a moment; but the truth is you couldn't do it. Yes, I will tell you about it if you think it worth hearing, at least in my way.

"I went down from Waterloo in the morning to bring up a train coming from Exeter on from Salisbury to London. It was blowing wild enough when we started, and the snow whirling round and round us—not in big flakes, like you see it fall when in still weather, but in a sharp fine dust, just like glass ground down into powder. Long before we got to our down journey's end the snow had begun to gather deep in the cuttings, the wind sweeping it down from the open country above, and laying it in a sloping bank, running down far across the rails. It is an odd sensation when you are cutting through snow that is not quite enough to stop you, but very near. It is as if you were off the rails, going over stony ground, and something all the time trying hard to shove you back, and then letting you go clean ahead for a minute or two.

"But the worst of it hadn't come yet. Our engine made her way through it very fair, and we were not much above half an hour behind when we went into Salisbury station. There we waited for the Exeter train, telegraphed from Gillingham only an hour late. When she came in I took her guard's place, and we started for Waterloo with nine or ten carriages, and a good many passengers, a little before five—just after dark, in fact. It had been snowing, snowing, snowing down there, as elsewhere, all day long; and as we went out of the lighted station right into the wild open country, I couldn't help thinking of what it would be like that night on the great chalk downs, or on the roads over Salisbury Plain, without a bit of shelter for miles and miles. Oh, how it did blow! and how the sharp snow-dust came sweeping down upon us as we went towards it in the teeth of the wind. We kept on at a good pace, at least on the embankments, where the line was swept by the gale as clean as twenty thousand brooms could have made it. On we went till we got into the cuttings the other side of Andover. There we were again rumbling as if over stones instead of iron rails, and being shoved back, and then again on with a start, and then rumbling and bumping, and then on again. I should think, with you, that the passengers found it unpleasant; but it was curious how quiet and contented they all seemed. Nobody cared apparently to peep out even for a moment. The ladies in the first-class carriages had got foot-warmers, and so had a good many people in the second and third class; but if they wanted anything more they didn't trouble themselves to make a sign, even when we stopped a moment at Andover. Somebody, I daresay, had tried to look out, and finding it took his breath away, and sent the snow flying in shovelfuls into the carriage, had shut the window quicker than he opened it. The frost on the panes made it impossible to see them from outside, and the lamps inside looked like little tips of yellow flame upon a tallow candle.

"So there they were, all invisible, huddling up together, I daresay, and longing to hear they were at Woking junction, or somewhere farther still on the way to Waterloo. I knew it would be worse when we got past Whitchurch, for the deep cuttings are about there; and so it was. Rumble, rumble we went again, and again something seemed shoving us back, and then on, and then back; and then we came to a dead stand in that comfortless hole, with the snow, that was continually sweeping down on us, now up above the foot-board and even against the lower part of the carriage doors. I got down with my lantern, and no sooner did I meet the cutting gale, than my beard and all the lower part of my face was covered over with a thick crust which you could neither rub nor pull off with the hand. The wind literally blew me backward, and forced me to keep my chin down on my chest, and grope along holding by the carriage handles.

"'How are you getting on, Jack?' I asked my mate beside the engine as soon as I could get near enough to his ear to be heard.

"'Bad enough, Bill,' he said. 'Turn your lantern down here, old man. It's the ash-pan all caked up with snow, and not a bit of draught can get into the fire.'

"And so it was—hard as flint, too, in spite of the warmth. There was nothing to be done but to rake away with a long bent iron bar—all three of us, stoker included—till we had cleared a bit; and we began to make steam again.

"'Can you get on now, do you think?' I says.

"'Look at that snow in front of my engine,' says he; 'she'll never go through with the train behind her.'

"'What'll you do, then?' I says.

"'You get into your van, Bill,' says he, 'and put the brake hard on while I unhook.'

"So I did; and when Jack Randall had backed a trifle, or tried to do it, he unhooked, and leaving us behind in that dismal place, whistled and went bang at the snow, and right on, ploughing and cutting into it for three hundred yards or so. Then he backed again, and down we were once more, stoker and all, hooking on and peering with the lantern, and clearing the ash-pan. That is the way we got on; and patience it wanted too, with our numbed fingers and half-frozen faces."

The troubles of the driver were greater even than those of the guard. Along the line the white ground reflected the light; but it was difficult to see any signal when the air was full of snow driving straight against him. He continually had to clear the snow off those two round glass spectacles in front of him, otherwise he could not see even a fogman, with his red or green light, against the signal post. And all down the lines there were similar difficulties. Trains got stuck fast in the stations themselves from the snow drifting in heaps up to the platforms.

"It is," continued the guard, "a hard life at times. But there's one comfort—at least for steady, sober guards and drivers—and no other kind of men will do in our trade, I can assure you. That's when they get home (for we do get home at last) and find the missus, late as it is, sitting up with a good fire and a bit of supper for them, as she always does, if she's one of the right sort. The women, you see, fidget a little bit when you're late; it's natural, and though they put the children to bed, they can't sleep themselves, for listening to the clock ticking, and counting the hours, wondering where you are, and hoping all's right."

A young lady has touchingly described her experiences during this storm in a journey from Oxford to London, and her words we cannot refrain from quoting. "At length," she said, "we came to a standstill, and on hearing voices upon the line, I opened the carriage window, and nervously inquired what was the matter, saying, 'Snowed up, I suppose,' and, receiving an answer in the affirmative, rejoined, in my simplicity, 'That we should all turn out and help clear the snow away,' to which a good-tempered man responded, 'If they was all like you, miss, we should soon get it out.' I closed the window, expecting every moment the train would proceed, and continued to amuse myself by reading; but hour after hour passed without the slightest indication of a movement, and I began to feel my lone and desolate position—cut off from all communication with my fellow-passengers, and with nothing visible on either side but snow, which insidiously crept in through the crevices of the windows and drifted to such an extent that I thought unless relief soon came I should become 'snowed in.'"

The light failed in the carriage. "Cold, benumbed, and hungry, I lay myself prostrate on the seat, unconscious of what was going on around me, until I was aroused by a knock at the window, and on opening it a 'Samaritan,' in the form of a labouring man, asked me to take a little 'whisky.' At first I refused his proffered kindness, but on his assuring me it would do me good, and that some other ladies had drunk some, I, much against my will, yielded to his kind-hearted solicitations, and for the first time in my life swallowed what I have heard my gentlemen friends term a drop of the 'crater.' That it did me good I have no doubt, although I should prefer to it many other alcoholic or non-intoxicating drinks. I offered a shilling to him, but, with a generosity I shall never forget, he declined to accept a farthing, and left me. On the departure of my well-intentioned benefactor, I took off my shoes and stockings and rubbed my feet, which were very benumbed, with all the energy I was possessed of. I made a pillow of some wraps strapped together, and tried to sleep; but in vain. Thoughts of home would come, and tears rolled down my cheeks, for up to this time I had not thoroughly realized my critical position. At 12.30 I heard some one talking to my next-door neighbours—some light-hearted youths going to Harrow—and asked where we were, for until then I had no idea, and was informed by the gentleman whose voice I had heard, that we were 200 yards from Radley station. He inquired if I was alone, and on telling him of my position he asked if he could do anything for me, and suiting the action to the word climbed up to my window, literally covered with frozen snow, supplied me with some biscuits, and took my foot-warmer away and refilled it from the engine, a matter of considerable difficulty, as the snow had blocked up the train on either side, and was very deep. I felt intensely grateful to him for his trouble, and, as he promised to return again with some hot tea and something to eat, if it was possible, saw a gleam of hope at last. He advised me to try to sleep, and for half an hour I managed to do so, when he returned with some warm tea and bread and butter, saying that he believed the train was to be cleared, and passengers were to go either to Radley station or the inn. He remained with me for several hours, and, a way having been cut through the snow, we reached the inn, where all my fortitude gave way, and I became dreadfully ill. Every room in the establishment was crammed with people, who seemed exceedingly thoughtful of each other, excepting one lady, who was more taken up with her lapdog, which she wrapped in a blanket, and sitting on a bed exclaimed frantically and continuously, 'Oh, my poor little darling, he has not been used to this sort of thing. I am sure it will kill him. What shall I do?' The supply of provisions was of such a limited nature that a bit of bread or a raw crumpet was a luxury; but whatever there was available the gentlemen placed at the disposal of the ladies.

"At length it was suggested we should go to Abingdon, and I started with a lady and her brother and the gentleman who had been so kind to me through a weary drag of nearly three miles in the snow. We arrived at the Crown and Thistle about noon, when my 'friend in need' left me, having seen me comfortably settled. The people at the hotel were very attentive, as also were two clergymen, who treated me with more than Christian kindness, entertaining me at their table to an excellent dinner (to which I need not inform you I did excellent justice), and tending me with fatherly care until ten o'clock, when I retired to bed and slept until eight o'clock on Thursday morning.

"I got home about half-past twelve on Thursday night, thankful to Providence that nothing serious had happened, and with a full sense of the great kindness I had received at the hands of those I had come in contact with, to one and all of whom I return my most heartfelt thanks." Amongst the blocked-in passengers were the Very Rev. the Dean of Christ Church, Dr. Acland, the Dean of Worcester, the Rev. Alwyne Compton, and others.

Such was the complete arrest at that time laid by these snow-storms upon the traffic, that the mail trains, with the mails for the west, were actually detained for twenty-four hours in the shed at Paddington, waiting till it was reported that the line was clear enough to get through—an unprecedented event.

Similarly, on Thursday, the 3rd of March, 1881, a snow-storm began to fall in West Yorkshire, Westmoreland, and around. So furious, in those higher elevations, was the wind, that it rocked the trains, even heavy Pullman carriages, as they paused at stations on the Settle and Carlisle line; and it swept the snow from the upper parts of the great fells "as clean as a broom." "During the day," said the engineer, "we kept the line open, but by ten o'clock at night the drifts entirely blocked the up road. We then worked the traffic for a short distance on the down line, till an engine, which had been taken from its train to make a run at the drift, bedded itself so fast in the snow

A MIDLAND TRAIN SNOWED UP, NEAR DENT.

that it could not back out. From that time till Sunday morning it was a continual fight with the drifts to try to keep the line clear. Two engines with a gang of nearly 600 men left Dent, and cut the drifts before them to Dent Head, and on their return had at once to repeat the process in order to get back, the drifts of snow filling every gully and cutting to a depth of thirty feet. During Saturday night it alternately rained and froze, so that the surface of the snow became firm and frozen; and on Sunday morning, when the gale ceased the masses of snow would bear." The engraving indicates the actual condition of affairs, showing all that was to be seen of an entire train, namely the top of the engine funnel, the snow around being hard. One man who walked over the train found the chimney top convenient as a spittoon. Meanwhile the moisture that had accumulated on the telegraph wires had become as thick as a man's wrist. The lamp-posts on the platform at Dent were buried in the snow. After the line was reopened, a train of ten locomotives that had "gone cold"—the trains of which had already been removed by fresh engines—was dug out of a drift thirty or forty feet deep and drawn away.

The railways in the Highlands of Scotland are in winter frequently exposed to obstruction from snow-falls and snow-drifts. The telegraph wires are broken down, and no one when he takes his seat in the train can tell when he will reach his destination. Even the steam-plough gives little help. Some years ago a number of travellers were snowed up on the high moorland at the bleak sources of the Gala, between Galashiels and Edinburgh. Some of them tried to wade through the snow to houses which, it was thought, existed in the neighbourhood. They had to return, wet to the skin, and to pass the night in the railway carriages. "The shepherd lost in the snow is a sufferer who has often attracted the notice of poets. The bagman lost in the snow appeared a topic for mockery to the Ettrick Shepherd. For a whole train to be swallowed up in the drift may be a very serious misfortune, but it is one which is rapidly becoming quite familiar on certain northern lines."

Travellers by rail to Sutherland may remember the desolation of the scenery between Dalnaspidal and Dalwhinnie. The landscape has the aspect of a high sour tableland, the prevailing colours are a sullen green and a dreary brown, while chill gleams of sunlight chase each other across the melancholy hills. The country seems starved. The rare houses are built of a dull grey stone, and have an inhospitable appearance. A suspicion of hail, even in summer, is mixed with the rain that is always scudding by. Here, in 1879, a train was snowed up. Towards Dalwhinnie the train struggled pluckily along. But before it arrived there, it was found that further progress was impossible. The snow was nearly on a level with the upper edges of the cutting. Fortunately there are a few houses in the neighbourhood, and so the outside world "believed that the officials and passengers would there have found refuge." Similarly from Inverness, during the same storm, it was announced that "the whereabouts of the 3.10 p.m. Sunday mail was to the officials on Monday night an absolute mystery." The train was known to have passed Altnabreac, and was believed to be probably somewhere between that station and Scot-scalder, a bleak and most inhospitable region—the very name of this home of the snow and the east wind tells of its desolation in its sound; one seems to hear the wind wailing through a forest of stunted and weather-bitten pines. "The most ordinary journey in Scotland seemed to partake of the nature of an Arctic expedition. Trains went into the darkness and the drift, and station masters, porters, and guards could not guess on Monday night where the mail that left on Sunday afternoon could be."

The issue of such events is, to the shareholders as well as to the public, practical enough. Sir E. W. Watkin, M.P., in 1876, stated to the South Eastern shareholders that the difference to them between a fine week or a wet week was something like £3,000. "A year with more than the average of sunshine, and a year with less than the average of sunshine, makes a difference to you of £100,000. We all know what sort of a half-year we have had. Now we are in the midst of reasonably hot weather, and for the first time we are beginning to perspire with pleasure. We almost forget that we have been going through a succession of winters. We have hardly had a spring; we have only had a little touch at the end of the half-year of a summer. Now, what really are the facts? I learnt from the Observatory at Greenwich that during the last half-year there have been no less than seventy-nine wet days, and no less than seventy-seven days on which, at four feet from the ground, the thermometer was less than 45 degrees Fahr. It is not to be expected that on a line which is to a large extent a pleasure line, as well as a business line, like ours, in that state of weather the trains will be very full."

But the burden devolving upon railways in dealing with great snow-storms is not only negative, by a loss of revenue: it is positive, by an enormous expenditure of labour and money. At the half-yearly meeting of the Great Western Railway Company, following the snow-storm of January, 1881, the chairman said: "We had every reason, up to the middle of January, to anticipate that we might have been able to offer the shareholders a dividend in excess of what they had previously received, but you all know in the middle of January a snow-storm occurred, the first we have had in the history of this railway to interfere with our traffic, and wiped off something like £56,000 of the amount available for dividend. Had we had that £56,000 in our pockets, we should have been able to give you from a half to three-quarters more dividend than we are now doing. We did not make the storm; we did our best under the circumstances; so I hope you will all be satisfied that the 5 per cent. we now offer you is as much as we could reasonably be expected to give. There is no doubt the storm was much more severe on our line than on any other. Its great weight fell in the counties of Berks, Wilts, and down towards Weymouth and that district. We had to excavate 111 miles of snow, varying according to the drift, from 3 feet down to 10 feet in depth. We had unfortunately fifty-one passenger trains and thirteen goods trains buried in the snow, making a total of sixty-four, and we had blocks on 141 different parts of the system. Great credit is due to the skill and zeal of our officers, and not only to the officers, but to every man engaged in the service, for accomplishing what they did. They had a very difficult service to perform, and we had no accident to any person during the whole period."

In Canada, and in some other parts of the world, special arrangements have to be made to prevent the interruption of railway traffic by snow-storms. The Central Pacific Railroad of California crosses the Sierra Nevada mountains at a height very near the perpetual snow-line; every winter the snow-fall is from sixteen to twenty feet deep; and in the spring mighty avalanches sweep down the mountain sides. Here the line has to be roofed over with solid structures of wood, called snow-sheds. One of them is 1,659 feet long; others range from 100 feet to 870 feet in length; and their aggregate length is no less than 45 miles. Over these sheds the "snow-slides" pass into the valleys below without injuring either the permanent way or the passing trains.

Having referred to some of the vicissitudes of railway travelling, we may advert to some of the means that are adopted for securing the safety of the public. That railway accidents are serious enough when they do take place, goes without saying. When steam locomotion began, a coachman is said to have drawn a distinction between coach accidents and railway accidents thus: "Why you see, sir, if a coach goes over and spills you in the road there you are; but if you are blown up by an engine, where are you?" The scene represented in the engraving, of an accident that happened to an empty goods train, may bring home to the mind of the reader the realities of such a contingency. In view, however, of the accidents on railways to passengers, from causes beyond their own control, we make bold to utter—what our readers may at first regard as a startling paradox—that, after all, as things now are, *it is safer to travel by railway than to stop at home.* Now is this statement true or untrue ?

Let us think for a moment of the number and the diversity of the casualties that occur to people who are not travelling

ACCIDENT TO AN EMPTY COAL TRAIN.
(*From a Photograph.*)

—casualties that do not happen to them when they are travelling. A person seated in a railway carriage is certainly free, for instance, from any danger of tumbling down stairs and breaking his neck, or of slipping over a piece of orange peel and dislocating his spine, or of being blown up in a coal pit, or of being torn by machinery, or of being burnt in bed, or of being thrown from a horse, or being run over, or being run away with, or getting drowned. Not very long ago it was mentioned in the newspapers how that a lad of sixteen became entangled with a cow's tail, and was dragged about a field by his leg till he was dead. A dog fell into a London dock, and a neighbour, who was passing, offered his aid in the rescue. In doing this the latter took hold of the hand of the owner, leaned over the side of the dock, and lifted the dog up to his master, who was so delighted to recover his property that he let go the hand of its deliverer, who dropped into the water, and was drowned. But such cases, it will be said, are exceptional. Doubtless; but "exceptional" accidents are always happening. Throughout the first six months of a recent year two persons were taken to the London hospitals *every day* who had been worried by dogs. M. Boutin informs us that in France three persons are struck dead by lightning every fortnight. Eight persons are burned or scalded to death in Great Britain every day. In South Wales a life is lost for every 66,000 tons of coals that are raised. In one week, recently, eleven persons were killed in London by street accidents; and the coroner declared that there are 300 fatal cases and 6,000 non-fatal cases of accidents from conveyances and horses in the metropolis every year. In fact, *nearly as many persons are slain in the streets of London every fortnight* as there were passengers killed on all the railways in Great Britain in a year from causes beyond their own control. Further, it is stated that "2,000 persons are lost in London every year, and only half of them found again, leaving annually 1,000 disappearances never accounted for." Again, above 1,000 lives are lost annually in the mines of the United Kingdom; and 500 lives are lost every year upon the coasts of the British isles by ship and boat wrecks.

So with other forms of injury in the country. The number of accidents occurring weekly in Bristol is 123; in Birmingham, 196; in Worcester, 32; in Stafford, 23; in Manchester, 246; in Northampton, 40. The proportion of these weekly accidents to the total population would show how large an amount of risk is incurred, which nobody sees, which nobody knows, and which nobody cares about, because the newspapers do not write on the subject in connection with the various industries carried on in this country, whereas concerning every railway accident they supply the amplest information.

Now, putting together many forms of accident, from which a railway passenger is for the time being exempt, remembering that the number of railway travellers last year in Great Britain was more than 620,000,000, that the average time occupied by a journey was about an hour, making 620,000,000 hours—equal to the whole population of a town of 500,000 inhabitants during twelve hours a day for more than three months, we believe it is not too much to say that there were fewer injuries received by passengers in railway carriages from causes beyond their own control than there were to a similar number of persons for a similar period who were not for that time railway travellers.

We may add that, at the half-yearly meeting of the London and North Western Railway, August, 1882, the chairman stated that there had not been a single passenger killed on that railway for the last two years and a half, and that for the last three years and a half only one passenger had been killed—a lady, who was killed by a beam breaking loose in one of the goods trains. Otherwise, in that period not a single passenger had been killed, although the company carry between fifty and sixty millions every year.

"I have in this room proved," said Sir E. Watkin, on one occasion, "that railway travelling is safer than walking, riding, driving, than going up and down stairs, than watching agricultural machinery, and even safer than eating, because it is a fact that *more people choke themselves in England than are killed on all the railways of the United Kingdom.*"

Our security in travelling, says Sir John Hawkshaw, depends on the perfection of the machine in all its parts, including the whole railway, with its movable plant, in that term; it depends also on the nature and quantity of traffic, and, lastly, on human care and attention. With regard to what is human, it may be said that so many of these accidents as arise from the fallibility of men will never be eliminated until the race be improved. And yet he adds: "There is only one passenger injured in every four million miles travelled. On an average, a person may travel 100,000 miles each year for forty years, and the chances are slightly in his favour of his not receiving the slightest injury." The marvel is, considering varying conditions, the imperfection of human nature, the intricacy of the machinery employed, and the high velocities attained, that railway travelling is so safe. Yet all this work is done, as the late Mr. Locke, C.E., expressed it, over "two thin parallel bars of iron." Hundreds of millions of passengers, and hundreds of millions of tons of goods, are moved over these same "thin parallel bars of iron," moved by the consumption of more than 10,000,000 tons of coal, burned by 13,000 locomotives, in all varieties of weather, by day, by night, in sunshine and fog, rain and storm, frost and snow; on level plains, through many miles of tunnel, over steep embankments and lofty viaducts, through long deep cuttings, over bridges spanning water and viaducts over the land, past innumerable junctions, and through crowded stations and level crossings. This immense number of passengers and enormous bulk of goods are drawn by engines of the most complicated mechanism, held together with millions of rivets, each engine containing an intricate network of tubes, numerous cranks, and other delicate pieces of workmanship, and the engines and vehicles are connected by chains and couplings. In every separate item of all these innumerable parts lurk elements of danger, and the slightest fracture might produce disaster. All this is done, and with what result? That there is no safer place in the world, as Professor De Morgan said some years ago, and it is still true, than a railway train.

It is a curious fact that, in at least two known instances, railway accidents have exercised a directly curative effect. The Rev. W. Woods, formerly of Leicester, assured the writer that a collision in which he had the good fortune to be had an immediate and most salutary influence upon his nervous system. Similarly a gentleman who wrote in November, 1869, to the *Times*, stated that a few days before he had been threatened "with a violent attack of rheumatic fever; in fact," he said, "my condition so alarmed me, and my dread of a sojourn in a Manchester hotel bed for two or three months was so great, that I resolved to make a bold *sortie* and, well wrapped up, start for London by the 3.30 p.m. Midland fast train. From the time of leaving that station to the time of the collision, my heart was going at express speed; my weak body was in a profuse perspiration; flashes of pain announced that the muscular fibres were under the tyrannical control of rheumatism, and I was almost beside myself with toothache. . . . From the moment of the collision to the present hour no ache, pain, sweat, or tremor has troubled me in the slightest degree, and instead of being, as I expected, and indeed intended, in bed, drinking *tinct. aurantii*, or absorbing through my pores oil of horse-chestnut, I am conscientiously bound to be at my office bodily sound." The writer humorously adds, "Don't print my name and address, or the Midland Company may come down on me for compensation."

We have already referred to the immense momentum of trains: we may now deal with the equally important subject of the best methods by which an arrest may be laid upon that momentum.

In June, 1876, horse-racing took a new turn in Nottinghamshire. In doing so, various innovations were introduced into the arrangements: the course was lengthened to nearly four miles; the speed was calculated and recorded by electricity; the spectators were strictly professional, and there was, we are assured, no betting.

But, to drop our metaphor, it is to the steam-horse, its paces and its races, that we refer. No panting flanks and furrowed ribs, no drooping heads and blood-red nostrils were seen upon that field; only ribs of steel, and bowels of brass, and breath of steam were tested in that contest; and, moreover, the problem to be solved was not so much how fast to run, but how soon to stop. It was, in fact, a trial of brakes.

Among the many proposed improvements that have occupied the attention of the railway world, has been how—with the greatest speed, certainty, and security—to stop a train. The enormous and increasing power and swiftness of our locomotives —which, despite their ponderous tread and massive burdens can clear, for long distances, a mile a minute—has necessarily involved the question: How shall a pace like this be controlled— a momentum like this be arrested? How soon, when a tire has come off, or a carriage has broken down, or an obstacle is in view upon the line, can the mighty mass, with its priceless living freight, be brought to rest?

The ordinary plan used to be to apply the pressure of blocks of wood to a few of the wheels, and to do this by means of screws worked by different men, at different moments, and in different parts of the train. The driver shuts off the steam, and the fireman applies the brake to the tender. What is the effect? The speed of the front part of the train is arrested; the remainder, with undiminished momentum, rushes forward upon the engine and tender. By this time the rear guard puts on his brakes; the last carriages are pulled back, and the tendency now is to snap the train in two in the middle. It is also found by experiment that with the hand brake a train of fourteen carriages and brake vans, weighing perhaps 180 tons, if running at 43 miles an hour, requires nearly a minute and a distance of some 700 yards before it can be stopped; that is to say, the wheels will "skid" along the rails for not much less than half a mile, with the inevitable tendency to grind the wheels into polygons, and to crush the upper surface of the rails into dust. All this would happen with the old brakes every time a stoppage at a station was required. But when unexpected stops had to be taken, the work was done under less favourable circumstances. The driver caught sight of a danger-signal or of an obstruction on the line, and what followed? He called to his fireman and whistled to his guards; but, though the former might obey as soon as he has had time to reach the handle of his brake and to turn it round, the guards could scarcely be so prompt. They might be sorting parcels, or making memoranda, or otherwise occupied, and a quarter of a minute might elapse before they take their brake screws in hand. Some seconds would still be necessary before the brake blocks were made to bear; and thus nearly a minute would elapse, and some six or seven hundred yards more would be traversed before the train would be brought to rest.

It is evident that any such arrangements and construction fall far short of a perfect brake. When an arrest of a train is attempted, it should be made equally upon every vehicle, and upon every wheel; it should be "continuous" throughout the train; it should be instantaneous and simultaneous. It should also not "skid" the wheels, but simply restrain them, with an elastic pressure which permits them to rotate, though more slowly than the speed of the train; in order that flat surfaces may not be worn upon them, nor vibration be communicated to the vehicles that are being stopped. It should, moreover, be capable of application by either the fireman or the guard; it should be unaffected by extreme changes of the temperature; it should admit of the carriages being coupled or uncoupled with facility; and, in the event of the train breaking in two, each portion should still be provided with a brake in complete order, which should also be automatically applied. Finally, the stoppage from a high velocity should not be made in too abrupt a manner, otherwise new mechanical disturbances may arise and new forms of accident be created. Such are the requirements of a perfect brake. From time to time inventors came forward with appliances which they averred would fulfil these conditions; and the period arrived when it was thought that their rival claims should be put to the test. The Railway Commission desired to be posted up on the subject; the Railway Association invited competitors into the field; the Midland Railway Company provided an eligible arena for the peaceful contest; and a series of trials were undertaken which, it was believed, would be fraught with benefit to the railway community and to the travelling public.

The trial ground stretched from about two miles west of Newark-upon-Trent for about four miles in the direction of Nottingham. It was nearly level; with the exception of one gentle curve it was perfectly straight; the permanent way was in excellent condition; and the ordinary traffic was not so considerable but that it could be relegated to one line while the experimental trains occupied the other. The distances were measured, and proclaimed in large letters on high posts; electrical and mechanical appliances were provided in order to ascertain the speed at which each train was running; platelayers were posted at every crossing, even of a field footpath, and every precaution of every kind appeared to be adopted to prevent accident or interruption. Splendid trains, with engines and carriages spick and span new, came in from various parts of England, and took preliminary canters over the course; and on the morning of the first trial day they were drawn up in apparently interminable line. In front was the London and North Western train, fitted with the chain brake of Clarke and Webb; then the Caledonian, with the automatic reaction brake; then the London, Brighton, and South Coast, with the Westinghouse vacuum brake; the Great Northern, with Smith's vacuum brake, was next; and there were others in line, including four from the Midland Company. Each train consisted of the regulation number of thirteen carriages and two vans, each carriage being loaded so as to represent the ordinary weight of passengers, and each van carrying two tons in lieu of luggage. At ten o'clock a train arrived bringing the Duke of Buckingham, the Earl of Aberdeen, and others officially connected with the Royal Commission, and also a hundred or two of the most eminent authorities in the railway world. As only one line of rail was at the service of the experimentalists, it was arranged that each train was to be tried, whether once or twice, in the order in which it stood; and that when its turn was over it should run forward to Thurgarton station, and wait there till, one by one, the others arrived, and then all could be brought back to the starting-point.

Our space forbids us to give any minute details of the results of the experiments thus made, but some approximate data may be mentioned. In the first trials the trains were brought up by the ordinary brakes, worked in the usual way by hand; and it is stated that the Great Northern train, for instance, when running at a speed of 47½ miles an hour, was not stopped till it had run a distance of nearly 1,200 yards in 86 seconds of time. But when the second series of trials was made with continuous brakes, the same train was pulled up, when at nearly the same speed, with Smith's vacuum brake in 400 yards and in 26 seconds—a whole minute of time being saved. A minute saved in an emergency might avert disaster.

Of the brakes themselves, we may say, without a word of disparagement to the rest, that there were two which it seemed hard to beat—the Westinghouse and Smith's vacuum. The Westinghouse is supplied with air, by a little "donkey engine" on the side of the locomotive, pumped into an air-chamber under the foot-plate. From this chamber two pipes run under the tender and communicate with a small cylinder containing a piston and rod under each carriage of the train. This piston, when pushed out, presses against the usual rods and fittings which apply the brake. All that is necessary to be done is for the driver to turn a tap in the communicating pipe; and the compressed air, flowing along the pipe, pushes out the piston under each carriage, and immediately the brake blocks are applied to every wheel, and the train is pulled up without jar or jolt. When the Midland train was running at about 54 miles an hour, it was stopped in some 330 yards of distance and in 23 seconds of time.

Many ingenious details have been provided in connection with the Westinghouse brakes. For instance, in the rapid making up of trains, it is important that the connecting-pipes should be easily fastened and unfastened, and still more important that there should be no leakage of the compressed air. This is done with the utmost simplicity of arrangement. There are no screws, cocks, or complex couplings. All that is necessary is "to stick one end of a pipe into another end of another pipe; to give the joint a half twist, and the joint is made good." A little india-rubber band is forced out by the pressure from within, and acts with perfect precision. "No joint," said the *Engineer*, "possessing anything like the advantages of this joint has ever been applied to a kindred purpose before;" and both pipes can be coupled in ten seconds.

Perhaps the most remarkable illustration of the power of this invention is seen in the following circumstance. Not long ago Mr. Needham gave instructions to the driver of a certain train that he was to go ahead, and, if the brakes should be applied, to take no notice, but push on at his utmost speed. He promised obedience; the train started; and when, as it was running at the rate of fifty miles an hour, Mr. Needham had the brakes put on, the effect was immediate and decisive; and though the machinery of the engine was in full forward gear, and though the steam was turned on at its highest pressure, the power of the brakes was too great for the mighty force of the locomotive, and engine and train were quietly and speedily dragged back to a full stop.

"Can any gentleman tell us," we inquired of a group who were standing on the line near the winning-post, "where Mr. Smith is, the patentee of the vacuum brake?" "Down yonder," was the reply; "ask for Vacuum Smith, that's his Christian name; only," added our informant, "it ought to be Vacuus to agree with Smith." But though we did not find Mr. Smith, his representative explained to us the peculiarity of his principle. It has two india-rubber tubes running under the carriages throughout the train, and attached by an ingenious form of coupling between them. By opening a steam valve on the engine, and ejecting steam from the boiler, which escapes up the funnel, a vacuum is formed, the air is suddenly drawn out of the tubes, a pressure approaching to fourteen pounds on the square inch is obtained, and this pressure acts on "sacks" shaped like accordions, under the carriages, and causes the "brake-blocks" to act on each wheel of every carriage in the train.

With reference to the relative powers of the Westinghouse and the vacuum brakes for stopping trains, the results at the Newark trial were thus given: the Westinghouse had its power in reserve and was always ready for instantaneous action, obeying the movement of its lever with almost electric speed; while the vacuum brake had to obtain its vacuum by the passage of steam through the whole length of the train before it came into play. The time lost might seem insignificant when expressed in seconds and estimated by ordinary rates; but seconds cease to be insignificant when an express train is being whirled at the rate of sixty miles an hour towards an obstacle which threatens to bring it to destruction. In such circumstances, a second means a run of seventy-nine feet; and its importance may be illustrated by mentioning that "a few nights previously, on the North British Railway, an express running at sixty miles an hour was stopped by a fog signal, which there had not been time to place as far back as could have been desired. The driver applied the Westinghouse brake, and the train was brought up nine yards in the rear of one which had broken down and was blocking the line. A repetition of the Abbot's Ripton accident was prevented."

After the series of brake trials near Newark, the Midland Railway Company put the several descriptions of brakes then exhibited into every-day work; their respective merits and defects were carefully studied; and exhaustive inquiries and experiments were made by the officers of the company. The result was that, in 1878, a very effective continuous brake, on the automatic vacuum principle, was brought out and patented by Mr. T. G. Clayton, the carriage and wagon superintendent. The automatic principle is, in a word, that in the event of anything going wrong with the brake-pipe, either by the severance of the train or otherwise, the brake is immediately self-applied.

The Midland Railway Company's apparatus is automatic, and otherwise conforms with the requirements of the Board of Trade. It has the advantage also of great simplicity, the action being obtained without the intervention of valves, cocks, or other devices usually inseparable from automatic action.

It may be said that the vacuum brake has only, as its maximum power, fourteen or fifteen pounds to the square inch—the amount of the pressure of the atmosphere; whereas the Westinghouse brake can create a pressure of seventy pounds on the inch. This disadvantage, it is replied, is got over by the vacuum brake using an 18-inch instead of the 8-inch cylinder of the Westinghouse. There is practically ample space in the under-frame of the carriages for this increase of the size of the cylinder. It is also remarked, in favour of the vacuum brake, that the constant pressure from within of the Westinghouse tends to open the joints, and therefore to create leakage in the pipes; while the pressure from without of the vacuum brake helps to close them, and to minimise any defects in them that may arise. Mr. Clayton's brake is now being fitted to all the Midland stock, the Westinghouse brake being confined to those Midland trains that run in connection with the Scotch railways.

A pleasant writer has described some of his experiences when riding on an engine with a train at a special trial of the earlier vacuum brake. "How the old engine," he says, "did rush, and roar, and seem to jump along! And as we near Marks Tey some one is on the line ahead, and the driver, our master, sounds his horn—screeching, yelling, and screaming out, 'Yoicks for'ard there, yoicks for'ard'—and we see a speck of a man looking no bigger in the distance than a fox, steal across the line, and with another bound we are through the station. The wind is so high, and the rush of the engine so noisy, that we can hardly hear each other speak, but Captain Tyler explains to us, as well as he can under such circumstances, the feat we are going to perform, and how it is to be accomplished; and as we near Witham we increase our speed to fifty miles an hour, and then the driver touches a little bit of metal before him, not bigger than the handle of an iron spoon, and all at once we hear a slight sucking sound beneath us, and along the train, and in twenty-two seconds, by the official's watch, we are brought up to a gentle trot! On again, through the curve at Witham, the worst on the line, and the most dangerous. But, luckily, those 'inside' don't see it as we did on Monday; we seem at first to be making full tilt towards the left-hand station, like a bull goes at a gate; then, with a sudden twist, we appear to go in the same way at the right-hand buildings; but we get through all right, nevertheless, and rush along with increased speed. How the wind searches out our very bones, and bits of coal and dust get into our eyes; yet we try to look cheerful, for the Captain is all on the *qui vive*—'Hark for'ard, there; hark for'ard; yoicks!' we are nearing Chelmsford, and shall put on another spurt, and then, turning the spoon-handle himself, he will bring us to a full stop!

"We ask how heavy the train is, and we are told 150 tons! 'And see,' says Captain Tyler, 'how easily by putting my little finger upon this strip of metal, this enormous weight, travelling at the rate of fifty miles an hour, can be "brought up!"'—there was again a grating or sucking noise beneath us, and in little more than twenty seconds we were standing still. It was something wonderful, and 'Locomotive' seemed to think so too, for she jibbed a bit, from the pressure of the curb, perhaps, and wouldn't start again all at once, and people in the train couldn't make it out, for as we looked back along the carriages every window had heads looking out, like rats peeping from their holes. 'Shove her back a bit,' says the Captain, 'and then give her her head,' and the driver backed, and then with another rush we went forward, and the heads of the people went in. No more experiments to-day, but the road is pretty and interesting. At some places we can see miles before us, and, as the road is spanned by numberless bridges, we seem to be rushing up the inside of a huge telescope from the big end, and never getting nearer to the small. Down the incline from Brentwood, our pace is a mile a minute, and then, as we near our crowded destination, signal posts greet us on all sides with various messages; and one with a red hand makes a slight inclination downwards—like a polite bow; and the Captain says, 'That means "Caution,"' and the driver touches the spoon-handle gently, and we ease our speed, and glide along carefully, until we run into Stratford—time, 1 hour 15 minutes, and only two 'vacuum' checks."

Efforts have been made in some quarters to compel railway companies to adopt, definitely and finally, a particular system of continuous brakes; and Earl de la Warr recently introduced a bill into Parliament to make it compulsory for railway companies to adopt such brake, the companies, however, taking all responsibility for the choice they made. Upon this proposal Earl Cairns remarked that "it was very desirable that a system of continuous brakes should be adopted, and if the Board of Trade had made up their minds as to the best system, and had come to Parliament for powers to compel its adoption, he, for one, should be very much disposed to grant their request. But that was just what they had not done. By the bill, Parliament was asked to stereotype, now and for ever, or at any rate until the Act was repealed, a sort of ideal brake, and to submit the question whether the brakes of the various companies answered the requirements of the Act to a body of gentlemen—the Railway Commissioners—who were utterly unfit to determine such matters."

A few years ago great efforts were made to provide some means of communication between the passengers and the guards of running trains. A committee was formed of the general managers of the leading railway companies, and they examined 193 inventions, "some of them patented, some of them registered; all of them," said Mr. S. Clarke, "considered very clever by the parties." The best of them was a delicate electric apparatus communicating between the guard and the driver, and the passengers and the driver; and it was soon afterwards used to some extent on the London and South Western line. It was found, however, more easy of application on a self-contained railway like the South Western, where there is little attaching and detaching of carriages at junctions, than on some of the northern lines, where the trains are remarshalled several times in a journey. Another proposal was the use of a tube, which was connected with the carriages so that a passenger could speak either to the guard or the driver without necessarily stopping the train. The tubes were of iron, except between the carriages, where they were of vulcanized wire, covered with vulcanized india-rubber. A metal mouthpiece was fixed at the end of each tube, the mouthpiece in the carriage being covered with a slide. Directly this slide was removed by a passenger, a red signal was displayed outside the carriage, which told from which compartment the communication was made. It also served as a check upon the needless or foolish use of the apparatus.

The only plan that eventually came into common use is "the cord system." Its practical value has not been as great as was expected. In one half-year on the South Eastern Railway the data were as follows:—"On the 14th June the up tidal passenger train was stopped at Chislehurst out of curiosity; on the 10th June the 12.15 Hastings train was stopped at London Bridge out of curiosity; on the 19th June the 7.40 mail was stopped by the Post-office clerks because they had put their baggage into the wrong van; on the 8th April the 12.15 Hastings train was stopped at Tonbridge out of curiosity; on the 16th April the 7.40 train was stopped at Dartford because of a hot axle; on the 2nd May the 12.15 Hastings train was stopped at Etchingham out of curiosity. The 7.40 train on May 17th was stopped at Ashford out of curiosity. On May 19th the 8.45 train was stopped by the guard at Staplehurst because a door had flown open; and on the 31st a train was stopped at Burton Green out of curiosity. On June 3rd the 1 p.m. Margate train was stopped at Chatham, again out of curiosity. On June 17th the 12.15 train from Hastings was stopped at Wadhurst out of curiosity." This was the history of six months' experience; and the result therefore was, that, out of a thousand trains a day run by this company, there were only two cases in which these means of communication between passenger, guard, and driver was of any direct practical value.

In July, 1880, Sir E. W. Watkin mentioned that in about a dozen years the electric communication had been used 177 times. "In this half-year, I suppose, we have run 1,000 trains a day—7,000 a week—and we have only had our trains stopped by this thing three times. The first was on the 20th March, when the 8.27 from Charing Cross to Tunbridge was stopped by a passenger in the Bletchingley tunnel out of curiosity. On the 12th of April the 4.20 from Charing Cross to Redhill was stopped in the Merstham tunnel out of curiosity; and on the 30th of May the 4.37 Ramsgate train was stopped by a passenger because he had got into the wrong train." With regard to some classes of accident, any communicator would be of little use. As Sir Daniel Gooch has said: "The first intimation that people in the train get of an accident where injury has arisen is the accident itself; it is all over before they have time to think of it." On the other hand, the presence of the communicator may prevent passengers annoying one another in the seclusion of a long run. The sense of security that its existence may inspire is itself a consideration not to be overlooked.

The rights of railway companies are not confined to their own estates, wide as many of them are. Parliament has provided * that lines that form part of a continuous route, or that have

* Railway and Canal Traffic Act, 17 and 18 Vic.

stations near one another, shall afford all due and reasonable facilities for receiving and forwarding traffic from and to one another; and a most complete and comprehensive system of through booking and rates, often without change of carriage or trans-shipment, has been arranged between the companies. "Working agreements" are also made between companies for their mutual convenience, by which the engines and servants of one company pass over the line of another company. Special statutory sanction may also, under certain circumstances, be obtained, called "running powers," or the right to work over and use with their engines, carriages, wagons, and servants, the lines, stations, watering places, and sidings of another company, on the payment of special tolls. Usually companies seeking such powers have done so for their mutual benefit; but in some cases they have been granted only after great opposition, and Parliament, in the public interest, has compelled a company to yield its road for the use of a rival. Other running powers have been obtained for politic reasons, but have been unexercised. The London and North Western has such powers over about 200 miles of the Caledonian system, and similarly the Caledonian over 100 miles of the London and North Western. The *Railway News* has given a list of the principal of these running powers, which shows how widespread they are. The Midland Company, for instance, has power to run over and use about 500 miles of other companies' lines, but these are exercised only on about 250; and the London and North Western has running powers over more than 1,200 miles of "foreign" line.

It must be allowed that all such powers are of value chiefly so far as the interests of the parties concerned are at one. When it is otherwise, "facility clauses" are of little worth. "I speak," said Mr. Allport in 1862, when giving evidence in support of the extension of the Midland to New Mills and Manchester, "from more than twenty years' practical experience in the management of railways, and I state that I never saw a facility clause yet drawn that would enable a competing company to avail itself of the line of the company which is required to give facilities, supposing that company to be determined not to give them."

The practical convenience of the exercise of these running powers is great, especially in the metropolis. Within six or seven miles of Charing Cross there are 260 miles of line in operation; and, allowing for double lines, sidings, and so forth, there are 750 miles—enough to make a single line from London to Thurso, in the extreme north of Scotland. These lines are the property of thirteen railway companies; but each possesses, by mutual arrangement or Parliamentary sanction, the power of collecting and distributing traffic over other lines. Thus the London and North Western trains run over forty-four miles of the lines of five other companies in the metropolis; the Great Northern over thirty-six miles of six other companies; and the Midland over thirty-one miles.

How convenient is the outcome may be illustrated by the case of a visitor to London, who takes a ticket for sevenpence-halfpenny from Broad Street station to the Mansion House. By road the distance is only a quarter of a mile; by rail the traveller rides for seventy minutes, over twenty miles of railway, and calls at thirty stations on his way, the property of no fewer than seven different railway companies, and makes the round of London.

Such, indeed, are the facilities afforded in the metropolis for the interchange of traffic, that if a body of troops were sent from Colchester to Portsmouth, there are seven different railway routes through London, any one of which could be taken. The Midland Company has eleven stations in the metropolis, the Great Western twelve, the London and North Western thirteen, the South Eastern twenty, and the Great Eastern forty. The different companies have of their own 245 stations, of joint stations 43, of stations on other companies' lines, 210; in all nearly 500, exclusive of goods, coal, and cattle depôts. It is estimated that the number of passengers using these stations is 750,000 a day, the Metropolitan alone averaging 180,000 every week-day; while the journeys taken by season-ticket holders are simply incalculable. Of the Metropolitan stations for long distance traffic, Paddington is the most important. With regard to the number of trains, several stations have 500 each, Liverpool Street has nearly 700, Moorgate Street over 800 a day, and Victoria more than 1,100—or an average of sixty-one an hour for eighteen hours a day. It has been estimated that in busy times of the day there are probably two movements of trains every minute. The passenger trains within the metropolis run a distance of 35,000 miles every week-day, or 11,000,000 in the year. The capital invested is more than £50,000,000.*

Besides those companies that have running powers over "foreign" lines, there are many others that are jointly owned by two or more different companies. These are of three kinds: those worked jointly; those worked by one of the owning companies; and those worked by a committee on behalf of the owning companies. The Ashby and Nuneaton, for instance, 29 miles long, is owned and also worked by the "L. & N. W. R." and the Midland Companies, and there are some 270 miles of line thus owned and worked by other companies. The Carnforth and Wennington, 9 miles long, is owned by the Midland and the Furness Companies, but is worked by the Midland, and the Macclesfield line is in a somewhat similar position; whereas the Cheshire lines, 104 miles in length, are owned jointly by the Great Northern, Midland, and "M. S. & L.," but are worked by a committee of the three companies. In addition to these there are several important lines that are "jointly leased"—the mileage, capital, and revenue of which are mixed up in the published accounts of larger companies. There are about twenty such companies, with about 400 miles of lines, and a capital of about £12,000,000, upon which the leasing companies provide the dividends.

In the vocabulary of railways there is one ugly word—ugly for all concerned—the word "compensation." It represents loss, injury, suffering; sometimes it means chicanery and fraud. The principle that has been acknowledged is that where accidents, causing injury to passengers, have resulted from carelessness on the part of railway officials, the company is liable for damages. From the first, charges for compensation to passengers have appeared in railway accounts; and in some years they have been so great as to cause a serious diminution in the dividends of shareholders. Two accidents on the Brighton Railway during one year cost that Company £100,000; and there have been many occasions on which £50,000 or £60,000 were required to meet the claims arising out of some great disaster. It is believed that, as a rule, railway directors are

---

* "Railway Revolutions," an article in the *Contemporary Review*. By Frederick S. Williams.

anxious to deal fairly with such cases; but it must be allowed that these liabilities of railway companies have sometimes had curious developments. A blind man went unattended into a station on the London and North Western, touched a nail on the top of the staircase, fell down, and claimed damages for injuries received. In another case, on the same line, a boy tried to climb on to the mantelpiece in a waiting-room, pulled it down, broke his arm, and obtained £150 from the company. A lady walking across the floor at Spalding station caught her foot in a hole in the carpet, fell, and received some injury, for which she was awarded by a jury £1,500 damages.

But there have been claims more surprising. Soon after the catastrophe at Abergele, a man, by his solicitor, claimed damages for injuries sustained in the collision. An officer of the company called upon him. He "appeared to be greatly suffering," and he said he claimed £4,000. When the case came on for trial he was short of funds, and the action was withdrawn. But soon afterwards the company procured conclusive evidence that he was never in the train at all. He was prosecuted, and sentenced to eighteen months' imprisonment. In another case a man who had been in a collision on the Midland line made a demand for compensation. He appeared in court wrapped in blankets; one friend supported his head, another his feet; and he gave his evidence in a pathetic whisper. The jury, touched by the sight of such suffering resignation, awarded him £750 damages, and £213 costs. The money was paid. Soon afterwards it was ascertained that on the Friday before the trial he had, with much agility, climbed over a five-barred gate; and that a few days after the trial he had been at the sea-side, had mounted rocks, had searched for crabs, had bathed, and had taken long walks. On the matter being once more submitted to a judge, he was thought sufficiently recovered to undergo fifteen months' imprisonment for perjury; but the railway company did not recover a penny of its nearly £1,000.

In another case a person who had met with a railway accident on the line of the London and Brighton Company sent in a claim for upwards of £4,000. The medical men called for on either side differed as to the cause of the symptoms from which the claimant was suffering, his medical advisers referring them to the accident, and the gentlemen who examined him on behalf of the company considering them solely due to fatigue subsequently undergone, to an attack of rheumatism, and to mercurial treatment. As to the amount of the claim, there was more agreement in the evidence. It was admitted by the plaintiff that the "loss on forced sale of livery stable business," which he had estimated at £600, was hardly fairly chargeable to the company, inasmuch as he had unsuccessfully attempted the said sale a year before the accident. Again, a claim for £300 for "loss from inability to go to the Continent for purchase of stock" could scarcely be defended in the face of his admission that he had discontinued his business on the Continent for a year and a half. An accountant who had examined into his affairs, found that one part of his business had not suffered, and that the other had improved since the accident. The jury diminished the compensation from £4,000 to £300!

"We would willingly pay," recently remarked a railway authority who has frequently to do with such cases, to the writer, "the uttermost farthing of all the damage we ever do, and five-and-twenty per cent. besides, if we could only be guaranteed against fraud." It is true, on the one hand, that no adequate compensation can be given for some injuries which may involve life-long disability or suffering; it is also true, on the other hand, that no condemnation can be too severe for those who attempt to defraud railway companies by claiming compensation for injuries they have never received.

We will conclude a subject which has both humorous and grave aspects by referring to an American case of compensation. A farmer, we are told, living on the line of the New York Central lost a cow by a collision with a train, and he at once started off to the office of the manager to effect a settlement. "I understand that she was thin and sick," said the manager, after the old man had explained his business. "Makes no difference," replied the farmer doggedly. "She was a cow, and I want pay for her." "How much?" asked the manager laconically. "Two hundred dollars!" returned the farmer. "Now, look here," said the manager kindly, "how much did the cow weigh?" "About four hundred, I suppose," answered the farmer. "And we will say that beef is worth ten cents a pound on the hoof." "It's worth a heap more than that on the cow-catcher!" retorted the old man. "But we'll call it that, what then?" "That makes forty dollars," said the manager quietly. "Shall I give you a cheque for forty dollars?" "I tell you I want two hundred dollars," persisted the old man. "But how do you make the difference?" inquired the manager politely. "I'm willing to pay full value, forty dollars. How do you make the one hundred and sixty dollars?" "Well, sir," replied the old man, rising in wrath, "I want this railroad to understand that I'm going to have something special for the goodwill of that cow!"

It must be allowed that there is a burden upon railway companies of an exceptional and scarcely equitable character. It used to be said by satirists, that an Englishman was always being taxed; that at his birth he was attended by a taxed doctor and laid in a taxed cradle, and that at his death he was carried in a taxed coffin in a taxed hearse to a taxed grave. Modern legislation, however, has been more enlightened. Our fiscal burdens have one after another been removed; locomotion has shared in the general remission, horse duties have been abolished, owners of vehicles have been relieved of charges, and toll-gates have been abolished by hundreds, in order to give a free current to the trade and traffic of town and country. But railways are still taxed through every moment of their being and every mile of their career. The changing policies of Parliament, the costs of law, the claims of the parishes through which they run, and the demands of the imperial exchequer, cause enormous, and often needless, charges to be laid upon the initiation, the construction, and the maintenance of railways. The railway has to pay its full share of local taxation, including the cost of the very highways along which carts and wagons, vans, omnibuses, and tramways, and all sorts of untaxed horses and vehicles, run in competition with itself. "We are taxed," said the Chairman of the Metropolitan District, "upon all our traffic; and yet we have the Thames running parallel with us nearly the whole length of our line, with comparatively no taxes and no maintenance of roads to pay; while we have also to contribute to the maintenance of the road for omnibuses, because since the turnpike trusts have been abolished the charge has come upon the ratepayers."

The local and imperial burdens thus laid upon railways are enormous. The London and Brighton Company, for instance, have during some recent years distributed to their ordinary shareholders the sum of £1,000,000 in dividends, but during the same period they have had to pay in the form of Government duty and taxes of various kinds not less than £670,000; in effect, an income tax of 67 per cent. The North Eastern directors recently complained that these charges levied upon them had greatly augmented. The amount of Government duty, they stated, had increased almost 30 per cent. on the gross passenger returns, equal to about 60 per cent. increase on the net receipts.

"The passenger duty alone," said the Chairman of the Metropolitan District, "is a serious matter for us. It is a matter of one per cent. to the preference shareholders."

By some it has been said that railways are rich, and can afford to be taxed. But if doubts arise whether it is fair even to the strong, what shall we say about the poor and the weak railways, and the impoverished shareholders which such concerns always represent? On the South Devon Railway, for instance, during a recent period of twenty-three years the income has been £644,000, and the amount paid for passenger duty has been £82,000; in other words, the Government received 12½ per cent. of the profits, although the company was able to pay its own shareholders only a 2 per cent. dividend. On the Cornwall line, also, £22,000 were paid under this tax, while the shareholders not only did not receive a farthing in dividend, but had to borrow something like £100,000 to meet their preference charges. "Then," said Mr. Mitchell, "there is the little line of Brixham and Torbay, which was made by a public-spirited individual who wished to give an impetus to the fishing industry on the coast. This result has been realized, but at the price of ruin to the man and his family. This line has never been able to pay either dividend or debenture interest; but the Inland Revenue carries off £50 every year for passenger duty, while the Post-office, with marvellous liberality, hands back £25 a year for carrying the mails five-and-twenty times a week. The reason why the duty is charged appears to be that while the line is 2¼ miles long, the Act of Parliament allows it to be reckoned as three miles, which thus brings up the charge of 3*d.* for a third-class ticket to more than a penny a mile." The magnitude of the injustice thus inflicted will be seen in the fact that there are many millions of railway capital that pay little or no dividend whatever; and yet all these lines are taxed to the amount of 5 per cent. per annum on their passenger receipts.

It is sometimes said that railways are monopolies, and may, therefore, be taxed exceptionally. On the contrary, not only are they in active competition with each other, but also with other rival carriers both on land and water, by coast and canal. This is especially the case in and around the metropolis, where the owners of tramways and omnibuses are not only free from passenger duty, but have had no land to buy for their roads, and have no duty to pay for their horses; and, so far as the omnibuses are concerned, no charges for the repair of the roads they wear out.

If, as Lord Bacon declared, the facilities for travelling in a country may be taken as a touchstone of its civilization, it cannot be sound statesmanship—apart from the inequity of laying upon railways an invidious and onerous liability—to cripple the free and full development of railway enterprise. That the great highways of a country ought to be as free as possible to the trade and traffic of the community is a truth that no one will deny whose lot happens to be cast in the neighbourhood of an impoverished and struggling railway. "Poverty," said Captain Huish, many years ago, and his words are true now, "causes railway companies to run things very fine." Trains are few and slow; accommodation for both passengers and goods is inadequate; fares and rates are high; shabbiness in appearance and in work is conspicuous; rival trades and rival towns on better lines of railway carry off the business of the district; and while the strong thus grow stronger the poor grow poorer. And, as with the district, so with the railway. "I believe that it is the greatest curse to any district," said Mr. Sherriff before the Royal Commission, "to have a railway company that does not pay a fair dividend." "I happen to have been connected with companies," says an eminent civil engineer, "in different phases of prosperity and poverty. In the case of a line that was not paying anything, I have always had the greatest difficulty in getting what was almost an absolute necessity, even to the rolling stock and the permanent way. I recollect having to apply for the relaying of a line which I did not consider safe; and I had it urged upon me whether it might not go on as it was for three months longer. That is drawing the line to the nicest possible degree. Even with reference to the simple question of painting the carriages and having them in a better state, it is always deferred, when you come to a line which is in a bad condition, to the very last moment. I suffered from these anxieties to an extent which it is impossible to describe. . . . But when you get to the next stage of a line—viz., one that is improving—everything looks up, and every application you make is treated in a totally different spirit." And all this, we may add, is not only natural, but inevitable.

The Government is not asked to recur to the policy of the time when Parliament conferred direct benefits upon commercial undertakings; when, for example, £130,000 was granted to put the road between London and Birmingham in such a condition as to enable it to compete with the new railroad, and when the workmen, paid for with Government money, were easing the gradients of a hill through which the railway engineers were tunnelling. But we agree with those who ask that "an act of justice and a great boon to the great body of railway shareholders throughout the kingdom" should be done to those "whose undertakings and profits are taxed heavily in other respects than the passenger duty."

We may here refer to the position of the Railway Commissioners. As far back as 1854, an Act was passed for the settlement of disputes relating to traffic. It was said, with some play of humour, that railway companies had become despots, whose despotism was tempered only by the fear of invasion. Their early history has been one of wars for the command of provinces—their later of amalgamations and agreements for the partition of the spoil. "Within certain limits," it was declared, "the companies were practically omnipotent. They shaped the destiny of a district to their will. Their time-bills were framed to favour one place, and keep down another. They were carriers, dock-owners, hotel-keepers, land speculators at once. They seized upon strategic points, and cut off communications. Their lines seldom worked harmoniously. By preferential rates on goods they made the fortune of one and crushed another. There was, indeed, a remedy at law, but so slow the process, and so difficult was it for the injured to get at the essential facts, that the appeal to justice was rarely ventured."

In all this there was, of course, much exaggeration, but it was at the same time felt that some suitable tribunal should be appointed, which could deal with matters at issue between the public and the companies. Hence the Railway Regulation Act of 1873, and the appointment of the Railway Commission. The Commissioners were to be three, "of whom one shall be of experience in the law, and one of experience in railway business." Their appointment was in the first place for five years, and has since been renewed.

The opinion expressed by the recent Select Committee with respect to the working of the Railway Commission is valuable. "The public approve of the Commission, and express the opinion that its beneficial effect has been much greater than indicated by the number of cases brought before it," whereas the representatives of the railway companies would prefer the jurisdiction of the ordinary courts. Whereupon the Committee remark, that inasmuch as the Railway Commission was established for the purpose of giving the public a more simple and direct control over railway companies, as well as to deal with questions of fact, if the object of appointing the Commission has been attained, "it may be only natural that the result should not be acceptable to the railway companies." They add that no really material change in the constitution of the court has been suggested "other than substantially a return to the jurisdiction of the ordinary courts, which was found so unsatisfactory as to necessitate the constitution of the Railway Commission."

Traders, however, ask that the functions of the Commission should be made more relevant to the public needs. Many witnesses stated that it is not for the interest or pecuniary advantage of almost any trader to take a railway company before the Commission : because of the expense of obtaining redress ; because railway companies are prepared to litigate to an extent which no trader would dare to contemplate ; and, because railway companies have so many opportunities of putting traders to inconvenience and loss by withholding ordinary trade facilities, that traders are afraid of the indirect consequences of taking a railway company into court.

The Committee stated that from the evidence submitted, there was ground for these apprehensions, and that it is to the pecuniary advantage of a trader to submit to overcharges, or to suffer from undue preference to others, rather than to take a railway company before the Commissioners.

The Committee accordingly recommended that a *locus standi* before the special Railway Tribunal should be given to Chambers of Commerce and Agriculture, and to similar associations of traders or agriculturists. The Committee was also of opinion that the establishment of the Railway Commission had been of great public advantage in causing justice to be speedily done in the cases which had been brought before it, in preventing differences from arising as between the railway companies and the public; and also by the deterrent and controlling influence of its mere existence. It accordingly recommended that it should be made a permanent tribunal.

With regard to the charges of railway companies for the carriage of goods, complaints were recently submitted to the Select Committee. It was stated that some rates were higher than the amounts authorized by law, "the authorized rate per mile multiplied by the distance" being taken as constituting the strictly legal charge. To this the companies replied that they were entitled under their special Acts to charge not only for carrying goods from point to point, but for services "incidental to conveyance." When the earlier Railway Acts were passed, it was supposed that the companies would be, like the canal com-

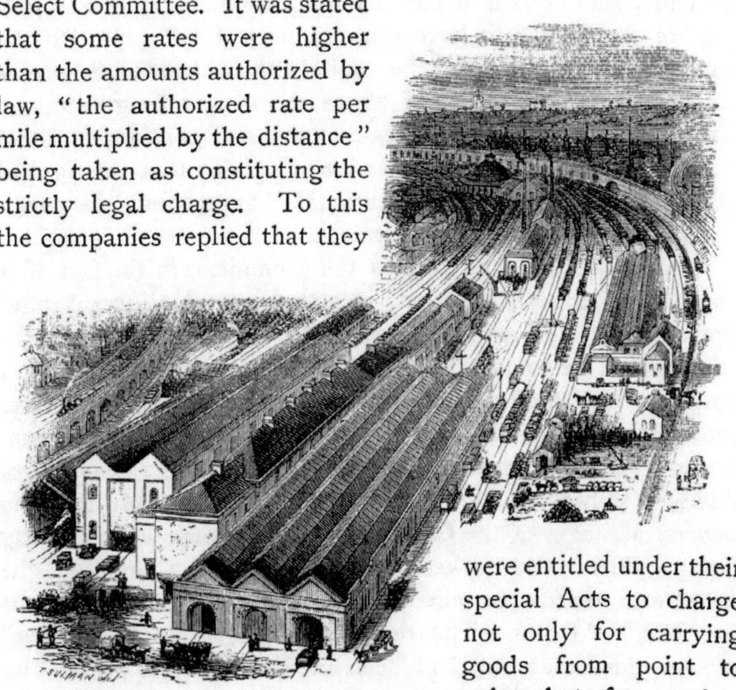

LAWLEY STREET GOODS STATION.

panies, mere owners of the route, and their maximum mileage charges were fixed accordingly. But they soon became carriers, and as carriers they had to undertake new and costly responsibilities. They had to expend capital on "land for stations and roads; on the cost of construction and maintenance of stations, sidings, sheds, platforms, warehouses, cranes, turntables, weighing machines, hydraulic power, fixed appliances, machinery, and other property, and also all the working charges, repairs, renewals, and insurance of station buildings, loading and unloading, clerkage, stores, covering, and other labour of all kinds; shunting by horses and engines, gas, rates and taxes, risk of damage in loading and unloading, and cartages, and all other services incidental to the duty of a carrier." Thus the case was put by Mr. Birt, the General Manager of the Great Eastern; and Mr. Noble, the General Manager of the Midland, subsequently said: "It is a fact that for every mile of line of railway we are obliged to have almost a mile of sidings." On the services thus rendered and the capital thus expended, a reasonable remuneration, over and above the mere mileage rates, is claimed. After hearing witnesses upon, and considering, these matters, the Select Committee were of opinion that the right of railway companies to these additional charges should be recognised in some declaratory enactment.

Another subject submitted to the Committee is the fact that goods are divided into various classes, for which different mileage rates are allowed, and that these vary from 1*d.* to 5*d.* a mile, except for coals. This classification is seriously lacking in simplicity and uniformity, some companies levying their rates under as many as fifty, or even seventy, Acts of Parliament. Nor is it easy to remedy this difficulty, since the rates chargeable by a railway amount to millions in number. Mr. Birt, the General Manager of the Great Eastern Company, when recently giving evidence, was asked, "Can you tell the Committee the lowest rate per ton per mile that you carry any goods upon your line for?" "I cannot," he replied; "we have 6,000,000 rates," and he added that they had been fixed as nearly as possible by what was believed to be the peculiar circumstances of each case. They had grown up gradually, with the view of meeting the wishes and requirements of the public. "So that," he was asked, "you have had to be the judges of 6,000,000 different circumstances?" "You may put it that that is so," he replied; "but, of course, it has been the work of very many years."

On the North British Railway the rates are more than 16,000,000 in number; and on the Midland about 30,000,000. "The way," said Mr. Noble, the General Manager, "in which rates are made, is by consultation between the traders and the railway companies; they have got to the figures at which they now stand after many years' experience. A railway company having ascertained the views and interests of a trader, and what he can afford to pay for the carriage of his goods to a certain market, meets him, if possible. We have a very large staff engaged daily upon the rates." The Select committee were of opinion that the charges made by companies should be entered in the rate book, or should be otherwise publicly notified; and that a revised classification of goods should be made between themselves and the public, so that any trader would be able to ascertain precisely what the company was entitled to demand from him for the transport of his goods.

Another class of complaints made was to the effect that certain places are "preferred" in the matter of rates—are "nursed" by railway companies to the prejudice of other places. Liverpool, for instance, stated that the railways from Barrow, Fleetwood, Holyhead, and other ports—at some of which the companies have docks of their own—carry goods to the inland manufacturing centres at lower rates than those at which they take them from Liverpool. Farmers, said the Committee, complain that imported agricultural produce is given a bounty over home produce, by being carried at a lower rate; that foreign corn and meat are carried from Liverpool to London for less than English corn and meat; that American cattle are conveyed from Glasgow to London for less than Scotch cattle; that cattle landed at Newcastle are carried inland for less than cattle reared in Northumberland and Durham; and that foreign fruit and hops are carried from Boulogne or Flushing to London for less than fruit and hops from Ashford or Sittingbourne. Ironmongers complain that Belgian wire and other goods are brought from Belgium to Birmingham for less than similar goods are charged from Birmingham to London. Bradford complains that the export trade from both Manchester and Bradford enjoys rates which are preferential as compared with those for the home consumption trade. In short, the complaint is frequently heard that railway companies prejudice home producers by low import and export rates.

How, we may ask, do these irregularities come about? and we may answer by stating a fact. Not long ago an ironmaster from the Erewash Valley went into the office of the General Manager of the Midland Railway. "I want," he said, "to tender for a contract for a large quantity of iron. It is for a foreign Government—25,000 tons to be delivered. The Cleveland district and South Wales will also tender, and they are on the sea. We find no fault with your ordinary rate for ordinary quantities; but this is special; and if you can for this large amount give us a special rate, we shall have a chance; otherwise we have none." "When do you want the rate?" was the inquiry. "To send off by to-night's post." The special rate was granted, and the tender was accepted. Now if, as some ask, a uniform and invariable rate were adopted, the only reply that could have been given in this case, and in all similar cases, would have been, "Our rules cannot be relaxed."

If the railways did not adjust their rates, they would lose much of their traffic. Mr. Allport was asked by Lord Derby, then Lord Stanley, if he considered it the duty of a Company "to endeavour so to regulate the trade as to distribute a certain share to each town in such a manner as seems to them just, or if it was not rather their business to take such traffic as might be offered them without asking further questions?" "I think it is the duty of managers of railways," replied Mr. Allport, "to develop the resources of their districts to the utmost possible extent; that is the principle that has influenced me. If I saw an opportunity of developing a trade at Gloucester, so long as the rates left a profit, I should most undoubtedly endeavour to do it, without reference to the rates from Liverpool, or London, or elsewhere; the only question would be whether the rates would leave a profit. I consider it my duty, as manager of the Midland Railway, to develop the resources of the district to the utmost extent that I can." Lord Stanley admitted the force of the proposition as thus put, and said: "So long as you only charge what the law of the land entitles you to charge, no one town or community has a right to complain because you happen, with a view to your own advantage, to charge a lower rate to another."

Even the cost of, and the traffic upon, a railway must be considered in the charges made. "I presume," said Lord Stanley to an advocate of uniform rates, "if one line is made between two great towns, say between Liverpool and Manchester, and if another line is made, say through the Highlands of Scotland, there would be a great deal more traffic on the former line than upon the latter; and where the traffic is greater, and the trains are fuller, it is possible to carry passengers and goods at a cheaper rate?" "Undoubtedly," was the reply. "Do you think," continued his lordship, "that an equal mileage rate in each of these cases would be just?" "No," replied the witness, "I cannot say that it would in that case; as a matter of course, I cannot say it would be." "Then you are not in favour of an uniform mileage rate throughout the kingdom?" "I cannot," he frankly added, "in the way in which your lordship puts it before me, say so."

But railway managers have to consider not only what is reasonable with some special consignment under some special contract, but also other conditions that affect the ordinary trade and traffic between one part of the country and another. Gloucester, for instance, is very inconveniently situated as a port, and the cost of landing goods on the quay at Gloucester is much greater than landing them at Liverpool. If, therefore, the Midland Company were to say to the people at Gloucester, "We shall charge you the same rate that is charged at Liverpool," the trade of Gloucester would at once severely suffer in its competition with Liverpool at many Midland towns, and the Midland Company would suffer too. Again, at first sight, it seems strange that a ton of sugar should be carried 76 miles, from Hull to Sheffield, for less money than 73 miles, from Liverpool to Sheffield. But the difference is accounted for by the fact that there is free water navigation from Hull to within a few miles of Sheffield, that the carriage rates are low by water, and that they must be low by land. To say to the railway company that they are bound to charge between Hull and Sheffield the maximum they charge for a similar distance to any other point, is to tell them that for the future all the work is to be done by the water navigation.

Similarly, there are low rates between Birmingham and Bristol, because there is a cheap navigation up the Severn to

Worcester and Stourport, and a cheap continuous navigation from Bristol to Birmingham.

To put an end to the "inequalities and contrarieties" that now exist by establishing uniformity of rates, according to distance, from everywhere to everywhere, would have the most injurious consequences on trade and on the country at large. Certain already rich districts on the coast would absorb foreign orders, and become overgorged with prosperity, while the staple trades of towns less advantageously situated would dwindle and die. The country, too, would suffer as much as the trade. London could no longer be fed every year with hundreds of tons of meat from Scotland, but must be satisfied with the flocks and herds of the Midland counties; vegetables could not be brought from the far west;* and the metropolis would have to look to the coasting trade and to Derbyshire for its supply of fuel. The producer and consumer alike would suffer; the trade and commerce of the whole country would have to be readjusted, at infinite loss and cost, to the new condition of charges; and the only individuals who would be gratified amid all this national ruin would be the admirers of a theoretical but disastrous uniformity.

Such was the conclusion at which the Select Committee arrived. To have an uniform rate would, they said, put an end to competition. "The result would probably be levelling up, and not levelling down." Parliament would never consent to take the lowest profit which a company now makes by its cheapest traffic as a standard, and fix maximum rates accordingly for all their traffic. Supposing such a standard fixed, the only result would be that the traffic which is now carried at a low rate in competition with a sea route would be driven from the railway to the competing route, whilst the railway, if it is to make as much aggregate profit as before, must charge a higher rate than is now charged on the traffic which remains to it. If, for in-

* "Between November and April in each season inclusive, the markets of London, and other large towns north of Bristol, are supplied from West Cornwall with from 16,000,000 to 20,000,000 of heads of brocoli, weighing about 15,000 tons, and in May, June, and July of each year the same markets are supplied with 12,000 tons of new potatoes. The average price for this season of brocoli in Covent Garden Market would be *7s.* a crate, each crate weighing from $1\frac{1}{2}$ cwt. to $1\frac{3}{4}$ cwt."—Evidence before Select Committee on Railways, 1882.

stance, Parliament were to take from the South Eastern Railway Company the power of charging on fruit and hops from Boulogne the low rate they now charge, the result would be that French fruit and hops would reach London by water. If Parliament were to say that the North Eastern shall make no greater profit on cattle or fish brought from Newcastle to London than they do on that brought from Scotland over the same lines to London, the Scotch goods would go by sea, or would not go at all. Or, again, if the Great Eastern were not allowed to have a cheap long distance to London, the trade of Norfolk and Suffolk in agricultural produce would almost disappear, since London is their market.

Pressed, before the Select Committee, by these difficulties, the proposers of equal mileage admitted that where there is sea competition,—which is the case at about three-fifths of the railway stations of the United Kingdom,—where low rates for long distances will bring a profit, and also where the article is, like coal, a necessary, exceptions must be made. But exceptions, so numerous and great, destroy the value of "equal mileage" as a principle, or the possibility of applying it as a general rule.

CHESTERFORD STATION, EASTERN COUNTIES RAILWAY.

CHAPTER XIV.

Financial Aspects of Railways.—Closing of Capital Accounts.—Enormous Demands on Railway Shareholders.—The Crucial Question.—Dividends on English Railways.—Capital Authorized.—A Profitable Line.—The State Purchase of Railways.—Financial Difficulties.—Increasing Value of Railways.—Captain Tyler's Proposal.—Cost of Purchase.—The Speculator.—Stupendous Financial Problems.—Logical Results.—Political Aspects of the Subject.—Political Pressure.—"Portentous Mischief."—Mr. Gladstone's Opinion.

WE may now turn to some of the financial aspects of railways. On the construction, maintenance, and enlargement of the railways of the United Kingdom £831,000,000 have been spent. The amount is stupendous; moreover, it is constantly increasing; and it has all been provided by private shareholders in a commercial enterprise.

And having done so much, they are compelled to do more. It is impossible for railway companies to stand still. Sometimes at shareholders' meetings the question is asked whether the directors cannot diminish their disbursements—cannot, it has been suggested, "close their capital account." Now what would a closing involve? We read the announcement that a railway company in a week has had an increased traffic above that of the corresponding week of last year of, say, £1,000. A locomotive can earn £100 a week; so it follows that, if this increased average is maintained, ten locomotives are required by that company alone, more than were necessary for its work of the same week of last year. But ten engines would cost some £2,800 each, or £28,000; in other words, £28,000 would have to be raised in capital, and spent on

The initial letter gives a sketch of Saltash Viaduct.

engines alone, in order to draw the mere increase of the traffic of this year; in addition to which there would be all the other expenditure for trucks, vans, sidings, and station accommodation which would necessarily be involved. But the increased amounts thus required by a railway company, even for engine power alone, are sometimes much larger than this. The Midland Company, for instance, has had an increase of £9,000 worth of traffic in a week, demanding an increased engine power costing about a quarter of a million sterling over and above what was sufficient a twelvemonth previously. And if that capital had not been spent on additional engines, and all the accessories consequent thereon had not been provided, the passengers and goods could not have been conveyed: in effect, a distinct public announcement would have gone forth that the existing railway accommodation for those districts was insufficient, and that some competing line would be welcome; an announcement the force of which would have been freely recognised by the first Parliamentary Committee to whom the claims of any new lines were submitted.

The demands made upon the resources of railway shareholders are enormous. A few years since there was a general revival of trade, and the ordinary growth of traffic and the special pressure put upon all the great railway companies was such as to necessitate an immense outlay of capital in the creation of new works. The London and North Western, for example, had to widen their road so as to admit a fourth line of rails for the forty-two miles between Willesden and Bletchley, necessitating an almost continuous series of excavations and embankments, masonry on a gigantic scale, and also two tunnels; and the widened line has since been continued through Northampton to Rugby. "We are spending," said Mr. Moon at the spring meeting of 1875, "*an awful lot of money.* We are," he continued, "spending a million at Liverpool, a large amount upon the Manchester stations, and even the London station is insufficient for the traffic, and we find it impossible to go on year after year giving facilities to the public without spending large sums of money." Similarly the London and South Western spent £500,000 in improving their stations, completing the block system, and for increased rolling stock. The Great Western widened their main line near London. The Lancashire and Yorkshire made a number of branch lines, and completed their block system. The Midland doubled their lines from Trent to Wigston, and from Chesterfield to Clay Cross, opened new lines in Notts and Derbyshire, made 20 miles of additional mineral branches, and meanwhile bore with what fortitude they could command the burden of more than £5,000,000 of unproductive capital on uncompleted works. The London and Brighton shareholders happily emerged, as their chairman expressed it, "from the depth of adversity" to "the position of a line paying a respectable dividend;" but the expenditure of capital during four years increased nearly £40,000 a year.

These enormous outlays were not a matter of choice upon the part of the companies: the traffic of the country compelled them. Complaints, for instance, had been made that the railway accommodation provided by the North Eastern Company was insufficient; and it might have been thought that Mr. Leeman and his board had been doing nothing. On the contrary, during the previous six months the North Eastern had spent on lines in course of construction, new sidings, working stock, engines, carriages, and wagons, nearly a million sterling; and in the course of one year, nearly two millions of money were spent for the better accommodation of traders and traffic. "It is," said Mr. Leeman, "a large expenditure—it is a fearful expenditure—and it is one which one would have thought would have brought a degree of satisfaction that we were, at all events, doing our best to meet the requirements of the district." Yet meanwhile there were complaints everywhere of the insufficiency of the accommodation provided.

In the four years ending June, 1875, twenty of our leading railway companies spent no less than £60,000,000. Of this, £22,000,000 went for improving the lines open for traffic; £12,000,000 for additional rolling stock; and the remaining £26,000,000 in constructing new lines, and in other objects which demanded the expenditure.

The period we have referred to was, no doubt, exceptional, and the rate of expenditure of capital has since diminished; but it still continues, and on an enormous scale. During the period extending from 1871 to 1881, the amount actually raised and expended by the London and North Western Company for additional accommodation, additional rolling stock, new lines, docks, and steamboats, has, in the ten years, been twenty millions. So with other railways. "We find," wrote a high authority on this subject, "that notwithstanding an outlay by railway directors of about twelve millions in the year, the estimates which appeared at the beginning of 1881 had to be exceeded. In other words, the amount wanted at the commencement of last year was *under-estimated* by about seventeen millions."

In the face of these facts it is idle to talk about the closing of railway capital accounts: the crucial, the only question is, not whether the expenditure of capital has gone on, and will go on, but how is it being spent? If to attempt to close the capital account would be to try to fossilize the railway system and the commercial life of the kingdom, we may, on the other hand, find consolation if it can be affirmed that the large expenditure during the last ten years has yielded as good a return to the companies as on their old capital. And this, we think, may be granted; while it is unquestionable that to the community at large the increased accommodation has been an immeasurable boon.

An important financial change has, during late years, been made by the consolidation of the guaranteed and preference stocks of several of our principal railway companies, and the result has proved of great advantage to the companies and to the holders of their stocks. In 1878 the London and North-Western Railway consolidated about fifty such stocks, of which the face or nominal value of the stocks amounted to as much as £94,000,000, exceeding that of any other corporation or joint-stock undertaking. The market value, as compared with the face value, was, however, much higher: the £94,000,000 being worth the enormous sum of more than £130,000,000, the excess being an actual aggregate premium.

Nor let it be forgotten that if the benefits conferred by railways have been vast—enriching every class of the community and making the trade of England the wonder and admiration of the world—the share of profit which railways generally have been permitted to appropriate is sufficiently modest; the capital expended having brought back to its owners only a little more interest than might have been obtained had the money been invested in consols.

During the last year a dividend of less than 1 per cent. has been paid on railway capital in England and Wales to the amount of £3,039,880;

							£
Exceeding	1	and not	exceeding	2	per cent.,	on	12,876,256
"	2	"	"	3	"	"	5,042,765
"	3	"	"	4	"	"	6,727,385
"	4	"	"	5	"	"	26,095,785
"	5	"	"	6	"	"	76,851,776
"	6	"	"	7	"	"	3,086,875
"	7	"	"	8	"	"	58,932,125
"	8	"	"	9	"	"	285,000
"	9	"	"	10	"	"	477,326
"	10	"	"	11	"	"	1,036,272
"	12	"	"	13	"	"	30,000

and 16½ per cent. on the £1,110,000 capital of the Taff Vale.

Some of the principal data touching the mileage, the capital, and the profits of the railways of the United Kingdom may here be given:—

Length of line open for traffic at the end of each year.	Miles.	Number of passengers besides season-ticket holders.
1854	8,053	111,180,165
1864	12,789	229,272,165
1874	16,449	477,840,411
1881	18,175	623,047,787

Capital authorized.	£
1854	368,384,308
1864	520,522,334
1874	704,338,299
1881	831,125,312

Receipts.		£	per cent.
From passenger traffic	1854	10,244,954	50·68
From goods "	"	9,970,770	49·32
From passenger "	1864	15,684,040	46·11
From goods "	"	18,331,524	53·89
From passenger "	1874	24,893,615	42·01
From goods "	"	32,005,883	84·01
From passenger "	1881	27,461,645	40·26
From goods "	"	36,446,592	54·76

We may add that probably the most profitable line in the world is the Marine Railway in Coney Island, the favourite suburban summer resort of New York. It is 2,000 feet in length, has two engines and four cars. It cost, including stations, 27,000 dollars, and it paid for itself a few weeks after it was opened. The expenses are said to be 50 dollars, and the average receipts 450 dollars a day. "The property paid a profit last year of 500 dollars per cent. on its cost."

We may now turn to a subject of great national moment—the proposal that there should be a transference of all railway property and administration from the present owners to the nation itself. The subject is one of the gravest importance. It is not one only for statesmen, or shareholders, or speculators—not one of merely theoretical interest or party politics. Every man who travels or who trades, every one who deals in or consumes the product of the manufactory or the soil or the sea, would be immediately affected, in every transaction of life, by the wise or the unwise solution of this problem. A property of almost incalculable value; interests, private and public, of the greatest magnitude and complexity, are directly involved. The rights of more than three hundred railway companies, of tens of thousands of shareholders, who employ some 400,000 officers and servants, and who receive a revenue of more than £60,000,000—all these claims would have to be adjusted before this vast and now divided property could be consolidated into one undertaking, and placed under the management and guarantee of the State.

Let us, in the first place, consider the subject *financially*.

The staple argument for the ownership of the railways by the State may be put thus:—"Government credit is better than private credit. Railways yield an average profit of about 4 per cent. per annum. Buy them up with money borrowed at about 3 per cent., and there will be a clear gain of 1 per cent. per annum on the transaction."

This estimate appears simple and satisfactory. But, in making it, some considerations have been overlooked and some facts have been ignored which would inevitably disturb the accuracy of the calculation. Let us suppose that the subject engages the attention of the Cabinet, that a Bill is laid before Parliament, and that in due course it becomes the law of the land. Now what are the principles and methods on which the

Government could equitably deal with the several kinds of property which constitute what is commonly described as the capital of a railway company? There is, for instance, the debenture stock, bearing interest on a good line at nearly 4 per cent., and worth rather more than £100. At the present moment the holder of such stock has a perpetual guaranteed dividend; and if the State took possession of this property by compulsory purchase, a smaller amount of interest could not be offered to the owner than that which he has been accustomed to receive. But, if so, a Government guaranteed debenture stock, at 4 per cent., would be worth more than par, if three per cent. consols are, say, at 100; in other words, a bonus would have to be given to debenture stock holders, to the detriment of all other creditors of the Crown. Meanwhile, the theory with which we started—that Government could borrow at about 3 per cent. —would have been compromised. How, too, we may inquire, would the Treasury provide a fair adjustment, under a compulsory scheme, for between thirty and forty different debenture stocks, which stand at different values in the market? Or would all stocks bearing the same interest be lumped together at the same price, the poorest properties being levelled up to the value of the richest?

When these difficulties had been overcome, would not others of a similar nature arise with regard to preference stocks? Of such stocks there are many kinds, some of them bearing a dividend contingent on the profits of the current year, others of which are free from this restriction; and others again are, at certain specified periods, convertible into the ordinary stock of the particular company—stock which may at the present moment be at a premium, at par, or at a discount. All these may have the one general designation of "preference stock," but they are very various in their real and relative values. A preference stock is merely one that is to be "preferred" to the ordinary; unless, therefore, a line is worked at a profit, its preference and its ordinary stock may, for the time being, be, in theory, valueless; and the precise degree of probability that the profits of a railway will yield enough to pay interest on the preference capital, is the measure of the market value of that stock. All these various degrees of probability would have to be considered, in order to estimate the values of the different preference stocks of different companies, before the claims of the owners of such properties could be equitably discharged.

But suppose that some principle were discovered by which these discrepancies were adjusted, by which the diversified claims of debenture holders, preference shareholders, and holders of fixed rents were satisfied, and by which the British public—who would have to pay the bill—was fairly dealt with; how shall the demands of the ordinary shareholder be met? Would it be enough to pay him the present market price of his shares, or their average worth during the last few years? No; because the value of railway property is increasing. "For the last ten years," said Mr. Dudley Baxter, some years ago, "there has been an annual increase of the gross profit of the railways of £2,000,000 sterling; and during the last five years there has been an increase of £1,300,000 a year in the net receipts." "Railways," remarks Captain, now Sir H. W. Tyler, "are an improving property." But, if so, it would not be enough for the State to offer the shareholder the mere present market price of his shares. If the sale of his property were optional, the price of the day would be enough; but what if he does not want to dispose of his property; what if, with the prospects that lie before him, he prefers to retain it, on what terms shall he be compelled to part with it, and to part with it confessedly for the good of other people? Many a shareholder might honestly say: I did not buy these shares, nor have I held them, nor do I keep them, for the interest they yield; but because I have reasonable ground to anticipate that since the construction of railways is limited, and the increase of population is unlimited, traffic will augment, and the profits of conducting that traffic will also augment. Who, for instance, would give £28 for a London, Chatham, and Dover share—a share that pays no interest, that has not paid interest for years, and that may be many years before it pays 5 per cent.—except because he is satisfied that that share will hereafter rise in value, and that then he will receive the reward of his patience? Was it not with the same anticipation—not of actual results, but of prospective profits—that a few years since North British stock, when it paid a dividend of only 12*s.* 6*d.* per £100 share, was worth £62? And even the best shares in the railway market are largely held, not simply for their present value; but because though they are costly to purchase to-day, they may be yet more valuable hereafter.

For the State, therefore, to tell the owner of such a property that he shall be compelled to surrender it to the public for the good of the public, at a price that does not take a full account of the future improvement for the sake of which he has been content with small interest or with no interest on his outlay, would be an injustice so palpable that no English Government would propose it, and no class of English people would sanction it. "Better far if the railways were paid for as the telegraphs were paid for," says a writer, "than incur the social dangers which confiscation would involve." But, if prospective advantages are to be discounted, then an amount will have to be paid to the present owners of the railways of this country greatly in excess of the market price of the day; and what with a clumsy bargainer, with a stupendous transaction, with forced sales, with the payment of cash or its equivalent for future and contingent profits, the account that would have to be discharged would probably exceed the anticipations of the boldest financier.

Some of these considerations came under the notice of the Joint Committee, and the Earl of Derby questioned Captain H. W. Tyler, R.E., Inspecting Officer of the Board of Trade, with regard to them. Assuming, at that time, that the purchase money would amount to only some £500,000,000, the earl asked Captain Tyler if he thought that those who had previously been receiving an average return of 4 or 4½ per cent. would accept a Government 3 per cent. stock in lieu thereof. "No," replied Captain Tyler, "I should not offer such terms." "Then," said the earl, "you would offer them a larger nominal stock than the amount of their present capital?" To this question Captain Tyler replied that he thought it might be undesirable to give "in public" a reply. But, to the further inquiry, whether in his judgment it would be possible "to substitute for the present railway stock, yielding an average of 4½ per cent., a Government stock to the same amount, yielding only 3¼ per cent.," Captain Tyler answered that it did seem "an enormous operation, no doubt;" but he appeared to find relief from the difficulty in the consideration that "when you come to look at it, you are only substituting one for another. You are only giving a man Government paper instead of company's paper for his holding in a particular railway." "Exactly," rejoined the earl; "but you are giving him $3\frac{1}{4}$ per cent. instead of $4\frac{1}{2}$ per cent.; and the success of your operation, as I understand it, depends upon his being willing to accept that change?" To which Captain Tyler assented so far as to say: "You must certainly not give him less than he is receiving at present. He would not take it, and it would not be fair to offer it to him."

Such are some of the preliminary financial problems that have to be considered before any action with regard to the purchase of railways could be contemplated; and by the time they had been equitably adjusted, the amount of the cost of the undertaking will be seen to have largely increased. If Sir R. Blennerhassett, in urging upon Parliament the adoption of the Irish railways, computed their value at twenty-two years' purchase, or £22,963,270, which he said was "an extravagant estimate," and yet candidly allowed that (with a couple of millions more to provide for re-stocking the lines, and for repairs) "the whole thing" would cost the country £30,000,000; if the Marquis of Clanricarde thought it worth while to make a formal application to the holders of Irish railway stock, whether they would be content to part with their property at an advance of 25 per cent. upon its present market value; if "the best authorities calculated that it would take something like £40,000,000, if not more, to buy the Irish lines;" then we leave the reader to estimate what would be the sum required to purchase on similar terms the railway property of the kingdom. No wonder, then, that Mr. Horatio Lloyd, more than ten years ago, estimated the cost of the purchase of such a property at not less than £800,000,000; that Mr. Newmarch, the banker, believed it would reach £1,000,000,000; and that Mr. Allport did not consider that it could be obtained for even that amount. The fact is, as the *Times* said, "We do not know within some hundreds of millions what the actual price might be;" and the *Daily News* truly remarked that "the magnitude of such a measure might well stagger the boldest financier. The cost, we believe, would not be far short of a thousand millions sterling, and the raising and payment of so vast a sum, though it would be substantially a conversion of railway securities into Government debt, would almost convulse Lombard Street, and would certainly require no little delicacy of management." All this was said when (in 1871) the total capital paid up on the railways of the United Kingdom was £552,661,551; this has since increased (in 1881) to £745,528,162; and the market value of our railways was said by Mr. Moon, Chairman of the London and North Western Company, in November, 1882, to be *a thousand millions sterling*.

The stupendous proportions of these financial problems appear sometimes to have staggered even so courageous a gentleman as Captain Tyler. When pressed by the Joint Committee with some of the "difficulties and disturbances" that would arise, he urged that, instead of the State by one supreme effort acquiring the ownership of the plant and powers of the railways of the kingdom, the work might be undertaken piecemeal.* The property of one company might, in the first instance, be purchased; and when the adjacent lines had begun to feel "all the disadvantage of competing with the Government," the State might proceed to buy up other lines "one line after another." But, "do you think it would be possible," inquired Mr. Hunt, "or do you think it would be allowed, that the Government should purchase a line running parallel with another line still left in the hands of a company?" "Yes," replied Captain Tyler; "I think if the Government makes terms with one company and buys it up; if another company felt itself aggrieved, it would come forward and say, 'You are going to do us an injury;' and then the Government might reply, 'Very well, if you think so, we are ready to buy you also on fair terms.'" "Supposing," said Mr. Hunt, "that the State purchased the Midland and worked it for some years, would not that have the effect of depreciating the property of the London and North Western?" "Not," replied Captain Tyler, "unless they worked it at reduced rates and fares, so as to oblige the other company to reduce their rates and fares in proportion." "Supposing," inquired Mr. Hunt, "that the State undertook the working of a railway, there would immediately be a demand on the part of the country that it should be worked to the advantage of the

* Sir H. W. Tyler's piecemeal plan reminds us of the gamekeeper who, wishing to reduce the proportions of his dog's tail, arrived at the conclusion that so severe an operation ought not to be performed all at once; and accordingly decided to get over the difficulty by what he considered the more humane method of cutting the tail off—*a joint at a time!*

public, and not to the profit of the Government or the State; would there not?" "Yes," said Captain Tyler, "clearly that would be the only object of the Government taking the railways." "Then," continued Mr. Hunt, "there would necessarily almost be a reduction in the rates and fares on the part of the Government?" "Yes; that would be so." "If that were so, the property of a competing company would be depreciated?" "Clearly," returned Captain Tyler. "Would it not be unfair to allow the Government to purchase that competing line, and to depreciate by means of its operations the property of the other company, and then to purchase it when they had depreciated it?" "I think," said Captain Tyler, "that it would be an unfair course for the Government to pursue, unquestionably, to go and buy up one line for the purpose of competing with others and bringing the price of their property down; but I do not think it would be unfair if it were done in a proper way, and if the Government were to offer both competing lines fair terms, and then to say, 'Well, if you will not accept fair terms, we will buy up only one line instead of both, and you must take the result.'" We must leave Captain Tyler to resolve the interesting problem of how what he admits to be "unquestionably" an "unfair course," would be made quite fair "*if it were done in a proper way!*"

We have thus far been considering the terms on which we have supposed that a bargain might be made between the Crown and the present owners of railway property. But there is another person, whose presence we have hitherto ignored, who would watch with eager interest every step in these proceedings, who would even anticipate every turn of events, and who, with astute calculation, adroit manipulation, and daring enterprise, would endeavour to turn every incident to the furtherance of his private advantage. We refer to the speculator. There is not a circumstance, from the first rumour of the intention of the Government down to the payment of the last pound to the last shareholder, in which, regardless of every interest but his own, he would not concern himself. Tens of thousands, too, who had never speculated before, would rush in to gamble for a part of the stupendous prize. No sooner was the earliest whisper heard that the State would perhaps purchase the telegraph companies, than the shares rose enormously in price; and mere priority of information, with regard to the progress of the negotiations, enabled men who previously never held a share, to make vast fortunes in a few weeks.* If, not long ago, a forged telegram, that the Sheffield Company was about to be absorbed into the Midland, led, in a few hours, to speculation in Sheffield stock to the extent of millions sterling, what would be the condition of the Stock Exchange when a thousand millions of money had become the football of gamblers? Is it, also, too much to say that at such a time, a little earlier private intelligence with regard to the development of affairs might be worth to the fortunate receiver of it—*millions!* Every change in that series of events would be discounted and speculated about on every Stock Exchange in England, and perhaps in the world. Property of enormous value would change hands. Capital to a yet more enormous sum would have to be created, or liabilities to a like amount would have to be incurred; the national debt of this country would stand at not less than £2,000,000,000 sterling; and even if, in the direction of so stupendous a transaction, every official were incorruptible in integrity, and inviolable in secrecy, nobody would believe it. The moral sense of the community would receive a shock from which it might never recover.

Let us imagine, however, that, as by the stroke of an enchanter's wand, all these difficulties are overcome. The bill, whatever it may be, is paid, and the State has possession of all the railways in the land. But if the Government is for the future to regulate the traffic of the country, would it be able to do this unless it controlled not only the railroads but the other great highways of the nation's commerce? When the Government undertook the charge of either the postal or the telegraphic

* Startling facts bearing on this subject have transpired, at which Mr. Allport hinted in a speech before the Statistical Society. "What," he asked, "did the Government do in the case of the telegraphs? They gave thirty years' purchase on the enhanced price of a property *which the sellers had not in their possession.* In the case of the Midland Company, for instance, the greater part of the wires and instruments belonged to the Company, which had an agreement with the Electric Telegraph Company expiring about the end of 1873 or the beginning of 1874. The Government gave the Telegraph Company thirty years' purchase; but the Government has yet to buy what belongs to the Midland Company, and an arbitration as to the amount to be paid is now pending."

business, it insisted on a monopoly: would it be possible to conduct public traffic in some directions without doing so in all directions—to control it in some ways without doing it in every way? There are great navigations that are worked in daily and direct connection or competition with the railroads: could any uniformity of system be devised on the land, if the conditions were constantly liable to be disturbed by the traffic on the water? In fact, would it not be inevitable that, if the Government took into its hands what Sir R. Blennerhassett calls "the great iron highway of modern civilization," it must also have possession of those great water highways which intersect these islands and wash their shores?

To this subject the attention of the Joint Committee was directed; and this problem was presented for the solution of a witness who may be presumed to be well qualified to deal with it, and who answered the questions proposed to him with, on the whole, a commendable consistency. Sir William Wright, chairman of the Hull Docks Company, admitted that the canals belonging to the railway companies should also be purchased by the State. But, it was asked, if the proprietors of other canals wished to dispose of their property to the Government, or if it were thought necessary, in order to regulate traffic rates, that control should be obtained over those navigations, should they not be purchased by the State? And Sir William gave an affirmative reply. But if the Government went thus far, must it not go farther? Mr. Childers pressed these inquiries, and obtained answers which indicate the goal to which State control of railways appears logically and inevitably to conduct. "Suppose," he said, "that railways and canals were placed under the Crown, ought not the docks—which are intimately connected with railways—to be similarly dealt with?" and the case of Hull, with which Sir William was connected, was cited. "I should," he replied, "have no objection whatever." "You are aware," continued Mr. Childers, "that some railways have also lines of steamers; should those steamers be purchased by the Government?" "I think," was the answer, "if they belong to the lines of railway they must follow;" and eventually he admitted that the docks at Fleetwood, Liverpool, and even London, must be included in the same category, and be purchased and amalgamated under Government control, along with the carrying trade and agencies connected therewith. But if railways are to be appropriated by the State, ought not the tramways and the small-gauge lines that have been contemplated, and the omnibuses, to be placed under the same control? "I do not know," said Sir William, deprecatorily, "that it is necessary to go down so low as that; but if you could not get omnibuses, you would have to provide them at the cost of the State." "You think it would be a public convenience that the omnibus system, the cartage system, the tramway system, and other proposed cheap systems of communication also, should all come under the control of the State?" And the emphatic answer was, "I do, decidedly." Broadly, he expressed his belief that "the carrying trade generally should be in the hands of the Government;" and with some qualification, he added, "both by land and by sea." He was asked whether "all the internal carrying trade, and all the foreign carrying trade, which either is in connection with railway companies, or which would not be established by private enterprise without that connection, should be in the hands of the State;" and his answer was "Yes." Under favourable circumstances he saw no objection to the State being the owner both of the home and of the foreign steam carrying trade; for, he added, "wherever the steamers which are absolutely required for the conveyance of traffic are not already in existence, I think the State ought to have the alternative of placing them there."

The consistency of Sir William's position we do not deny; but our readers will admit that by the time the State had undertaken these responsibilities—railways, tramways, canals, docks, home and foreign steam carrying trade—or even any considerable part of them, the estimate of the capital that had to be paid by the State for their purchase would have passed out of the region of arithmetic into that of imagination.

Having dealt with the subject in some of its financial bearings, we might, in the second place, look at various *effects that would be likely to flow* from the substitution of Governmental for private administration; but we will refer to only one or two. Would there not, as Mr. Hugh Mason suggests, be "great danger of an entire absence of that elasticity which characterizes the present management of railway property? In other words, before the public could get relief from any particular grievance, there would have to be unrolled an enormous quantity of red tape. There would be the laying down of hard and fast lines for the government of railways, which would be found incompatible with the ebbs and flows of railway traffic." Again, would an English Government be willing, after all ordinary questions of the patronage and promotion of their men had been determined, to come into contact with Trades' Unions, and to deal practically with the constant agitation going on among all classes of railway servants for shorter hours of duty and higher pay? The free warehousing of goods, clearing and shipping at the ports, long credits, and other kindred problems would have to be considered, and would probably end in the withdrawal of existing facilities, and in the introduction of all the other objectionable modes of dealing with goods traffic which are found to prevail in France, Belgium, and Germany. Would it, too, be prudent "to allow a system of private lines to grow up that might form a nucleus of larger undertakings which must either enter into competition with State railways, or be bought up hereafter? There is more than one instance on record of a combination of colliery owners constructing railways and docks in competition with existing lines, and doing it successfully. Would this be allowed or not?" These and many other problems would have to be solved before it could be shown to be advantageous for the State to undertake the administration of our railways.

But thirdly, we may refer to the bearings of this subject *politically*.

We will take, for example, the proposal to purchase the railways of Ireland, and that the Government had consented. Suppose that the State had become the common carrier of that country; and that it was now the largest employer of labour in Ireland. "Does anybody believe," asked the *Daily News*, "that it would be good either for Ireland or the Government that ministers should have a whole army of railway officials in their employment? Again, as soon as it had assumed the management of the railways of Ireland, the Government would be regarded as responsible for the prosperity of every undertaking which is in any degree dependent on railway locomotion. Ireland has many mines and other undertakings, the success of which is a simple question of carriage. Imagine a Government being told, at a time when the price of ore or any other produce falls in the market, and profits are ready to vanish, that the alternative of the continued employment or discharge of bodies of men depends on its resolution." As Sir Francis Goldsmid has said, "the lowering of the rates would become a hustings cry."

And if anything like this were true—and true it would be on even a much larger scale with regard to the railways of Eng land and Scotland—would it be possible to administer so vas a machinery witnout some contingencies arising that would affect the theory and practice of constitutional government itself? "How many supply nights," naïvely inquired Lord Redesdale, "do you suppose would be required for railway business?" And would there be no danger of the conduct of the traffic and trade of the kingdom being affected by political and party influences? If a certain amount of political pressure could secure to a population, however scanty, and to a region, however barren, the enormous benefits of railway communication —the sale of land at an enhanced price, the augmented value of every building and every acre near which the line would pass, the vast outlay of capital in the construction of works, the means of conveyance of agricultural produce, of goods, of minerals, not to say of passengers—surely every part of the country would assert its claim, and would press that claim with an importunity and persistency which it might be hard, or even impossible, to resist.

Similarly, even the minor matters affecting local accommodation might become the parents of political agitation. "Every town in the country," said the Earl of Derby to Captain Tyler, "would come to the Government to ask a favour, which might be granted or refused at the option of Government." Captain Tyler, shrinking from the word "favour," replied: "I do not think they would ask 'favours'; but the department which managed the railways would see what extensions were required from time to time, and would carry them on as a matter of necessity, not as a matter of favour." "But I presume," rejoined the earl, "that it would be a matter of 'disfavour' if the traffic in one place were not accommodated as well as in another. You cannot lay down any such self-acting rules as would exclude the discretion of the executive." "The question of political pressure," Captain Tyler eventually admitted, "is perhaps the greatest difficulty in the way of State purchase." "All Governments," Professor Fawcett has said, "tried to strengthen their position by patronage; and the more patronage a Government has to bestow, the more will pecuniary and political corruption flourish."

With sound political sagacity, Mr. Hugh Mason, President of the Manchester Chamber of Commerce, has declared that he "viewed with uneasiness the slightest prospect of the Government of the country obtaining the vast amount of political power and patronage which would necessarily follow the acquisition of railways by the State." Even Mr. Biddulph Martin allowed, "that the habit of relying on co-operation either in the shape of limited partnership or Government aid is a most enervating and pernicious national habit;" and the *Times* declared that "the consequences of placing so vast an amount of patronage in the hands of the ministry of the day would be almost incalculable."

By the State-ownership of the railways every tradesman and every traveller would be brought, in all his transactions, into what Sir Edward Watkin has characterized as "a compulsory partnership with the State. Every day the railway service is becoming more and more an integral portion of almost every action or transaction of our lives; and therefore to arm the State with the power of regulating the whole movement of the population, the whole carriage of goods, and all the varied transactions which railways involve, is just to say to every man who is a manufacturer, or to every man who moves about, that he must from that day forward be a partner with the State. What is the State? In this free country it simply means the party government of the day; and the moment you give the control of this vast system of carrying to the State, you practically hand over the management of railways to party government."

"It had been held in Manchester as a cardinal principle," said Mr. Mitchell Henry, M.P., "that the prosperity of the country must depend upon individual enterprise, and as a Manchester man he should be ashamed if it were possible that they should desire the Government to acquire the railways, in order to their greater success." Similarly, Mr. Hugh Mason thought that the country owed an immense amount of its prosperity to the enterprise, skill, and wisdom with which our great railway system had been brought to its present state of perfection; and he was very much afraid that if railways were thrown into the hands of the State, "we should have a much worse master to deal with than with a board of directors." Mr. Chadwick also declared that he "dreaded anything in the shape of Government interference with the industry or the commercial operations of this country;" and the *Times* deprecated "all the portentous mischiefs of commercial enterprise on so colossal a scale conducted by the State."

We trust that "our transit and our traffic, like our liberties, will remain free and independent of Government and State control; that this nation will refuse to rest on the rotten support which all Government assistance to commercial undertakings in reality is;" and that, like the Manchester Chamber of Commerce, we shall "view with disfavour, both on economic and political grounds, the project of the purchase and working of railways by the State." "It is the business of a Government," Mr. Gladstone has said, "not to trade, but to govern."

CHEE VALE TUNNELS.

CHAPTER XV.

Continental Railways.—Belgian Railways.—Railways in France.—Railway up Vesuvius.—Spanish Railways.—Railways in India.—American Railways.

SOME attention might now be given to the progress of railway construction and the conduct of railway administration in other lands; and many a strange tale and many a startling fact might be told thereon. A few brief glances must, however, suffice.

The successful results of railway locomotion in England quickly attracted the attention of various parts of Europe. Belgium was the first of the continental nations to avail herself of the new agency. Political, as well as social and general considerations, led to the establishment of a system of railways in which great skill in design and energy in execution were developed.

The first proposal was that two trunk lines should be made, which, with some secondary lines, were 347 miles in length. The project was at once adopted by the legislature; the necessary enactment was passed on the 1st of May, 1834; and it was undertaken as a national work, to be carried on under national management.

The railways of France may be regarded as national enterprises. Private energy and resource in that country are inferior to those of England; and though special encouragements were given for the undertaking of railways by the people, they were inadequate, and the French companies stand in the relation of tenants or lessees of lines which the State principally made.

The initial letter gives a view of part of the Righi railway.

Continental railways have peculiarities unknown in this country, which appear strange, and are sometimes annoying, to Mr. Bull. In England, the traveller goes to the station when he pleases; lounges in the waiting-room, eats and drinks when he pleases; wanders about the platform, and superintends his luggage as he pleases; and, in fact, so long as he does not interfere with the convenience of other people, and does not violate the "bye-laws" of the company, he may do what he likes. In France, instead of the traveller managing himself, he is managed. On procuring his ticket, he delivers up his luggage, is marched into a waiting-room, according to the class of his fare; as if the company were afraid that, having paid his money, he should not have his ride. When the train is ready, the first-class passengers are liberated, and every one scrambles to his seat with as much agility as circumstances will admit; and then the second-class and the third are allowed to follow.

THE CARRIAGE.

We pass by those modern wonders of European railways—the Righi incline, the Mont Cenis and St. Gothard tunnels (to which we have already referred at length), but must mention the railway up Vesuvius. At the foot of the cone, on the west side of the mountain, stands the new station of the railway, which ascends to the summit of the old crater. The constructors of the railway have adopted the American double iron rope system. There are two lines of rails, each provided with a carriage divided into two compartments, and capable of holding six persons. While one carriage goes up the other comes down, thus economizing the steam of the stationary traction engine. The incline is extremely steep, commencing at 40 degrees, increasing to 63 degrees, and continuing at 50 degrees to the summit.

The railway is protected against possible flows of lava by an enormous wall. The ascent occupies seven or eight minutes. A supply of water is preserved in large covered cisterns, which in winter are filled with the snow that often falls heavily on Vesuvius. A writer says that at every step one feels the proximity of the great storehouse of heat. Great pillars of smoke frequently burst up from the ground, close to the spot where the railroad ends, and great chasms open, swallowing up anything which may be on the spot, so that the expedition may sometimes not be wholly free from danger. The view from the summit repays all the trouble taken and the risk incurred.

THE RAILWAY UP VESUVIUS.

In many parts of Spain there are great difficulties in the formation of any considerable scheme of railways. Leaving out of sight the fact that Spain has never yet been able to construct even a sufficient number of common roads and canals for her poor and passive trade, the geological formation of the country presents serious obstacles to engineering skill. Spain is a land of mountains, which wall off one district from another. The mighty cloud-capped Sierras are masses of hard rock, and tunnelling, if attempted, would be requisite on a scale which would reduce that of Box or Kilsby to the delving of the poor mole. Spain, again, is a land where travellers are occasionally attacked by brigands; by whom, during the Carlist times, expresses were run off the line, railway men were murdered, and against whom the passengers and their escorts of soldiers had to barricade themselves in houses till assistance arrived. One travels in a "stiff, straight-backed, narrow-seated first-class carriage," through what seems to be "a death-stricken, God-forsaken, irreclaimable solitude," where the absence of present life is enhanced by the vestiges of a former greatness visible in the lofty aqueducts, temples, and theatres, such as those that cumber the ground for miles around the Merida railway station.

Some time ago a German authority calculated that the railways of Europe were upwards of 70,000 miles in length, and that they had 60,000 bridges and 40 miles of tunnel; that some 20,000 locomotives were employed; and that the engines and vehicles might be formed into a train that would reach from St. Petersburg to Paris.

Our dwindling space forbids us to dwell upon the revolutions that railways have effected in India. "There," says a traveller, "it used to take a man three months to ascend the Ganges from Calcutta to Cawnpore, a distance I have now travelled by rail in about six-and-thirty hours." There it is now customary to telegraph ahead how many guests are coming to dine at the next refreshment station; and there (such are the refinements of civilization) the once easy-going Bengalees, who were well content to travel at the rate of four miles an hour, now "write to the papers" to complain of want of speed and punctuality on the railways.

The wonders of American lines might well form a delightful volume. Railways have created new cities in the East, and have surprised, if they have not always gladdened, the solitudes of the Far West. A border newspaper tells us—and we receive the narrative according to the measure of faith—that on the Union Pacific road, not long ago, a Kickapoo Indian saw a locomotive coming down the track at the rate of forty miles an hour. He thought it was an imported breed of buffalo, and was anxious to secure one. So he fastened one end of his lasso to his waist-belt, and, when the engine got near enough he threw the noose nicely over the smoke-stack. The locomotive did not stop; but the engineer and fireman witnessed the most

LEWISTOWN NARROWS.

successful attempt to do the flying trapeze made by any Kickapoo Indian upon the plains. Subsequently, near a hamlet further on the line, a small piece of copper-coloured meat tied to a string was found, and was duly enclosed in a sardine box, and interred.

The appearance of many American railways is very different from that of our English lines. As he travels along, an Englishman opens his eyes to find the greater part of the line entirely open, and unprotected on both sides. There is no embankment or fence to prevent children or cows from wandering on to it. "The train dashes fearlessly through villages and towns, cutting the streets at right angles, and if people get in its way, why, they must take the consequences, and do duty as an awful example for others." "Mile after mile," said Charles Dickens in his time, and in some districts the facts are the same to-day, "we pass stunted trees, some hewn down by the axe, some blown down by the wind, some half fallen and resting on their neighbours, some mere logs half hidden in the swamp, others moulded away to spongy chips. The very soil of the earth is made up of minute fragments such as these ; each pool of stagnant water has its crust of vegetable rottenness ; on every side there are the boughs, and trunks, and stumps of trees, in every possible stage of decay, decomposition, and neglect. Now you emerge for a few brief minutes on an open country, glittering with some bright lake or pool, broad as many an English river, but so small here that it scarcely has a name ; now catch hasty glimpses of a distant town, with its clean, white houses, and their cool piazzas, its prim New England church and school-house ; when, whir-r-r-r ! almost before you have seen them, comes the same dark scene : the stunted trees, the stumps, the logs, the stagnant water—all so like the last, that you seem to have been transported back again by magic." On, still on, the train advances, traversing roads where there are no gates, policemen, nor signals —nothing but a rough wooden arch, on which is painted the important "Notice.—When the bell rings, look out for the locomotive."

The roughness of the American railroad sometimes leads to contingencies more or less pleasant. A traveller tells us that he had proceeded the greater part of the journey smoothly enough, but when within about ten miles of his destination, a violent jolt apprised the passengers that they had run against something. The engine-driver slackened speed; and, on the stoppage of the train, it was discovered that a cow had trespassed on the line. "Sure out," said the driver, as soon as he had satisfied his curiosity. "You seem familiar with such accidents," observed the traveller; "are they frequent?" "Now and then of a night," said he, "we do run agin somethin' of the kind, but they ginirally manage to get the worst on't." "But do they never throw you off the rail?" "They seem to take a pleasure in doin' it when they find us without the cow-ketcher," he replied.

That veracious historian, Artemus Ward, implies that the mechanical arrangements of American trains are sometimes defective. "I was," he says, "on a slow California train, and I went to the conductor and suggested that the cow-ketcher was on the wrong end of the train; for I said, 'You will never overtake a cow, you know; but if you'd put it on the other end it might be useful, for now there's nothin' on earth to hinder a cow from walkin' right in and bitin' the folks!'"

In the American world of locomotion, novelties and wonders never cease. It is a land where we travel by "track" instead of line, by "car" instead of carriage, from "depôts" instead of stations, attended by "baggage cars" instead of luggage vans; where mountains, 8,000 feet above the sea level, are climbed by Pullman cars, in which as luxurious a meal is served as can be provided by a first-class hotel; a country in which occasionally "railway highwaymen" are found who remove a rail, pour in a volley of bullets, ransack the dollars from the "express safe," cut open the mail bags, and ride off across the prairie with their booty; where "elevated railways" pass over the crowded streets of cities, and run in keen competition with the tramway cars beneath; where strikes of workmen have been celebrated on the largest and fiercest scale, petroleum cars have been fired, train after train destroyed, and the populations of cities have been thrown into paroxysms of terror; where new lines are laid down at the rate of fifteen miles a day and of 5,000 a year; where there are already 100,000 miles of railroad, and where it is expected that in 1884 there will be 140,000 miles; where railway "rings" and "corners" have been carried out by daring and unscrupulous speculators, "utterly and shamelessly," and where "the intrigues, conspiracies, and pernicious influence of Wall Street debauch the moral sense of the community, and convert the most solemn processes of justice into the weapons of a mere personal contest of the lowest kind;"—a land where the dull monotony of meetings of railway shareholders is sometimes diversified by "a struggle for the possession of the records," when "coats are torn, hair is pulled, windows are broken, pictures pulled down and envelope the combatants, when seats and benches are broken, and personal encounters take place."

CONESTOGA BRIDGE,
ON THE PENNSYLVANIA RAILROAD.

CHAPTER XVI.

Railway Revolutions.—Increased Comfort and Convenience of our Locomotion.—English Locomotion Fifty Years Ago.—Wealth-creating Power of Railways.—New Industries brought into Existence.—Improvements in Country Towns and Country Life.—Lowestoft and Harwich.—Crewe and Swindon.—Railway Companies as Landowners.—Increased Value of Land in Scotland through Railways.—Residential Area of London Enlarged by Railways.—Diminished Cost of Locomotion.—Numbers of Passengers who Travel by Railway.—Goods and Mineral Traffic.—Conclusion.

THE opinion has been expressed by Mr. Bright that railways have rendered more services and have received less gratitude than any other institution in the land. It is somewhat difficult to account for the asperity of the tone in which railway administration is criticised. A letter in a newspaper that frankly expressed thankfulness for a new benefit conferred by a railway would be almost a novelty; an acrimonious complaint from a correspondent—whose sharp-nibbed pen has been dipped in ink of which the principal ingredient is gall—is more common. Whether this is to be attributed to a general belief that railway "boards" are wooden, and therefore incapable of feeling; or that, being "corporations," they have, as Sidney Smith said, neither a body to be kicked nor a soul to be lost; or that, as "monopolies," they ought to excite in every properly constituted British mind a feeling akin to that which inspires an orthodox British bull at the sight of a red rag, we

The initial letter is from a sketch of the embankment of the London and North Western line as it approaches Lancaster from the south.

cannot tell. But the fact remains that a railway, from the very commencement of its career, has to fight for its life against landlords and lessees, who charge and surcharge it; against lawyers and jurymen, who mulct it; and against speculators, who toss it with their horns into the air, and then tread it with their hoofs into the mire.

In a tone thus adverse much was recently said about "Railway Revolutions." The decision of the Midland Company that third-class carriages should be attached to all trains was said to be "a revolution." When, by the same board, the first-class fares were lowered to the amount that had been charged for second-class, we were assured that this was "a financial revolution." To permit the second-class passenger to encroach upon what had previously been the exclusive privileges of the first-class, was angrily affirmed to be not only a mingling in hopeless confusion of classes of carriages, but of classes of society—"a democratic and social revolution."

Now, of course, when we have stigmatized anything as "revolutionary," it is enough. There is nothing left to be said or done. Argument would be irrelevant, and declamation only idle air. Every well-constituted British mind shrinks with moral loathing from "revolution." The French Revolution, which happened a good way off and a long while ago, was bad enough; but to have a revolution in our midst, though it be only a railway revolution, must, it is implied, involve calamities, not perhaps so conspicuous, but possibly, on that account, all the more dangerous. To reduce our railway fares, to cushion all our carriages, and to ask second and first-class passengers to travel together and behave themselves well—all this may, in the judgment of some, have constituted a revolution; yet we venture to think that there are other revolutions—economical, social, political, and international, revolutions in every department of business, in every rank of society, and in every relationship of life—which railways have already wrought out, even in England, more mighty and more minute than perhaps have been generally supposed. At some of these, laying aside our humour, we propose to look. In doing so we will notice, first, the revolution that railways have effected in *the comfort and convenience of our locomotion.*

Let us endeavour to picture to ourselves what the means of

communication were in England before the introduction of railways. We will not go back so far as the time of Sir Walter Scott, when he solemnly deprecated any use of that then modern innovation, a gig. "On no account," he says to his son, "keep a gig. You know of old how I detest that mania of driving wheelbarrows up and down, when a man has a handsome horse and can ride him. They are childish and expensive things, and in my opinion are only fit for English bagmen; therefore, gig it not, I pray you." We will simply look back to less than fifty years ago.

Here the surprising fact confronts us how "very modern" are all our skilled industries. English engineering itself is only about a century old; and all our most powerful, widespread, and facile means of locomotion—the very breath of the life of trade and commerce—and all the magnitude and multitude of the issues that flow therefrom, are the creation of less than half a century. We listen almost with incredulity to men still living who tell us how when they went on a business journey they were wont to put their money in their purse, to mount their horse, and to ride fifty or a hundred miles to a market or a fair, although the gold in their pocket and the goods in their saddle-bags did chafe them a little; how hosiery sent from Leicester into some parts of that county were conveyed in panniers on the backs of donkeys; and how, when the roads in certain districts were sufficiently improved to allow a cart to pass, the new facilities for business thus created amounted to almost a revolution.

It was not till the 30th of May, 1839, that the Midland Counties Railway was opened. Till then the only modes of conveyance were three: the canal, the fly wagon, and the coach; and the charges made were proportionate to the speed. Only three coaches ran daily each way from Leicester to Nottingham, in addition to those that passed to and from more distant points, and on which little reliance could be placed by local travellers. So with goods. Wool required two days to travel the fifteen miles between Leicester and Market Harborough, a special price being charged because the distance was "so short, and the traffic so unimportant." It frequently happened also that conveyances were unable to carry the quantity of goods offered. A woolstapler stated, in evidence, that he frequently had from 200 to 500 bags of wool lying at Bristol, which could not be brought forward by land, and he had to divide the bulk and send it by different routes; that which went by road occupied from seven to ten days in the transit, and that by water from three weeks to a month. Further west, the difficulties increased, so that goods from Plymouth had to come by sea to London, and were not unfrequently a great length of time on the voyage and the land journey, and often arrived in a wet and damaged condition. Such was the condition of affairs when the new era was inaugurated in 1839; and stupendous have been the revolutions that have since been silently and peacefully accomplished.

One of the most remarkable of these is the wealth-creating power of railways. In their construction in the United Kingdom no less a sum than £831,000,000 of capital have been authorized by Parliament, and £745,000,000 have been paid up. It may be true that some of these railways "do not pay," in the sense that they do not give a reasonable dividend, or, in some cases, any dividend at all, to the shareholders who have provided the capital; but the poorest line that runs in the poorest district is of value to the trade and to the people among whom it passes. The construction of every mile of every railway—unlike money lavished in war—has at almost every stage enriched somebody, has enriched the nation and the world. Wealth employed on armies and fleets, or squandered in the destruction of life or property, or wasted in the luxuries of despotic rulers, is unproductive. Not so with railways, every pound of which honestly spent, in due time yields a reward. The navvy "who receives his wages for building up embankments, forming cuttings, driving tunnels, or preparing the surface of the railways;—the men who are employed on the permanent way, and who keep the ballast and the rails in order;—the pointsmen and the signalmen, whose duty it is to watch over the running of the trains;—the drivers, the guards, the porters, and the station-masters,—these all expend the wages which they receive in the purchase of the necessaries, and, in not a few instances, what but a short time since would have been regarded as the luxuries, of life. The producer of the goods thus distributed makes his profit on their production, and in his turn secures a share of the money which the working of the railway system causes to be circulated throughout the country. In like manner the coal-owner or the ironmaster who supplies the coal and iron, the various manufacturers who build the rolling stock; each in his turn realizes profits and accumulates some fraction of the great total of national wealth. The profits thus realized become in their turn invested in reproductive works."

In the early days of railways those who watched the coming events anticipated that the great centres of population would grow to immense proportions and would overshadow the whole of the smaller towns. Small towns on the lines of railway, it was thought, would be bodily carried to London, or Liverpool, or Manchester; their shops would be deserted, their manufactories transferred, and the grass would grow in their streets. These results have only in small part been realized; and, on the other hand, railway enterprise has not only brought about the enlargement and enrichment of innumerable towns: it has led to the actual creation of several. When the Stockton and Darlington line was opened, the Corporation welcomed the railway to their port, but it acted in so short-sighted a manner with regard to the accommodation it provided for the traffic brought, that the company resolved to provide for themselves elsewhere. A few miles below Stockton, on the mudbanks of the river, stood, among green fields, a solitary farmhouse; here 500 acres of land were purchased; here staiths and other conveniences for the shipment of coal were erected; and here, as if by magic, the great town of Middlesbrough, "a land whose stones are iron," arose,—the "youngest born town," as Mr. Gladstone called it some years ago, of Britain. All along that line, too, new populations arose: Bishop Auckland became threefold what it was; from one farmhouse, Wilton Park became a little town; Shildon, called by an engineer the "hospital of the locomotive," received from its patient a new life for itself; the little linen-weaving and Quaker town of Darlington started upon a new career. Eastwards is "Urby Nook, where bibulous coach-drivers in the line's early days stopped to gain refreshment for man and beast; Preston, where 'Mr. Fowler's covers' were of yore a snare to the drivers; Redcar, away to the east, became rejuvenescent; Marske, the home of the workers in one of the largest iron mines in the world, Saltburn has given name to a bathing-place of note, and Lofthouse has found a newer treasure than its 'alum stored,'"—here are towns which, the other day, were mining villages. Other and allied trades have felt the impulse: lead mining is in the Durham dales; shipbuilding on the Tees; chemical factories and woollen mills are on and near the Skerne; coke-ovens to the north-west of the county, each and all have fresh life-blood coursing through their veins. Railways have revolutionized the populations of wide districts of England; and especially so in the north—"birthplace of railway and locomotive."

The improvement made in the position of a town may be great even through the diversion of a railway. "You have done a great thing," said a gentleman to the Chairman of the Midland Company as they stood together on the down platform of the Nottingham station, alongside one of the new London and North expresses, on the 1st of July, 1880: "You have for the first time placed Nottingham, with its 200,000 inhabitants, on the main line of the Midland system." For on that day Nottingham rose to a new dignity and entered on new advantages. "Henceforth," as a writer in a local journal remarked, "the great tide of traffic that flows from south to north and north to south through the Midlands of England need not suffer by diversion among the cross currents and eddies that converge at Leicester and Trent, but may move swiftly and uninterruptedly along the new channel across the county and through the county town that has been prepared for it; and no one can stand to-day at our busy but well-ordered station, and see the splendidly-appointed trains—the spacious and easy bogie carriages, the continuous brakes and the swift and powerful engines—without thankfully confessing that Nottingham, placed near the heart of the Midland system, is now in the enjoyment of advantages of locomotion that are equalled by few and surpassed by none." *

Railways, too, have brought changes to our county towns and our county life. Many of these have become little capitals; and where, in former days, a few coaches came bustling in, and the carriages of neighbouring gentry occasionally enlivened their streets, there are now all the bustle and activity and all the signs of wealth and luxury which before railway times were seen only in great cities. The wealth and trade of the country have kept

* *The Nottingham Daily Express.*

pace with the railway development, and it has not merely increased in a wonderful manner the facilities for intercourse, but has developed in far more than corresponding proportions the industrial activity, the trade capital, and the mineral wealth of our country districts and our county towns.

Many seaports have received special activity and wealth from the incoming of railways. The Great Eastern Company has constructed the harbour at Lowestoft. In the year 1862 the tonnage to and from that town by rail was 35,000 tons, and the population was 9,500; in 1881 the tonnage had risen to 83,000 tons, and the population to 20,500; and the town has made "very considerable headway during the last few years," which is largely to be attributed to the enterprise of the railway company. So also with Harwich, with reference to which Mr. Birt, the General Manager of the Great Eastern, recently gave evidence: "We are developing a very large trade in the port of Harwich; so that it is now something like the twelfth port of the United Kingdom, and we attach so much importance to it that we are spending over £250,000 in providing additional waterside works at Harwich for the traffic with the Continent. Attempts had been made several times to attract additional trade to the port of Harwich by the establishment of docks by outsiders; but they had not been successful; and unless the railway company had found the means required for the purpose, I do not believe they ever would have been found." And what is thus said of Lowestoft and Harwich, may be declared of numberless other seaport towns which railways have created or re-created.

Some towns have been the distinct creation of railway establishments. It is so with Crewe. Here stood one farmhouse: now there is a railway establishment that employs 5,000 or 6,000 men; and between 2,000 and 3,000 locomotives have been here erected. So with Swindon. Some five-and-forty years ago, a little party of gentlemen sat down on the greensward to take their luncheon. "The furze was in blossom around them; the rabbits frisked in and out of their burrows; two or three distant farmhouses, one or two cottages, these were all the signs of human habitation, except a few cart-ruts, indicating a track used for field purposes." Where that luncheon was that day eaten by Isambard Brunel and Daniel Gooch, the platform of the Swindon station is to-day, and hard by are Swindon junction and the vast locomotive establishments.

Railway companies are themselves great landowners. In December, 1868, it was estimated that the average quantity of land held by railways was "about twelve acres to each mile of railway, or a belt as many miles long as there are miles of railway of 102 feet wide, including land for stations, sidings, and other purposes, and surplus land." The railway companies of England then occupied no less than 213 square miles of land; those of Scotland and Ireland, 38 square miles each; and the total amounted to what was equal to *a belt of land a mile broad that would extend between Brighton and Newcastle.* The acreage must, since that time, have enormously increased; since, instead of 14,628 miles of line then open, there are now 18,175 miles.

Nor is it only that railway companies have given a high price for the land they have bought, they have also greatly enhanced the value of all the property into the neighbourhood of which they have come. For example, the late Mr. Smith, of Deanston, who was a good agriculturist and agricultural engineer, showed that the formation of a certain proposed line of railway would add *2s. 6d.* per annum to the valued rental of each acre of the land five miles on either side; that this sum capitalised would pay for the formation of the line, which might be given over to be worked as a turnpike road. The evidence, too, recently placed before the Select Committee with regard to the increased value of land in some considerable districts of Scotland is still more remarkable. "I had the curiosity," said Mr. Walker, the General Manager of the North British Railway, "to look into the valuation rolls of several counties of Scotland, namely, Midlothian, Peebles, Selkirk, Roxburgh, East Lothian, and Berwick, and I find that in the valuation for the year 1877, as compared with that for 1862, there is an average increase of 30 per cent. in the rent roll. In the pastoral county of Peebles the increase has been no less than 33½ per cent." After giving other data to a somewhat like effect, Mr. Walker was asked: "What inference do you wish drawn from these figures?" With Scotch caution and suggestiveness he replied: "I wish the inference to be drawn that the railway companies have done a great deal to improve Scotland."

Railways have created important changes in the life and wealth even of London. They have made it more than ever the intellectual and social centre of the land. "The country gentry no longer go into the county towns to form a charming provincial society there, as they did at Norwich and Nottingham and Derby and similar places half a century ago. They come to London for the season, and their houses in the county towns are let as shops, or warehouses, or banks." When the London and Birmingham Railway had been opened seventeen years, it was found that within a circle of two miles of each station between the metropolis and Tring the total amount that had been expended in new buildings was only £22,000. It was then suggested that if a first-class pass, available for a few years, were presented to every person who erected a residence of a certain annual value near the line, all parties would be benefited. In eight years £240,000 or £250,000 were spent in house-building in these localities; the increased population largely contributed to the passenger, goods, and parcels traffic of the line; and the amount since expended in building has been enormous.

Similarly, but on an incomparably larger scale, the residential area of the metropolis has been increased in all directions, and especially along the southern lines. Business men, not many years since, were accustomed to live within a moderate omnibus ride of their offices; but numerous trains, low fares, and season-tickets have created traffic; millions of capital have been expended in house-building; new towns have arisen as if by magic; every station near London has become the centre of a large population, until there are now some 3,000,000 of inhabitants within the registration limits, and "beyond this central mass there is a ring of life growing rapidly and extending along railway lines over a circle of fifteen miles from Charing Cross." The district formerly inhabited by Londoners stretched from Clapham to Highgate, and from Bow to Kensington; it is now from Reigate and Tunbridge Wells, and even from Brighton, to Watford, and from Epping and Blackheath to Richmond.

Another of the beneficent revolutions effected by railways is in the *diminished cost of locomotion.* A favourable change in this respect was produced at the outset. The coach fares between Liverpool and Manchester had been 5*s.* outside and

10*s.* inside; the railway fares were 3*s.* 6*d.* outside and 5*s.* inside; and soon the carrying of outside passengers was discontinued—all were conveyed under cover. Thirty years ago the usual fare of a passenger was 5*d.* a mile; now it is little more than a penny.

Similar reductions have been made with respect to goods. When the Stockton and Darlington line was opened, the rate per ton for the carriage of ordinary merchandise was reduced from 5*d.* to a fifth of a penny a mile; in other words, the trader was charged a shilling for what he had before paid 25*s.* Similarly, the reduction in the price of the carriage of minerals was from 7*d.* to 1½*d.* per ton per mile, and the market price of coals at Darlington fell from 18*s.* to 8*s.* 6*d.* per ton. The rate of carriage between Liverpool and Manchester had been about 18*s.* a ton; after the line was opened the rate was about 10*s.*, and it has since been reduced, as the costs involved in conveyance have diminished. Instead of paying £5 a ton for bale goods between Manchester and London, the merchant now pays less than 30*s.*; instead of 13*d.* a ton a mile for goods of various kinds, the amount is perhaps only 2*d.* Within a year after the opening of the Liverpool and Manchester line the reduction in the charges in cotton was £20,000 a year; some firms saved £500 annually in this one item; and when the Leicester and Swannington Railway was made, Leicester effected a saving of £40,000 a year in coals alone—enough to pay all the rates and taxes of the town.

To all this the reduction and simplification of railway fares themselves have further contributed. At the time when Mr. Allport joined the Midland Company there were express fares, first and second-class ordinary fares, third-class, and Parliamentary or fourth-class, fares. He soon abolished express fares, and then third-class fares as distinguished from Parliamentary. This was first done on one selected portion of the line, and the effect was carefully watched; in twelve months it was ascertained that no loss had been sustained, and the experiment was extended to another section. The third-class fare was then made a penny a mile, and was gradually spread over the system, so that eventually the fares were, for the three classes, 2*d.*, 1½*d.*, and 1*d.* a mile. The next step was to put third-class carriages on all trains, and the last was to abolish second-class fares, and to reduce the first-class to the former price of second-class. The increase that has thereby been effected in the comfort and convenience of travelling, not only on the part of the working classes, but of all who deem it right to avail themselves of the cheaper services of trains, is enormous.

The reduction of the cost of locomotion that railways have secured is enormous. Startling as it may seem, it may yet be said that all our railway travelling costs the country *nothing at all.* If we put to the credit of railways the diminution in the expense of traffic since they were introduced, it may be declared that our railways do their work for *less than nothing.* The reduction, for instance, in the rate of the conveyance of coal to London, Mr. Allport has said, "for the last fifteen or twenty years is equivalent to the total value of the coals themselves. Twelve months ago people were paying for coals in London less than they paid for the carriage of the coals before railways came into operation;" and so it has been with other kinds of traffic. All the railway locomotion of this country for passengers, goods, and minerals, for raw materials and manufactured, for export trade and import, is paid for by the people of this country by a gross outlay by each of *a penny a day;* while all the passenger traffic is carried on for *a third of a penny a day.* "I venture to assert," Mr. Allport has remarked, "that the reduction in carriage by the railways, as compared with the former charges and quantities carried, has effected a saving to the country of an amount equal to more than double the entire gross receipts of all the railways of the kingdom, or *more than* £100,000,000 *sterling annually.*"

Nor is the direct saving and cost effected by railway locomotion alone to be estimated; there is the indirect saving of time, both with passengers and goods; and "time is money." Assuming, for instance, that the 600,000,000, who (besides season-ticket holders) travelled last year, would have saved 300,000,000 hours; and supposing a working year to consist of 300 days of eight hours each, the years of life and labour saved would be 125,000, and the industrial energies of the nation would have been economized proportionately. A similar test of money value might, by imagination, if not by arithmetic, be extended to the goods and mineral traffic of our railways, and the total would probably be more remarkable still:—"Coal is raised from the mine, delivered to the consumer, paid for, and burned at least a week or ten days earlier than would have been the case had it been sent by sea or by the sluggish route of the canals. The manufacturer now sends his goods from Manchester to London by rail. They are packed overnight, put into the railway trucks, and delivered in London simultaneously with, and in many cases before, the letter or invoice advising the despatch of the goods is received by the consignee. A week would probably be taken up by the carriage and delivery of the same goods by canal. The manufacturer can now draw upon his customer for the goods sent a week earlier than would have been the case if the canals were the only mode of conveyance offered. What is the value to the manufacturer of this economy in point of time? He receives payment for his goods a week earlier than he would do if the railways did not exist. By the joint aid of the telegraph and the railways, the merchant, manufacturer, vendor, or consumer is enabled to save, in the shape of interest and discounts, a sum which in the aggregate must amount to many millions."

Another revolution that has been effected in our social condition by railways is in *the amount of our locomotion.* Nowhere have these effects been more noteworthy than in the neighbourhood of London itself. People who live in the country, and who know of the metropolitan railways only through the occasional eruptions of criticism and complaint that appear in newspaper correspondence, might naturally conclude that, on the whole, the London lines are a failure: let their work be actually witnessed and their effects be examined, and it will be allowed that they have wrought a peaceful and beneficial revolution in the life of the metropolis. Apart from the main-line traffic, and the fifteen great termini, and their magnificent stations and splendid expresses, the mere suburban work is one of the marvels of the age. Lines costing half a million or a million of money a mile; railway bridges spanning the Thames; underground lines running perhaps under underground lines; innumerable trains passing all day to and fro with almost the constancy and precision of the weaver's shuttle, and at night, gas-lit, flashing out of the darkness and into the darkness, and making one wonder where they can all be coming from and where they can all be going to: these are sights which have become as familiar to the Londoner as Hansom cabs.

Or, if we wish to form some estimate of the amount of our railway locomotion, we may look at the traffic of, for instance, the London and North Western Company, with its 1,766 miles of continuous railway, more than 10,000 miles in all, along which flows the trade of several of the chief towns and cities of the Empire; carrying 50,000,000 passengers a year, or a million a week, equal in a month to the population of London; conveying 8,000,000 tons of general merchandise, and nearly 26,000,000 of minerals; with 2,300 locomotives, 3,500 carriages, and over 50,000 other vehicles, that run a distance of more than 36,000,000 miles a year, equal to 1,458 times round the world; to say nothing of a magnificent fleet of steamships; and estimate, if it were possible, what all this means in the traffic of that one line of railway. Such an institution, with its policies, its negotiations, its responsibilities, its revenue, its 40,000 servants, its power, and its authorized capital of more than £102,000,000, is more like a kingdom than a company.

Or take the Midland, which has gradually spread its 1,365 miles of railway, north and south and east and west, through half the counties of England, till they stretch from the Severn to the Humber, the Wash to the Mersey, and the English Channel to the Solway Firth; that has cost £60,000,000; that has an authorized capital of more than £72,000,000 of money; that receives a revenue of nearly £7,000,000 a year; that carries 29,000,000 of passengers, and more than 31,000,000 tons of goods; and the engines of which run a distance equal to four and a half times round the world every day; and imagine how stupendous a revolution in the amount of locomotion has been accomplished in the districts through which that one line runs.

So vast are the results of railway enterprise that we are lost in the number and magnitude of the terms that express them. Words and figures are inadequate to the task of conveying intelligible and proportionate ideas. Sir Henry Bessemer has dwelt on the impossibility of realizing what is meant by a billion; and the difficulty seems almost as great when we talk of a million. When we learn that last year our British railway companies ran their trains a distance of nearly 250,000,000 miles, the impression conveyed to the mind must fall immeasurably short of what is required by the stupendous fact; and we try, however ineffectually, to simplify the statement. We are aware that a journey round the world would be 24,000 miles long; the distance, therefore, run by our trains equals more than 10,000 journeys round the world; or, to speak astronomically, equals two and a half times the distance from the earth to the sun!

We are equally embarrassed by the numbers that tell us of the multitudes of passengers who travel. Instead of the 80,000 persons who, thirty years ago, went by coach, 1,500,000 passengers are now carried every day by railway in a fraction of the time and at a fraction of the cost previously required; passengers who would require 70,000 coaches to hold them, and 700,000 horses to draw them. Exclusive of season-ticket holders there were—in 1870, 336,000,000 passengers; in 1880, 604,000,000; in 1881, more than 623,000,000, or considerably more than 10,000,000 a week the year through. Now, what do 10,000,000 of passengers mean? They mean a number two and a half times the population of London. They mean that so many persons travel that in three weeks the railway passengers are as numerous as the whole population of England and Wales. Ten millions a week means nearly a million and a half a day, who would fill 60,000 first-class carriages, which, if each is eight yards long, would make a train which would stretch nearly 300 miles in length, or from London to Newcastle; while the passengers who travelled last year in Great Britain would form a procession 100 abreast a yard apart—extending across Africa from Tripoli to the Cape Colony; or from London across the Channel, France, Switzerland, Italy, the Mediterranean, Egypt, Nubia, and Abyssinia to Aden, at the southern mouth of the Red Sea, a distance of nearly 3,500 miles; and all this in addition to the journeyings of season-ticket holders, who last year numbered 500,000, many of whom probably travelled 200 or 300 journeys each. "Figures like these," remarked the *Times*, "ought to overpower the pardonable dislike of statistics which the reader may entertain. They are more eloquent than many descriptions of the increasing wealth and welfare of the country; and the growth of intercommunication, of which they are evidence, must be exerting the most vital influence upon the feelings and habits of the people."

Moreover, these astounding facts and figures of the augmented facilities for our locomotion mean much more than they say. They mean the more frequent intercourse of families who otherwise would be separated, perhaps, for months or years ; the promotion of the domestic happiness of hundreds of thousands of homes. They mean the increased activity and intelligence of society. They mean that business is done better, more effectively, cheaply, and widely. They mean that trade, manufacture, and commerce become possible that otherwise would have been impossible. They mean that England has become the distributive centre of Europe ; and they explain how it is that, whereas thirty years ago the exports of this country amounted to £1,000,000 a week, and great authorities were deprecating the inflated speculation of the times, they have since risen to £5,000,000 a week.

The proportions to which goods traffic has extended is also enormous. During the year 1881 the weight of minerals carried was 174,000,000 tons on the railways of the United Kingdom. If the average load is estimated at, say, seven tons a truck, the minerals conveyed would fill more than 24,000,000 trucks ; and, as the ordinary length of a truck is about five yards, these wagons would every day form a train 190 miles long, reaching from London as far as York, and in the course of a year these trucks would stretch from one end to another of a railway 68,000 miles long, or nearly three times round the world. If we similarly estimate the goods traffic of the United Kingdom, we shall learn that the amount conveyed by railway in 1881 was more than 70,000,000 tons ; and that if we average six tons to fill a truck, there would be 11,000,000 trucks full of general merchandise. Now, as a truck is five yards long, the amount would fill a fresh train every day 86 miles in length, and these trains in a year would be 31,000 miles long. In fact, the minerals and and goods trains of the United Kingdom (if every mineral truck were quite filled with seven tons of minerals, and every goods truck with six tons of goods) would stretch a distance of nearly 100,000 miles, and would be long enough to form a gigantic necklace hanging four times round the world. Add to these figures the fact that on our railways we have nearly 14,000 locomotives, 42,000 carriages and other vehicles for passenger trains ; that we have also more than 400,000 other vehicles for goods and mineral traffic ; that the rolling stock of our British railways would, if placed in line, form a train 2,000 miles long ; and we have data before us of which it is hard indeed to realize the momentous significance.

Such are some of the silent and gradual but mighty revolutions that have been effected in this country, and in other lands, by railways ; augmenting in ever-increasing proportion and with ever-enlarging result, the intelligence, the wealth, and the welfare of the nation and the world. It is railways alone that have made our postal system possible. It is easy, for instance, to put on six or eight additional vans to a night mail ; but if we were still dependent on coaches, we were told by Sir Robert Stephenson, that in his day fourteen or fifteen would be needed to carry the bags between London and Birmingham. Instead of the productions of one district, or of one land, supplying itself, perhaps to satiety, they are being distributed far and wide, to the enrichment of both the producer and the consumer. Pastoral plains are turning into mineral fields of priceless worth. The extremities of the kingdom are as accessible to the metropolis as were its suburbs two hundred years ago. Europe has united its great cities and ports together by links of iron. The physician will soon be ordering his patient a change of air in the ancient Garden of Eden, or a fishing trip to the Euphrates. An acquaintance may give point to his after-dinner conversation by reciting an adventure he had the other day as he was on an excursion about such a degree of longitude. The valetudinarian may live, like the swallow, in perpetual summer. We shall all increasingly sympathise with the saying of Burton concerning the traveller: " He took great content, exceeding delight, in that his voyage. And who doth not, who shall attempt the like ? For peregrination charms our senses with such unspeakable and sweet variety, that some count him unhappy who never travelled, a kind of prisoner, and pity his case, that from his cradle to his old age, he beholds the same ; still, still, still the same, the same ! "

Let us then cherish the spirit and indulge the hope of the poet, Dr. Charles Mackay, when he sang :—

" No poetry in Railways ! foolish thought
Of a dull brain, to no fine music wrought,
By Mammon dazzled, though the people prize

The gold untold ; yet shall not we despise
The triumphs of our time, or fail to see,
Of pregnant mind, the fruitful progeny
Ushering the daylight of the world's new morn.

" Lay down your rails, ye nations, near and far ;
Yoke your full trains to Steam's triumphal car ;
Link town to town ; and in these iron bands
Unite the strange and oft-embattled lands.
Peace and Improvement round each train shall soar,
And Knowledge light the Ignorance of yore :
Men, joined in amity, shall wonder long
That Hate had power to lead their fathers wrong ;
Or that false glory lured their hearts astray,
And made it virtuous and sublime to slay.

" Blessings on Science, and her handmaid, Steam !
They make Utopia only half a dream ;
And show the fervent, of capacious souls,
Who watch the ball of Progress as it rolls,
Thatall as yet completed, or begun,
Is but the dawning that precedes the sun."

A "DEAD END."

INDEX.